EXPLORING RELIGIOUS MEANING

third edition

ROBERT C. MONK
WALTER C. HOFHEINZ
KENNETH T. LAWRENCE
JOSEPH D. STAMEY
BERT AFFLECK
TETSUNAO YAMAMORI

PRENTICE HALL REGENTS, Englewood Cliffs, NJ 07632

Library of Congress Cataloging-in-Publication Data

Exploring religious meaning.

Includes biographical references and index.
1. Religion.   2. Religious literature.   I. Monk,
Robert C.
BL48.E95 1987   200   86-9381
ISBN 0-13-297524-6

Editorial/production supervision and
    interior design: **Marjorie Borden**
Cover design: **Ben Santora**
Manufacturing buyer: **Harry P. Baisley**

Printed in the United States of America

10   9   8   7

ISBN 0-13-297524-6   01

Prentice-Hall International (UK) Limited, *London*
Prentice-Hall of Australia Pty. Limited, *Sydney*
Prentice-Hall Canada Inc., *Toronto*
Prentice-Hall Hispanoamericana, S.A., *Mexico*
Prentice-Hall of India Private Limited, *New Delhi*
Prentice-Hall of Japan, Inc., *Tokyo*
Prentice-Hall of Southeast Asia Pte. Ltd., *Singapore*
Editora Prentice-Hall do Brasil, Ltda., *Rio de Janeiro*

To the memory of

Mary Ida and Walter C. Hofheinz

with gratitude to

Carolyn Monk
Carol Lawrence
Sarah Stamey
Patsy Affleck
Judy Yamamori

Contents

PART II EXPERIENCING RELIGION

3 Cases of Religious Experience 50

4 Elements of Religious Experience 65

5 Religion in Artistic Expression 89

PART III THE DIVINE

6 History, Revelation, and the Knowledge of God 106

PART VI   UNDERSTANDING RELIGIOUS KNOWLEDGE

PART VII   RELIGION AND THE NATURAL ORDER

Preface

This book is intended to serve as a set of tools and resources for exploring the many dimensions of religion as a central activity of human beings. It was designed with introductory courses in religion, religion and culture, and the humanities in mind. It is useful as a supplementary text for courses in comparative religion, philosophy of religion, and sociology of religion. It is indexed in ways that suggest a variety of uses in classroom settings or for independent research. Both instructors and individuals interested in independent study will find the indexes useful.

The design of *Exploring Religious Meaning* suggests an approach to inquiry that may be called inductive and integrative. Many of the readings are taken from the Scriptures and classic literature of the world's great religions. Others are drawn from classic and contemporary sources that seek to interpret religion in its various dimensions—theological, philosophical, psychological, sociological, cultural. Some materials are drawn from areas of contemporary culture where religious experience and stances of religious commitment are actualized, appreciated, or criticized: cartoons, poetry, drama, motion pictures, news stories, song lyrics. The materials are presented in a variety of ways—in juxtaposition with interpretative commentary and questions—that seek to evoke encounter and insight.

Just as the authors of *Exploring Religious Meaning* do not always agree among themselves on questions of interpretation, readers will no doubt find themselves disagreeing with points of view expressed in the sources and in the interpretative commentary included in this book. We hope that readers will confront these materials, and the issues they raise, with questions and responses that arise from their own experiences. We hope that each individual reader will be stimulated to address uniquely personal questions and formulate personal responses in studying the issues.

To understand religion, religious phenomena must be seen in their wholeness, as they are manifested in society and in the lives of individuals. Religion is first of all something alive. Doctrinal formulations, institutional structures, traditional patterns and practices handed down from generation to generation—these are important aspects of religion. These aspects of religious experience probably receive more emphasis in this edition than in the previous ones. But important too are highly individual elements of feeling, movements of protest and reform, the emergence of new patterns that may modify, give new life to, or put into eclipse the old and the established. We hope that the materials included in *Exploring Religious Meaning* will guide the reader to explore sources and issues that will lead to deeper understanding of and greater appreciation for the enduring and perennially renewed impact of religion on human life.

In the Introduction a functional definition of *religion* is proposed. This definition suggests that religion is important to everyone because each person's life is shaped by—and all persons respond to—critical events that confront them in individual life and in society in terms of basic commitments. An individual's most basic commitments express what the individual values most, how that person defines the meaning and value of existence. Basic commitments, those involving a person's deepest loyalties and ideas about what is valuable and worthwhile, are—according to our proposed definition of religion—*religious*. The reality and meaningfulness of such commitments can finally be determined, expressed, and actualized only by the individuals who make them. But the study of religion—of religious traditions and religious phenomena—even as an academic discipline, may help persons clarify their own basic commitments and come to appreciate them more fully. The study of religion can also help persons come to understand and appreciate the religious commitments, attitudes, and behavior of others. As in all life, from the turbulent arenas of social and political controversy to the sometimes lonely realms of scientific and artistic creation, one must decide for oneself what is best in the realm of the good and the true.

We have been pleased with the response to the first and second editions of *Exploring Religious Meaning*. Instructors and students from a wide variety of academic settings indicate that they have found the book stimulating and useful. In preparing the third edition, we have taken seriously suggestions by those who have used the book about ways to improve or strengthen it. We have retained the general structure of the book and much of the original material. We have tried to remove features of its layout and organization that were found to be distracting. There has been reorganization and updating of material and a thorough revision of some chapters and units.

Perhaps the most important change in the third edition is an expanded and more systematic treatment of the central concepts involved in the analysis of religion. We believe that the story is now a more complete and connected one.

Instructors will see that updating is reflected as much in use of recent theoretical studies as in use of newer illustrative materials.

In the third edition more attention is given to religion in modernized and modernizing societies, but there is also additional material dealing with non-Western traditions. There are several completely new and other significantly updated units dealing with contemporary issues where religion and society interact: intensified religious concern about the threat of nuclear war and world hunger, the quest for human liberation, the rise of new or renewed religious movements, the new religious conservativism, issues related to the status of ethnic culture, women, minorities and pluralism in contemporary societies.

We continue to be indebted to Jacques Bakke for the illustrations that add so much to *Exploring Religious Meaning*. We are greatly indebted to Professors William Barrick and Johnnie Kahl, colleagues at McMurry College, who have given us the benefit of their use of this text. Acknowledgement is long overdue to Professor Joyce Carroll of McMurry College for advice on earlier editions relating to contemporary films dealing with moral and religious issues, and to Professor Nell Senter of Texas Christian University for providing valuable information relating to contemporary moral problems, particularly those concerned with the status of women in society.

The secretarial assistance we have received from Ms. Pat Shackelford, whose dedication is matched only by her skills and diligence, has been invaluable.

We express sincere appreciation to the many persons—especially those professors in a variety of academic settings—who have offered suggestions for improving the text. We also received—and incorporated into the text—many extremely valuable suggestions from the readers who reviewed our proposal for the revision leading to this edition. Finally, to our many students in the different colleges and universities where we teach, and to former students, some of whom are themselves now graduate students or professors engaged in the academic study and teaching of religion, we express sincere and abiding gratitude for suggestions, criticism, and encouragement.

Throughout *Exploring Religious Meaning*, dates of historical events are, for the most part, designated by the abbreviations B.C.E. ("before the common era") and C.E. ("common era"), which in most older sources and in some more recent ones were commonly abbreviated as B.C. and A.D.

1

Toward a Definition of Religion

INTRODUCTION

From earliest times religion has been a pervasive social phenomenon. In our own complex society there are evidences of religion everywhere: religious holidays of particular groups (Christmas, Hanuka, Mardi Gras, Ash Wednesday, Passover, Good Friday, Easter), national holidays that have a distinctively religious component (Thanksgiving, the Fourth of July, Memorial Day), church buildings and synagogues, and even controversial social and political issues, such as those concerning abortion, the Equal Rights Amendment, and capital punishment. Officials of religious denominations take part in public ceremonies, such as Presidential inaugurations—and officials of organizations and private citizens advocating separation of church and state protest such participation.

There is evidence that in our own society, participation in the activities of organized religion is, after a slight decline during the early 1970s, on the increase. But there is also in our society, increasingly, a new awareness of religious *pluralism*, and an increasing *diversity* of religious groups. There seems to be, also, on the part of many individuals, both a return to traditional religious practices—an interest in finding one's roots—and a new individualism in religion—the individual wants to be his or her own kind of Baptist or Catholic or Jew.

At the individual level, many who have turned away from traditional religious answers, or who have turned away from "organized religion" entirely, give evidence of deep religious concern. Contemporary American Jews who observe *Havurah*—

religious celebrations that bring several families together in the setting of a home—or Protestant or Catholic charismatics may participate in new forms of religious expression that both renew and depart from traditional affiliations. In seeming paradox, there also appears to be a trend toward more traditional religious participation in the return of many to traditional patterns of worship (as in marriage ceremonies) and affirmation of traditional forms of belief. On the other hand, commitments to social justice, to peace, to the rights of women, minority groups, the threatened environment, and animal life, and to helping the starving, famine-threatened human populations of the world give evidence of a *religious* fervor. The many who have responded to the promise of transcendental meditation, or to seminars that promise growth in human potential, assertiveness, and the quest for identity share the basic religious preoccupation with the question of what makes human life meaningful.

Investigation of religion must be broad enough to incorporate the most individualistic and nontraditional expressions of religious concern. While examining the major forms of established and emerging institutional patterns, it must be able to comprehend traditional patterns of religious expression, including those of societies other than our own. Affirming the need for such a broad perspective in religious inquiry makes especially necessary a concrete identification of the ways in which the term *religion* will be used in this book.

Religion is defined in many ways. Radoslav Tsanoff, in his book *Religious Crossroads*, conveniently summarized the linguistic data concerning the terminology used in various cultures to designate what we call "religion." Tsanoff surveyed the major language stocks of the modern world and noted that no language group has a word meaning "religion" as a universal, inclusive phenomenon. Some languages have terms that designate "law," "devotion," "knowledge," and other components of what in the West has been termed religion. In fact, the Latin *religio* itself originally designated the ancestral customs and rituals of the early Romans. It was not until the emergence of a Greco-Roman culture, encompassing the area from North Africa to the British Isles and from India to the Atlantic Ocean, that the term *religio* began to denote a phenomenon of universal import. Tsanoff considered various ways of defining religion. Several are enumerated and discussed: (1) theistic and other belief, (2) practices, (3) mystical feeling, (4) worship of the holy, (5) conviction of the conservation of values.[1]

Everyone has had some experience of religion. Most people use the term on the basis of past experience, acquired beliefs, and favorable or unfavorable impressions. To one person, the word *religion* may produce good feelings. It may connote a close relationship to God—to the benevolent Being or Beings believed to provide life, security, meaning, and purpose. To another, the term may evoke feelings of fear or inadequacy or guilt. It may connote a threatening relationship to stern or hostile and judging Power or Powers. People often reflect their own positive or negative feelings toward religion and toward their own past experiences of it when

---

[1]Radoslav A. Tsanoff, *Religious Crossroads* (New York: E. P. Dutton & Co., Inc., 1942), pp. 13–25.

stating what they conceive it to be. On the one hand, the behavioral scientist—the psychologist, sociologist, anthropologist—may emphasize religion's *functional* aspect; psychologists may be interested in the role of religion in providing integration or in causing conflict in the individual personality and in the individual's group relationships. Sociologists may attempt to study ways in which religion may be a source of stability or change, unity or conflict, in societies. On the other hand, philosophers may be primarily interested in the *cognitive* claims of religion, in trying to understand the belief statements of particular religious traditions and in trying to discover what the functions and significance of those statements may be, and how one might discover whether they are true. Theologians may seek to explicate the "meaning" aspect of religion, or at least of their own religious tradition. They will perhaps try to show that the religious tradition *is* meaningful and will provide for the adherent a framework, an orientation that makes sense of life.

The anthropologist Clifford Geertz has pointed to two major functions of religion: providing a comprehensive system of symbols for understanding the nature of reality, and providing a system of values that demand complete devotion.[2] He sees these as inseparable. We may express his view by saying that ultimately we value the things we do because we see them as rooted in ultimate reality, and we see them as rooted in ultimate reality because we have learned to value them as having ultimate significance.

Accordingly, in *Exploring Religious Meaning* we will define *religion* as *any person's reliance upon a pivotal value in which that person finds essential wholeness as an individual and as a person-in-community. For that person all other values are subordinate to this central value.* The pivotal value spoken of in the definition is authentic to the individual, though it may not be meaningful to others. Here, "reliance upon a pivotal value" includes trust in an unrivaled power or being. The pivotal value may be shared by others. In such cases we speak of a "religious tradition," such as Christianity, Buddhism, Hinduism.

For a person's professed religious commitment to be authentic, the person's life must be governed by the religion's pivotal value. Persons from very different religious traditions, where the pivotal values at least seem to differ greatly, may therefore have great difficulty in understanding one another. An Orthodox Jew who emphasizes (whose pivotal value is) the living of all life in accordance with God's revealed law (the Torah) may find it difficult to understand or to sympathize with a Hindu mystic or a Christian Pentecostalist for whom an overwhelming sense of the presence of God within is the ultimate goal. Even within the same religious tradition this difficulty may appear. A Christian fundamentalist and a theologically liberal Christian may have a difficult time understanding and accepting the authenticity of the other's differing religious commitments, conduct, and belief.

However, a religiously committed person with an open and searching attitude may understand and empathize with a person of another faith by turning inward, to his or her own experience of religious commitment. At that moment a dialogue—in

[2]See Clifford Geertz, *The Interpretation of Culture: Selected Essays* (New York: Basic Books, 1973), pp. 89, 126, 140.

its truest sense—between human beings with different idiosyncrasies and different self- and world-understandings can become real. What is demanded is willingness of the participants in dialogue to open to each other.

This definition must be seen as a preliminary one. It will receive much qualification in the following units and sections of *Exploring Religious Meaning*. The immediately following units will both attempt to illustrate the definition of religion as "reliance on a pivotal value" and begin to qualify it.

UNIT 1

> We define religion as any person's **reliance upon a pivotal value** in which that person finds essential wholeness as an individual . . .

A (*Lolly* by Pete Hansen. Copyright © *The Chicago Tribune*. New York News Syndicate; Inc. Used by permission.)

In answer to the question: "What does it mean to have a god?" Martin Luther wrote, "Trust and faith of the heart alone make both God and idol. . . . Whatever . . . your heart clings to . . . and relies on, that is what really is your God."[3] It is sometimes said by religious persons that there are in reality no atheists. In what way is this statement true? In what ways— bearing in mind the definition of religion we have accepted—might it not be true? Do you think that the way Luther talks about what a person's "real" god is makes sense? Is this a useful way of talking about "religious" commitment?

H. Richard Niebuhr was a twentieth-century Protestant thinker who accepted Martin Luther's definition of the concept of "God"—what one relies on, puts his or her trust in. Commenting on the definition, Niebuhr wrote: "If this be true, that the word 'god' means the object of human faith in life's worthwhileness, it is evident that men have many gods, that our natural religion is polytheistic."[4] Mr. Quimby, the golfer in the comic strip, might illustrate this. In the accompanying cartoon, the

[3]Martin Luther as quoted by H. Richard Niebuhr, *Radical Monotheism and Western Culture* (New York: Harper and Row, Pub., 1960), p. 119.
[4]Ibid.

object of his supreme devotion—his pivotal value—seems to be to do well at golf. In other cartoons in the "Lolly" series, he was equally concerned about wealth—he experienced severe emotional crises when the stock market fell, or when it was time to pay his income taxes, or when an employee asked for a raise. Are people frequently "polytheistic"? Do the terms *theism*, *polytheism*, and *monotheism* acquire new meanings—or at least other possible meanings—when "religion" is defined as "pivotal value"?

H. R. Niebuhr pointed out that an individual's pivotal value—that which the individual seeks or adheres to as the source of ultimate meaning or fulfillment—may shift from one value to another, or may be composed of a group of values (such as "health, wealth, and wisdom"). The religions of the world propose supreme or pivotal values to their adherents as that which will bring fulfillment and security. In later units we will focus on some major religious orientations toward pivotal value. For instance, there is a *moral* orientation which holds obedience to the will of a Divine Being (for many adherents of Judaism) or to an eternal code of right behavior (as in Confucianism) as the supreme value to be sought. There are also *mystical* religious orientations which hold that a very intense sense of union with the Divine (Hinduism) or experience of the ultimate, overwhelming, transforming presence of God to worshippers whose will and personality are united to God in love (Christian mysticism) is the pivotal goal of life. We will speak also of esthetic and magical orientations to religion. These need not be exclusive of one another, and this way of classifying orientations to pivotal value is only a conceptual tool; it is not the only way of approaching the role of religion as the center of value and meaning in the lives of groups and individuals.

The following materials illustrate how the concept of pivotal value is present in three of the world's great religious traditions. In a passage from the Hindu *Bhagavad-Gita* (c. 100), the Lord Krishna calls for the entire devotion and loyalty of his devotee Arjuna. In effect, the Divine Krishna asks his follower to make devotion to Krishna the supreme, the pivotal, value of Arjuna's life.

B
> Cling thou to me!
> Clasp Me with heart and mind! so shalt thou dwell
> Surely with Me on high. But if thy thought
> Droops from such height; if you be'st weak to set
> Body and soul upon Me constantly,
> Despair not! give Me lower service! seek
> To read Me, worshipping with steadfast will;
> And, if thou canst not worship steadfastly
> Work for Me, toil in works pleasing to Me!
> For he that laboreth right for love of Me
> Shall finally attain! But, if in this
> Thy faint heart fails, bring Me thy failure! find
> Refuge in Me! Let fruits of labor go,
> Renouncing all for Me, with lowliest heart,
> So shalt thou come; for, though to know is more
> than diligence, yet worship better is

Than knowing, and renouncing better still.
Near to renunciation—very near—
Dwelleth eternal Peace! . . .

Take my last work, most utmost meaning have!
Give Me thy heart! adore Me! serve Me! cling
In faith and love and reverence to Me!
So shalt thou come to Me! I promise true.
Make Me thy single refuge! I will free
Thy soul from all its sins! Be of good Cheer.[5]

In the Christian Apostle's Creed (c. 500), powerful expression is given to the Christian belief that the God of Christian worship is Lord of all life. He is confessed as being Creator, Savior and Redeemer, Deliverer, and Lord of life in the present and in his eternal Kingdom beyond the present.

C   "I believe in God the Father Almighty, Maker of heaven and earth. And in Jesus Christ his only Son our Lord; Who was conceived by the Holy Ghost, born of the Virgin Mary; suffered under Pontius Pilate, was crucified, dead, and buried; he descended into hell; the third day he rose from the dead; he ascended into heaven; and sitteth at the right hand of God the Father Almighty; from thence he shall come to judge the quick and the dead. I believe in the Holy Ghost; the holy catholic Church; the communion of saints; the forgiveness of sins; the resurrection of the body; and the life everlasting. Amen.

The following Muslim prayer gives graphic expression to the adherent's reliance on Allah as the Supreme Source of wholeness for the individual.

D   Thanks be to my Lord; He the Adorable, and only to be adored. My Lord, the Eternal, The Ever-existing, the Cherisher, the True Sovereign whose mercy and might overshadow the universe; the Regulator of the world, and Light of the creation. His is our worship; to Him belongs all worship; He existed before all things, and will exist after all that is living has ceased. Thou art the adored, my Lord; Thou art the Master. the Loving and Forgiving. . . .
O my Lord, Thou art the Helper of the afflicted, the Reliever of all distress, the Consoler of the broken-hearted; Thou art present everywhere to help Thy servants. . . .

O my Lord, Thou art the Creator, I am only created;
     Thou art my Sovereign, I am only thy servant;
     Thou art the Helper, I am the beseecher;
     Thou art the Forgiver, I am the sinner;
Thou, my Lord, art the merciful. All-knowing, All-loving.

[5]*The Song Celestial or Bhagavad-Gita*, trans. Sir Edwin Arnold (London: Routledge & Kegan Paul Ltd., 1955), 12.8, 18.64–66. Used by permission.

UNIT 2

> We define religion as any person's reliance upon a pivotal value in which that person finds essential wholeness ... as **a person-in-community**. ...

A

TAOS, N.M. (AP)—An aging spiritual leader of the Taos Pueblo Indians, the sight in his 90-year-old eyes dimming, plans to take his tribe's plea for a religious sanctuary to the white man's Capitol.

He will renew the plea of the Taos Indians for title to 48,000 acres of forest land surrounding Blue Lake, high in the Sangre de Cristo Mountains of northern New Mexico, and sacred to the tribe.

"Our Blue Lake wilderness," Romero said, "keeps our water holy and by this water we are baptized. Without this, we have no life."

"If our land is not returned to us," Romero said, "if it is turned over to the government for its use, then it is the end of Indian life."

"Our people will scatter as the people of other nations have scattered. It is our religion that holds us together."

In religion humans find wholeness not only as individuals, but also as persons-in-community—persons unavoidably related to others, with whom the individual shares identity, purposes, and experience.

B After experiencing the Risen Christ on the road to Damascus, Paul in time felt compelled to preach to the Gentiles, despised by all good Pharisaic Jews. Sent by the church at Antioch, of which Paul had become a part, he went out into the Greco-Roman world with the message of salvation for all nations. For Paul the community was essential: "For just as the body is one and has many members, and all the members of the body, though many, are one body, so it is with Christ. For by one Spirit we were all baptized into one body—Jews or Greeks, slaves or free—and all were made to drink of one Spirit. . . . Now you are the body of Christ and individually members of it." (I Corinthians 12:12, 13, 27, RSV)

C

After the ecstasy (Enlightenment) had passed, Gautama was immediately confronted with a problem, a temptation. . . . He had attained to a Doctrine that was "profound, recondite, hard to comprehend." Were he to preach this Doctrine or Dhamma, and were others not to understand it, that would be labor and annoyance to him. After some struggle with himself, whether he should remain a Buddha for his own sake or become a Buddha for all, a teaching Buddha, he rose and went back into the world to communicate to others his sav-

ing truth. He sought out the five ascetics who had deserted him at Uruvela. He found them in the Deer Park at Benares. . . . He opened to them his own experience and challenged them to believe his testimony, to admit that he was an "arahat" (a monk who had experienced enlightenment), and to try the "middle way" he now advocated. The five ascetics were converted, and thus the Sangha (the Buddhist monastic order) came into being. . . . "I take refuge in the Sangha."[6]

[6]John B. Noss, *Man's Religions*, 4th ed. (New York: Macmillan, Inc., 1969), pp. 130–32, © 1949, 1956, 1963 by Macmillan, Inc., © John B. Noss, 1969.

This aspect of religion—in which the individual finds personal wholeness in community—raises profound questions about the significance of the individual's relationships to other human beings and about the meaning of human existence, about human nature generally. In addition, it raises questions about the nature of our avenues to truth: How much of what we consider knowledge, the belief systems of society, is simply the result of shared assumptions and a shared way of life? The point has often been stressed that most newborn animals are far better equipped biologically to begin life than humans are. Human beings, with their long period of dependency, literally have to learn from their human group how to be human.

The reality of human interdependency is clearly expressed by a student in her journal:

> So many people think that they can be an island and not depend on anyone else. But we have to have help; God did not mean for us to exist separately. I think that we can only find self-happiness when we can find happiness together.

UNIT 3

> We define religion as any person's reliance upon a pivotal value in which that person finds essential wholeness **as an individual and as a person-in-community.**

For the Apostle Paul, living in an idol-worshiping society, commitment to Christ—as the pivotal value—eliminated the efficacy of idols. Therefore, it made no difference for Christians if the meat sold in the marketplace had been offered to idols. Nevertheless, Paul saw that, although this might be true for him as an individual, as a person-in-community he had to consider other factors. "There are some who have been so accustomed to idolatry that even now they eat this food with a sense of its heathen consecration, and their conscience, being weak, is polluted by the eating." Paul as an individual was at liberty to eat such meat, but as a member of the Christian community he was ready to restrain himself. "If food be the downfall of my brother, I will never eat meat any more, for I will not be the cause of my brother's downfall." (I Corinthians 8:7, 13, *New English Bible*)[7]

Martin Luther King's last public speech was delivered in support of a sanitation workers' strike in Memphis, Tennessee. Adapting Jesus' Good Samaritan story to the current scene, King pointed out not only the social need of the time but also that individual wholeness is never separate from corporate wholeness.

A

> And you know, it's possible that the priest and the Levite looked over that man on the ground and wondered if the robbers were still around. Or it's possible that they felt that the man on the ground was merely faking. And he was acting like he had been robbed and hurt, in order to seize them over there, lure them there for

[7]Scripture quotations in this publication identified by the letters NEB are from *The New English Bible*. © the Delegates of the Oxford University Press and the Syndics of the Cambridge University Press 1961, 1970.

quick and easy seizure. And so the first question that the Levite asked was, "If I stop to help this man, what will happen to me?" But then the good Samaritan came by. And he reversed the question: "If I do not stop to help this man, what will happen to him?"

That's the question before you to-night. Not, "If I stop to help the sanita-tion workers, what will happen to all of the hours that I usually spend in my of-fice every day and every week as a pas-tor?" The question is not, "If I stop to help this man in need, what will happen to me?" "If I do not stop to help the sani-tation workers, what will happen to them?" That's the question.

The speech ends with King's premonition of his own death. Nevertheless, the dominant note is a firm confidence that, no matter what happens to the individual, there is an abiding triumph that the individual shares when, under God, individual and group faith and action issue in corporate and individual wholeness—"the Promised Land."

Well, I don't know what will happen now. We've got some difficult days ahead. But it doesn't matter with me now. Because I've been to the mountain-top. And I don't mind. Like anybody, I would like to live a long life. Longevity has its place. But I'm not concerned about that now. I just want to do God's will. And He's allowed me to go up to the mountain. And I've looked over. And I've seen the promised land. I may not get there with you. But I want you to know tonight, that we, as a people will get to the promised land. And I'm happy, to-night. I'm not worried about anything. I'm not fearing any man. Mine eyes have seen the glory of the coming of the Lord.[8]

King's personal commitment led to direct social action. Essential wholeness, how-ever, manifests itself in various ways. This is seen in the experience of Dietrich Bonhoeffer. Bonhoeffer sought meaningful wholeness as he wrote from his German prison. A committed Christian preacher who would not silence his public witness for Christ despite Nazi commands to do so, Bonhoeffer was locked away from his people and finally martyred. Till his death, however, he maintained his faith and his loving concern for others. Affirming Christ as the Man for others, Bonhoeffer interpreted faith as "Something whole, involving the whole of one's life."[9] Faith meant "taking risks for others."[10] For such a faith in Christ, Bonhoeffer risked himself—gave himself for others—and in this way, as he believed, experienced wholeness as an individual.

UNIT 4

> We define religion as any person's reliance upon a pivotal value. . . . **for that person all other values are subordinate to this central value.**

---

[8]Martin Luther King, "A View from the Mountaintop." Reprinted by permission of Joan Daves. Copyright © 1968 by The Estate of Martin Luther King, Jr.
[9]Dietrich Bonhoeffer, *Letters and Papers from Prison* (New York: Macmillan, Inc., 1958), p. 199
[10]Ibid., p. 209.

Leon Trotsky, who, with Lenin, led the revolutionary movement that produced a Communist government in Russia in 1917, was one of the most brilliant Marxist thinkers of the twentieth century. He did not become a Marxist all at once, however. The son of a prosperous farmer, Trotsky was drawn to various revolutionary movements popular among students who were concerned with improving the lot of peasants and industrial workers. After a period during which he argued strongly against the Marxist position, while in prison for revolutionary activities, Trotsky was "converted" to Marxism. In the following passage of his autobiography, Trotsky describes how, during a period of exile, he found in his new position the key to understanding all the major aspects of life.

A

Since 1896, when I had tried to oppose all revolutionary ideas, and the following year, when I opposed Marxism even though I was by that time already carrying on revolutionary activity, I had come a long way. By the time I was sent into exile, Marxism had definitely become the basis of my whole philosophy. During my exile, I tried to consider, from the new point of view I had acquired, the so-called "eternal" problems of life: love, death, friendship, optimism, pessimism, and so forth. In different epochs, and in varying social surroundings, man loves and hates and hopes differently. Just as the tree feeds its leaves, flowers, and fruits with the extracts absorbed from the soil by its roots, so does the individual find food for his sentiments, and ideas, even the most "sublime" ones—as Marxism states —in the economic roots of society.[11]

In Marxism, Trotsky found the key to the understanding of all life. He never deviated from this position. Even after his expulsion from Russia and from the Russian Communist party, he believed that the Marxist theory fully explained why backward economic and social conditions in Russia had inevitably produced a deterioration of Russian Communism into the Stalinist dictatorship. Trotsky remained a committed Marxist revolutionary. He was assassinated in 1940 by a Stalinist agent in Mexico.

We have stressed that religions provide a unifying value or system of values by means of which all other values and all parts of life may be interpreted. Did Trotsky's Marxist theory—his Marxist beliefs—express this kind of value orientation? Could Marxism for Trotsky be called a religious orientation? Note how Trotsky's beliefs about the central questions of life are interpreted by and subordinated to the central, unifying beliefs provided by Marxist theory.

The sociologist J. Milton Yinger has written:

B

Major religious differences can persist in a functionally unified society only at the cost of sharp conflict on the one hand or by the reduction of the significance of these religions to their adherents on the other, or by some mixture of these processes. Insofar as it is reduction in the significance of traditional beliefs that occurs, men do not thereby give up the search for a unifying system of values. They develop a quasireligion to do the job. Most often in our time it is nationalism, sometimes pursued with an almost desperate sense of urgency for the conviction of unity.[12]

[11]Leon Trotsky, *My Life* (New York: Grosset and Dunlap, Inc., 1960), p. 127.

[12]J. Milton Yinger, *Sociology Looks at Religion* (New York: Macmillan, Inc., 1963), p. 31. © J. Milton Yinger 1961, 1963. Used by permission.

Sociologists often use the term "quasireligion" to describe something—like nationalism or Marxism—that is ordinarily thought of as "nonreligious" in content, but that *functions* or *acts like* a religion. What analogies are there between the unifying role that Marxism played in the life of Trotsky and the role that Marxism or nationalism might play in the life of a society? The cartoon comments on this.

For both traditional religions and secular quasireligions there will usually be *symbols* that express the meaning and importance of the religion's pivotal value or system of values. What might happen to adherents of a religion or quasireligion when they perceive conflicts among the values their religious tradition or political movement advocates?

C

"Listen, I *love* my country and I'm *proud* of the flag, but do we *have* to pledge allegiance every time we get into the car?" (Drawing by D. Fradon; © 1969, *The New Yorker Magazine, Inc.*, October 25, 1969.)

Religious symbols usually express and appeal to the emotions of the adherents of the religion in a powerful way. The cross for Christians; the words of the sacred Scriptures, the Torah, for Jews; the city of Mecca for Muslims; the red flag or the tomb of Lenin for Marxists—these are powerful religious symbols. Is the American flag as used in the cartoon seen by the cartoon characters as a religious symbol expressing a pivotal value?

UNIT 5

> **This pivotal value . . . is authentic to the individual though it may not be meaningful to others.**

In 1961 Dag Hammarskjöld, Secretary General of the United Nations, was killed in an airplane crash while on a mission seeking peace in a war-torn region of Africa. After Hammarskjöld's death, his personal journals and diaries revealed him as a man who had been motivated in his political career by insights of a deeply personal religious mysticism. He wrote: "In our era, the road to holiness necessarily passes through the world of action."[13] Others may not share this particular primary value. Nevertheless, we believe it may be useful to consider that all human beings have this in common—for each person there are values that are pivotal. The way these values fit together to become *the* pivotal value—if they do fit together—is the basis of the unity, the wholeness, of that person's life. We hinted in Unit 4 that conflicts within the values in the system of pivotal values in an individual's or group's life may result in the sense that *wholeness* is lacking. This may result in distress and a feeling of meaninglessness.

Cartoonists graphically reflect this awareness and at times draw their humor from unexpected conflicts in values. Consider the accompanying "Snuffy" cartoon.

(*Snuffy* by Fred Lasswell. © 1970 King Features Syndicate.)

A

Is there any doubt as to what is important to Lukey on this occasion? Are most persons as honest as Lukey in revealing their pivotal value?

UNIT 6

The pivotal value may be shared by others. In such cases we speak of a "religious tradition." . . .

Religion may be an intensely personal dimension of an individual's life, but even the most personal and individualistic religious experiences will have drawn from the social setting. New religious movements, movements of reform or renewal or new direction in religious life, draw to some extent on a common body of belief and practice in the larger society. Thus we can speak of at least two important phases of religious tradition. First, "religious tradition" refers to those things handed down from the past that are shared to some extent by the members of a social group. In this phase, religious tradition becomes the basis of present and future religious life, for whatever new or deeper or repetitive elements an individual or group may experience. In a second phase, "religious tradition" may refer to that which, on the

---

[13]From *Markings* by Dag Hammarskjöld, p. 12:6, trans. Leif Sjöberg and W. H. Auden. © 1964, Alfred A. Knopf, Inc., and Faber & Faber Ltd.

basis of the old traditions—perhaps in opposition to them, perhaps in the desire to renew them—becomes in a new way a religious possibility for people.

In the New Testament accounts of the origins of the Christian movement there is an interesting blending of these two phases of religious tradition. On the basis of traditional and newly interpreted expectations of Judaism for deliverance from foreign oppressors, for God's Messiah who would bring justice and salvation to God's people, many contemporary Jews responded to a call by John the Baptist for repentance, for a renewal of life and intention in expectation of God's soon-to-be-accomplished act of judgment and deliverance. According to the earliest Christian accounts, some of those who first responded to John's interpretation and reinterpretation of the traditional Messianic hope of Israel then responded to the message and activity of Jesus. In the Gospel according to John there is the following account of how some of Jesus' first disciples or followers began to spread or hand on the beliefs and hopes they had acquired about Jesus:

> One of the two who followed Jesus after hearing what John said was Andrew, Simon Peter's brother. The first thing he did was to find his brother Simon. He said to him, "We have found the Messiah" (which is the Hebrew for "Christ"). He brought Simon to Jesus, who looked at him and said, "You are Simon son of John. You shall be called Cephas" (that is, Peter, the Rock).
>
> The next day Jesus decided to leave for Galilee. He met Philip, who, like Andrew and Peter, came from Bethsaida, and said to him, "Follow me." Philip went to find Nathanael, and told him, "We have met the man spoken of by Moses in the Law, and by the prophets: it is Jesus son of Joseph, from Nazareth." "Nazareth!" Nathanael exclaimed; "Can anything good come from Nazareth?" Philip said, "Come and see." When Jesus saw Nathanael coming, he said, "Here is an Israelite worthy of the name; there is nothing false in him." Nathanael asked him, "How do you come to know me?" Jesus replied, "I saw you under the fig-tree before Philip spoke to you." "Rabbi," said Nathanael, "you are the Son of God; you are king of Israel." Jesus answered, "Is this the ground of your faith, that I told you I saw you under the fig-tree? You shall see greater things than that." Then he added, "In truth, in very truth I tell you all, you shall see heaven wide open, and God's angels ascending and descending upon the Son of Man." (John 1:40-51, NEB)

In a similar way, later units in the text (Units 12 and 20) describe how the Prince Gautama, dissatisfied with life, tortured by unanswered questions about human suffering, began the kind of religious quest that the Hinduism of his day taught those seeking religious enlightenment to pursue. He sought answers from the holy men and the teachers of philosophy. He withdrew to the forest, fasted, and meditated. A number of other seekers after enlightenment were so impressed by his devotion and his efforts to find the answers he was seeking that they attached themselves to him, hoping that, when the answers came, they too would be enlightened through their contact with Gautama. When Gautama modified his approach, rejecting the prescribed fasting, mortification, and asceticism, these disciples were shocked and withdrew from him. But when the experience of enlightenment did come, they returned, became his disciples, and began to be part of a community that eventually preserved and handed on the teachings of Gautama.

A new religious tradition very often arises as a result of the activity and teachings of a powerful personality who has reinterpreted an older body of tradition. In later units of the book, such figures as Confucius, Martin Luther, Mohammed, and Teresa of Avila will be examined. In each case the pattern just described is present: Through a powerful reinterpretation of existing religious tradition, something new emerged, followers were attracted, and a new or renewed religious tradition began to be an effective influence in the societies and lives of individuals reached. Other such renewers, reformers, or initiators of religious tradition include Bernard of Clairvaux, George Fox, John Wesley, Alexander Campbell, Radhakrishnan, Joseph Smith, Brigham Young, and Charles Taze Russell. In more recent times there have been Mohandas Gandhi, Leo Tolstoy, Mary Baker Eddy, Sun Myung Moon, and Dorothy Day. From the work of each of these individuals who responded with various degrees of affirmation or rejection to existing religious tradition, new religious movements arose, and new and living religious traditions resulted.

UNIT 7

For a person's professed religious commitment to be authentic, the person's life must **be governed by the religion's pivotal value.**

The value systems we consciously espouse as authentic may fail to coincide with those from which we subconsciously act. This inauthenticity is often transparent.

(*Peanuts* by Charles Schulz. © 1959 United Features Syndicate, Inc.)

A

The Hebrew prophet Amos lived in a time when many of his coreligionists made a show of devotion to God. Amos believed that their acts of worship often failed to express an inner reality of commitment to the God they claimed to worship, since they were not concerned about God's demands for justice and compassion in society. Speaking for God, Amos condemned outward practices of religion that did not express authentic inner commitment.

B   I hate, I despise your feasts,
            and I take no delight in your solemn assemblies.
        Even though you offer me your burnt offerings
            and cereal offerings,

I will not accept them,
    and the peace offerings of your fatted beasts
I will not look upon.
Take away from me the noise of your songs;
    to the melody of your harps I will not listen.
But let justice roll down like waters, and
    righteousness like an everflowing stream.

Amos 5:21-24 (RSV)

Current criticism of religion usually concentrates on the hypocrisy of unauthentic religion or pseudoreligion. A song popularized by the singing group Peter, Paul, and Mary two decades ago is a good example:

C

Sunday morning very bright
I read your books by colored light
that came in through the pretty window picture.

I visited some houses where they said that you were living
and they talked a lot about you
and they spoke about your giving.
They passed a basket with some envelopes.
I just had time to write a note and all it said was
"I believe in you."

Passing conversations where they mentioned your existence
and the fact that you had been replaced by your assistants.
The discussion was theology
and when they smiled and turned to me
all that I could say was
"I believe in you."

I visited your house again on Christmas or Thanksgiving
and a balded man said you were dead
—the house would go on living.
He recited poetry
and as he saw me stand to leave
he shook his head and said
I'd never find you.

My mother used to dress me up
and while my dad was sleeping
we would walk down to your house
without speaking.[14]

Buildings, money, position, theology, and all the outward signs of religion are here subordinated to complete trust. But the song also seems to indicate that much that occurs in the worship service is not authentic. What one might do on the basis of an

---

[14]"Hymn" by Karen Gold, James Mason, and Paul Stookey. ©1968 Pepamar Music Corp. All rights reserved. Used by permission of Warner Bros. Music.

authentic religious commitment within this (Christian) religious tradition is not indicated in the song but possibly is expressed in a New Testament passage:

D   Tell them [who trust in this world's goods and goals] to hoard a wealth of noble actions by doing good, to be ready to give away and to share, and so acquire a trea- sure which will form a good foundation for the future. Thus they will grasp the life which is life indeed.
(I Timothy 6:18-19, NEB)

As should be clear from earlier units, though frequently people are not genuinely or fully committed to the religious values they profess, there are many examples of persons who *have* been authentically and powerfully committed to the values espoused by religious traditions. Hammarskjöld, Martin Luther King, and Bonhoeffer have already been cited, as well as others. In succeeding units others from a great variety of traditions—among them St. Teresa and St. Francis, Martin Luther, Gandhi, Moses, Martin Buber, and Gautama—will be presented, persons whose lives were transformed in and through wholehearted commitment to the central values of one or another of the world's great religious traditions.

UNIT 8

> For its adherents a religion usually is held to be absolute, not relative. This means **it is often difficult for one to understand the faith commitment of someone with a different faith perspective,** either within or outside one's own religious group of tradition.

Contemporary society is becoming more religiously pluralistic. Sometimes this means that religious groups and individuals within groups are more willing to be tolerant of differing groups, and of differing individuals within them or within their own group, than once was the case. Not only have the three major religious groups in contemporary America—Catholics, Protestants, and Jews—become more knowledgeable about one another and in many ways more tolerant, but each group also recognizes pluralism within its own ranks. In the past there was often bitterness, and sometimes in the present there is bitterness, between different religious groups *and* between differing individuals within the same group. The following quotation gives us some feeling for the way religious walls have affected people:

A   Thomas Sugrue recalls from his childhood: "I began to hear what came to be familiar phrases: 'those people,' 'the Prods,' 'our own kind,' 'they don't want us.' I became aware that we did not live in a community of friendly neighbors, but that as Catholics we were camped instead in the middle of war-like Protestants, who didn't want us and wouldn't let us 'get ahead.' . . . When I was twelve, a Protestant boy invited me to the Boy Scouts . . . I asked my mother and she said no. 'They don't want you,' she added, 'they're all Protestants.' . . . About this time, too, I began to hear the phrase, 'They have everything.' The Protestants, of course, were 'They.' "[15]

[15]Will Herberg, *Protestant-Catholic-Jew* (New York: Doubleday and Co., Inc., 1955), pp. 232–33.

These feelings of rejection may not abound as they did years ago in America, but sometimes it takes a long time for such wounds to heal.

Subtler kinds of misunderstandings develop among different religious groups. Different denominations stress certain doctrines and practices and thus distinguish themselves from one another. *Peanuts* illustrates this reality.

(*Peanuts* by Charles Schulz. © 1963 United Features Syndicate, Inc.)

B

UNIT 9

> In this situation a religiously committed person with an open and searching attitude may understand and empathize with a person of another faith by turning inward, to his or her own experience of religious commitment. **What is demanded is willingness of the participants in dialogue to open to each other.**

Martin Buber, a twentieth-century Jewish philosopher and religious writer who had great influence on Protestant and Catholic as well as Jewish thought, recounted in the introduction to his book *Eclipse of God* two talks he had that involved him in religious disagreement with others. In the first, after one of Buber's public lectures, a French workingman presented an argument favoring atheism. Buber refuted the man's position. Then

A

When I was through . . . the man . . . raised his lids, which had been lowered the whole time, and said slowly and impressively, " 'You are right.' . . ." Buber was dismayed. "What had I done? I had led the man to the threshold beyond which there sat enthroned the majestic image which the great physicist, the great man of faith, Pascal, called the God of the Philosophers. Had I wished for that? Had I not rather wished to lead him to the other, Him whom Pascal called the God of Abraham, Isaac, and Jacob, Him to whom one can say Thou? . . ."

On another occasion, Buber and an older man whom he greatly admired ar-gued about religion and never came to verbal agreement with each other. The older man criticized Buber for clinging to the use of the word "God." "What you mean by the name of God is something above all human grasp and comprehension, but in speaking about it you have lowered it to human conceptualization. What word of human speech is so misused, so defiled, so desecrated as this! All the innocent blood that has been shed for it has robbed it of its radiance. All the injustice that it has been used to cover has effaced its features. When I hear the highest called 'God,' it sometimes seems almost blasphemous. . . ."

Buber replied:

"Yes," I said, "it is the most heavy laden of all human words. None has become so soiled, so mutilated. Just for this reason I may not abandon it. Generations of men have laid the burden of their anxious lives upon this word and weighed it to the ground: it lies in the dust and bears their whole burden. The races of man with their religious factions have torn the word to pieces; they have killed for it and died for it, and it bears their fingermarks and their blood. Where might I find a word like it to describe the highest? If I took the purest, most sparkling concept from the inner treasure-chamber of the philosophers, I could only capture thereby an unbinding product of thought. I could not capture the presence of Him whom the generations of men have honoured and degraded with their awesome living and dying. I do indeed mean Him whom the hell-tormented and heaven-storming generations of men mean. Certainly, they draw caricatures and write 'God' underneath; they murder one another and say 'in God's name.' But when all madness and delusion fall to dust, when they stand over against Him in the loneliest darkness and no longer say 'He, He' but rather sigh 'Thou,' shout 'Thou,' all of them the one word, and when they then add 'God,' is it not the real God whom they all implore, the One living God, the God of the children of man? Is it not He who *hears* them? . . ."

We cannot cleanse the word "God" and we cannot make it whole; but defiled and multilated as it is, we can raise it from the ground and set it over an hour of great care.

It had become very light in the room. It was no longer dawning, it was light. The old man stood up, came over to me, laid his hand on my shoulder and spoke: "Let us be friends." The conversation was completed.[16]

Buber believed that the first of these two talks had been a failure. Although he had communicated with the man on the level of *ideas*, the two had failed to meet at the deeper level which gave force and meaning to the ideas. In the second talk there was apparently little or no agreement at the intellectual level, but Buber and the older man had come to *understand* each other. Each had come to understand the force of meaning and personal depth of the other's beliefs and ideas about religion and the term *God*.

UNIT 10   The following cartoon illustrates an attempt at communication that fails because of the attitude of one participant toward the other. Failure to achieve meaningful communication generally rests on the inability of the persons involved to respect and trust each other. True dialogue and honest encounter mean willingness to respect each other and to share ideas without an attempt to minimize honest disagreements.

Some may wonder whether it is valuable or necessary for persons holding to different religious traditions or beliefs to discuss religion with each other. Won't differences and disagreements be minimized if people simply agree to be different in

[16]Specified excerpts from pp. 5–9 in *Eclipse of God* (Harper Torchbook edition) by Martin Buber. Copyright 1952 by Harper & Row, Publishers, Inc. Reprinted by permission of the publisher.

A

(The Born Loser by Art Sansom. Reprinted by permission of Newspaper Enterprise Association (NEA).)

religion and concentrate on areas in which they *do* agree? In some cases, if the differences are great and mutually disturbing, can't people simply keep entirely apart from each other? (Can you think of other options besides these—agreeing to disagree while leaving religious differences undiscussed, or keeping entirely separate from those whose religious beliefs or practices disturb us?)

In the unit on the Islamic religion in Chapter 2 of *Exploring Religious Meaning*, it is suggested that if there had been better understanding of the meaning of Islamic religious beliefs and the value placed on them by their adherents, some present conflicts between the United States and the nations and groups in the Middle East might have been avoided or at least lessened in scope and intensity. Many believe that in a world that is increasingly interconnected, and in a society as increasingly diverse and pluralistic in ethnic and cultural make-up as the contemporary United States, we cannot afford the luxury of failing to understand diverse and contrasting religious positions.

In addition, some ethical or religious positions adhere to and advocate the need to try to understand, in both of Buber's senses—at the level of ideas and at the level of personal depth—those who differ from us religiously, as the Christians did who formulated the following statement concerning dialogue with persons committed to other religious traditions or positions. (Participation in the process does not assume that agreement in belief will be achieved or that all differences will be found to be unimportant.)

B

Love always seeks to communicate. Our experience of God's communion with us constrains us to communion with men of other beliefs. Only so can the Christian live the "with-ness" which was shown him in the Incarnation. His intercourse takes the form of dialogue, since he respects the differences between him and others, and because he wishes to hear as well as to speak. The fundamental nature of dialogue is this genuine readiness to listen to the man with whom we desire to communicate. Our concern should not be to win arguments.

We believe that Christ is present whenever a Christian sincerely enters into dialogue with another man: the Christian is confident that Christ can speak to him through his neighbour, as well as to his neighbour through him.

Dialogue means a positive effort to attain a deeper understanding of the truth through mutual awareness of one another's convictions and witness. It involves an expectation of something new happening—the opening of a new dimension of which one was not aware before. Dialogue implies a readiness to be changed as well as to influence others. Good dialogue develops when one partner speaks in such a way that the other feels drawn to listen, and likewise when one listens so that the other is drawn to speak. The outcome of the dialogue is the work of the spirit.[17]

[17]The Kandy Consultation on "Christians in Dialogue with Men of Other Faiths" was held from February 27–March 3, 1967, at Kandy, Ceylon, under the sponsorship of the Division of Studies, Department of World Mission and Evangelism. World Council of Churches.

2

Religious Traditions

INTRODUCTION

In the introductory chapter of *Exploring Religious Meaning* the term "religion" was given a functional definition. That is, "religion" was defined in terms of what religion does, of how it functions in the life of an individual or a group. It was defined as that which provides unifying power, a center of meaning, a supreme, or pivotal, value in the life of the individual or group.

It was also stressed, however, that religious traditions, clustered around the unifying center of a pivotal value, tend to crystallize, to develop and attain objective status, so that a religious tradition can be defined in terms of a number of characteristic features: (1) a set of beliefs (creed) which may be highly articulated and specific or may be informal and relatively indefinite but still important in shaping the lives of the religion's adherents; (2) a code of conduct (code) which, again, may be rigidly formulated in terms of taboos or may be relatively undefined, more a matter of life-style; (3) a number of devotional or ritual practices for corporate or individual worship, meditation, or self-discipline (cult); and (4) conceptions of inclusiveness or exclusiveness of the religious group and the significance of belonging to it (community). In this chapter we briefly examine seven of the major religious traditions of the world. This chapter has two major purposes. The first is to provide relevant background material about seven of the "world religions" that are frequently referred to, discussed, or utilized in the later sections of the book. (Here the reader should note that the appendix to this chapter contains a table that lists, under the headings of creed, code, cult, and community, major aspects of these seven religious traditions, as well as another table that attempts to contrast major emphases of Western and Eastern religious traditions.) A second purpose of this chapter is to illustrate the way in which the various features or elements of a religious tradition may cluster around the central emphasis or emphases—the pivotal value—of that tradition.

It must be clearly stated at this point that the following seven units are extremely brief. Material in later chapters will add to the information included in them, as will the two tables in the appendixes.

UNIT 11   Hinduism

Many would insist that oversimplification is always involved in trying to define the "essence" of a living religious tradition, that every living religion is a cluster of beliefs, practices, and attitudes held together in a certain bond of resemblance but without definable or essential identity. The philosopher Wittgenstein used the term *family resemblance* to characterize the way in which similar things—for example, games (football, baseball, chess, capture the flag)—may be like each other without necessarily sharing a group of precisely identifiable common features. Wittgenstein's term applies to religions, and to no religion more than to Hinduism, which in one sense is not a religion at all (see the remarks about Tsanoff's discussion of the term *religion* in the introductory chapter) and in another sense is a whole family of religions—sects, cults, and creeds—and of religious practices.

Unlike some of the historic world religions—Buddhism, Christianity, Islam, Confucianism—no founder or group of founders can be assigned Hinduism. The complex of rites, images of the gods, and beliefs that characterize it stretch very far back into human history. Of the hundreds of millions of Hindus in the world today, the vast majority live on the subcontinent of India, though there are Hindus in other parts of Asia. During the nineteenth and early twentieth centuries, Hinduism, responding to contact with Western Christian missionaries, experienced a resurgence of vitality. Some intellectuals in Europe and America, attached to Hindu philosophy and spirituality, were converted to Hinduism. The broader world contact that has occurred since World War II has allowed various forms of Hinduism to become more widely known and accepted. Hindu sects, such as Krishna Consciousness (also known as Hare Krishna), have been particularly successful among young Americans and Europeans, and claim adherents around the world.

To say that Hinduism has made converts itself involves a difficulty. The doctrines and cults of Hinduism are not exclusive, as are those of some religions of the world, nor is Hinduism dogmatic or doctrinaire in creed or code. It is not organized in any institutional way, though many of its sects, cults, and movements are so organized. Perhaps the prime characteristic of Hinduism is its tolerance. Willing to recognize truth in any religious creed or way of life, Hinduism grants that anyone who is sincerely religious—a Jew, a Christian, or a member of some other faith—is by the very fact of this religious sincerity also a devout Hindu. (Both Gautama the Buddha and Jesus the Christ are recognized by Hindus as among the *avatara*—incarnations—of the great God Vishnu.) Along with Hinduism's religious tolerance goes a certain skepticism and permissiveness in doctrinal formulation and practice. Since the ultimate Divine One—Brahman—is beyond all finite characterizations, almost *anything* asserted about the Divine is both true and false (incomplete). Hinduism has shown a remarkable ability to absorb and transform—to incorporate into itself—elements of other religions. Thus, though Buddhism began as a reforming, and in some ways secessionist, movement in the India of the sixth century B.C.E., Hinduism was able to transform and incorporate elements of Buddhism, as it was to do millennia later with elements of Christianity.

Westerners may find Hinduism bewildering. In one sense it is extremely polytheistic, to the extent that there are literally millions of gods worshiped in Hindu cults, but in another sense Hinduism is so purely monotheistic as to be monistic or pantheistic. There is One Divine Reality and nothing else exists at all, since *every* reality—individual human being, cow, rock, tree—in its deepest essence *(Atman)* is not a separate entity or soul at all, but is identical with the universal Self or Soul *(Brahman)*.

The many gods, whose stories are told in bewildering detail in the Hindu Scriptures, are themselves held philosophically to be aspects of the One Underlying Reality (Brahman) who is beyond all distinctions and characteristics, even beyond personality or personal existence. Though Brahman is described as the One or Supreme Self, Brahman is not to be thought of as a literal being or person, certainly not as having sexual character or personality. This nonpersonal understanding of the Divine is often difficult for Westerners, since the Divine is almost always understood in the West as having personal characteristics.

Some of the complexity involving Hindu gods results from the fact that Indian culture, like that of classical Greece, was shaped by the interaction of the culture of an original, conquered (Dravidian) population of India with the culture of conquering Aryan invaders. The gods of both cultures, certainly not identical, tended to mingle with each other and to preserve names and functions, as well as to exchange or share functions. The gods of Hinduism are closely related to nature, to natural functions and natural processes. They tend to merge and also to duplicate one another. There are gods from the realms of animal life—for example, elephant gods and monkey gods—and the cow is recognized as having divine significance.

Most important among the gods is the so-called Trinity of Brahma (Creator), Vishnu (Preserver), and Śiva (Destroyer and Renewer); each represents Brahman, the Supreme Self. Brahma, as the Creator, is rarely an object of cultic worship and is often depicted as dependent on, or derived from, Vishnu. Vishnu and Śiva, in their many forms, and with their female consorts, are, of all Hindu divinities, the most frequent objects of devotion.

Śiva is a god closely identified with the forces of the natural world, with fertility, with the river and the monsoon rains. Though a part of the great Hindu

Trinity, Śiva is presented as having several aspects. Known as the "destroyer," his destruction is for the purpose of renewal or purification, so that he not only destroys but also creates; he is often considered life itself—the force or energy that sustains life. He and his many female consorts, such as Kali, a goddess particularly worshiped in her destructive and violent character, are popular objects of cultic worship.

Vishnu, the other god of the Trinity, is known for his compassion and is most often represented as the "preserver" of life. In the role of preserver, he intervenes in human history by means of *avatara*—divine representatives in animal or human form—showering humanity with benevolent love and compassion and exerting his influence on their behalf. Krishna and Rama, as principal avatara of Vishnu, are celebrated in legend and ritual, and their stories, along with those of their female consorts, are told in Hindu scripture and art. They themselves are objects of cultic devotion, even though they are derivative figures representing Vishnu.

The patterns found in the worship of these and the many other gods of Hinduism are varied. There are important daily rites in the home and at the numerous temples where gods are honored. Elaborate religious festivals commemorate important events in history, honor natural phenomena, and celebrate the activities of divine beings. Purification rites are important in all worship, and pilgrimages to temple shrines and other sacred places, such as the river Ganges, are central in Hindu worship.

The Hindu Scriptures are an enormous body of literature of different types—from epic poetry to cultic rites and prayers—composed over several centuries. The name given the Hindu Scripture is the *Vedas*, among which the *Upanishads* contain the most characteristic statement of the philosophical concepts underlying Hinduism.

Some scholars have suggested that the basis of all later Hinduism is to be found in early rites of sacrifice from which the concept of *karma* developed. Be that as it may, the concept of karma is essential to Hinduism. It is related to a belief that the universe is strictly governed by a law of cause and effect. Individual existence is the result of a kind of ignorance (nescience) on the part of the individual. Individual entities become separated from the great ground of Being, Brahman. Wrong attitudes and actions by these individual entities produce karma, resulting in a further separation from the true Reality. The proper goal of any individual or entity is that through one of the ways of salvation (each is called a *yoga* or *yoke*)—the way of religious devotion *(Bhakti-yoga)* to a particular deity like Vishnu or Śiva, the way of action or good works *(karma yoga)*, the way of knowledge or intellectual enlightenment *(jnana Yoga)*, the way of spiritual self-discipline (meditation) *(raja yoga)*—that individual should achieve ultimate release *(moksha)* from the karmic wheel of bondage to the round of birth, death, and rebirth *(samsara)* in the world of unreality or illusion *(maya)* which separates the individual from complete union of the deepest self (Atman) with Brahman.

The theory sketched above underlies the traditional Hindu caste system. According to the theory of karma, many incarnations—many births, lives, and deaths—may be required before an individual achieves enlightenment and reunion with Brahman. The status one has in any particular existence depends upon the accumulated karma, bad or good, of previous lives. One may be born into any level of life, animal or human. Among humans, four major states or levels of caste were recognized, though there developed over centuries a multitude of subcastes within the major groupings. One was born into a caste and could not leave it, except by becoming a complete outcaste, during a given lifetime. One's caste status determined what one's vocation would be, whom one could marry, and one's religious and social duties. Highest among the castes, traditionally, was that of the *Brahmins*, the priestly and intellectual leaders of India. Next came the *Kshatriyas*, the caste of political rulers and military leaders. Third were the *Vaisyas*, the caste of persons engaged in commerce and agriculture. Fourth were the *Śudras*, the servant caste. Below these and their numerous subcastes were the outcastes, those who had sunk to a level that excluded them from most opportunities to participate in society, whose very presence was religiously contaminating to members of the higher castes, and to whom only the most degrading and menial forms of livelihood were allowed.

Since India gained independence from British rule shortly after the end of the Second World War, the Indian government has attempted to correct some features of the caste system—outlawing, for instance, the outcaste status. Social change has also greatly modified the caste system; nevertheless, the caste system continues to have great impact on Indian life.

Basically one's caste status specified one's religious duties. A vast number of rituals—often involving rites of washing for purification, of sacrifices of various kinds, and of prayers to be said or chanted—were associated with the various castes, particularly with the Brahmins. Also, though many Hindus might choose a life of perpetual religious quest or devotion, a typical pattern of life for Hindus of the three highest castes, again particularly for those of the highest, Brahmin caste, was (and to some extent still is) to close a life that had passed through several stages (student, married person, head of family, householder, and participant in economic and public life—according to one's caste status) by finally adopting the life of a religious pilgrim or hermit—a life of complete religious devotion or meditation.

Among the important rites of almost every religious tradition are rites of passage. These are ceremonies marking significant transitions from one stage of life to another. The most important rites of passage in Hinduism are those commemorating (1) the assumption by an adolescent or preadolescent boy of the religious duties of an adult, (2) marriage, and (3) funeral ceremonies, the ostensible goal of which is to liberate the soul of the deceased individual to assist in its transition to a new stage of life, either preparation for a new incarnation or final liberation.

Among the characteristic emphases of Hinduism, along with the stress on doing one's duty—moral, social, and religious—as defined by one's caste status or by one's social roles, is emphasis on the kinship and interconnection of all things. According to Hinduism, one whose eyes have been opened, one who is sufficiently enlightened, always sees only the one true reality, the one divine and wondrous

Brahman. From the lowest to the highest, everything is God, and life is therefore full of beauty and sacredness.

UNIT 12   Buddhism

Buddhism, emerging in the sixth century B.C.E., began as a reform movement within Hinduism which sought to renew the essential spiritual core of the older faith during a period when Hindu vitality had become static and ritualized. Accepted by powerful political leaders and understood to have relevance to all people, it became a missionary religion. Over several centuries it spread through Asia, where it became an important, if not dominant, religion in China, Japan, Korea, Indochina, Nepal, Tibet, and Sri Lanka. Hinduism ultimately absorbed Indian Buddhism, so that in the modern world Buddhism is hardly represented in India. Buddhist groups in other countries were to become the conveyors and molders of modern Buddhism. Buddhism, in the last century, has experienced a resurgence of missionary zeal, spreading in some forms throughout the world.

The founder of Buddhism, Siddhartha Gautama, lived from 563 to 480 B.C.E. His life is surrounded by legend, yet it would appear that he was a member of the Kshatriya Caste. His father protected him in his youth from the realities of suffering and evil in life—from *dukkha*, life's disjointedness and dislocation. Once Gautama discovered the realities of the world, he set out on a quest to discover why life should include such things and what they meant. Lasting several years, the quest led him through the disciplines of philosophy and asceticism, but he found no lasting solace in these. Eventually, through meditation, he became "enlightened"—that is, he found answers to the riddles of life—and subsequently began a new way of life. (For a more detailed discussion of his experience, see Unit 20.) He later would be called "The Buddha," or the enlightened or awakened one; he became Gautama the Buddha and is referred to throughout history as Buddha.

Having found for himself release from the anxieties of life, Buddha chose to share this knowledge with others who had shared his quest. Five ascetics who had been with him accepted his new insights and joined with him to form a *sangha*, a monastic order, the nascent Buddhist movement. Enlightened at approximately thirty-five years of age, he spent the rest of his life in a wandering existence, teaching others the insights he had gained. Although he had gathered a large following by the end of his life, even to the extent of establishing orders for women, the development of Buddhism as a distinct religion became the work of his disciples.

Some of Buddha's insights certainly contrasted with the philosophical and popular Hinduism of that time; nevertheless, he also began with certain assumptions inherent in Hinduism. Hinduism's basic understanding of the universe was accepted: (1) the concept of the material world as an illusion *(maya)* to be ultimately discarded by the true believer; (2) the belief in reincarnation in a continuous round of existence *(samsara)* from which one is to be freed; (3) the law of karma—the universe is governed by cause and effect, and all actions have their reward, good or evil; therefore, one's actions determine what one will be. Accepting this framework, however, Buddha made major transformations in the religious thought of his own day. He was convinced that all persons, whatever their stage or station in life, could achieve the enlightenment he enjoyed. Consequently, he rejected the caste system of Hinduism, which required that one advance through a large number of reincarnations to a status where release would be possible. Philosophy in Buddha's time was also highly complex and intricate. Since Buddha saw no practical applications through these avenues that would offer enlightenment to ordinary persons, he summarily rejected metaphysical speculation. He went so far as to reject even any comment or speculation on the Divine, leaving belief in the Divine questionable in some forms of Buddhism.

The principal teachings of Buddha revolved around several insights into the nature of humanity and its life. He was particularly interested in helping persons become "aware" of themselves and the world—the *dukkha* of life—and how they might overcome this disorientation. He is reputed to have said, "I teach only two things, O disciples, the fact of suffering and the possibility of escape from suffering." According to Buddha, one must recognize not only the reality of suffering but also that it is caused by ego-centered patterns—selfish desires *(tanha)*. To alleviate suffering one must learn to redirect these desires until ultimately they are extinguished—so that one is not bound by mental, emotional, or physical desires but is released simply to "be." To achieve release was not, however, a simple matter, for one must redirect one's whole attitude toward reality. The method was formulated in two direct steps. The first of these was the recognition of the truth discovered by the Buddha as expressed in the Four Noble Truths: (1) suffering is an all-pervasive fact of life, (2) suffering is caused by self-centered desire, (3) suffering can be overcome only if attitudes of self-centered desire are eliminated, and (4) attitudes of self-centered desire can be eliminated only through a comprehensive and systematic effort. The second step of the method taught by the Buddha involved a commitment to the required, systematic effort to overcome self-centeredness, an embarking on an "Eightfold Path" leading to enlightenment and ultimately to *Nirvana* (see Unit 20). Such insights into life and its realities meant that Buddha was far more interested in the ethical patterns of life than in religious rites, rituals, and theologies. In Buddha's teachings one is challenged to work out one's own "salvation," or release—others may help by pointing the way, but each person is personally responsible for the attitudes and patterns that determine one's ultimate existence. Though high ethical action is the method for moving toward enlightenment, that enlightenment is far more than simply a matter of ethics; rather, it is insight into the very essence of life and freedom to live on the basis of that insight.

A person who has experienced this insight or enlightenment has entered into a state of being most often described as *Nirvana* (extinction of desire). According to Buddha, when one enters Nirvana there is no need for a continuing soul or self; one simply *is*. Enlightenment also ends the round of reincarnations since, for Buddha, what is passed from life to life is the accumulated karma attached to one's consciousness. Having entered Nirvana, one no longer has need of individual consciousness.

Buddha's forty years of teaching elaborated these insights and others into a wealth of sayings and instructions. In his own eyes and in those of his immediate successors, he was only "the enlightened one," giving insights into life. In his own life he treated all persons and living things with compassion and taught others to do the same. Later, others were to make much more of his role and teachings—in some cases elevating him to divine status.

Immediately after his death, some of the leading monks among his followers joined in council and began to recite and memorize his teachings. The result was the formulation of dogma and tradition, which Buddha had criticized in Hinduism. These developments led first to the standardization of the teachings into scriptural writings and second to the formulation of two great branches or patterns of Buddhism.

The Scriptures were written forms of the oral tradition passed down through the centuries. First written after a fourth council in the first century, they were recorded in the Pali tongue (an ancient Indic language). Today this text is a basic orthodox version of the Scriptures. Other forms of the scripture also emerged in Sanskrit, another ancient Indian language and the official language of the northern branch of Buddhism. Codifications of these scriptural texts have been numerous and controversial.

The branches of Buddhism developed early. They arose over differences of understanding of the Buddha and his role. Theravada, or the School of the Elders, understood Buddha to be one who pointed the way to enlightenment; he was a teacher who helped others by giving instruction, but ultimately it was by the individual's efforts alone that enlightenment could be reached. As a result, the Theravadist tended to adhere to a strict interpretation of Buddha's teachings, insisting upon an austere following of rules and disciplines. The ideal followers of Buddhism were the monks (known as *arhats*), who gave themselves fully to the pursuit of enlightenment, usually through meditation. The laypersons in Theravada understood their religious role primarily as supportive of the monks' quest, yet any person might become a monk. In return for material support, the monks performed for the laypersons ritual and festival functions on such occasions as holidays, weddings, and funerals—functions often carried by priests in other religions. The monks still stressed meditation rather than these duties. Theravada became the religion of Ceylon, Burma, Thailand, and Indochina—the southern branch. Theravada, because of its austerity, is also known (by its adversaries) as *Hinayana* (the small vehicle or raft), since relatively few people (the monks) would be expected to follow its path immediately to ultimate enlightenment.

Mahayana (the large vehicle) developed from a different impulse within Buddhism. Stressing the infinite compassion of Buddha's willingness to share his insights, it stresses how he helped others achieve Nirvana. The goal is still the same—release—but within Mahayana, Buddha assumes the role of a savior and becomes deified, for he and others assist persons toward enlightenment. Buddha shares with others his divine grace or compassion. This branch tended to be much more flexible and allowed a permissive attitude toward a number of developments in ritual and theology. A most significant development within Mahayana was the concept of the *bodhisattva*, which refers to persons or beings who are "awakening" and are far along the path to full enlightenment such as that enjoyed by the Buddha. They have not fully achieved Nirvana but are close. What is distinctive about them is that they have chosen to share their insights and help those who have just begun their quest for enlightenment. The bodhisattvas are many and as bearers of a divine grace offer immense help to the ordinary believer, strength to achieve enlightenment. Compassion is their chief characteristic and they are destined to be future Buddhas. Mahayana also found a larger role for the layperson and developed elaborate and exquisite ritual patterns and art. This form of Buddhism more readily adapted itself to native patterns and forms, often incorporating national or cultural emphases. As a result it took significantly different patterns in differing cultures. This pattern of Buddhism spread north and east into China, Japan, and Korea. It is called the large vehicle, or raft, for the obvious reason that many more might expect salvation.

Although these two branches of Buddhism have dominated the development of the religion, other forms have arisen over the centuries, and all branches have adapted many native customs and practices into the religion as it has moved through the various countries of the East. In the seventh century B.C.E., Buddhism was introduced into Tibet, where it took on significantly different forms, coming to be referred to as a distinct branch, taking several names, such as *Lamaism* (referring to the central place of the Dalai Lama), *Mantrayana* (the Vehicle of the Mantras), or *Vajrayana* (the Vehicle of the Thunderbolt). In more recent times, other forms of Buddhism have arisen, such as Zen, which combines insights of both older branches, as well as elements of Chinese Taoist tradition and practice.

The diversity of Buddhism is evident, yet Buddha's basic insistence upon enlightenment, which leads one from selfish desire to a state of selfless bliss and compassion for others, binds the various branches and interpretations together.

UNIT 13　Taoism

For centuries, the religious tradition called *Taoism* (usually pronounced "Dowism") has been intertwined with dominant attitudes and themes of Chinese life and culture. The term *Tao* itself designates both a way of living that humans should follow to be in harmony with nature and the Power or Principle or Overall Governing Presence that is manifested in the universe. Thus, to follow the Tao is to live in harmony with the Governing Power or Principle that brings harmony, unity, and balance to all things. For human beings to be striving, ambitious, self-seeking, overly refined, or overly civilized (artificial) disrupts the natural harmony according to which they should, unaggressively, blend into the life that flows through all things. Understood in this manner, the Tao, or "the way," lies at the core of all Chinese culture and is claimed by the two major religious traditions that arose in China, Taoism and Confucianism. The religious tradition which took the name of Taoism is often traced to the writings and doctrines of Lao-Tzu, a teacher who is supposed to have lived during the first half of the sixth century B.C.E., yet it incorporates elements of much earlier Chinese tradition and has also greatly influenced, and been influenced by, later religious movements, especially Buddhism.

Little, if anything, is known with certainty of the life of Lao-Tzu. This name literally means "the Old Boy" and is used affectionately to designate one who is revered as a Master, Teacher, or Sage, whose life-style was marked by spontaneity, lack of pretense or pretentiousness, and a mischievous, paradoxical manner. According to tradition, Lao-Tzu was a government official who resigned his post after becoming convinced of the futility of a life of ambition, striving, and conformity to artificial social conventions. For Lao-Tzu a life of harmony with nature in its unvarnished simplicity was best. Again according to tradition, he was prevailed upon, before leaving the borders of the civilized world for good, to commit his doctrine to writing. This he is supposed to have done in the thin volume called the *Tao Te Ching*, one of the classics of the world's religious and mystical literature.

The *Tao Te Ching* is characterized by a style of thought and writing that is crisp, playful, profound, and paradoxical. In it, the central concepts of Taoism are expressed in ways that show their continuity with earlier and later Chinese attitudes, foremost of which is a feeling of harmony and kinship with nature. From very early times, Chinese society has been characterized by a reverence and a positive appreciation for nature and the powers—spirits—supposed to inhabit it. Good and evil spirits were worshiped with rites and sacrifices to secure good fortune and ward off evil. The spirits of departed ancestors were worshiped in the belief that this would ensure good fortune in the present life. A failure to worship the ancestors would turn them into avenging Furies. Many natural phenomena, both real and legendary, were worshiped as manifestations of powers and spirits—mountains, rivers, and various kinds of animals. For instance, building one's home above the nest of a dragon was supposed to bring good luck. Ritual—sacrifices, celebrations, colorful festivals—was very important, both in placating the spirits and as enactments of the harmony between the earthly (human) and the heavenly realms, both seen as parts of one whole.

Later Taoism incorporates all these elements. The worship of ancestors and sacrifices to them (though increasingly the sacrifices came to be *symbolic* in nature—a model of a house rather than a real house, or token offerings of food that might actually be eaten by the human worshipers were offered to the spirits), as well as magical rites and all kinds of charms and spells and incantations supposed to bring good luck, became parts of its tradition. The doctrine as taught by Lao-Tzu was somewhat more philosophical and mystical, but Lao-Tzu also stressed the harmony between the human and the heavenly and the place of human life in the overall unity of a nature governed by Tao.

A basic virtue or positive quality stressed by Lao-Tzu's Taoism is *wu wei*, a kind of creative passivity, an attitude of selfless nonaction according to which one flows with the life present in all things. Just as Lao-Tzu is supposed to have withdrawn from the corrupt and artificially overcivilized world of his day to return to the simplicity of nature, there are many such stories of Taoist "conversions." In one such story, a harried government official, impressed by the teachings of Lao-Tzu, is supposed to have resigned his office and titles, stripped off his clothes, and walked naked into the woods to spend the rest of his days beside a stream quietly fishing without using bait (in order not to disturb the fish, the stream, or the peaceful harmony of the natural setting). Passivity, nonaction, the absence of striving, and the utility of quiet receptiveness, spontaneity, and appreciation of the simple beauty of life—these are the qualities exalted in the *Tao Te Ching*. In a sense, *nothing*—nonaction, nonbeing—is more useful than being: it is the empty space that makes a cup useful. The hardness of a rock may impress us, but a steady stream of water—what could be more yielding than water?—can wear down the hardest rock.

Very important to Taoism is the concept of *Yin* and *Yang*. Yin and Yang are the two major components or principles that must be blended to give reality to everything. When they are blended harmoniously in accordance with Tao, peace, harmony, and fruitfulness result. Yang (in representations it is given the color red) is the positive, assertive, masculine force. It is the source of warmth, brightness, hardness, dryness, firmness, strength. Fire and sunlight are particularly associated with Yang. Yin is feminine and dark, passive, cold, moist, mysterious. Water, shadow, shade, and night are associated with Yin. Neither of these is seen as evil.

Yin and Yang.
(*Jacques Bakke*)

Both are necessary ingredients of all that exists. Yin and Yang, in fact, contain each other in a hidden or scarcely discernible way. Anything possesses its own natural goodness and health when there is a proper balance of Yin and Yang in its makeup.

Lao-Tzu apparently emphasized Yin more than Yang as a corrective device; he seemed to see too much Yang—too much of the masculine, the assertive, the rationally manipulative—in the society of his day. He wanted a right balance and therefore called for more intuitive spontaneity, mystery, and sympathetic receptiveness. For Lao-Tzu, this kind of naturalness was everything. The truly moral life was not one governed by a system of abstract moral rules or principles—one needed such a system only if one was morally corrupt. True morality meant to respond to the actual presence of things, to be in undisturbed kinship and harmony with the world and to manifest harmony in all that one did.

The Taoist doctrine taught by Lao-Tzu and later Chinese sages is sometimes referred to as *philosophical Taoism* to distinguish it from the *popular Taoism* that, for centuries, involved worship of ancestral and other spirits and belief in and practice of magical and other rituals oriented to good luck and prosperity. A third form of (or really a third element within) Taoist tradition is sometimes designated by the term *esoteric Taoism*, which refers to teachings and practices of physical and spiritual self-discipline, resembling the meditation of Buddhist monks and Hindu yogis. This aspect of Taoism was indeed influenced by Buddhism, introduced into China during the first century.

Techniques of concentration and meditation, and claims of methods of attaining remarkable physical as well occult spiritual powers, are characteristic of this element of Taoism. Taoism developed a priesthood, shrines, temples, cultic worship, and a number of divine beings to be worshiped, all to some extent modeled on Buddhist counterparts. Taoism also interacted with, sometimes complementing and at times criticizing, Confucianism, the other religious tradition which arose in the same century and emphasized the social hierarchy, law, and rational order. If Lao-Tzu emphasized Yin in order to temper an overemphasis on Yang, Confucius was the great champion of Yang tempered with Yin. For many centuries, Chinese culture was characterized by the two traditions of Taoism and Confucianism that more or less balanced or complemented each other. In fact, for most Chinese there was no inconsistency in being Confucian (with respect to one's social duties), Taoist (with respect to elements of personal life-style as well as in order to secure good fortune in the present life), and Buddhist (particularly since many of the sects of Chinese Buddhism dealt with one's fate in a life *after* the present life).

Elements of Taoist philosophy influenced Buddhist thought, too, particularly Chinese and Japanese Zen sects, and elements of popular Taoism can perhaps be recognized in the traditional Japanese popular religion called *Shinto*. With the rise of Mao Tse-tung's version of Marxism in China after the Second World War, there were strong efforts to eradicate Chinese popular religion, including Taoism, Buddhism, and Christianity, as well as religious philosophies such as Philosophical Taoism and Confucianism, because they seemed to be obstacles to the Marxist transformation, or modernization, of Chinese society. With the emergence of more permissive attitudes in post-Maoist Communism, the opposition to traditional and popular religion has lessened. Citizens are now allowed to practice religion openly, although the official position of the regime remains atheistic.

UNIT 14 Confucianism

Of the two major Chinese religious traditions, Taoism and Confucianism, Confucianism, with its emphasis on the virtues of propriety and reverence for tradition, has been the more influential in Chinese civilization. The teachings of Confucius and his disciples and later interpreters molded the social patterns and mores that were to dominate the culture for centuries. Because Confucian teachings sustained the traditional and, in Mao's view, decadent governmental and social patterns, Mao Tse-tung frequently attacked the influence of Confucius and Confucianism, declaring that it had to be rooted out before China could be transformed into a progressive, politically and technologically modernized society. (At times he insisted that some of the Confucian virtues, such as certain forms of courtesy, were nevertheless necessary.) More recently the Chinese government has stressed the importance of Confucius and his teachings as an important part of China's cultural heritage.

Confucius was born during the middle of the sixth century (c. 551) B.C.E., apparently in humble circumstances. He worked diligently to acquire an education, studying the classics of Chinese literature and music and meditating on the virtues of the great teachers and sages of an earlier period, which he took to have been more virtuous and noble than his own time. The period into which Confucius was born was one which he believed to be characterized by moral and social anarchy caused by crude and selfish behavior, especially on the part of rulers motivated by vain personal ambitions—greed, desire for prestige and power, self-indulgence. Confucius conceived the idea of a reformation of society through a reformation of its rulers. He believed that if princes could be persuaded to live exemplary lives and to show justice and compassion to their subjects, the whole of society might be reshaped in accordance with the good, tested ways of the past. Here Confucius reflected, in a more sophisticated way, the ancient and later Chinese belief that there should be a harmony between the heavenly and the earthly kingdoms, and that the ability of the ruler to conform to the eternal pattern of the heavenly sphere determined whether his subjects would be blessed with peace and prosperity. Confucius himself sought positions in government in order to try to influence princes by precept and example. According to tradition, his moral standards, his insistence on propriety, were felt to be overly rigorous, and he spent most of his life outside government service as a teacher whose doctrines and personality attracted and influenced an increasing number of disciples.

The primary emphasis of Confucianism is on sincere adherence to a moral and social code of propriety. The Chinese term *li* designates one of the primary concepts (and virtues) exalted by Confucius. *Li* means propriety—the way things should be done. It refers to good behavior, conformity to a moral and social code of appropriate behavior, doing what is customary, traditional, and required by social usage. In a more limited usage, *li* means rite or ritual. Confucius taught that the rites of Chinese traditional religion should be observed, not so much because he believed in the ancestral and other spirits to whom sacrifices were offered as because he believed in the value of ritual, rite, and ceremony—a stylized pattern of life—as good for a society's stability. Confucius hoped to correct the anarchy of his own time by establishing a highly stylized, ritualized code of conduct according to which each individual at each moment of life and in any conceivable relationship or situation would know exactly what to do and would do exactly what was expected. Thus, the two meanings of *li* tend to converge in Confucian teaching.

Crucial to the Confucian concept of propriety are the five great relationships. These are relationships of ruler to subject, father to son, husband to wife, older brother to younger brother, and older friend to younger friend. In each case, one member of the relationship is dominant and the other subordinate, yet ideally there is reciprocity of respect in the relationship. The ruler, the father, the husband, the older brother, and the older friend should show concern, courtesy, and consideration for the subordinate partner. The subject, son, wife, younger brother, and younger friend should show respect, reverence, and obedience to the dominant partner. The Confucian code is not unlike codes of chivalry of medieval Europe, in which the highborn and strong were supposed to protect the lowborn and weak, to care for them and show courtesy in all things, whereas the lowborn and weak were supposed to obey uncomplainingly and with gratitude.

The question is frequently raised about the appropriateness of regarding Confucianism as a *religious* tradition. Is it not primarily a code of ethics and a social philosophy? Bearing in mind the definition of religion as "pivotal value" given in the introduction to *Exploring Religious Meaning*, one can see that Confucianism can be regarded as having a profoundly religious dimension. Being in harmony with, being in conformity to, the eternal moral code, being in conformity with "heaven" *was* a pivotal value for Confucius. It should be remembered that for him even the rites of traditional religion were of value because observing them was demanded by the code, by propriety. In the same way, about religious beliefs— about the nature of heaven and the origin of things—Confucius had nothing to say. But he did treat the moral code as having a status in the very nature of things.

In addition to li, Confucius spoke of other virtues and characteristics that one should possess. *Jên*, which he valued so highly that he spoke of it less frequently than he did of some other virtues, designates an attitude of benevolence that produces courtesy, good will towards others, and loyalty to those to whom loyalty is due. *Jên*, for instance, produces service to one's parents and to one's ruler. It includes an attitude of respect and good will toward others and a proper respect for oneself, for one's own dignity and value as a human being.

Another important Confucian concept is that of *Chun-tzu*, which designates a kind of ideal humanity—the kind of fulfilled humanity that one should seek to achieve in one's own life. *Chun-tzu* is sometimes translated as "Superior Manhood," "Ideal Man," "Man-at-his-Best" or even as "the Gentleman." The person who is a *Chun-tzu* is someone who possesses the Confucian virtues, who conforms to the code of propriety, who is generous, unselfish, benevolent, loyal, and courteous—the opposite of someone who is petty, selfish, grasping, and untrustworthy. Confucius was convinced that the major means of acquiring this virtue, of becoming a *Chun-tzu*, was through study of and meditation on the classics of Chinese literature and music and through study of the ancient rites. Thus, Confucius placed great emphasis on correct education to create good character in individuals and to restore good order to society. Confucius, partly reflecting positive Chinese attitudes toward nature and the natural realm, believed in the essential goodness of human nature, an innate potential that can be realized through correct education in a well-ordered society. Confucius left sayings of his own as well as edited versions of earlier Chinese writings to provide a basis for an educational curriculum that for more than two thousand years shaped Chinese civilization. Mencius, a later interpreter of Confucius, did much to systematize the Confucian teachings, classifying the virtues—Li, Jên, *Chih* (wisdom), and *I* (justice). Mencius taught that the seeds or origins of the virtues were "in the nature of things," the way the world was, and that their effects would restore harmony to the present world.

The influence of the Confucian writings (some going back to Confucius himself; others, though attributed to him, probably coming from other hands) as a foundation of Chinese culture cannot be overestimated. Among these, perhaps the best known outside China is the *Lun yü* (translated into English as *The Sayings of Confucius*), though in recent years the *I Ching* (sometimes translated as *The Book of Changes*) has received much attention in the West. In fact, the sayings of Confucius—many of them memorable proverbs and epigrams—as well as the other "canonical" Confucian writings, functioned in China in ways similar to those in which sacred writings have functioned in other societies—certainly as the basis of a moral and social code, as folk wisdom, as history, and as literary models, even (as the *I Ching* did and does) providing methods of divination, foretelling and deciding about conduct to meet future situations.

UNIT 15   Judaism

Judaism, for the purposes of this unit, refers to faith, worship, and life of the Jewish people. Judaism arose among Semitic peoples who lived in the ancient Near East around the eastern edges of the Arabian desert. Migrating to the West, they settled in the Palestinian area of the Eastern Mediterranean now occupied by Israel, Jordan, and Syria. After occupying this land for a number of centuries, the Jews began to scatter through the ancient Mediterranean world after an exile period in Babylon. Their Palestinian community was destroyed by the Romans in 70 and 135 C.E., and Judaism thus became a religious community spread throughout parts of Asia, Africa—and, later, Europe and America. Its Palestinian homeland was not restored until 1948, with the establishment of the modern state of Israel. Modern Jews, bound together by their religious and cultural heritage, live over much of the world, with Israel itself comprising a relatively small number of the total.

Historically, Judaism traces its heritage to one patriarch, Abraham, and his family. Abraham was a Semitic wanderer who migrated into Palestine around 2000–1800 B.C.E. Central to his family tradition was the belief that he had been led into this migration by a God who promised him both a land and that his family would become a "mighty nation." Some centuries later (1290 B.C.E.), again at God's instigation, Moses led the descendants of Abraham out of a period of slavery in Egypt. It is as a result of this exodus from Egypt and subsequent developments that the distinctive patterns of Jewish faith and life began to emerge. Whereas Abraham and his sons were patriarchs of the community, Moses emerged as the architect of later Judaism. Beginning as a familial and tribal grouping, Judaism later incorporated others into the community if they were willing to accept the requirements of the "covenant" which bound them to God.

The basic beliefs of Judaism are rooted in the historical events that created the community. In Jewish understanding the God who led Moses and Abraham, Yahweh, chose Abraham and his descendants (the Israelites) to be his unique and particular people. By acting in their history both in the formation of the community and since that time, he has revealed himself as a God intimately related to the world and involved in its activities. Judaism also came to affirm that this God was *the* God of the universe (creator, all-powerful), thereby establishing a monotheistic faith. In the Exodus from Egyptian slavery, he further revealed himself and the nature of complete life through the giving of the Ten Commandments and the laws of Moses—the Pentateuch—the first five books of what Christians refer to as the Old Testament. He bound himself to the Israelites by giving promises of being "their God," and expecting that they in return would be "his people" by following the commandments and laws given. Created in this manner, Judaism expresses its loyalty and solidarity by a corporate life in which every aspect of life, public and private, is permeated by God's presence and human response to that presence. Through this relationship, Yahweh, although transcendent in the fullest sense, is revealed as being personal and exhibiting characteristics of love and concern, as well as justice (when disobedience occurs). For Judaism this choice by Yahweh has yet another implication: Through Israel God reveals himself and his nature to all humanity so that the estrangement that exists between himself and humanity can be overcome.

In Jewish understanding, humanity is created to be responsible for its actions. As such, humanity is given freedom of will—freedom to be obedient or disobedient to the universal laws established by God. Given this freedom, humanity has a propensity to be disobedient or self-oriented, thereby becoming evil. In receiving God's commandments and responding in faithfulness, Israel overcomes this propensity, thus becoming truly a "light to the nations." According to Jewish understanding, the Israelites have not always been faithful to this ideal and have been disobedient; yet the uniqueness of the relationship to God remains. In its best sense this is to be a source not of pride, but of responsibility for the Israelites. Historically the relationship has produced among Israelites two perspectives often held in tension—an extreme exclusiveness and a sense of world mission.

The relationship depends ultimately upon God's choice and upon His giving to the Israelites the *Torah*—"the teachings," or, more commonly, "the law." Incorporated in the concept is the understanding that for the Jew all of life is given a normative pattern by God's gracious guidance. In the broadest sense, the Torah is that guidance expressed in every aspect of life. In its written form it refers to Jewish Scripture—Pentateuch, Prophets, and Writings. It may also refer to an oral tradition of revelation as well as to oral and written interpretations of the tradition *(Talmud)*. This understanding of the Torah as a source of guidance is representative of Rabbinic Judaism, that form of Judaism which survived the Roman destruction of Jerusalem in 70 and 135 and was dominated by the rabbis—the teachers, ultimately the religious, social, and political leaders of the community. Rabbinic Judaism concentrated on interpretation of the law to adapt it to ever-changing social conditions and yet to retain its uniqueness. In the community, civil and religious law were not distinguishable from each other. Rabbinic Judaism took a traditionalist approach protective of distinctive Jewish ethical and ritual patterns. This set the members of this particular community apart from their non-Jewish neighbors (creating in Europe Jewish "ghettos," where the Jews lived separated from others), while at the same time guaranteeing the survival of the tradition that was severely tested through intense persecution in the medieval and modern periods. Ancient ritual and ethical practices, as well as demanding and exacting food laws established in the Exodus period and later, have survived into the modern day through this insistence upon obedience to the Torah.

Within Judaism, other significant features characteristic of the religion have emerged. The assumption that all of life is guided by God, added to the familial origins of Judaism, meant that the family emerged as a central element in the religion. Primary religious services and teachings, as well as the enforcement of ethical codes, take place in the home. Here the community of the faithful has its roots; therefore, some major religious festivals, as well as regular worship, take place in the home. Arising in the family is another central concern—insistence on education: to know and interpret the Torah and to prepare oneself as completely as possible for life. Related to the familial emphasis are several rites of passage: circumcision for male children as a sign of the covenant relationship; Bar Mitzvah, when the son, at age thirteen, recites Torah benedictions in the synagogue to mark his acceptance of the responsibilities of the covenant (also practiced among some Jews is Bas Mitzvah for girls); marriage, with appropriate rites and scripture readings; and burial, a simple but significant service. Each of these events, though a milestone in the individual life cycle, is also a family, and often a community, event celebrated in the synagogue. (The synagogue, formed by any ten adult male Jews, first arose as a place of teaching the Torah, but became also a place of worship.)

In addition to these ceremonies, the feasts and festivals of Judaism play an important part in the religious life of the community: Pesach (Passover), commemorating the exodus from Egypt; Shavuot (Pentecost), celebrating the grain harvest and commemorating the giving of the Torah; Sukkot (tabernacles), an autumn harvest festival; Simchat Torah, concluding and beginning a new annual round of Torah readings; Rosh Hashana, celebrating the New Year; Yom Kippur, the Day of Atonement; Hanuka, a feast of dedication celebrating victory in 165 B.C. over the Syrians; and Purim, celebrating deliverance from the Persian Empire. Other lesser festivals and fasts are also observed by many Jews. Central to all such cycles and to the regular life of the Jew is the Sabbath, instituted in earliest times as a day of rest and worship.

The impact of cultural and intellectual developments in Western civilization during the eighteenth and nineteenth centuries drastically changed the economic and political situation of European and American Jews. For the first time they were able to move freely, and they gradually abandoned the ghettos to be amalgamated into the larger society. The results have been varied. Among the traditionalists, the heritage of Rabbinic Judaism has survived to become incorporated into modern Orthodox synagogues, where ancient ritual and ethical practices are still understood to be operative, though some modifications have been allowed in order to meet urban and nonghetto situations. Nevertheless, every decision and situation in life can be the topic of Rabbinic interpretation. The intellectual ferment of the Enlightenment and its aftermath led some Jews, however, to question the ancient traditions and abandon certain of the laws (such as food laws and exclusive dependence upon the Hebrew language in religious services) and to change some elements of their theological positions. These and other changes led to the establishment of Reform synagogues—those of the more liberal Jewish religious community. Reform Judaism basically abandoned dependence upon a total religious-political-ethical code but retained emphasis upon the moral law along with traditional religious practices when appropriate. Conservative Judaism forms a third major Jewish community, which, though willing to make concessions regarding certain aspects of the law, nevertheless insists on a more conservative formulation and practice than that found within the Reform community. Each of these major groups contains many smaller subgroups which often reflect ethnic differences. With this diversification, there is still a strong cohesiveness among the Jewish community. The sense of a unique culture and relation to God is present. Although the unifying core of Jewish culture has traditionally been its religion, many modern Jews, through identification with patterns of Jewish culture, affirm their continuing identity as Jews without actively participating in, or necessarily accepting, the theological implications of the religious tradition.

UNIT 16 Christianity

Christianity began in the first century, arising within Palestinian Judaism but soon separating itself from Judaism. It gradually spread throughout the Mediterranean, becoming the religion of the Roman Empire in the fourth century and eventually the major religion of Europe. Within the past three hundred years it has experienced phenomenal growth, expanding through most of the world, and presently is the world's largest religion (with over one billion adherents).

Foundations for the religion were laid in the teachings and ministry of Jesus of Nazareth, a Palestinian Jew, who lived during the reigns of Augustus and Tiberius Caesar. Although Jesus taught in the patterns and some of the traditions of the Jewish rabbis, he also reinterpreted the Jewish law on the basis of his own authority, healed the sick and infirm, and proclaimed the long expected "kingdom of God" to have begun. The Jewish expectation of a Messiah (anointed one) who would manifest God's graciousness historically was greatly modified by Jesus' teachings. For him, God's kingdom would be established when God's will was done in the lives of the people. Jesus also taught that obeying the will of God meant loving God and one's neighbor completely. Therefore, according to Jesus, the long-expected kingdom had already begun in those who did God's will and would come to final fruition in the future. Though much more is included in Jesus' teachings, this insistence upon love to signal the coming of the kingdom was central.

Jesus' teachings and life-style were controversial, leading him to gather a number of followers but also making him an adversary of many, particularly the leaders of the religious community. Charged with blasphemy by the Jewish leaders because of his claim to be speaking by God's authority, he was handed over to Roman authorities and crucified for treason (his supposed claim to be "King of the Jews"). His followers proclaimed that he was resurrected on the third day after death and appeared to them on several occasions. The later Christian community would make the belief in his life (teachings), death, and resurrection the central affirmation of the religion, for in their understanding, through him God had uniquely appeared to humanity manifesting the nature of his love.

Because this religion has so many followers, it is not surprising to find Christians differing widely in their interpretations of the meaning of these events and of other beliefs, yet several central concepts are accepted by most believers. Basically Christianity accepted without major modification a number of Jewish beliefs: a monotheistic faith in one God of the universe, a confidence that this God acts significantly and graciously in the history of humanity, a belief in humanity's propensity to disobey the will of God and a concept of God's gracious offer of salvation to humanity by which disobedience will be overcome. As previously noted, Jesus' teachings on the kingdom did modify the normal Jewish expectations of that kingdom, as did his insistence on looking behind the multitudinous applications and interpretations of the Torah to the *intent* of the law—what theological and ethical principles were fundamental to it and what it indicated about God and his relationship to humanity.

Christianity, accepting these Jewish beliefs and Jesus' modifications of others, broke most distinctly from Judaism, however, in its proclamation that in Jesus' life, death, and resurrection he was manifested to be the Messiah (in Greek translation—the Christ). Here, for the Christian, God has revealed in a unique manner his gracious love for all humanity through Jesus' life and teachings but most certainly in the triumph over death proclaimed in the resurrection of Jesus from the dead. In this resurrection God acted out of his graciousness. For the Christian, this event, along with the life and teaching, came to mean that Jesus was the very incarnation of God himself in human form (a unique and unrepeatable event); that the power of death was broken not only for Jesus but for all believers; that believers were offered the promise of this gracious love in their lives and the hope that it would continue beyond life; and that through this event God offers salvation to all humanity by overcoming their disobedience and its consequences. Another belief arose among early Christians. In their lives and community the God who revealed himself in Jesus continued to be uniquely present in the form of a spiritual presence, the Holy Spirit. The later church would combine these insights into a doctrine of the Trinity: belief in God the Father (and Creator), God the Son (God manifest in Jesus the Christ), and God the Holy Spirit (God present in history)—a triune manifestation of one God. Subject to a great variety of interpretations, these concepts form the core of Christian theology.

Immediately after the death of Jesus, his followers formed themselves into a community to give a continuing embodiment to the teachings and experiences of Jesus. Although at first made up of Jews, the community soon began to expand so that by the end of the first century after Jesus' birth, various communities of Christians were found throughout the Mediterranean, and non-Jews had become the majority in the movement. These churches, as they came to be called, understood themselves to be the continuation of Jesus' life and mission in the world. This missionary understanding, in which Christians were to spread the "Good News" (Gospel) of Jesus, became a characteristic of the religion.

As Jews, the first Christians retained profound respect for and dependence on the Hebrew Scriptures—the Torah, the written forms of Jewish law, writings of the prophets, and historical writings. These became for the Christians the Old Testament (Covenant), embodying basic truths about humanity and God. Alongside these Scriptures arose Christian writings recounting Jesus' life and teachings, expositions of the faith such as those found in Paul's letters (Paul was a highly influential early Christian leader), sermons, and apocalyptic materials. The most significant of these became the New Testament (Covenant) and were understood to be divinely inspired. Within the community these Scriptures constitute a principal source of information, inspiration, and interpretation of the gospel. For some Christians, they are the sole authority in matters of faith. For others, they, along with faithful church tradition and the inspiration of the Holy Spirit, form the sources of authority.

The diversity of the Christian community and its accommodation to hundreds of social settings have meant a great diversification of practices and patterns of worship. Most Christians accept at least two sacraments: baptism, an initiation rite recognizing God's gift of his love and forgiveness to the person and the acceptance by the believer of that grace, and the Eucharist (the Lord's Supper, Holy Communion), a rite in which the partaking of bread and wine commemorates the life, death, and resurrection of Jesus and provides the opportunity for the believer to participate symbolically in that life and death. Interpretations of the meaning and form of these sacraments have been numerous and often divisive, yet these sacraments remain characteristic of Christianity. Certain branches of the church (particularly the Roman Catholic and Orthodox) recognize other sacraments in addition to these two (usually seven in all). Though there is also great diversity among Christian celebrations, the commemorating of Jesus' death and resurrection is incorporated in the Easter celebrations of various churches. His birth is also recognized by most Christians at Christmas, as is the coming of the Holy Spirit to the first disciples at Pentecost.

Patterns of church organization, governance, and theology have also been diverse. From the earliest period, the church found itself ministering to variant groups with differing intellectual, cultural, and ethical impulses. The result has been the formation of many subgroupings or separate groups, but most of them can be incorporated into three major branches: Orthodox, Roman Catholic, and Protestant.

During its first several hundred years, the church was a loosely organized community with local leaders (bishops) carrying responsibility and authority in local questions of doctrine and practice. When a universal or churchwide issue arose, representatives from the various local churches formed a council to make authoritative decisions. However, because the eastern and western sections of the Mediterranean represented differing cultural traditions, distinct theological and ritual practices emerged. During the first five hundred years the authority of the Bishop of Rome also spread, particularly in the West. The differences between the eastern and western sections ultimately became acute, and two branches of Christianity emerged: Orthodoxy in the East and Roman Catholicism in the West. The process was slow, and an official final split did not occur until 1091.

Orthodoxy emphasized the spiritual aspects of worship by stressing the poetic and the mystical, accepted a loose regional autonomy of "equal" metropolitans (archbishops), and saw the Eucharist as the celebration of Christ's resurrection from the dead. Roman Catholicism insisted on a more precise rationalistic theology and on the authority of one bishop over the church (the Pope), and understood the Eucharist as a remembrance and reenactment of Christ's redemptive death on the cross. Once separated, these branches had little contact with each other until modern times.

In the West, the medieval Roman Catholic church dominated Western culture and religious life. In the sixteenth century, various groups broke from this monolithic church to form new and separate churches in what came to be known as the Protestant Reformation. Although the causes were numerous, a chief Protestant concern was the abuse of spiritual and political power in the Roman church. Basic to the protest were the rejection of the power of the Pope, the insistence by Protestants that God's grace was available through faithful trust in him as well as through the sacraments, and the belief that the sole or primary authority resides in Scripture rather than the church. Accompanying such protest was the concept that one is saved on the basis of voluntary commitment to God, setting the stage for the development of numerous independent voluntary congregations and churches. Proliferation of separate denominations with their own interpretations, beliefs, and practices has been evident ever since in Protestantism. Although this tendency to separate has been characteristic of Protestantism, there have also arisen, within the past hundred years, movements toward unity. Protestant denominations have merged, downplaying their differences; national and world councils have arisen, expressing unifying concerns of Protestants and Orthodox Christians; and there has been much more contact and discussion between Protestants and Roman Catholics, as well as between Roman Catholics and Orthodox Christians.

UNIT 17   Islam

The term *Islam* literally means "submission." In the context of the Islamic religion, the term is used to describe submission to the will of *Allah*, as God is designated in the Arabic language. An adherent of the religion, a *Muslim* is "one who submits" (to the will of Allah).

Perhaps more is known with certainty about the origins and the historical founder of Islam than about those of any of the other major world religions. Muslims are sometimes incorrectly referred to as Mohammedans, because Mohammed (born in A.D. 570), a native of the city of Mecca, is regarded as the founder of the religion. Mecca was both an important center of trade and a site of religious pilgrimage. The religion of the Arabian tribes was polytheistic, and in Mecca numerous deities and spirits were worshiped. Some of the Arab tribes worshiped a god called Allah as the most important god among many other gods. A rectangular structure in Mecca called the *Ka'ba* contained many religious relics and images of gods which were objects of religious devotion. It also contained a large black stone, or meteorite, which had religious significance.

Mohammed was born into the clan that had responsibility for taking care of the Ka'ba. He is said to have been repelled by the polytheism of his own culture. As a boy and young man, he encountered adherents of Judaism and Christianity. Mohammed was impressed by the monotheism of these two traditions, by their emphasis on the revealed will of the *one* God through spokesmen (prophets) whose messages had been written down in the Jewish and Christian Scriptures.

In his maturity, he married Khadija, a wealthy woman several years older than Mohammed. He managed business affairs connected with his wife's property, but he did not forget his religious concerns. For reflection and meditation, he often withdrew to a cave in the desert, where, on one occasion, the angel Gabriel appeared to him in a vision and commanded him to "recite." Mohammed understood this recitation as a unique revelation of Allah's will. He shared this revelation with his wife, and she became the first convert to a new religion. Others joined her, and a small community of believers emerged. Mohammed experienced subsequent revelations which were written down, possibly after his death, and became the 114 *suras* (chapters) of the *Koran*, the Islamic scriptures. These revelations and the Koran are looked upon by Muslims as revelation from Allah given through his greatest prophet, not as the original thoughts of Mohammed.

Mohammed began to preach the message of Islam to the citizens of Mecca. His message was that they should abandon the worship of many gods and the idols that represented them and give complete devotion to the one God, Allah. The citizens responded with hostility, in part because they felt that Mohammed's message represented a threat to the economic benefits of the religious rites and shrines that attracted pilgrims to Mecca. For his own safety, Mohammed had to leave the city. He took refuge in another city, then called Yathrib, where he was welcomed. There his teachings were received and Mohammed was made governor of the city. Later, the name Yathrib was changed to Madinat an-Nabi (Medina), which means "City of the Prophet," in honor of Mohammed. Mohammed's escape from Mecca to Medina in the year 622 is known as the *Hegira*. From the Hegira, or Flight, Muslim calendars are dated. The city of Medina soon became involved in warfare with Mecca. Under the leadership of Mohammed, Mecca was conquered, its polytheistic worship suppressed, and the Ka'ba—with all religious images and relics except the black stone removed—became the holiest shrine of Islam. Mecca became the spiritual center and holiest city of the new religion, with Medina, and later Jerusalem, recognized also as holy cities.

During the remainder of Mohammed's life and in the years after his death, the Islamic religion spread rapidly across the Eastern Mediterranean and North Africa and into parts of Europe. Islam forbade wars of aggression, but recognized the right of defensive war and did not hesitate to suppress polytheism, while tolerating other monotheistic religions, among conquered populations. During the seventh and eighth centuries Muslims occupied Portugal and Spain and a part of present-day France. Islam also spread across all of the Arabian peninsula, across large parts of Asia—covering present-day Turkey, Syria, Iraq, Iran, Afghanistan, Pakistan and parts of India, Malaya, and Indonesia—and into China. Though Muslims were later driven from France, Spain, and Portugal, Muslim influence remained in the architecture, medicine, and philosophy of medieval Europe. At present, there are large numbers of Muslims in parts of southern Europe—Yugoslavia, Albania, and Bulgaria—as well as in Africa and in the parts of Asia just mentioned.

Mohammed is regarded by Muslims as the last and greatest of the prophets in a line extending from Abraham and other figures whose lives and teachings are recorded in the Jewish Scriptures down through Jesus. Mohammed is called "the Seal of the Prophets." He is not regarded in any sense as a divine being. (Muslims recognize a kinship with Christians as well as with Jews, since all worship the same God in a monotheistic way; nevertheless, Muslims are critical of elements that they consider polytheistic in Christianity—including the doctrine of the Trinity and the recognition of Jesus as in some sense divine, the unique Son of God—and of what they see as the unfaithfulness of the Jews to the revelation that they received through their prophets.)

Doctrinally, Islam is based on the belief in one supreme, all-powerful, eternal God, the creator of all things, and in the belief that this God has revealed His will to humanity through prophets, among whom Mohammed gave the greatest and culminating revelation. Muslims are enjoined in the Koran to observe five supreme duties, called "the Five Pillars of Islam." The first of these duties is to confess (to profess) and sincerely hold belief in the one God and in the revelation of his will through Mohammed. Anyone who can confess sincerely that "There is no God but Allah, and Mohammed is his Prophet" is regarded as a Muslim and has fulfilled the first duty of the Islamic religion.

A second duty is to offer prayer to Allah, at prescribed times, five times daily. Although ideally prayer is best offered in a *mosque* (a building dedicated to the worship of Allah), Muslims can pray anywhere. In Muslim countries followers are summoned to prayer by the chant of a *muezzin* (one who calls the populace to prayer, usually from the tower of a mosque). In prayer, Muslims, facing toward Mecca, prostrate themselves to symbolize their total submission to Allah, usually on a specially designed prayer rug (to symbolize or confer sacredness on the site where the prayer is made). Though women may attend services at mosques, it is especially important for men to do so, and if at all possible, men and boys are present in the mosque for prayer at midday on Fridays, when an *imam*—a mosque official—leads the worship.

A third duty prescribed for Muslims is to give alms for the benefit of the poor and for the upkeep of the mosque.

A fourth duty is to observe a strict fast during daylight hours of the Muslim month of Ramadan, the month which marks the anniversary of the beginning of Allah's revelations to Mohammed. The month is intended to be marked also by special conscientiousness in fulfilling one's moral and religious duties. As much daylight time as possible is supposed to be devoted to prayer and meditation. At night, feasting frequently takes place.

A fifth duty—the Fifth Pillar of Islam—is the duty of making, at least once during one's lifetime, a pilgrimage (called a *hadj*) to the holy city of Mecca. The hadj is supposed to be made with great reverence and with strict obedience to all moral and ritual requirements of the Islamic religion. A number of ritual duties must be performed during the trip to Mecca and after arrival if the hadj is to fulfill its purpose. For instance, on arrival, the pilgrim must run around the Ka'ba seven times, each time kissing or touching the black stone. Only Muslims are allowed inside the sacred city. Muslim pilgrims often testify to the sense of brotherhood present and experienced by Muslims of many different national, racial, and cultural backgrounds during the hadj.

In addition to the Five Pillars, there are many moral and cultic requirements binding on Muslims. Demanded of Muslims are justice, truthfulness, abstention from alcoholic beverages, abstention from eating pork, and above all, abstention from anything that seems remotely connected with idolatry; no representations of divine, human, or animal beings may be made.

To those who are faithful to its moral and cultic demands, Islam promises endless rewards in a blissful Paradise after the present earthly life. The rewards are often presented as involving both material and spiritual benefits. Those who are unfaithful are threatened with endless punishment in Hell, represented in graphic physical detail in the Koran (see Unit 60).

The rapid spread of Islam after Mohammed's death was accompanied by schism among Muslims. Some of these persist to the present day. For instance, *Sunnis* derive from those followers of Mohammed who accepted Abu Bakr, one of Mohammed's chief followers, as his legitimate successor. Abu Bakr was elected to succeed Mohammed after Mohammed's death and was given the title *caliph* (leader). Abu Bakr and his successor caliphs were largely responsible for the effective and energetic spread of Islam. Minority groups, however, rejected the authority of the caliphs. The Shiites felt that the true successor of Mohammed should be one of his descendants.

In most Muslim countries there are rival Muslim groups and rival interpretations of the meanings of important aspects of the Islamic religion. There have recently been militant revivals of traditional, or "fundamentalistic," Islamic practices and beliefs in some Islamic countries, particularly Iran, in opposition to adoption of Western non-Islamic influence. The necessity of developing technological societies to meet the challenges of the modern world has created great tension with the strongly felt need to resist Western encroachment and to retain distinctive Muslim patterns and traditions. The intensity of feeling among Muslims who have felt traditional patterns of belief and practice threatened by non-Muslim influence has often surprised outsiders, as has the bitterness between competing Muslim groups, Iran, for instance, is predominantly Shiite and has supported efforts, sometimes including violence, of Shiite minorities to secure greater influence in Muslim countries where the Sunni tradition is predominant.

Another major strand of Islamic faith that has been influential in many forms of Islam is that of the *Sufis*, a pattern of religious mysticism which first arose in the ninth century and continues to the present. The influence and strength of the Sufi tradition has been varied throughout history and was strongly criticized and persecuted by more traditionally oriented Muslims in the nineteenth century.

Muslim contact with the Christian West has often involved great tension, yet Muslim theologians and philosophers helped to preserve the teachings of the great Greek philosophers of antiquity, transmitting them, with monotheistic elaboration and interpretation, to the Christian philosophers and theologians of the Middle Ages. To the outside observer, the Islamic tradition may appear stern and demanding, yet rich and varied. It has supported and encouraged subtle and powerful expressions of religious devotion and creativity in the arts, in science, in poetry, and in speculative philosophical and religious thought.

APPENDIX A, CHAPTER 2

Since this book does not seek to consider exhaustively the *content* of all the varied living religions, the charts that follow are intended to serve as aids in comparing and differentiating basic concepts and thrusts in today's major religions.

The material in these categories cannot be considered complete or fully representative of any of the religions in terms of content and practice. One must constantly remember that there are problems in oversimplification. If one keeps in mind the complexity that is characteristic of any religious perspective, then the chart may be helpful in reminding the reader of important emphases in the various religions.

In addition to the seven religious traditions discussed in Chapter 2, information is included here on the native Japanese religion Shinto, which is discussed in several units of *Exploring Religious Meaning*.

	TAOISM	CONFUCIANISM	SHINTO
Creed What is the divine?	Tao: the Way.	Cosmic order.	*Kami:* Spiritual force in all things.
What is man?	One among many natural beings. Corrupted by aggressiveness and self-assertiveness.	One among many natural beings. Rational. Able to do good or evil. Moral. Educable.	One among many natural beings in whom kami is present.
What is nature?	Ever-changing process in which the harmony and unity of the Tao is ever present.	Real and dependable order in which harmony may be realized.	Expression of the kami.
What is salvation?	Becoming one with the Tao through mystical union and passivity.	Restoring harmony within society and the universe by restoring the old ways.	Recognition and veneration of the kami: the gods of the way.
Code How should one live?	Social passivity. intuitive, mystical oneness with Tao.	Harmonious relations with living, dead, and nature.	Doing one's duty and honoring the kami.
Cult How should one worship?	——	Prayers Offerings Sacrifices Hymns Scriptures Ritual Learning directed toward Heaven, ancestral spirits.	Prayers Offerings Sacrifices Hymns Scriptures Ritual directed toward the kami.
What should one worship?	——	Heaven Ancestors Spirits.	Kami, which may or may not be symbolized by images.
Community How is the religious group understood?	Any who seek union with Tao.	Every thinking, sensitive person in society.	Everyone.
How is it related to others?	Withdraws from society.	Is part of society seeking to establish harmony for all.	Includes all society.

JUDAISM	CHRISTIANITY	ISLAM

Yahweh
  (One God with personal
  attributes.)
 	
A being created in the image of
  God and directly dependent
  upon him.
	One God with personal attributes
	  characterized by love and justice
	  (often conceived of as triune unity—
	  Father, Son, Holy Spirit).
	A being created in the image of God,
	  renewed in relationship to God and
	  all men through Christ.
		Allah (one God with personal
		  attributes).
		
		A being created by Allah and
		  dependent upon him.

Created physical order with a
  specific beginning, end, and
  purpose.
 	
Proper recognition of Yahweh
  and following his will.
	Created physical order with specific
	  beginning, end, and purpose.
	
	Freedom from alienation to participation
	  in the Divine Love through
	  relationship to Christ.
		Created physical order with a
		  specific beginning, end, and
		  purpose.
		
		Heavenly eternal reward for
		  obeying Allah.

Following the commandments
  of the Torah.
	In loving fellowship with man and God.	Maintaining active obedience
		  by following the *Five Pillars*
		  and the instruction of the
		  Koran.

Prayer Ritual Scriptures Offerings Festivals.	Prayer Ritual Scriptures Offerings Festivals Preaching.	Prayer Alms Scriptures Pilgrimage.
Yahweh.	God.	Allah.

Those who recognize Yahweh
  and follow his laws.
Family.
Lives peaceably with other
  faiths.
	Those who affirm the Lordship of Christ
	  and live by his precepts of love in
	  community.
	Recognizes various approaches
	  but seeks to convert others through
	  basic message of faith.
		Those who recognize Allah and
		  Mohammed as his prophet.
		
		Recognizes Christianity and
		  Judaism as legitimate
		  religions; tolerated others.

| | HINDUISM | BUDDHISM | |
		Hinayana	Mahayana
Creed			
What is the divine?	Brahman-Atman. Eternal Spirit in world and individual.	——	Cosmic compassion.
What is man?	Eternal soul in bondage to a physical body through ignorance.		
	Reincarnation	Reincarnation	
	Karma: reap what you sow.	Karma: reap what you sow.	
What is nature?	Illusion arising from ignorance. Unreal.	Illusion arising from ignorance. Unreal.	Illusion yet reality, through which many may know compassion.
What is salvation?	Being freed from bondage to illusion through: Knowledge Works Devotion Asceticism.	Achieving enlightenment through: Four Noble Truths Eightfold Path.	
Code			
How should one live?	Meditation. Doing one's duties. Devotion to deity or deities.	Eightfold Path. Discipline. Gentleness and kindness.	Gentleness. Kindness and Discipline.
Cult			
How should one worship?	Prayers Offerings Sacrifices Hymns Scriptures Meditation Ritual directed to deity or deities.	Prayers Offerings Sacrifices Hymns Scriptures Meditation Ritual for the sake of discipline.	Prayers Offerings Sacrifices Hymns Scriptures Meditation Ritual directed toward divine beings.
What should one worship?	Powers of nature. Brahman-Atman symbolized by images.	——	Divine beings embodying cosmic compassion symbolized by images.
Community			
How is the religious group understood?	Everyone.	Those seeking enlightenment through self-discipline (monks) and, to a lesser extent, laymen abiding by the rules.	Those who express compassion.
How is it related to others?	Tolerates others. Holiest withdraw to live the life of religious hermits.	Tolerates others. Expresses wisdom to all.	Tolerates others. Expresses compassion to all.

APPENDIX B, CHAPTER 2

EASTERN RELIGIONS	WESTERN RELIGIONS
Hinduism *Buddhism* *Taoism* *Confucianism* *Shinto*	*Judaism* *Christianity* *Islam*
Oriented toward nature. Conceives of Divine Power(s) as impersonal. Places little emphasis on time. Believes world and man eternal and uncreated. Believes truth is not bound to particular persons. Tends to be inclusive. Has little interest in clearly defined doctrine. Tends toward unity of reality. Downgrades individual will.	Oriented toward history. Conceives of Divine Power as personal. Places great emphasis on time. Believes world and man created and not eternal. Believes truth comes through particular persons. Tends to be exclusive. Has strong interest in clearly defined doctrine. Tends toward duality of reality. Exalts individual will.

3 _____

Cases of Religious Experience

INTRODUCTION

A flash of insight dawns as the Zen Buddhist is engaged in strenuous silent meditation; the Christian Pentecostal cries out in joyous ecstasy, in language unintelligible to the average listener, at the height of a highly active group experience. Through rational consideration and observation, the religious intellectual apprehends an orderly interrelationship of life forms, and places this in the context of an awesome universe—such are the enormous wide-ranging personal experiences that may be termed religious.

Religious experience may be broadly divided into two basic forms—the intensely personal experience, and group experiences, in which one joins with others. These may also be distinguished as spontaneous experiences (those which occur without conscious, recognizable motivation or preparation) or formal experiences (those structured to produce particular types of religious experience). The spontaneous experience is generally identified with that of the individual and the formal experience with that of the group. These experiences need not be exclusive of each other; an individual while participating in a formal group worship service may have a spontaneous individual experience. Also, individuals who see their own experience as unique may find it shared by a group. This is a natural basis for the creation of religious groups—shared or similar individual experiences. Examples of both individual and group experiences, as well as spontaneous and formal experiences, are examined in this section.

This chapter presents representative examples of individual religious experiences. They have been selected from a number of traditions and periods not only to show the richness of diversity but also to allow the reader to observe the intensity and significance that the experiences held for the persons involved. Corporate expressions of religious experience are included in the study of structural elements in Chapter 4. Our purpose here is to begin with specific individuals who were historically influential but typical of the "varieties of religious experience."

The following questions may provide a framework for examination of the cases of religious experience given in this chapter. They will also be relevant to the instances of religious experience described throughout the book.

1. How did the experience initiate, maintain, strengthen (intensify), or weaken the relationship of the individual or group to (a) pivotal value(s)?
2. What specific features did the experience have?
   Was it an experience of conversion/nurture/intensification?
   Was it sudden or gradual?
   Was it expected or unexpected?
   Was it sought (a quest) or unsought (a call)?
3. In what context did the experience occur?
   Did it occur in familiar or in unfamiliar surroundings?
   Did it occur in relation to familiar or unfamiliar persons?
4. Where was the religious experience centered—that is, what areas of the individual's or the group's life did it affect most? Least?
5. How did it affect the individual's or the group's relationships? How did it affect the roles the individual had in the group or the roles the group had in the larger society?

It should be remembered that many factors influence and are affected by individual or group experience. Most religions involve a belief, or credal component. Similarly, every religion contains some directives, moral or legal, relating to the way of life, or code of conduct, advocated for its adherents or the world at large. Most religions contain practices and prescriptions for public and private devotion, its worship or cultic aspect. Finally, every religious tradition contains some concept of limits of the community—who is included and how one becomes included, who is excluded—united in (or divided by) their adherence to the particular tradition. Note how each of these factors, and others, may or may not be present in the cases that follow.

UNIT 18   God's Call, Moses' Response

Moses was the leader of the Hebrews during their exodus from Egypt, perhaps sometime during the fourteenth to thirteenth centuries B.C.E. Born to a Hebrew woman but reared in Pharaoh's court, Moses enjoyed Egyptian favor until he impulsively killed an Egyptian taskmaster whom he saw mistreating one of his Hebrew kinsmen. Fearing Egyptian punishment for murder, he fled to "the land of

Midian," where he became a shepherd and married the daughter of Jethro, "the priest of Midian" (Exodus 2:15–22). While in Midian, Moses received a "call" from God. As the following passage indicates, God initiates the relationship with Moses and defines its purposes.

While keeping his father-in-law's flock, Moses approaches the traditional holy mountain of God, Horeb. There he encounters a burning bush which is not consumed by the fire, and, having paused to investigate this phenomenon, finds God speaking to him.

> When the Lord saw that he turned to see, God called to him out of the bush, "Moses, Moses!" And he said, "Here am I." Then he said, "Do not come near; put off your shoes from your feet, for the place on which you are standing is holy ground." And he said, "I am the God of your father, the God of Abraham, the God of Isaac, and the God of Jacob." And Moses hid his face, for he was afraid to look at God. (Exodus 3:4–6, RSV)

Note that this is a personal direct encounter with God. Moses does not observe God himself but is clearly aware of his holy presence. In Hebrew tradition such encounters are normally for a particular purpose—a call to mission or an instruction to the people. The Lord makes the purpose of this call clear.

> Then the Lord said, "I have seen the affliction of my people who are in Egypt, and have heard their cry because of their taskmasters; I know their sufferings, and I have come down to deliver them out of the hand of the Egyptians, and to bring them up out of that land to a good and broad land, a land flowing with milk and honey. . . . Come, I will send you to Pharoah that you may bring forth my people, the sons of Israel, out of Egypt." (Exodus 3:7–10, RSV)

Moses then responds in typical human fashion with a series of reasons why he should not be God's messenger. Moses wants to know "Who am I that I should go to Pharoah?" The question is never answered directly. He is simply God's choice. Next Moses objects that he does not even know the name of the God who is giving the call. God then identifies himself as "I AM WHO I AM" and the "God of your fathers—Abraham, Isaac, and Jacob." The "I AM" designation indicates that Moses is here encountered by the transcendent, holy God whom the Hebrews had once followed, but had forgotten. In giving Moses this "new" name, God is asserting that no explanatory name is adequate or necessary—he simply "is"—yet he is also identifying himself with the ancient God of the Hebrews and renewing his promises to Israel. Convinced that the Israelites will never believe what he has heard from God, Moses further objects.

God promises a sign to the people—a shepherd's rod or staff will become a serpent. Moses then points out that he is "not eloquent . . . slow of speech and tongue." God chides Moses, pointing out that he had made Moses' tongue, and he promises to be with Moses in his speech. Finally, Moses, driven to no more excuses, cries out, "Oh, My Lord, send, I pray, some other person." God, relentless in his call, only promises to use Moses' brother, Aaron, as his spokesman. Moses reluctantly submits to the call.

God establishes the relationship, and yet Moses is free to struggle with his response to that call. Based upon a personal encounter, the call is to a much broader community responsibility—the saving of all of Israel. The experience changes the direction of Moses' life and the immediate relationship of God to the people of Israel. In submitting to God's will, Moses becomes one of the central figures through whom the relationship of Israel and God is revealed and clarified.

UNIT 19 Luther's Religious Experience

A vivid description of personal religious pilgrimage comes from the writings of Martin Luther, a leading figure of the sixteenth-century Protestant Reformation.

Following the wishes of his strong-willed father, Martin began as a young man to prepare himself for a law career in order to assist in his father's business. This changed, however, when he was struck to the ground by a bolt of lightning in a thunderstorm. At that moment Luther vowed, "Help me, Saint Anne, I will become a monk!" Entering the Augustinian Convent at Erfurt in 1505, against his father's will, he assiduously pursued the monastic life. He had no doubt been troubled for some time by religious questions, especially by the problem of how one could come into the saving relationship with God, who in those medieval times was often depicted as the condemning judge of the unrighteous. Luther gave himself unstintingly in seeking to experience God's grace. He quickly rose in his order and became a professor in the University of Wittenburg in 1512. Nevertheless, for all his close observance of the medieval way to salvation (serious good intentions, repentance, confession of sins, good works, and sacramental observance), he found no satisfying answer to his own growing question: How can one stand in holiness before the demanding righteousness of a just God?

During the period 1513–19, Luther lectured at Wittenburg on the Psalms and Paul's letters to the Romans and Galatians. Through his constant dealing with these Scriptures, he discovered a new and vital meaning in the Gospel of Christ. He experienced what is classically known as justification by grace through faith—trusting in God's merciful love rather than one's own good works for salvation. His account of this religious experience follows:

Though I lived as a monk without reproach, I felt that I was a sinner before God with an extremely disturbed conscience. I could not believe that he was placated by my satisfaction. I did not love, yes, I hated the righteous God who punishes sinners, and secretly, if not blasphemously, certainly murmuring greatly, I was angry with God, and said, "As if, indeed, it is not enough, that miserable sinners, eternally lost through original sin, are crushed by every kind of calamity by the law of the decalogue, without having God add pain to pain by the gospel and also by the gospel threatening us with his righteousness and wrath!" Thus I raged with a fierce and troubled conscience. Nevertheless, I beat importunately upon Paul at that place, most ardently desiring to know what St. Paul wanted.

At last, by the mercy of God, meditating day and night, I gave heed to the context of the words, namely, "In it the righteousness of God is revealed, as it is written, 'He who through faith is righteous shall live.' " There I began to understand that the righteousness of God is that by which the righteous lives by a gift of God, namely by faith. And this is the meaning: the righteousness of God is revealed by the gospel, namely, the passive righteousness with which merciful God justifies us by faith, as it is written, "He who through faith is righteous shall live." Here I felt that I was altogether born

again and had entered paradise itself through open gates. There a totally other face of the entire Scripture showed itself to me. Thereupon I ran through the Scriptures from memory. I also found in other terms an analogy, as, the work of God, that is, what God does in us, the power of God, with which he makes us strong, the wisdom of God, with which he makes us wise, the strength of God, the salvation of God, the glory of God.[1]

Are there elements in Luther's experience that are also found in the experience of Gautama Buddha as described in Unit 20? What is different about these two experiences? What similarities and differences do you see in this experience and that of Augustine's conversion as described in Unit 26? What was it in the experience that was most important for Luther, in your opinion?

UNIT 20   Gautama's Quest for Nirvana

Siddharta Gautama is reputed to have been reared in a noble family in India, where he was protected from many harsh realities of the world. As a young man, he ventured forth into that world, only to discover and be staggered by extreme human suffering, disease, and death. Resolved to find answers to these realities of the human condition, he began a quest.

Like many before him in India, Gautama (born c. 560 B.C.E.), a contemporary of Confucius, began the life of spiritual sojourn, now studying with the Brahmins and then joining in the company of the ascetics, now gaining knowledge in Hindu philosophy and then experiencing extreme asceticism. Even after six years of striving, his quest was not satisfied. Having exhausted the means suggested by the holy men of India, Gautama sat under the Bodhi Tree (the Tree of Wisdom) in meditation, determined to find a solution to the riddle of existence. During this meditation, it is said that Gautama received an illumination. Thereafter he was called Buddha, the Enlightened One. In the following are described Gautama's religious experience and the Buddhist concept of Nirvana.

Gautama's Religious Experience

A

Then I thought, it is not easy to gain that happy state while my body is so very lean. What if I now take solid food, rice and sour milk. . . . Now at that time five monks were attending me, thinking,

"When the ascetic Gautama gains the Doctrine, he will tell it to us." But when I took solid food, rice and sour milk, then the five monks left me in disgust, saying, "The ascetic Gautama lives in abun-

[1]Excerpt from *Martin Luther, Selections from His Writings*, ed. John Dillenberger, p. 11. Copyright © 1961 by John Dillenberger. Reprinted by permission of Doubleday & Company, Inc.

B

Amida Nyorai (Amitabha), known as
Great Buddha of Kamakura, thirteenth
century. Kotokuin Temple, Kamukura,
Japan (Photo by M. Sakamoto; repro-
duced by permission of Sakamoto
Photo Research Lab., Tokyo, Japan.)

dance, he has given up striving, and has turned to a life of abundance."

Now having taken solid food and gained strength, without sensual desires, without evil ideas I attained and abode in the first trance of joy and pleasure, arising from seclusion and combined with reasoning and investigation. Nevertheless such pleasant feeling as arose did not overpower my mind. With the ceasing of reasoning and investigation I attained and abode in the second trance of joy and pleasure arising from concentration, with internal serenity and fixing of the mind on one point without reasoning and investigation. With equanimity towards joy and aversion I abode mindful and conscious, and experienced bodily pleasure, what the noble ones describe as "dwelling with equanimity, mindful, and happily," and attained and abode in the third trance. Abandoning pleasure and abandoning pain, even before the disappearance of elation and depression, I attained and abode in the fourth trance, which is without pain and pleasure, and with purity of mindfulness and equanimity.[2]

Having progressed to a state of pure consciousness, Gautama came to several states of knowledge. First, he reviewed his many former existences, in which he had gone through thousands of rebirths. In these he came to understand each of his former lives and the truth that there is rebirth in the normal order of life. Second, he came

[2]Edward J. Thomas, *The Life of Buddha as Legend and History* (London: Routledge and Kegan Paul, Ltd., 1927), pp. 66–68.

to realize that the reason for this constant rebirth is the law of karma, wherein those who lead evil lives "in deed, word, and thought . . . are reborn in a state of misery and suffering." Those who live good lives are "reborn in a happy state." Having become aware of this truth, Gautama had arrived at the basic Buddhist understanding of the nature of the world: Life contains suffering brought about by desire, and this suffering can be overcome through elimination of desire—an insight which comes to be known among Buddhists as the Four Noble Truths (see p. 57). This awareness of the nature of the universe, or "enlightenment," brought Gautama an immense sense of freedom and emancipation.

C   As I thus knew and thus perceived, my mind was emancipated from the āsava of sensual desire, from the āsava of desire for existence, and from the āsava of ignorance. And in me emancipated arose the knowledge of my emancipation. I realized that destroyed is rebirth, the religious life has been led, done is what was to be done, there is nought (for me) beyond this world. This was the third knowledge that I gained in the last watch of the night. Ignorance was dispelled, knowledge arose. Darkness was dispelled, light arose. So is it with him who abides vigilant, strenuous, and resolute.[3]

The freedom and knowledge obtained in this enlightenment Gautama then chose to share with others. His experience and the teachings that arose from it became the basis of Buddhism. An ultimate state of freedom from the world and eternal bliss was taught by Gautama and is known as Nirvana. Following are descriptions of this state and suggestions as to how it might be achieved.

D   A wanderer who ate rose-apples spoke thus to the venerable Sariputta:
"Reverend Sariputta, it is said: 'Nirvana, Nirvana.' Now, what, your reverence, is Nirvana?"
"Whatever, your reverence, is the extinction of passion, of aversion, of confusion, this is called Nirvana."
(*Samyutta-nikāya* IV, 251-52)

E   The stopping of becoming is Nirvana.
Samyutta-nikāya II, 117
It is called Nirvana because of the getting rid of craving.
Samyutta-nikāya I, 39[4]

F   We are told that Nirvana is permanent, stable, imperishable, immovable, ageless, deathless, unborn, and unbecome, that it is power, bliss, and happiness, the secure refuge, the shelter, and the place of unassailable safety; that it is the real
Truth and the supreme Reality; that it is the *Good*, the supreme goal, and the one and only consummation of our life, the eternal, hidden and incomprehensible Peace.[5]

[3]Ibid., p. 68.
[4]Edward Conze, ed., *Buddhist Texts Through the Ages* (New York: Harper & Row, 1964), pp. 92, 94.
[5]Edward Conze, *Buddhism: Its Essence and Development* (New York: Harper & Row, 1959), p. 40.

Gautama's *Four Noble Truths:*

---

1. That life inevitably involves *dukkha* (suffering)
2. That the cause of suffering is *tanha* (desire or selfish craving)
3. That the suffering can be cured by overcoming selfish craving
4. That the way to overcome selfish craving is through following the eightfold Way, or Path

---

The following steps constitute the *Eightfold Path* and led one to Nirvana:

---

1. Right View—Awareness of life's problem.
2. Right Thought—Determination to solve this problem.
3. Right Speech—Abstention from lies and evil language.
4. Right Action—Abstention from killing, stealing, and immoral conduct.
5. Right Mode of Livelihood—Noninvolvement in the professions that harm living things.
6. Right Endeavor—Suppression of wrong states of mind and creation of right states of mind.
7. Right Mindfulness—Self-knowledge and self-mastery.
8. Right Concentration—The understanding of truths about human existence and of Gautama's insight that emerged from his experience under the Bodhi Tree.

How does Gautama's religious experience compare with Luther's?

Is your understanding of "salvation" similar to what is described as Nirvana?

The Eightfold Path regulates how the Buddhist should live. How does it resemble or differ from your ethical codes?

UNIT 21 Saint Francis

To describe the religious experience of Saint Francis of Assisi is to recount the story of a series of events that led to a life of humble service to others and continual awareness of God's presence in every aspect of the created world.

Francesco Bernardone was born in Assisi in 1182, a time of prosperity during which many people felt that the love of wealth had replaced the love of Christ. Francis was the son of a wealthy merchant. As a young man he took part in celebrations and festivities that provided the main occupation for sons of the wealthy. He was often named "king of the feasts," an office that included responsibility for footing the bill for entertainment. His goal in life, however, was more ambitious. He was never fully satisfied with the life of pleasure. He wanted to become a knight—a possibility at this time open to sons of the wealthy middle class—living by the knightly code. He saw himself becoming a great hero who would win fame and fortune by his brilliant conquests.

In 1205 Francis set out for Apulia to enlist in the army of Gualtieri of Brienne. With characteristic generosity, he gave his own military equipment to a nobleman who was too poor to buy a suit of armor. That night he had a dream in which he saw a magnificent palace filled with weapons and military trophies and heard a voice calling him by name. He took the dream to be a sign that he would succeed in his military career. On the next night the voice spoke to him again, asking him why he had left the service of his Lord for the service of a vassal. The voice told him to return to Assisi.

Francis did return to Assisi and was welcomed with ridicule by his friends and relatives, who felt he had abandoned a military career because of faint-heartedness.

While riding one day, he found himself among lepers, who were at that time still rejected by society. Dismounting, he ministered to them, thus beginning his career of service to those in need. Soon after this event he felt an irresistible urge to enter a church he was passing, the Church of Saint Damiano. He knelt in front of a crucifix, and to his amazement, the figure of Christ on the cross seemed to begin talking to him: "Francis, repair my house because it is falling into ruin." Francis interpreted this as a command to rebuild the crumbling church in which he found himself, not suspecting that the call had much wider implications. His interest in service and religion now heightened, he took a roll of cloth from his father's shop, sold it, and gave the money to a priest.

Francis's father was outraged. He wanted his son to achieve success in a secular career; he was angry because he had taken the material from his shop, and brought legal proceedings against his son. During the hearing, Francis renounced his hereditary rights, even stripping off the garments he was wearing to return them to his father. When Francis made this gesture, demonstrating his willingness to give all to Christ, Bishop Guido, who was presiding at the hearing, took the young man under his protection.

Francis began to rebuild the Church of Saint Damiano, using his own labor and whatever materials he could gather. One day, while attending mass, he heard a passage from the Gospel giving Christ's instructions to his disciples for a preaching mission they were to undertake. He heard in this passage that Christ's disciples must possess no money, no gold or silver, no wallets or purses, no footwear, and only one tunic, and that they must devote their lives to proclaiming the Kingdom of God and the necessity of repentance. Thereupon he dedicated himself to such a life of poverty and witnessing, finding in this life a satisfaction he had never known in the life of pleasure and worldly ambition.

He soon found many followers. At first, most of them came from the wealthy middle class and the nobility; some had tried the joys of wealth and pleasure and had found them flat and tasteless. Soon they were joined by persons from all sectors of society, including the poor. Poverty was a strict requirement for every Franciscan. The order itself was intended by its founder neither to acquire nor to own property.

Toward the end of his life, after having journeyed to Egypt in an attempt to end the armed conflict between Muslims and Christians by an appeal to the Sultan, Francis, in a state of ecstasy, experienced a vision of the crucified Christ descending from heaven in angelic form. It is said that after receiving this vision, Francis bore on his own body, in his hands and side, the stigmata, the marks of the wounds of Christ. Not long after this, he wrote the famous "Canticle of the Creatures," a poem calling on all the creatures of the natural order, including humankind, to praise God for his goodness and love. Francis told his followers to sing the canticle in public squares after their sermons to lift the hearts of people so that they might be led to God "in gladness of spirit."

St. Francis died on October 3, 1226, at the age of forty-two. Just before his death, he recited a verse from one of the Psalms: "Free my soul from prison, so that I may praise Thy name."

The Canticle of the Creatures (in part)

All creatures of our God and King,
Lift up your voice and with us sing
Alleluia! Alleluia!
Thou burning sun with golden beam,
Thou silver moon with softer gleam!
O praise Him, O praise Him!
Alleluia! Alleluia! Alleluia!

ST. FRANCIS OF ASSISI
Translated by William H. Draper[6]

UNIT 22 Saint Teresa's Ecstasy

Christian mysticism has never been more highly developed or widely appreciated than it was in sixteenth-century Spain. Central figures in the reforms brought to the life of the church by this mystical tradition were Saint Teresa of Avila and her younger colleague, Saint John of the Cross. Their writings on mysticism provide for the Roman church standards for mystical discipline and have greatly influenced the tradition in all its phases. For her preeminence in this field, Saint Teresa was declared a "Doctor of the Church" in 1970—a distinction granted to only two women by the Roman Catholic church.

Born in 1515, Teresa was a member of a prominent Spanish family. On her mother's death when she was fourteen, she began to turn to a more serious religious life, although its full fruition was a long time in coming. At the age of twenty, over

[6]Used by permission of J. Curwen & Sons, Ltd.

her father's objections, she entered the Carmelite Monastery of the Incarnation at Avila. Except for periods of illness, she remained there until 1562. The Carmelite convent at that time allowed a rather lax religious life with a good deal of interaction with the secular community. From her early years Teresa had experienced visions, trances, and other spiritual experiences, which intensified through the years and made her uncomfortable with the convent's lack of a rigorous spiritual life. Beginning in 1555, as a result of an experience of intense compassion and sorrow at the sight of a statue of Christ's scourging, she turned to a life of spiritual perfection. Over considerable opposition, she was granted permission in 1562 to establish the Convent of Saint Joseph, in order to follow more strictly the original disciplines of poverty and spiritual life of the Carmelite order. The community became known as the Discalced (Barefooted) Carmelites, and over the next twenty years some thirty-two houses were established for both nuns and monks. The ultimate influence of the reforms instituted was to be felt throughout the whole Carmelite order. Teresa's mysticism became the example for dedicated spiritual life and, at the same time, was combined with an extremely active participation in religious reform. In later life her mysticism provided the motivation and power for her involvement in establishing and controlling an increasingly influential religious order. Mysticism did not lead her to become inactive or passive.

To share her experiences, she wrote, at the urging of her superiors, several books. Her *Life* is both a recounting of her own early experiences and a manual for her sisters in the disciplined spiritual life. In this work, she describes several states of prayer, from the first beginnings in meditation to union with God. The metaphor of water is used to illustrate her experience. The first state of prayer is like drawing water from a well. It is difficult, requiring discipline when the result is small and slow. The second state is like the introduction of an irrigation pump. Divine aid is given and the reward is much greater. The third state is compared to a running stream. The stream runs at God's instigation and not that of the individual; one's faculties are reduced, in that one may participate in directing the flow but may have little other function. The final stage is likened to a gentle shower of rain, wherein the soul is freely watered by God without human effort. One's usual faculties are transcended so that the experience becomes indescribable. Ecstasy comes at God's instigation, is not granted to many, and results in influencing the person's subsequent life (this was the way Teresa distinguished between true and hallucinatory experience). Teresa insisted that, though such experiences were of the greatest importance, they were not ends in themselves—the goal of life remained to do God's will.

The following passage from her *Life* recounts one of Teresa's best known descriptions of an ecstatic mystical experience.

A   It pleased the Lord that I should sometimes see the following vision. I would see beside me, on my left hand, an angel in bodily form—a type of vision which I am not in the habit of seeing, except very rarely. Though I often see representations of angels, my visions of them are of the type which I first mentioned. It pleased the Lord that I should see this angel in the following way. He was not tall, but short, and very beautiful, his face so aflame that he appeared to be one of the highest types of angel who seem to be all afire. . . . In his hands I saw a long golden spear and at the end of the iron tip I seemed to see a point of fire. With this he seemed to pierce my heart several times so that it penetrated to my entrails. When he drew it out, I thought he was drawing them out with it and he left me completely afire with a great love for God. The pain was so sharp that it made me utter several moans; and so excessive was the sweetness caused me by this intense pain that one can never wish to lose it, nor will one's soul be content with anything less than God. It is not bodily pain, but spiritual, though the body has a share in it—indeed, a great share. So sweet are the colloquies of love which pass between the soul and God that if anyone thinks I am lying I beseech God, in His goodness, to give him the same experience.[7]

In the seventeenth century Saint Teresa's experience of the pierced heart was depicted in sculpture by Gianlorenzo Bernini. This piece was to become one of the most well-known religious art works of the day and the most famous representation of Saint Teresa.

B

The Ecstasy of St. Theresa by Gianlorenzo Bernini, in Sta. Maria della Vittoria, Rome. (Reproduced by permission of Alinari—Art Reference Bureau.)

What distinctions do you see between Teresa's experience, described here, and those of Gautama (Unit 20)? How does it compare to Luther's or Moses' experience?

[7]*The Life of Teresa of Jesus: The Autobiography of St. Teresa of Avila*, trans. and ed. by E. Allison Peers (New York, Doubleday & Co. Inc., 1960) pp. 274–75. Reprinted by permission.

UNIT 23   Juan Diego and Our Lady of Guadalupe

In April 1519, Hernando Cortez and his Spanish army entered Mexico. The natives of Mexico were subjugated by the conquerors, who sought to force their culture and religion upon the indigenous people in the name of the Cross of Catholicism and the Crown of Spain. The priests who accompanied Cortez represented the Roman Catholic mandate to missionize, evangelize, and win pagans to Christianity. During the decade following the conquest by Cortez, the Indians of Mexico resisted the Catholic faith. Then, in 1531, a mysterious event happened—one that caused the Indians of Mexico by the thousands to embrace Catholicism. Virgilio Elizondo writes about this religious experience as follows:

There is no scientific proof or disproof, or explanation, of the "apparition" of Our Lady of Guadalupe, but there can be no denying its impact on the Mexican people from that time to the present. Its inner meaning has been recorded in the collective memory of the people.

According to the legend, as Juan Diego, a Christian Indian of common status, was going from his home in the *barriada* ("district") near Tepeyac, a hill northwest of Mexico City, he suddenly heard beautiful music. As he approached the source of the music, a lady appeared to him. Speaking in Nahuatl, the language of the conquered, she ordered Juan Diego to go to the palace of the archbishop of Mexico, at Tlatelolco, and tell him that the Virgin Mary, "Mother of the true God through whom one lives," wanted a temple to be built on that site so that in it she could "communicate all her love, compassion, help, and defense to all the inhabitants of this land . . . to hear their lamentations and remedy their miseries, pain, and suffering."

After two unsuccessful attempts by Juan Diego to convince the bishop of the Lady's authenticity, the Virgin wrought a miracle. She sent Juan Diego to pick roses in a place where only desert plants grew. She then arranged the roses in his cloak and sent him to the bishop with the sign he had demanded. As Juan Diego unfolded his cloak in the presence of the bishop, the roses fell to the floor and the painted image of the Lady appeared on his cloak.

The subjugated Mexican people came to life again because of Guadalupe. The response of the Indians was a spontaneous explosion of pilgrimages, festivals, and conversions to the religion of the Virgin. Out of their meaningless and chaotic existence of the postconquest years, a new meaning had erupted.

The real miracle was not the apparition but what happened to the defeated Indian. In the person of Juan Diego was represented the Indian nations defeated and slaughtered, but now brought to life. They who had been robbed of their lands and of their way of life and even of their gods were now coming to life. They who had been silenced were now speaking again through the voice of the Lady. They who wanted only to die now wanted to live.

As at Bethlehem when the Son of God was born as Jesus and signaled the reversal of the power of the Roman empire, so at Tepeyac Christ set foot on the soil of the Americas and signaled the reversal of European domination. Tepeyac symbolized the birth of the Mexican people and the birth of Mexican Christianity. They were no longer an orphaned people and the new religion was no longer that of foreign gods.[8]

[8]Virgilio Elizondo, *Galilean Journey: The Mexican-American Promise* (Maryknoll, New York: Orbis Books, 1983), pp. 11, 12.

Every year, thousands of persons make a pilgrimage to the Basilica de Guadalupe in Mexico City, where Juan Diego's apparition is believed to have happened. There they recall the story and worship Our Lady of Guadalupe. The centrality of this story for the people of Mexico and Latin America cannot be overemphasized. One cannot understand the people of Mexico and the religious roots of Mexico without reference to Juan Diego, whose experience represents in an exemplary way how many Mexican people believe in God.

UNIT 24 Mahatma Gandhi's Religious Journey

Mahatma Gandhi led India to independence from England, not by the power and might of military strength, but by *Satyagraha* (nonviolent direct action). A world-renowned figure in his own lifetime, Gandhi was revered and admired by millions in both the East and West for his courage to renounce violence and his tremendous spiritual strength. Born in India in 1869 and reared a Hindu, he trained in England to be a lawyer and practiced law in South Africa for twenty years before returning to India. There, with creative power, he led his people to spiritual renewal and to political independence. In 1948, while on his way to prayer, Gandhi was assassinated. His last words, murmured as he was shot, were, "Hey Rama (oh God)."[9]

Gandhi's early glimpses of religion came from the Vaishnava faith, but that interpretation of Hinduism repelled him because of too much "pomp and glitter."[10] While a law student in England he studied the *Bhagavad Gita* and then the Bible, reading the Old Testament in boredom but the New Testament with deep interest, especially the "Sermon on the Mount," which he compared to the *Gita*. He was particularly impressed by Jesus' teaching:

> "But I say unto you, that ye resist not evil: but whosoever shall smite thee on thy cheek turn to him the other also. And if any man take away thy coat let him have thy cloak too," delighted me beyond measure and put me in mind of Shamal Bhatt's "for a bowl of water give a goodly meal," etc. . . . My young mind tried to unify the teaching of the *Gita*, the *Light of Asia* and the Sermon on the Mount. That renunciation was the highest form of religion appealed to me greatly.[11]

From that time forward, Gandhi increased his interest in religion, studying various religious writers.

While he was practicing law in South Africa, friends and colleagues sought to convert Gandhi to Christianity. He willingly submitted to hearing the Gospel, discussing doctrine, and being the subject of Christian prayers. He told a colleague, a Protestant lay preacher, that "nothing could prevent me from embracing Christianity should I feel the call. . . . I had long since taught myself to follow the inner

[9]Homer A. Jack, ed. *The Gandhi Reader* (Bloomington: Indiana University Press, 1956), p. 475.
[10]Ibid., p. 14.
[11]Ibid., p. 23.

voice."[12] He even attended a convention for Protestants, during which friends prayed fervently for him, but Gandhi saw no reason to convert, for he could not believe that Christianity provided the only way to salvation. Although he did not feel that Christianity was the supreme religion, neither did he hold Hinduism as perfect. He saw great value in both religious as well as in Islam, which he also studied.

Clearly, Gandhi believed in divine power and in the life-changing implications of commitment to God. The spirituality of both Hinduism and Christianity intersected in his religious quest to undergird the principle of nonviolence by which India's freedom was won from the British empire. The insights he gained from his religious studies reinforced *Satyagraha*, meaning the "Force which is born by truth and love of non-violence. . . ."[13] For *Satyagraha*, Gandhi suffered imprisonment, attacks on his life, long fasts that nearly killed him, and, finally, a martyr's death. Gandhi was rooted in a tradition of Indian spirituality that came to life when he studied and encountered the love taught by Jesus.

Until the end, Gandhi lived with the conviction that commitment to God, and the keeping of an oath in God's name, is paramount. He said as much to a gathering of Indians who had decided to exercise nonviolent disobedience of the South African ordinance discriminating against Indians. He exhorted them to pledge such resistance with only the deepest resolve:

> We all believe in one and the same God, the differences of nomenclature in Hinduism and Islam notwithstanding. To pledge ourselves or to take an oath in the name of that God or with Him as witness is not something to be trifled with. If having taken such an oath we violate our pledge we are guilty before God and man. Personally I hold that a man, who deliberately and intelligently takes a pledge and then breaks it, forfeits his manhood.[14]

Gandhi's commitment to keep an oath to God may have been expressed when he was killed. One might wonder whether Gandhi's last words, "Oh God," meant more than that he realized he was facing tragedy. To refer to God in that moment of death certainly was congruent with the tenor of his whole life, for he had been led by his vow to keep faith with the highest and deepest Truth, the Truth which he held to be not only divine but also essential for being human.

How do you interpret Gandhi's religious pilgrimage?

How do you understand that he could be influenced by both Hinduism and Christianity to come to his religious convictions concerning nonviolent power as the force of love?

---

[12]Ibid., p. 35.
[13]Ibid., pp. 65, 66.
[14]Ibid., p. 62.

4 ____

Elements of Religious Experience

INTRODUCTION

As evidenced in the preceding chapter, religious experience may be characterized in varied ways. It may be highly emotional or quietly mystical, ecstatic or born of suffering, gradually and rationally developed or sudden in origin. In this chapter we consider some categories of religious experience. The materials included focus on a number of aspects characteristic of a broad range of religious traditions. There are units that deal with the role of ritual, symbols, and myth in religion. There are also units that examine a number of contrasting religious orientations. These orientations—the mystical, the magical, and the aesthetic—may be present to various degrees within a given experience of religion, or any one of them may be sought and valued exclusively by a group or an individual as *the* desirable mode of religious experience. No doubt there are other such approaches to religion. For example, some experiences involve a moral or legal outlook, in which the individual or group seeks to subordinate self and world to a code of life and conduct expressive of the Divine Will. Conformity to this code becomes the pivotal value, or at least is closely connected with it. Confucianism is perhaps a good example of this type. Several units in other sections of the text (see especially Chapter 14) give examples of moral or legal approaches to religion. Definitions of the major approaches discussed in the present chapter are provided in relevant units. The questions listed in the introduction to Chapter 3 may help one understand the nature of the experiences recounted in this chapter.

In studying religion, no aspect of religious concern should be neglected. Theologies, creeds, organizations, institutions, traditions—all are important. But it is probably at the level of personal experience—what happens to the individual or to the group, what is done or felt or believed—that the vitality of religion is most evident. Thus units in Chapter 3 are intended to give a variety of individual cases of the experience of religion. The units in this chapter are intended to provide a framework for understanding these and other instances of personal and group experience.

UNIT 25   The Role of Ritual in Religion

Ritual acts of piety and worship have been associated with all recognized religions. Their variety is unlimited and their functions are as numerous. In early cultures it was only natural that ordinary events taking place in orderly patterns should become "ritualized." Since religion permeated all aspects of life and was not separated from any event, the rites and rituals that emerged in life naturally had religious overtones and functions. Thus, planting crops, passage from one stage of life to another, death, tribal celebrations, and all other events in the life of a people carried ritual forms to recognize the gifts and guidance of the deities in these events. Because such rites and rituals had religious implications, they often became elaborate, beautiful, and central to the culture. As with symbols (see Unit 27), their importance and power were not limited to their particular form or ritual pattern. They came to have a vitality and reality that transcended the form itself. People often understood the rites to be humanity's part of participation in the divine drama of life itself.

Such an understanding continues into very sophisticated cultures, as reflected in the words of Hzün Tzu, a Chinese philosopher of the third century.

A

In general, rites begin with primitive practices, attain cultured forms, and finally achieve beauty and felicity. When rites are at their best, men's emotions and sense of beauty are both fully expressed. When they are at the next level, either the emotion or the sense of beauty oversteps the others. When they are at still the next level, emotion reverts to the state of primitivity.

It is through rites that Heaven and earth are harmonious and sun and moon are bright, that the four seasons are ordered and the stars are on their courses, that rivers flow and that things prosper, that love and hatred are tempered and joy and anger are in keeping. They cause the lowly to be obedient and those on high to be illustrious. He who holds to the rites is never confused in the midst of multifarious change; he who deviates therefrom is lost. Rites—are they not the culmination of culture? . . .[1]

While in many cultures every event and act in life has its religious aspects often celebrated in ritual patterns, every religion has also developed specific patterns

---

[1] Hzsün Tzu, "Rationalism and Realism in Hzŭn Tzu," trans. Y. P. Mei, as quoted in William Theodore de Bary, ed., *Sources of Chinese Tradition* (New York: Columbia University Press, 1960), pp. 123–24.

of worship and celebration to publicly show devotion and commitment. Often these rituals are obligatory for pious believers. The Koran, the Muslim holy scripture, clearly illuminates this aspect of ritual. In the following passage Allah (God) is speaking of the pilgrimage all Muslims should make at least once to the Ka'ba, or Holy Mosque, in Mecca.

B

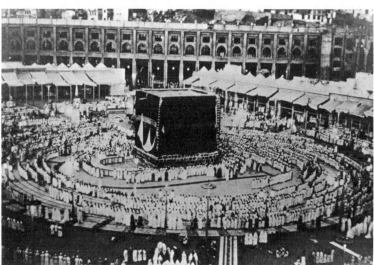

Pilgrims at the Ka'ba in Mecca. (Used through courtesy of Saudi Arabian Public Relations Bureau.)

C

And when We settled for Abraham the place of the House [Ka'ba] We said: "Thou shall not associate with Me anything [idols or other Gods]. And do thou purify My House for those that shall go about it and those that stand, for those that bow and prostrate themselves; and proclaim among men the Pilgrimage, and they shall come unto thee on foot and upon every lean beast, they shall come from every deep ravine that they may witness things profitable to them and mention God's Name on days well-known. . . . Let them then finish with their self-neglect and let them fulfil their vows, and go about the Ancient House." All that; and whosoever venerates the sacred things of God, it shall be better for him with his Lord.

We have appointed for every nation a holy rite, that they may mention God's Name over such beasts of the flocks as He has provided them. Your God is One God, so to Him surrender. . . .

O men, bow you down and prostrate yourselves, and serve your Lord, and do good; haply so you shall prosper; and struggle for God as is His due, for He has chosen you, and has laid on you no impediment in your religion, being the creed of your father Abraham; He named you Muslims aforetime and in this, that the Messenger might be a witness against you, and that you might be witnesses against mankind. So perform the prayer, and pay the alms, and hold you fast to God; He is your Protector—an excellent Protector, an excellent Helper.[2] (*The Koran*, Sura XXII)

[2]Reprinted with permission of Macmillan Inc., from *The Koran Interpreted*, Arthur J. Arberry, translator, Sura XXII, verses 26–38, 75–77. © 1955 George Allen & Unwin, Ltd.

Another aspect of ritual is the commemoration of a central act or event in the religious history of a community. Such is the Christian Eucharist, also known as the Lord's Supper, Communion, and the Mass. The basis of the ritual is Jesus' last meal with his disciples. The bread and wine became Christian symbols of Jesus' suffering and death, revealing to the believer God's unbounded love. In the accompanying passage Paul passes on instruction for ritual practice that he had received from his predecessors in the faith.

D For the tradition which I handed on to you came to me from the Lord himself: that the Lord Jesus, on the night of his arrest, took bread and, after giving thanks to God, broke it and said: "This is my body, which is for you; do this as a memorial of me." In the same way, he took the cup after supper, and said: "This cup is the new covenant sealed by my blood. Whenever you drink it, do this as a memorial of me." For every time you eat this bread and drink the cup, you proclaim the death of the Lord, until he comes. (I Corinthians 11:23–26, NEB)

In some modern cultures religion has become only one element among many others, often losing its central place in ordinary life. Consequently, religious rituals have been modified and often limited to specifically religious functions, or sometimes completely lost. This has also meant that religious rituals have sometimes been reduced to particular rites or patterns, losing much of their dynamic quality.

Are ritual forms and practices necessary for religious expression?

What rituals or rites are widely practiced in our own society?

Are all rituals public, or are there private rituals?

Why have most religions stressed that participation in public rites of worship is a duty for the believer?

UNIT 26 Religious Nurture and Conversion

The term *conversion* is used in several different senses to characterize religious experience. It may be used to refer to a person's leaving one religious group and becoming an adherent of another, as when someone is said to have converted from Protestantism to Catholicism, or from Christianity to Islam. A second sense of *conversion* is present when someone who has not been an adherent or participant in *any* religious group or tradition joins one, as when someone speaks of the *conversion* of an atheist or a skeptic or agnostic. In Europe or America, such usage usually carries the implication that the convert has become a member of some Christian group, though it may only mean that the person has become a believer in God or in some form of Christian faith. Finally, especially among some groups of Protestant Christians, the term *conversion* may be used to describe an event of deepened or internalized participation in a religious tradition, or adherence to its doctrines or way of life by someone who has previously participated in a more superficial or less committed way. For many Protestant groups, this experience is characterized as being "born again" and signifies that, according to the group's understanding, the individual has for the first time made a full personal commitment to the truths that the group holds.

The development within Christianity, particularly in the last few centuries, of emphasis on a distinctive religious conversion has helped focus study of religious experience on this particular manifestation. Historically, however, conversion is only one form of religious experience. A far more common experience is that of nurture, wherein one's religious faith is gradually matured through a variety of events, including religious education. A person is nurtured in religion by participation in numerous experiences within a faithful community. The older or more traditional Christian church bodies—Roman Catholic, Anglican, Lutheran—most often stress this form.

Horace Bushnell, a nineteenth-century American theologian, vigorously argued that religious experience and commitment are as legitimately the result of Christian nurture as they might be of a dynamic conversion experience.

A

Christian piety should begin in other and milder forms of exercise than those which commonly distinguish the conversion of adults; that Christ himself, by that renewing Spirit who can sanctify from the womb, should be practically infused into the childish mind; in other words, that the house, having a domestic Spirit of grace dwelling in it, should become the church of childhood, the table and hearth a holy rite, and life an element of saving power. Something is wanted that is better than teaching, something that transcends mere effort and will-work— the loveliness of a good life, the repose of faith, the confidence of righteous expectation, the sacred and cheerful liberty of the Spirit—all glowing about the young soul, as a warm and genial nurture, and forming in it, by methods that are silent and imperceptible, a spirit of duty and religious obedience to God. This only is Christian nurture, the nurture of the Lord. . . .

Children have been so trained as never to remember the time when they began to be religious. Baxter was, at one time, greatly troubled concerning himself, because he could recollect no time when there was a gracious change in his character. But he discovered, at length, that "education is as properly a means of grace as preaching," and thus found the sweeter comfort in his love to God, that he learned to love him so early.[3]

John Betjeman, a modern British poet, although raised a Christian, demonstrates that one can reject or lose the nurture Bushnell stresses but still return by a series of events to faith. For Betjeman, none of the events was identifiable as *conversion*, but each was part of a clear progression toward belief and commitment that may be described as a conversion process.

B

I was brought up Church of England, you know, and baptized and then, at Marlborough, I suddenly decided I was an atheist and refused to be confirmed. I used to think that religion was hymn singing and feeling good and not being immoral and always having a high moral tone and really rather priggish. Until . . . I remember one summer bicycling about in Cornwall and coming to a church, St.

[3]Horace Bushnell, *Christian Nurture* (New Haven: Yale University Press, 1916), pp 12–13, 17.

Irvin, in North Cornwall and meeting the vicar there who was a nice eccentric, and he said, I suppose you think religion is hymn singing in the chapel at Marlborough. And I said—Yes. And he said: Well—read this. And he gave me a book—Arthur Machens' *Secret Glory*, which suddenly showed me there were the Sacraments, and then I became very interested in ritual and I was first, I suppose, brought to belief by my eyes and ears and nose. The smell of incense, and the sight of candles, High Church services, they attracted me and I liked them. And at Oxford I got confirmed at Pusey House and went to Confession and lived the full life of a Catholic in the Church of England. And then found that one had gone so much off the rails one didn't dare to go to Confession any more, so I gave it up for a bit, and then went back again, holding on. Not finding it very easy to believe until only just lately. I do see that behind all the ritual and everything like that, the one fundamental thing is that Christ was God. And it's very hard to believe—it's a very hard thing to swallow. But if you can believe it, it gives some point to everything and really I don't think life would be worth living if it weren't true.[4]

These examples express a confidence in the developmental idea of Christian experience that has been most common. Yet the phenomenon of religious conversion characterized by a unique experience of enlightenment and change is a clear and significant tradition within Christianity. The experience of Augustine is a classic example.

C   So was I speaking and weeping in the most bitter contrition of my heart, when lo! I heard from a neighbouring house a voice, as of boy or girl, I know not, chanting, and oft repeating, "Take up and read; Take up and read." Instantly, my countenance altered, I began to think most intently whether children were wont in any kind of play to sing such words: nor could I remember ever to have heard the like. So checking the torrent of my tears, I arose; interpreting it to be no other than a command from God to open the book, and read the first chapter I should find. . . . I seized, opened, and in silence read that section on which my eyes first fell: Not in rioting and drunkenness, not in chambering and wontonness, not in strife and envying; but put ye on the Lord Jesus Christ, and make not provision for the flesh, in concupiscence. No further would I read; nor needed I: for instantly at the end of this sentence, by a light as it were of serenity infused into my heart, all the darkness of doubt vanished away.[5]

In this passage, a renowned Christian leader describes an event wherein an extraordinary religious experience served as a vehicle of confirmation of faith and trust in God. Augustine can call this his conversion. He had accepted some Christian beliefs and principles before this time, but now he could fully commit himself to God. In this description the crucial element is an awareness of acceptance by God, whatever one might be or have been. The concept that one's personal acts—one's own sins—are not a detriment to being accepted by God is that which allows total commitment and change of understanding and direction. Earl Ferguson has defined this type of religious experience as follows:

[4]From John Betjeman's Diary as quoted in Derek Stanford, *John Betjeman* (London: Neville Spearman, 1961), pp. 25–26.

[5]Saint Augustine, *The Confessions of Saint Augustine*, trans. Edward B. Pusey (New York: Random House, 1949), pp. 166–67.

D Religious conversion, from the psychological point of view, is an abrupt, involuntary change in personality in which the subject, under the pressure of resolving internal conflict or tension, surrenders the control of his life to beliefs and sentiments previously peripheral or repressed; the change occurs suddenly at a time of crisis and is not psychologically identical with the gradual process of growth or development.[6]

The categories of religious experience just discussed certainly are not exhaustive or exclusive, but do illustrate common experiences among the Christian communities of Europe and America. Neither of these modes excludes the other, and they are often combined in a person's experience even if one may be emphasized more than another. Many other religions have similar experiences of religious nurture and conversion.

> *How well does Ferguson's definition of conversion apply to each of the three senses of the term discussed at the beginning of the unit? How well does it apply to the individual experiences cited in the unit?*
>
> *Is an identifiable religious experience—whether by gradual nurture or conversion— necessary for religious consciousness and commitment?*
>
> *Why in certain areas of America has conversion been the predominant form of experience?*
>
> *Why among traditional and established churches would Christian nurture be predominant?*
>
> *Does one type of experience provide a more personal sense of security than the other? Why?*

UNIT 27 The Role of Symbols in Religion

Symbols have traditionally been relied on by religions to express truths and insights that may not be simply rational. The root word in Greek for symbol is *symballo*, which means "to bring together," so a central function of symbols in religion has been to unite or join truths with graphic representations. Yet one problem in dealing with symbols is a semantic one. Some persons may use the terms *symbol*, *allegory*, *metaphor*, and other terms as interchangeable. But a careful consideration of the *functions* of symbols requires that they be differentiated from other signifying phenomena.

Many modes of expression serve a primarily communicative function. In such communication, one frequently can separate the meaning from its vehicle. Consider a well-known metaphor, *the ship of state*. The intention of the phrase is readily apparent. Few would confuse a nation with a ship, that is, the vehicle with its meaning. Therefore, what distinguishes a symbol from this or any other signifying process is its peculiarly representative function. That which is pointed to becomes

[6]Earl Ferguson, "The Definition of Religious Conversion," *Pastoral Psychology*, 16, no. 156 (September 1965), 16.

one with the vehicle which serves as pointer. Reality can become condensed in its symbol. This can enable persons to grasp part of a transcendent reality so that they can participate in its symbolic form. Metaphor, then, is especially concerned with a linguistic procedure. It is developed by us to indicate what something *is like*. But the symbol is two-dimensional; it takes us beyond the semantic to roots deep in experience which can be beyond words.[7]

If symbols point to something beyond themselves, they also go further. A symbol *participates in* that to which it points. Since a symbol may be understood to become a kind of autonomous reality by pointing to *and* being a part of larger dimensions of reality, it elicits response that is both deep and strong from the person who perceives it. The symbol demands more than cognitive recognition; it functions at the affective (emotional) level as well. Therefore, one may encounter symbols at the conscious and unconscious levels. Symbols bring these levels together in experience.[8]

Indeed, symbols often may not be constructed by intention. They may arise from individual and group unconscious experience. Further, symbols change as individual and group needs change. Symbols grow and sometimes are replaced by new and more functional ones.

Specifically religious symbols may represent the ultimate, that which is God. They can serve to make the vast, the transcendent, perceptible. They are part of the language of faith. Religious symbols can have a power that distinguishes them from other symbols; they deal with issues about which one is ultimately concerned—the absolute.

Religious symbols are supported by communities and therefore are socially rooted. Most societies give support to special institutions such as churches, whose function is to maintain and develop the tradition of religious symbols supported by that society.

The more primitive religious image can become an idol for a person or group when it does not *represent* the deity for a worshiper. It can be perceived and treated as the deity itself. Such an image can function as a symbol only when some difference is discerned between the representation and the represented, between the object and the actual ultimate. When this is known, a person becomes capable of employing a symbol to *point* to the ultimate, to serve as an "arrow" to the Divine. It is *in* and *through* the symbol that the divine is encountered, known. The symbol serves to telescope the transcendent Divine, to make it accessible, to serve as vessel or vehicle and yet not *be* the totality of the Divine. The symbol serves functionally as a revealer, though it may not be complete. In many living religions, the symbol is "of God" in terms of its intermediary, representational function, but the image and the words remain less than that to which they point.

Many contemporary commentators on the role of religious symbols have observed that humans sometimes become so immersed in the models and symbols

---

[7]For a more complete discussion, see Paul Ricoeur, *Interpretation Theory: Discourse and the Surplus of Meaning* (Ft. Worth, Texas: Texas Christian University Press, 1976), pp. 45–69.

[8]See also Rollo May, "The Significance of Symbols," in *Symbolism in Religion and Literature*, Rollo May, ed. (New York: George Braziller, Inc., 1960), pp. 11–49.

that they produce or inherit that they forget their function. A symbol represents that which it is not itself. It is a form which arises from the depths of human experience and serves as it stands for something vast, something not fully under rational control, something at the edge of one's ability to comprehend. Yet the symbol embodies some essential characteristic or quality of that which it represents. As has been suggested, it "telescopes" that which it represents into a manageable form; hence, the represented is encountered within the symbol; it is there. Yet the symbol always points beyond itself to the represented. Both models and symbols are functional. They facilitate connections. They are not *absolute* substitutes for what they represent, but the essential of the represented may be contained in them.

Acutely aware of the signal importance of images and symbol in religion and of how they function and change, Martin Buber has addressed some of the central issues.

A

There is a story, that during the reign of the emperor Tiberius, people on a ship passing close to Epirus heard a mournful voice from one of the islands which bade the helmsman carry to another coast the tidings that great Pan had died. Men of all eras have heard tidings of the death of gods. But it was reserved for our era to have a philosopher feel called upon to announce that God himself had died. Whether or not we know it, what we really mean when we say that a god is dead is that the images of God vanish, and that therefore an image which up to now was regarded and worshipped as God, can no longer be so regarded and so worshipped. For what we call gods are nothing but images of God and must suffer the fate of such images. But Nietzsche manifestly wished to say something different, and that something different is terribly wrong in a way characteristic of our time. For it means confusing an image, confusing one of the many images of God that are born and perish, with the real God whose reality men could never shake with any one of these images, no matter what forms they might honestly invent for the objects of their particular adoration. Time after time, the images must be broken, the iconoclasts must have their way. For the iconoclast is the soul of man which rebels against having an image that can no longer be believed in, elevated above the heads of man as a thing that demands to be worshipped.

In their longing for a god, men try again and again to set up a greater, more genuine and more just image, which is intended to be more glorious than the last and only proves the more unsatisfactory. The commandment, "Thou shalt not make unto thee an image," means at the same time, "Thou canst not make an image." This does not, of course, refer merely to sculptured or painted images, but to our fantasy, to all the power of our imagination as well. But man is forced time and again to make images, and forced to destroy them when he realizes that he has not succeeded. The images topple, but the voice is never silenced. "Ye heard the voice of words but ye saw no form" (Deut. 4:12). The voice speaks in the guise of everything that happens, in the guise of all world events; it speaks to the men of all generations, makes demands upon them, and summons them to accept their responsibility. I have pointed out that it is of the utmost importance not to lose one's openness. But to be open means not to shut out the voice—call it what you will. It does not matter what you call it. All that matters is that you hear it.[9]

[9]Reprinted by permission of Schocken Books Inc. from *Israel and the World* by Martin Buber. Copyright © 1948 by Schocken Books, Inc. Copyright renewed © 1976 by Schocken Books, Inc.

B

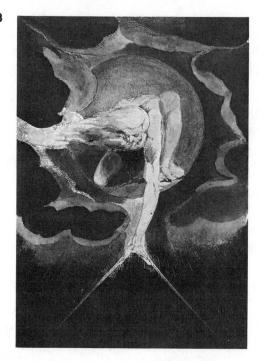

The Ancient of Days, by William Blake, 1794. (Reproduced with permission of the Library of Congress, Lessing J. Rosenwald Collection.)

Certainly, a large part of human religious experience is mediated through symbols. The cross, the Bible, the Wailing Wall in Jerusalem, the Ka'ba in Mecca, a footprint of the Buddha, the sacred Ganges River in India—all are powerful religious symbols, expressive of the Divine that is apprehended through them, in them, or behind them by adherents of the religious traditions involved—Christian, Jewish, Muslim, Mahayana Buddhist, and Hindu, respectively. The same may be true of works of religious art and architecture. They often function powerfully in human religious experience.

A recent suggestion is that one primary mode of religious orientation, the aesthetic, may be particularly closely dependent on symbols, on seeing the religious-symbolic significance of things—parts of the natural and human world, persons and historical events as well as works of art—as the intrinsic element in religious experience. According to this view, the aesthetic type of religious orientation is that which seeks to discover the presence and disclosure of God or the Divine Powers in the world, others, and the self.

Most modes of religion depend heavily on symbols as expressions of God or the Divine, even though it may be held that no finite symbol—thing or work of art—can fully or adequately express the Divine that transcends all symbols. The magical mode of religion and magic generally are heavily dependent on symbols. Perhaps only the mystical mode of religion attempts finally to dispense with all symbols and to know God directly. But even in the mystical mode, symbols may have an important role in the preliminary stages of the religious life. Later they may be used to communicate some sense of the mystic's experience to others.

UNIT 28 Mysticism in Religious Experience

I

An account of the religious experience of Teresa of Avila is given in a previous chapter (Unit 22). Teresa's experience is a classic instance of religious mysticism.

A

One day, being in orison, . . . it was granted me to perceive in one instant how all things are seen and contained in God. I did not perceive them in their proper form, and nevertheless the view I had of them was of a sovereign clearness, and has remained vividly impressed upon my soul. It is one of the most signal of all the graces which the Lord has granted me. . . . The view was so subtle and delicate that the understanding cannot grasp it.[10]

Mysticism as a type of religious experience has been frequent in Christianity. Mysticism is also highly characteristic of the Eastern religions—Buddhism, Hinduism, and Taoism—and has been represented by the Sufis in Islamic religion. The Greek philosopher Plato believed that the highest knowledge of reality must be gained in a flash of mystical insight.

B

Even so, this organ of knowledge must be turned around from the world of becoming together with the entire soul, like the scene-shifting periact in the theater, until the soul is able to endure the contemplation of essence and the brightest region of being.[11]

A recent suggestion is that mysticism is one of the major forms of religious experience. According to this view, in the mystical mode of religion, one attempts to negate the relation to self, others, and the world in order to give God or the Divine Reality complete power in and over the self. The result is that the self is completely surrendered to, or in union with, the Divine.

C

As a hart longs
for flowing streams,
so longs my soul
    for thee, O God. . . .
When shall I come and behold
    the face of God?
My tears have been my food
    day and night,
while men say to me continually,
    "Where is your God?"

Why are you cast down, O my soul,
    and why are you disquieted within me?
Hope in God; for I shall again praise him,
    my help and my God.

Psalm 42 (RSV)

[10]Saint Teresa of Avila, as quoted in James, *The Varieties of Religious Experience*, p. 411.
[11]Plato, quoted in Walter Houston Clark, *The Psychology of Religion*, (New York: Macmillan, Inc., 1958), p. 261.

Evelyn Underhill, an important twentieth-century British writer on mysticism who was herself a Christian mystic, defined mysticism as follows:

D

Mysticism, according to its historical and psychological definitions, is the direct intuition or experience of God; and a mystic is a person who has, to greater or less degree, such a direct experience—one whose religion and life are centered, not merely on an accepted belief or practice, but on that which he regards as first-hand personal knowledge.[12]

In describing the phenomenon of mysticism in religious experience, the psychologist and philosopher William James found these four characteristics:

E

1. *Ineffability.*—The handiest of the marks by which I classify a state of mind as mystical is negative. The subject of it immediately says that it defies expression, that no adequate report of its contents can be given in words. It follows from this that its quality must be directly experienced; it cannot be imparted or transferred to others. In this peculiarity mystical states are more like states of feeling than like states of intellect. No one can make clear to another who has never had a certain feeling, in what the quality or worth of it consists. One must have musical ears to know the value of a symphony; one must have been in love one's self to understand a lover's state of mind. Lacking the heart or ear, we cannot interpret the musician or the lover justly, and are even likely to consider him weak-minded or absurd. The mystic finds that most of us accord to his experiences an equally incompetent treatment.

2. *Noetic quality.*—Although so similar to states of feeling, mystical states seem to those who experience them to be also states of knowledge. They are states of insight into depths of truth unplumbed by the discursive intellect. They are illuminations, revelations, full of significance and importance, all inarticulate though they remain: and as a rule they carry with them a curious sense of authority for after-time. . . .

3. *Transiency.*—Mystical states cannot be sustained for long. Except in rare instances, half an hour, or at most an hour or two, seems to be the limit beyond which they fade into the light of common day. Often, when faded, their quality can but imperfectly be reproduced in memory; but when they recur it is recognized; and from one recurrence to another it is susceptible of continuous development in what is felt as inner richness and importance.

4. *Passivity.*—Although the oncoming of mystical states may be facilitated by preliminary voluntary operations, as by fixing the attention, or going through certain bodily performances, or in other ways which manuals of mysticism prescribe; yet when the characteristic sort of consciousness once has set in, the mystic feels as if his own will were in abeyance, and indeed sometimes as if he were grasped and held by a superior power. . . .[13]

R. C. Zaehner, in a classification of three types of mysticism, feels that in all of them, the quality or kind of experience is perhaps similar—like that described by William James—but that the object or *content* is different. The first type of mystical experience described by Zaehner is *nature mysticism*, sometimes called pantheism—the feeling of union or identity of the self with objects in the natural world or "nature" as a whole.

[12]Evelyn Underhill, *The Mystics of the Church* (New York: Schocken Books, 1964), pp. 9–10.
[13]James, *The Varieties of Religious Experience*, pp. 380–81.

F

A vision of the resurrected Christ is presented by an artist of the High Renaissance, Matthias Grünewald, in this section of his triptych, the *Isenheim Altarpiece* in Musée Unterlinden, Colmar. (Photo courtesy Musée d'Unterlinden.)

A second type of mysticism is that typical of certain Eastern religious traditions, particularly Vedantic Hinduism, in which the self feels itself as identical with the Absolute Self, Brahman, the One Reality *beyond* the natural world of mere appearance, and in which the individual self is *totally* merged with, absorbed in, the Absolute.

Zaehner continues:

Thirdly there is the normal type Christian mystical experience in which the soul feels itself to be united with God by love. The theological premise from which this experience starts is that the individual soul is created by God in His own image and likeness from nothing and that it has the capacity of being united to God, of being "oned" to Him as the medieval English mystics put it. Here again we have a third type, distinct, it would appear, from the other two. . . . No orthodox Christian mystic, unless he is speaking figuratively or in poetry as Angelus Silesius does, can well go farther than to say that his individual ego is melted away in God by love: something of the soul must clearly remain if only to experience the mystical experience. The individual is not annihilated, though transformed and "deified" as St. John of the Cross says: it remains a distinct entity though permeated through and through with the divine substance.[14]

What difference does Zaehner see between Christian and Vedantic mystical experience? Between both and nature mysticism?

[14]R. C. Zaehner, *Mysticism: Sacred and Profane* (London: Oxford University Press, 1961), p. 29.

II

Although Zaehner's threefold division of the types of religious mysticism is useful, it probably represents a simplification that, taken too far, is misleading. This can easily be seen by considering Zen Buddhism, which is based on a form of mystical experience, prepared for by instruction in rigorous techniques of meditation by a Zen teacher (or Master), and leads to an experience of enlightenment called *satori*. In many ways Zen enlightenment results in attitudes similar to those of nature mysticism, a sense of the overcoming of the division between the self and the whole, as well as between the self and the individual concrete presence of things. Zen is rooted in Buddhist traditions that derive from Hindu pantheism (though Buddhism generally and Zen particularly do not have theological or metaphysical theories of pantheism or, for that matter, of the nature of things). Finally, recent Christian writers have found profound analogies between the Zen approach and that of the Hebrew-Christian Scriptures and parts of Christian mystical tradition and practice.[15]

Following is a Zen play presenting the experience leading to the Zen enlightenment of Bodhidharma, an Indian Buddhist monk who became the founder of Zen, a movement which spread to China and is now most frequently associated with Japan. The play, entitled *Bodhidharma*, is by Saneatsu Mushakōji. It is a good illustration of Zen mysticism, which is in some sense uncategorizable as one of Zaehner's types. Nevertheless, it resembles all of them, particularly if one realizes that, even with the emphasis in Christian mysticism on devotion to an absolute object, God, most Christian mystics have stressed that God as experienced in mystical union cannot be conceptualized as "known" (as a subject-knower might know—perceive or understand—an object of finite experience). Note that entrance into enlightenment is the culmination of extreme personal discipline but does not depend upon that discipline or reason; it comes in the intuitive moment, in this case symbolized by a blow on the head.

G The characters are A, B. and Dharma. In front of a small temple where Dharma sits in meditation, A and B enter.

> A: Do you know the fellow that lives here?
>
> B: I don't.
>
> A: Don't you? There's a peculiar fellow living in this temple.
>
> B: What is he like?
>
> A: A fellow who has sat staring at nothing but the wall for eight or nine years.
>
> B: Staring at the wall for eight or nine years? What for?
>
> A: If we knew what he was doing that for, he would no longer be considered peculiar. But there isn't anyone who knows what he is staring at the wall for. People say he must be an idiot.
>
> B: If you talk in such a loud voice, the fellow inside will hear you.
>
> A: No fear. He's an idiot, and besides, he's deaf.

[15]See Thomas Merton, *Mystics and Zen Masters* (New York: Farrar, Straus & Giroux, Inc., 1967) and J. K. Kadowaki S. J., *Zen and the Bible: A Priest's Experience* (London: Routledge and Kegan Paul, Ltd., 1980).

B: Is he deaf?

A: He is deaf.

B: Is that why he only stares at the wall?

A: Yes, that's why he only stares at the wall.

B: How does he eat?

A: His neighbors make a point of bringing meals to him, it seems.

B: How thoughtful of them!

A: I suppose they sometimes forget to bring the meals. They told me that once they purposely didn't bring his meals for three or four days, but he stared at the wall as usual as if nothing had happened. . . .

B: But is he really an idiot? I can't believe that he is.

A: But an intelligent person could not go on doing such a thing for eight or nine years at a time like this, could he? For what is the good of staring at a wall? It can't do any good, can it?

B: I think you're right. However, are you sure he didn't change color when he was beaten? Don't you think he was just pretending?

A: No, I assure you he didn't change color. I watched him intently.

B: But you saw him at some distance didn't you? Then you couldn't possibly see him roll his eyes.

A: Then I'll strike him on the head now, so watch closely.

B: Is it all right to strike him? If the fellow should suddenly roar you look as though you'd be paralyzed with terror. For we seldom see such a fearful face, you know.

A: Don't worry. Now watch me, I'll strike him.

B: Are you sure it's all right?

A: Of course it is. Watch me closely.

B: The more I look at him the stranger his face looks. He looks as if he'd choke you to death and eat you if he once got angry.

A: No, he is a mild fellow really. He looks terrible only in the face. Now I'll strike him.

B: All right.

        [A strikes Dharma on the head.]

A: How was it?

B: Strange. It surely is strange. Please strike him again. [He draws nearer.]

A: All right. [He strikes him again.] . . .

        [He approaches Dharma . . . and raises his arm. Dharma turns his head]

A: [falling on his knees.] Please forgive me. Please forgive me.

DHARMA: What day is it today?

        [A and B are struck dumb. They try to say something but cannot.]

DHARMA: Are you two deaf?

A: No, no.

DHARMA: What day is it today?

A: Yes, sir. Today is the twelfth day of December.

DHARMA: Is it? Then I have been here exactly nine years!

A: Yes sir.

DHARMA: [Standing up.] Dullard as I am, I have at last attained enlightenment after nine years! What the Buddha said was true. Thanks! Thanks!

        [The two watched in amazement.]

A: Then you are not deaf?

DHARMA: No, I am not deaf.

A: Please forgive us our rudeness a while ago.

DHARMA: You haven't done anything rude to me.

A: But we struck you on the head . . .

DHARMA: Oh, then it was you? I must thank you for it. I was able to attain enlightenment because you struck me on the head. The Buddha kindly entered into you and beat me.[16]

H   Zen as a religion is purely a religion of human realization, or self-awakening. It teaches us, human beings, to attain *satori* and live a new life in this world as new men of *satori*. It insists that this inner conversion should be carried out by oneself, that one can attain his Zen personality by oneself by searching inwardly, not relying on anything outside. It declares that man has the potentiality for attaining *satori*. This should be happy tidings for human beings.[17]

The following excerpt from a longer poem expresses in poetic form the classic Zen insight into the universe and life.

I   All beings are primarily Buddhas
Like water and ice,
There is no ice apart from water;
There are no Buddhas apart from beings.[18]

UNIT 29 Pentecostal Experience

In the past half century, Pentecostalism has swept the globe, growing to over ten million advocates. Professor Frederick Bruner of Union Seminary in the Philippines suggests that some church leaders recognize Pentecostalism as "the Third Force in Christendom, ranging it alongside Roman Catholicism and historic Protestantism."[19]

As this unit shows, present-day Christian Pentecostalism grew out of the dissatisfaction of some Christians with what they felt to be a lack of vitality in the established Protestant denominations and a sense of need for a deeper, more intense source of spiritual meaning and life within themselves. It began largely as a North American movement, resulting in several new denominations, including the Assemblies of God and the Churches of God. It is now a worldwide movement, but it

---

[16]Umeyo Hirano, trans., *Buddhist Plays from Japanese Literature* (Tokyo: The Cultural Interchange Institute for Buddhists, 1962), pp. 1–2, 4–5, 7–8. Used by permission.

[17]Zenkei Shibayama, *A Flower Does Not Talk* (Rutland, Vt.: Charles E. Tuttle Co., 1970), pp. 30–31.

[18]Shibayama, *A Flower Does Not Talk*, pp. 65.

[19]Frederick D. Bruner, *A Theology of the Holy Spirit* (Grand Rapids, Mich.: William B. Eerdmans, 1970), p. 29.

is especially strong in Latin America. During the past thirty years, Pentecostalism, often called the charismatic movement, has become influential among some of the established (sometimes called "mainline") Protestant denominations, including Lutheran, Presbyterian, Episcopalian, and Methodist, as well as among Roman Catholics.

Pentecostals take as their central reference point the following passage from Acts 2:4, interpreting it to mean that the Pentecostal experience of the early disciples can be and still is evident in the lives of Christians today.

> And they were filled with the Holy Spirit
> and began to speak in other tongues.
> (RSV)

Convinced that the early church lost its power by neglecting the Pentecostal experience of the Holy Spirit, modern Pentecostals believe the church will receive new power only by baptism in the Holy Spirit. This baptism in the Holy Spirit serves as the fulfillment of Christ's promise in The Acts of the Apostles: "You shall receive power when the Holy Spirit has come upon you. . . ." (Acts 1:8 RSV) Pentecostals believe that this experience is available to all Christians and that it includes the "remarkable spiritual manifestations recorded in the New Testament such as speaking in tongues, prophecy, healing, nature miracles, and visions. . . ."[20]

While granting that initial conversion to Christianity represents an authentic faith for the Christian, Pentecostals emphasize the need for the full baptism in the Spirit. "That is, Pentecostals believe that the Spirit has baptized every believer into Christ (conversion), but that Christ has not yet baptized every believer into the Spirit (Pentecost)."[21]

The locus of the gifts of the Spirit, for modern Pentecostals, is the Pentecostal meeting, in which believers share their gifts of tongues, interpretation of tongues, prophecy, healing, and so forth. A highly participational experience, the meeting includes singing of gospel songs and choruses, music of an amateur church orchestra, joyous shouting, hearty handclapping, ecstatic prayer, communal witness, and testifying. A mood of joy prevails as Pentecostals "sing not only with their voices but with their hands, and their feet and their bodies." The rhythm of the distinctive "American folk beat" prompts the people to become one with the orchestra in praising God. In utter abandon the whole congregation may at some points in the service "descend to its knees" to pray "in vocal concert or cacophony." The sanctuary may fill up with sound during prayer as the people pray in tongues. In a time of mutual sharing the believers in the Spirit witness to the Spirit of God filling their lives with power. Their preaching of the Word becomes a thorough-going community affair.[22]

[20]Ibid., pp. 22, 23.
[21]Ibid., p. 60.
[22]Ibid., pp. 133–36.

A   Contemporary Neo-Pentecostal Experiences

I stand as one of the group of pastors who are desperately concerned and deeply disturbed and confused over the lack of power . . . there has been a growing concern in my heart, for I knew that something ought to be there which was not there, and could not be found. . . . I read in the Bible about the early church and its supernatural power and I so longed for such as that. . . . This was about two years ago. Between seventy and eighty of our people have received this glorious experience. Men and women who wearily trudged to prayer meeting and drove themselves to be faithful have becoming flaming evangels for Jesus![23]

B   *Another Pentecostal Experience.* I continued to tarry for the Baptism. . . . On Sunday . . . I received the Baptism. The Holy Spirit came like a torrent, as though He would tear my body to pieces. One of my besetting sins has been my unwillingness to speak out boldly for Christ, but when the Holy Spirit came in He made me shout the praises of Jesus until He verily split my throat. However, as one brother said to me, the Lord is able to repair any damage He does to the old temple. After being tossed about violently for quite awhile until I was panting for breath and wet with perspiration, I then lay for quite awhile in blessed quietness and poured forth praise to God in tongues for over half an hour.[24]

Does Pentecostalism (charismatic Christianity) seem similar to or different from Christian mystical experience?

UNIT 30   Myth and Religious Insight

The term *myth* is often used in ordinary conversation to mean "something that is widely accepted or believed but that is in fact false." A second common use of *myth* is to designate stories that arose in primitive or naive societies that involve personified forces of nature, gods and goddesses, and legendary heroes—for example, the familiar Greek myths. In a third sense, *myth* is sometimes used to mean "primitive" beliefs about nature and the universe—"prescientific science"; for instance, the Babylonian cosmology (still the basis for systems of astrology) is sometimes called a "mythological" scientific system. Finally, the term *myth* has been used by recent political or social thinkers—R. M. MacIver and Bronislaw Malinowski among them—to refer to any *basic* belief or system of beliefs involving value claims and commitments. Thus, MacIver defined *myth* as "the value-impregnated beliefs and notions" that sustain and give unity to society. Malinowski called such myths the "charters of belief" that validate the customs and practices and code of society.[25]

We will suggest in this unit that a simpler and better way of trying to understand the term *myth* is to begin by remembering that the word often does refer to a

[23]Ibid., p. 127.
[24]Ibid., p. 126.
[25]See David Bidney, *Theoretical Anthropology* (New York: Columbia University Press, 1953), p. 297.

kind of story, though not always a story about gods and goddesses, or personified forces of nature, or even legendary heroes. There is an American myth associated with the life of Abraham Lincoln—the myth (or story) of a man who grew up in poverty, who experienced hardship and failure, but who, through determination, hard work, and personal integrity, rose to the highest office in the land. This story embodies one of the great myths of American society, but it is a myth based on historical truth.

Myth does have an important role in social and individual life. It is often by means of myths that societies and individuals define or acquire their sense of identity. This is why myths have an important role in most of the world's religions. However, it is very misleading, as the present unit attempts to make clear, to think that myths necessarily involve falsity.

The following description of a Vietnamese myth shows the story aspect of myth. It also illustrates some of the features that make myth a special kind of story.

A
The Myth of the Birth of the Vietnamese Race

The myth of the birth of the Vietnamese race goes back to the misty Bronze Age during which De Minh (a great grandson of Than Nong, the God of Agriculture) met, in the course of one of his inspection tours in the southern part of China, a Tien (fairy), and married her. From this union a son, Loc Tuc, was born. And when De Minh was too old to rule his vast empire, he divided it into two territories: the North, which he gave to his eldest son, De Nghi, child of his first marriage, and the South (Vietnam), which he gave to Loc Tuc. Loc Tuc became Emperor Kinh Duong Vuong and married the daughter of Than Long (the Dragon God). From this marriage between the descendant of a fairy and a dragon there came a son who would be Emperor Lac Long Quan. Indeed, the Vietnamese often call themselves the children and grandchildren of a dragon and a fairy. Lac Long Quan's marriage to Au Co, another fairy, resulted in the birth of one hundred male children. He told his wife one day: "I came from the race of Rong (Dragon), you came from the race of Tien. We are as different as water is to fire, and it would be unwise for us to continue to live together. We have to part." Fifty children then followed their mother to the mountains and fifty marched with their father to the south seas. Lac Long Quan then handed over his throne to his son Rung Vuong, who founded the Rong Bang Dynasty and named his kingdom Van Lang.

About the "Myth of the Birth of the Vietnamese Race," the author Tran Van Dinh comments as follows:

From this recital of legendary origins, one can see that Vietnam considers its fate determined by:

1. A contradiction—the marriage between the descendant of a fairy (sweet, gracious, beautiful) and a dragon (powerful, aggressive, and hard-featured). These two contradictory aspects still prevail both physically and mentally in the Vietnamese people, and especially among the women who are slender but tough, durable and aggressive but romantic and gracious. The fairy virtues seem to be most apparent and persistent, however. . . .

2. An internal division—the first Vietnamese family was a divided one (fifty children went with their mother to

the mountains and fifty accompanied their father to the seas). Division and disunity became Vietnamese national problems in the past as well as at the present time. And the division is not only between North and South but also between the minorities which live in the mountains (Montagnards) and the majority dwelling in the pallins of the sea coasts. . . .[26]

This myth of Vietnamese origins incorporates a story, but goes beyond being a simple story to express a truth found in the very fabric of the Vietnamese culture. It is then more than a story. Preliterate societies often communicate their most important truths and beliefs through myths.

In modern Western religions, faith has often been equated with the acceptance of certain beliefs or propositions and the rejection of others. Yet religious faith may involve more than the acceptance or rejection of facts, including the types of facts with which science concerns itself. "Religious faith is an awareness of the depths in our existence and a certain kind of response to what reveals itself in them.[27] Such awareness is often best captured in stories or narratives—biographical, autobiographical, historical, or even legendary—that persons pass from one generation to the next in order to *interpret* what is most significant to them.

Henri Frankfort has explored one way in which myth is cultivated and transmitted:

B

The irrational aspect of myth becomes especially clear when we remember that the ancients were not content merely to recount their myths as stories conveying information. They dramatized them, acknowledging in them a special virtue which could be activated by recital.

Of the dramatization of myth, Holy Communion is a well-known example. Another example is found in Babylonia. During each New Year's festival the Babylonians re-enacted the victory which Marduk had won over the powers of chaos on the first New Year's Day, when the world was created. At the annual festival the Epic of Creation was recited. It is clear that the Babylonians did not regard their story of creation as we might accept the theory of Laplace, for instance, as an intellectually satisfying account of how the world came to be as it is. Ancient man had not thought out an answer; an answer had been revealed to him in a reciprocal relationship with nature. If a question had been answered, man shared that answer with the "Thou" which had revealed itself. Hence, it seemed wise that man, each year, at the critical turn of the seasons, should proclaim the knowledge which he shared with the powers, in order to involve them once more in its potent truth.

In this statement Frankfort stresses the crucial role of *participation* in the truth expressed through the myth. Do we see this same role in the experience of many modern persons with music, drama, video recordings, television drama, or even televised accounts of public events, the news?

Frankfort summarizes the character of myth:

[26]Tran Van Dinh, "The Foundation of Man," in *"Story" in Politics*, Michael Novak, ed. (New York: Council on Religion and International Affairs, 1970), pp. 55–59. Used by permission.

[27]John Knox, *Myth and Truth* (Charlottesville, Va.: University Press of Virginia, 1964), p. 2.

We may, then, summarize the complex character of myth in the following words: Myth is a form of poetry which transcends poetry in that it proclaims a truth; a form of reasoning which transcends reasoning in that it wants to bring about the truth it proclaims; a form of action, of ritual behaviour, which does not find its fulfilment in the act but must proclaim and elaborate a poetic form of truth.[28]

Another contemporary student of myth in both preliterate and literate societies, the anthropologist Claude Lévi-Strauss, has given an account of the nature and functioning of myth. Lévi-Strauss's account supplements and reinforces Frankfort's discussion.

According to Lévi-Strauss, the essential characteristic of myth is that its structure is historical or narrative in character. A myth is the narration of a sequence of events. These events may be historical or legendary, but they are presented as being, and are felt to be, ahistorical and "eternally valid." A myth is a pattern of timeless relationships combined in a temporal sequence and related to one another by means of transformations. The result of the transformation of the elements of myth is that unlike or contradictory elements of human experience (including life and death, and agriculture and warfare, and maleness and femaleness) are enacted and felt as being essentially identical. The myth allows the integration into experience of differences that are potentially disruptive to society or to the individual because of their contradiction with other elements (such as beliefs, values, interests, expectations, and desires). The mythical resolution of the contradictions of life is not reached or apprehended reflectively or discursively; it is enacted and lived in feeling, imaginatively and affectively.

Contemporary biblical scholars have written extensively about the use of myth in the Jewish and Christian Scriptures. John Knox, a contemporary Christian New Testament scholar, has referred to such biblical images as "the pre-existence of Christ, his decision to come into this world as a man, his struggle with demonic powers and his triumph over them, his ascension to heaven, where he reigns at God's right hand" as part of a mythological framework used by early Christian writers to express the *meaning* of the *historical* events of the life, death, and resurrection of Jesus.[29]

Some Christians have objected to the use of the term *mythological* to characterize these or any parts of the Biblical message. Others, including Rudolf Bultmann, have asserted that mythological elements must be interpreted in such a way that the message of the New Testament can come alive in a meaningful form for contemporary persons. The Bible must be "demythologized." Still others, including Paul Tillich, have insisted that all religious expression must involve mythological elements, since myth is a necessary symbolic medium in expressing transcendental reality. Such Christian commentators agree with the anthropologists

---

[28]H. Frankfort and H. A. Frankfort, "Myth and Reality," in *Before Philosophy, the Intellectual Adventure of Ancient Man* (Penguin Edition), pp. 14–16. Copyright © 1946 by University of Chicago Press. Used by permission.

[29]John Knox, *Jesus Lord and Christ* (New York: Harper & Row, 1958), pp. 51–53; 255–59.

that myth functions to preserve and reinforce "unexpressible" truths. *Myth* in its religious use, according to them, does not denote that which is false or fabricated, but that which is most significant.

> *What insights do Lévi-Strauss's view of myth give into the purposes or functions of "The Myth of the Birth of the Vietnamese Race"?*

> *Examine the Babylonian and Japanese creation myths presented in Unit 85, and also examine some of the familiar Greek and American Indian myths in the light of Lévi-Strauss's discussion of the way myth functions.*

UNIT 31   Magic: Theory and Practice

As myth plays a unique role in culture and is often related to religion, so too has magic frequently been associated with religion. Many recent authors have argued that there is a fundamental difference between magic and religion and between religious and magical orientations to our lives and transcendent reality—divine beings or powers.

The anthropologist Bronislaw Malinowski, in *Magic, Science and Religion*, argued that:

A   There are no peoples however primitive without religion and magic. Nor are there, it must be added at once, any savage races lacking either in the scientific attitude or in science, though this lack has been frequently attributed to them. In every primitive community, studied by trustworthy and competent observers, there have been found two clearly distinguishable domains, the Sacred and the Profane; in other words, the domain of Magic and Religion and that of science.

On the one hand there are traditional acts and observances, regarded by the natives as sacred, carried out with reverence and awe, hedged around with prohibitions and special rules of behavior. Such acts and observances are always associated with beliefs in supernatural forces, especially those of magic, or with ideas about beings, spirits, ghosts, dead ancestors, or gods. On the other hand, a moment's reflection is sufficient to show that no art or craft however primitive could have been invented or maintained, no organized form of hunting, fishing, tilling, or search for food could be carried out without the careful observation of natural processes and a firm belief in its regularity, without confidence in the power of reason: that is, without the rudiments of science.[30]

In the societies that Malinowski studied, he found that people used scientific—or technical—procedures in situations in which there was little natural danger or unpredictability. They used magic only in situations that involved uncertainty, great difficulty, or hazard:

B   "It is most significant that in lagoon fishing, when man can rely completely upon his knowledge and skill, magic does not exist, while in the open-sea fishing, full of danger and uncertainty, there is extensive magical ritual to secure safety and

[30]Bronislaw Malinowski, "Magic, Science and Religion," in *Science, Religion and Reality*, ed. Joseph Needham (London: Society for Promoting Christian Knowledge, 1925), pp. 17–18.

good results." Further, even when magic is used, the individual "never relies on magic alone, while, on the contrary, he sometimes dispenses with it completely, as in fire-making and a number of crafts and pursuits. But he clings to it, whenever he has to recognize the impotence of his knowledge and of his rational technique."[31]

While Malinowski saw a significant role for magic in dealing with the unknown and dangerous elements of life, he believed that there is a clear differece between magic and religion:

C   While in the magical act the underlying idea and aim is always clear, straightforward, and definite, in the religious ceremony there is no purpose directed toward a subsequent event. It is only possible for the sociologist to establish the function, the sociological *raison d'être* of the act. The native can always state the end of the magical rite, but he will say of a religious ceremony that it is done because such is the usage, or because it has been ordained, or he will narrate an explanatory myth.[32]

The sociologist, Malinowski thought, will see that whereas magic is directed to specific ends—for example, a good catch of fish—religion is less specific in terms of goals. But religion will tend to express and promote the cohesiveness of the community. This can be seen by considering the social function of the funeral ceremony, a religious rite found in most societies.

D   The mortuary proceedings show a striking similarity throughout the world. As death approaches, the nearest relatives in any case, sometimes the whole community, forgather by the dying man, and dying, the most private act which a man can perform, is transformed into a public, tribal event. . . . There is always a more or less conventionalized and dramatized outburst of grief and wailing in sorrow, which often passes among savages into bodily lacerations and the tearing of hair. This is always done in a public display and is associated with visible signs of mourning, such as black or white daubs on the body, shaven or disheveled hair, strange or torn garments. The immediate mourning goes on round the corpse. This, far from being shunned or dreaded, is usually the center of pious attention. . . .

. . . Man's conviction of continued life is one of the supreme gifts of religion, which judges and selects the better of the two alternatives suggested by self-preservation—the hope of continued life and the fear of annihilation. . . .

Thus the rites of mourning, the ritual behavior immediately after death, can be taken as pattern of the religious act, while the belief in immortality, in the continuity of life and in the nether world, can be taken as the prototype of an act of faith.[33]

According to Malinowski, then, magic and religion can be sharply distinguished. Magic seeks to tap transcendent or mysterious powers for specific goals (safety, health, wealth, love, success) of groups or individuals in order to manipulate the environment when technological or common-sense knowledge is not available

[31]Ibid., pp. 48–52.
[32]Ibid., p. 38.
[33]Ibid.

to achieve these goals. Religion is directed toward transcendent powers, or beings, or even a Being, by a community for relatively nonspecific goals—or perhaps for no goals at all but merely out of a sense of obligation or necessity, perhaps to obey the will of, or to express reverence toward, some transcendent Being. However, we spoke earlier of a *magical* orientation (in contrast to moral, mystical, and aesthetic orientations) toward religion, and many religious traditions contain magical elements or at least allow their adherents to participate in semimagical practices. We may define the *magical orientation* toward religion as one in which control of transcendent or divine power is sought in order that it may be used for manipulation of the religious adherent's environment for personal or group purposes. Because of this manipulative element in magic, many modern and some ancient religious traditions, such as Judaism, have rejected, or have come to suspect and repress, magical elements.

5

Religion in Artistic Expression

INTRODUCTION

The two previous chapters of this section concentrated upon the nature of religious experience. The examples used in those units generally were verbal descriptions and discussions of religious experience. Such experience is not, however, confined to verbal expression. In fact, human religious experience probably has been as readily expressed, perhaps even more adequately expressed, in art. Persons and groups in all ages and in various cultures have sought to express in painting, sculpture, architecture, and other artistic forms their deepest values, the symbols arising from their sense of encounter with the Divine.

Some persons suggest that artistic expression is the most reliable of all expression. In the nineteenth century, John Ruskin said that a culture presents its autobiography in three books. The first is the book of its deeds; the second, the book of its words; and the third, the book of its arts. He argued that not one of these books can be understood unless we read the other two. Of the three, he claimed the only trustworthy one to be the last: the arts. In the contemporary era, British art historian Kenneth Clark has indicated that he agrees. "Writers and politicians may come out with all sorts of edifying sentiments, but they are what is known as declarations of intent. If I had to say which was telling the truth about society, a speech by a

Minister of Housing or the actual buildings put up in his time, I should believe the buildings."[1]

The purpose of this chapter is to look at some ways in which religious experience and meaning are communicated in visual arts such as painting, sculpture, and architecture. The first unit in the chapter explores ways in which art as a symbolic vehicle expressing religious meaning can evoke participational responses in its interpreters. How the changing religious experiences of the early Christian church are reflected in its representations of Jesus is discussed in Unit 33. Unit 34 investigates the expression in Western medieval architecture of religious themes and understandings. The chapter is intended to encourage the reader to examine ways in which the many and varied art forms one encounters daily may communicate religious meaning.

UNIT 32 Art As Symbolic Vehicle

One can argue that the arts are among the most reliable means of knowing the true characteristics of a culture or a time. The twentieth century Spanish painter Pablo Picasso is reported to have said, in a rare moment of theorizing about his work, that "art is a lie that makes us realize the truth."[2] Like many seeming paradoxes, this one teases and should arrest the mind. How can truth, of all things, be realized by means of deliberate invention or a carefully constructed illusion? Picasso's remark is more than a playful and provocative turn of phrase. It may be that Picasso is saying something of primary importance about the form and intention of all art. Its *form* is given to it by human imagination. An *intention* of art is to declare the way things really are for us, to provide a breakthrough to significance. If what Picasso said is true, then the artist is one who skillfully, insightfully, does create a fabrication, something not literally real, which, as a symbol, reaches into us in such a way as to disclose the depths of our experience, the profound and the deeply true. One might suggest, then, that of the many things that it is, art is *disclosure*.[3]

The person to whom it first occurred to *fix permanently* that which surrounded him or her probably did not intend to create a mere reproduction. It is true that some art objects may be extraordinarily true to life, but no less frequently we find art objects that agree with "reality" only in a few points. Therefore, *representation is not reproduction*. Humans have the ability to invent *other* forms besides themselves and the forms which they come upon. *We create symbols and through them represent the surrounding vast reality. We create images of that reality in which the form we perceive and the form we create fall together.*

Thus we are dealing with representation, not reproduction. The concept of "representation" in art involves not just external display but internalization, participation on the part of audience or viewers.

[1]Kenneth Clark, *Civilization* (New York: Harper & Row), p. 1.
[2]Roger Hazelton, *A Theological Approach to Art* (Nashville: Abingdon Press, 1968), p. 16.
[3]Ibid.

Much contemporary art has highlighted this participational characteristic. Some plays, films, paintings, and sculpture in order to be fully understood *require* involvement. Widely varied responses have been educed by the works of the contemporary surrealist artist Salvador Dali. In 1955, he painted *The Sacrament of the Last Supper*. No doubt persons viewing the painting have verbalized perceptions and responses to it that Dali did not have in mind when he painted it. For most viewers, the work evokes response; some enter into it, participate in it. They may see a truth to which this symbolic representation points.

A   Salvador Dali, *The Sacrament of the Last Supper*, 1955, The National Gallery of Art, Washington, D.C. (Photo by Kenneth Lawrence.)

Works of art often function powerfully as religious symbols. The following selection describes the response by a student, Judy Covington, to Dali's *The Last Supper*, a painting in which subject matter, form, and style all convey religious meaning.

B

I saw this painting for the first time while I was still in junior high school, and the thing that grabbed me then is what still grabs me now—it's so realistic that it's unreal. I thought at first it was a retouched photograph, because of the preciseness and detail with which the scene is portrayed—the refraction of light within the cup and the foldmarks on the tablecloth, as well as the sharp lines of light and shadow across the table and the disciples' robes. But I realized that the figure of Christ, although very human-looking, was transparent. And even though it seems logical to assume that the light would have its source in him—he casts no shadow on the table in front of him—the shadows of the disciples indi-

C   Dali, *The Sacrament of the Last Supper*, detail. (Photo by Kenneth Lawrence.)

cate that the light comes from somewhere behind him, from what would be the body of the enlarged arms and chest visible above and behind Christ. That caught my attention, too—it was the first time I had ever seen "a painting of God" as such. I was a little overawed—who was this Dali character to think he could imprison a likeness of the Almighty on canvas? But looking at it now, I can understand that Dali must have felt that men need a "see-able" God, and not some vague apparition floating around in the clouds. Most of the body is invisible, but the chest, shoulders, and arms seem firmly anchored—there's nothing vague about them. Dali does not go further than the shoulders—I imagine he did not quite feel up to painting a face—that would have been nearly profane. Just from that part of the body which is there comes a sense of peace. There is a feeling of anticipation, not necessarily sorrowful, either. It is as though Christ has raised his hand and stopped time for a moment, stopped to remember himself and so that the disciples may remember, too. The transparent beams which support without enclosing add to the contrast between real and unreal. Christ is definitely the center of the painting, with the lines of light on the table and the beams on either side and above Him outlining the nucleus of the painting. His is the only visible face, and his expression is one of calm. There is no sorrow in his eyes, only certainty. He looks as if he is remembering all the good things in his life, as if he will not die in vain. Dali has taken a traditional scene out of the structured, dark upper room, out of an anxious, melancholy mood, and set it on a plateau overlooking the world, almost, with God the Comforter watching over. The painting is so personal a statement of faith and painted with such clarity that it almost hurts to look at it. I wanted to sit still so as not to disturb anything or spoil the image.[4]

In addition to this response, there are a number of possible interpretations. The background of dawn in the picture, the Sea of Galilee, and the fishing boats may

[4]Used by permission.

point to the Easter event. The outstretched arms of the raised figure could represent the crucifixion of Jesus. Thus, the painting encapsulates the Last Supper, Crucifixion, and Resurrection sequence. Therefore, the painting powerfully expresses both the historical events and the symbolic-interpretive dimensions.

UNIT 33   Images of Jesus as Christ in the Early Church

Conceptions of the incarnation of deity have played an important role in several of the religions of the world. Yet, one could conclude that in no other religion has the incarnation of God been more central than in Christianity. From the affirmation that the essential quality of the divine was fully present in the man Jesus, all the rest of Christian doctrine proceeds.

Pivotal in the Christian perspective is Jesus of Nazareth's affirmation that unqualified love has the power within itself eventually to elicit a response of the same kind. His capacity to express this "no-strings-attached" love (in the Greek, *agape*) was exemplified in his forgiveness of the persons who were crucifying him even while they were doing it. The early Christians saw in this the presence of God fully manifest in the man. Hence, the cross representing crucifixion became the central symbol of the religion, though several hundred years would pass before it did so.

The earliest Christians seemed to take the position that Jesus had taught that the one God in whom they placed their trust was the sovereign, moral, personal deity ruling the universe, perfectly just, and that God could be characterized most centrally by unconditional love *(agape)*. They further observed that Jesus *was* what he had taught, that he exemplified perfectly what he had taught about the nature of deity. Thus, the faith claim emerged that God was *incarnate* in Jesus, to whom they gave the title, Christ.

Throughout the history of Christianity, followers of the faith have developed conceptions of Jesus the Christ as saviour and as mediator of God's love and will for mankind. Soon after Jesus' time, Christians began to express their understanding and experience of Christ in verbal *and* visual statements.

Controversies have arisen and have continually recurred in the church regarding Christology. Historic creeds were devised affirming both the humanity and divinity of Christ. Just *how* these characteristics were mingled, without confusion, in Christ has remained a point of continued discussion, although orthodox Christianity affirmed that Jesus was fully a man in whom God was fully present.

Artists have expressed varied understandings of Christ and his ministry through painting, mosaic, and sculpture. Particular characteristics are emphasized in these works of art, which sometimes communicate with greater depth than can words. The combination of the figure of Jesus Christ (especially the manner in which he is portrayed) along with various symbols and actions can be one of the most effective means of communicating conceptions of his significance.

One of the most frequent modes of depiction of Jesus Christ in the early church was as the Good Shepherd. Jesus was consistently presented as youthful, a common mode at that time to suggest continual height of power, vigor. He was also shown as cleanshaven, with a Caesarian haircut, and in the *contraposto* pose frequently employed in Greek and Roman art to present heroes or deity figures. The clothing and general appearance were quite familiar in the Greco-Roman world. Such depictions of Christ began to appear as early as the second century.

A

The Good Shepherd, fresco, third century. Detail from the ceiling of the Vault of Lucina, Catacomb of Callixtus, Rome. (Photo by Kenneth Lawrence.)

In illustration A, Jesus Christ is the shepherd, the deliverer from death, of his flock (the Christian community). He is depicted carrying a sheep over his shoulders, an idea that may have as its scriptual source the parable of the lost sheep. (The style of this presentation was familiar at that time because it had been employed in non-Christian art.) Further, Jesus is shown carrying a container of water (the water of new life or baptism?), and his arm is extended in a very natural manner because of the weight of the object. He is surrounded by other sheep which represent the community of the faithful (the church). Frequently, such scenes are placed in a pastoral setting. The whole scene is enclosed by a circle, which helps to complete part of the total design. Circles were frequently used symbolically to represent eternality.

Figures called *orants* often appear in enclosed sections adjacent to the outer perimeters of the circle. (They are similar to the orant figure in illustration B.) The orant, in early Christian art, was a symbolic representation of the disembodied soul and consistently was presented in an attitude of prayer with the hands uplifted, as illustrated here. Indeed, the orant expresses faith, since prayer is an expression of it. It can be argued that the orant in such catacomb depictions prays for himself and asks for God's deliverance or gives thanks for it.[5] Thus, the disembodied souls of the faithful are related to the eternal Christ, their shepherd and deliverer from death to eternal life.

In the fresco painting in a lunette above a crypt in the Catacomb of Saint Domitilla at Rome, we begin to notice important changes in the depiction of Jesus Christ (see illustration C). It may be dated approximately a century after the inter-

B

Orant, fresco, Rome, Catacomb of Priscilla, late third century. (Photo by Max Hirmer. Used by permission.)

[5] Walter Lowrie, *Art in the Early Church* (New York: W. W. Norton and Co., Inc., 1969), p. 46.

pretative statement in illustration A. The artist has employed depictions of the twelve Apostles arranged in a manner to center attention upon the Christ figure. Their gestures and their gaze suggest his importance in their company and have the effect of exaltation. Christ is presented with an air of authority; his right hand is extended in a gesture. His eyes look out with intensity. Christ is depicted as the teacher and lawgiver. Two figures stand behind him, holding up and extending what appears to be a kind of mantle, similar to the modern conception of a type of cape. The interior fabric is a field of blue with stars scattered as a design. The blue field with stars was subsequently used in Christian art to refer symbolically to the cosmos; and by being placed behind the figure of Christ, it came to refer to his universal significance. The position of these figures and the way they seem to lift the object suggests the possibility that they will place it on the shoulders of Jesus Christ. If this is the case, this gesture was associated with a kind of investiture; in the church, it eventually became one act in the investment of Christ's authority in his vicars (representatives), the bishops of the church, who were already being set aside, even in New Testament times. A more exalted Christology is suggested by the entire composition.

C

Christ Teaching, with Apostles, fresco, Catacomb of St. Domitilla, Rome. (Photo by Max Hirmer. Used by permission.)

In 313, the Roman Emperor Constantine issued the Edict of Toleration at Milan. Through this act, the Christian religion was officially recognized by the state. Though the emperor seems to have adopted the new religion, and members of his family, especially his mother, Helena, were active in it, there remained for a long time many who were opposed to it, including some important senatorial families. Nevertheless, with imperial sanction made official, the church could openly grow and organize itself throughout the empire. It would officially supplant the old Roman religions in 380.

In the next several hundred years, magnificent churches were erected and decorated, often in a splendid manner. After Emperor Constantine moved the imperial capital from Rome to Byzantium (and named the capital city Constantinople), Latin *and* Eastern Byzantine influences began to appear in churches. They blended a bit at times because of the interaction between Eastern and Western parts of the Empire.

At Ravenna, on the Adriatic coast of Italy, some of the finest examples of Christian art of the fifth and sixth centuries are preserved. Among these is the little Mausoleum of Galla Placidia, erected in 424 or 425. Originally a chapel dedicated to Saint Lawrence, the structure was probably employed as a mausoleum for the husband of Galla Placidia, Constantius III, as well as her brother, Emperor Honorius. In a lunette above the entrance to the building, a mosaic depiction of Christ as Good Shepherd with sheep is presented. (See illustration D.)

In this mosaic, we see exhibited some of the finer workmanship of the period, and although Byzantine influences are present in this somewhat transitional work, the Good Shepherd figure recalls Roman catacomb presentations. Christ is shown tending and caring for the flock (the community of faith). His face might be said to be rather Roman, instead of Eastern, in character—classical art style still is present. However, this representation exhibits him in a different, more priestly garb than that depicted in other such works. He holds a cross; the scene is very orderly in a more strictly balanced style.

D Christ as Good Shepherd, mosaic, Mausoleum of Galla Placidia, Ravenna, Italy, ca. 424–435. (Photo by Don C. Wilson. Used by permission.)

Jesus is seated on rocks which are three in number and graduated in size, more thronelike. The sheep are three on each side and geometrically arranged. Christ the Shepherd warmly responds to one of the sheep with a "chin chuck," an intimate gesture. Nevertheless, the overall effect of this visual statement may be said to be "colder" in quality. A more exalted interpretation of Christ is being made in this era. An aureole or halo[6] appears about his head. In the vault we see a strictly ordered vault decoration with a deep blue background and starlike designs (a symbol of the cosmos?). The colors, geometric balance, and concern for order blend with those of the lunette.

E   Christ glorified with Saint Vitalis, Saint Ecclesius, and archangels Michael and Gabriel. Mosaic in apse of Church of San Vitale, Ravenna, ca. 547. (Photo by Lawrence D. White. Used by permission.)

During the reign of Emperor Justinian II (from Byzantine Constantinople), a remarkable, if small, church was constructed in Ravenna and completed about 547. In the mosaic-encrusted sanctuary apse of this church, the scene in illustration E appears. Heavily influenced by imperial court ceremony, the mosaic includes, at the center, Christ enthroned as Pantocrator (sovereign, universal judge). In the formal scene, Christ presents a martyr's crown to Saint Vitalis (at left), to whom the church is dedicated. An angel presents the saint to Christ. Another angel presents

[6]In classical mythology, an aureole was a shining cloud sometimes surrounding a deity when on earth.

Saint Ecclesius (at right), the founder of the church, who in turn ceremonially presents a model of the church to Christ. By this time, saints and martyrs are being represented in the clothing of the court in some of the very formal, ceremonial church art of the time.

Christ himself, now much exalted in the thought of the church, is shown seated on a sphere while the other figures stand with their feet on the ground. Below the Christ, the four rivers of Heaven flow. He holds the Book of Life and is endowed with a bejeweled halo which incorporates the shape of the cross. The light depicted by brilliant colors on the clouds behind Christ possibly suggests sunrise. The brilliant gold background (which becomes a convention in art of this type) and the strong colors have a dazzling effect upon the viewer below and connote both the preciousness of the function of Christ's church and its authority.

UNIT 34 Luminous Wholeness in Medieval Architecture

How are perspectives of religious meaning expressed in physical structures? Many examples might be cited to illustrate a response to this question. Several can help us understand the phenomenon.

Western Gothic church architecture was born between 1137 and 1144, when the royal Abbey Church of Saint-Denis was reconstructed near the city of Paris. An abbot by the name of Suger was at that time an adviser to the King, Louis VI. Suger played a role in accomplishing an alliance between the French Monarchy and the church, creating a new closeness between the efforts of the church and the goals of the monarchy.[7] Abbot Suger was also conscious of an underlying dissension within the political structure of the country, caused by the traditional independent behavior of the dukes. Seeking to cement the new closeness of state and church and to undergird political accord, Suger dreamed of creating a dynamic symbol of unity.

The relics of Saint Denis, the missionary who is credited with bringing Christianity to France, are entombed in the Royal Abbey church which bears his name. Abbot Suger wanted to make this Church of Saint-Denis the center of both spiritual and patriotic emotion in France. He set out to achieve this goal partly through the restructuring of this building, and from the project emerged a striking architectural accomplishment: the new style since called *Gothic*.

Two salient features of Gothic architecture which are especially revelatory of religious meaning are (1) *harmony*: the careful emphasis on strict geometric planning, perfect mathematical ratios, and (2) *luminosity*: the use of light to emphasize the building's features. Harmony, achieved in this architectural form in the carefully planned balance of ratios, was understood as the source of beauty. In this harmony the laws by which divine reason created the universe were exemplified. Within this structure, the enlarged windows (made possible by this new form)

[7]H. W. Janson, *History of Art* (New York: Harry Abrams, Inc., 1962), pp. 229–30. Used by permission.

provided much more than the simple utility of admitting light into these often vast, vertical structures. The deep coloration of the stained glass of this period served to transform the light, to diffuse and filter, to change the very quality of daylight and endow it with special character. The luminosity was like the "light Divine," the revelation of God within the universe as represented by the whole structure.

Such a symbolic interpretation of numerical harmony and light had existed in Christian thought for centuries. It was believed that the concept came directly from Dionysius the Areopagite, an Athenian disciple of Saint Paul the Evangelist. In twelfth century France, Dionysius was thought to have been Saint Denis, the Apostle to France and its special protector.

As a Frenchman, the abbot was thoroughly steeped in this thought. Further, it was a perfect way to attempt to embody in a building what could be considered at that time peculiarly French Christian thought. Suger gathered architects and artisans to carry out his goals for "building theology" in stone and glass. That they succeeded is testified to by the first edifice in the new style. Visitors to the new church of Saint Denis were overwhelmed by the achievement. Soon, the new architectural statement spread not only throughout but far beyond the region.[8]

The cathedral of Notre Dame de Paris, which was begun in 1163, "reflects the salient features of Suger's Saint-Denis more directly than any other."[9] The new

A

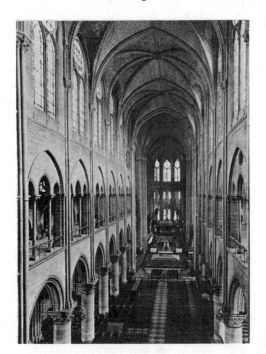

View looking down on choir and nave, Cathedral of Notre Dame, Paris. (Seton Lloyd et al., *World Architecture* (New York: McGraw-Hill, 1963), p. 22. © The Hamlyn Group. Used by permission. Photograph by Michael Holford.)

[8]Janson, *History of Art* pp. 230–34.
[9]Ibid., p. 233.

architecture combined harmony, balance, light, massiveness, and verticality to represent concepts of God.

The sense of splendid balance of ratios, harmony, and the invasion of space by dazzling light is exhibited especially well by the Cathedral Church of St. Andrew at Wells, England. Smaller than many of the Gothic cathedral churches, Wells may be judged a superlative statement of the Gothic perspective. Upon entering the nave of the church, one immediately perceives the two major ideas of the Gothic conception. (See illustration B.)

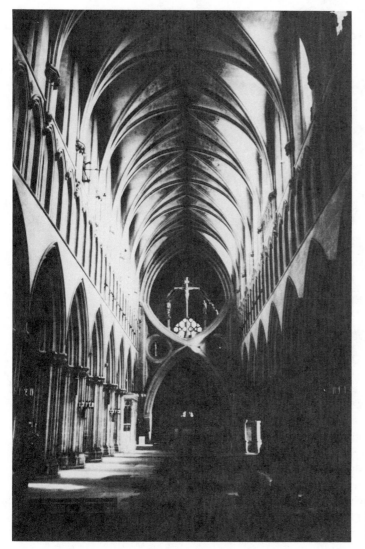

B

Nave, with choir and sanctuary beyond double arch, Cathedral Church of St. Andrew, Wells, England. (Photo by Kenneth Lawrence.)

C

Facade, Cathedral of Siena, Italy.
(Photo by Kenneth Lawrence.)

Striving for a coherent and balanced whole is characteristic of the facade of the Cathedral of Siena, Italy. The formal architectural discipline embraces both the mosaics and sculpture. Each part has a definite role within the unity of the total framework.

Paul Tillich, in his discussion of the thought of the Pseudo-Dionysius, describes the use of light as a symbol. Tillich refers to this light as emanating from the source and substance of all being and suggests that the light is the good in all things. "Light is a symbol not only for knowing but also for being."[10]

Especially notable in the planned use of light as a religious expression is the Cathedral of Notre Dame de Paris. Indeed, a black and white photograph (illustration D) cannot begin to present the power of the light admitted through the dense colors of the stained glass. Actually, the windows admit a much smaller amount of light than one would expect and function in the filtering manner described earlier. As we have said, they serve to transform the quality of daylight; this gives to the light the symbolic meaning intended.

D

Transept rose and lancet windows, Notre Dame, Paris. (Photo by Kenneth Lawrence.)

The extreme verticality which developed as the Gothic style was further elaborated through the centuries, coupled with the intricate structure of ratios in the thrust and counterthrust of roof and wall with flying buttress, and the admission of light through highly placed windows, is well exemplified in the Cathedral at Köln (Cologne), Germany.

[10]Paul Tillich, A *History of Christian Thought* (New York: Harper & Row, 1968), p. 93.

E

Exterior, south transept, Köln Cathedral, Germany. (Photo by Kenneth Lawrence.)

While Christian thinkers created the theological systems of the High Medieval period, the schools and cathedrals influenced the religious experience of the populace. One can imagine the communicative effect of these structures upon the worshippers as they participated in the mass and, awed by light filtering into the gloom below (where they were), perceived the massive intricacy of these houses of God. Their massiveness, beauty, and luminosity all express through the structure itself religious meaning—the majesty and power of the Divine.

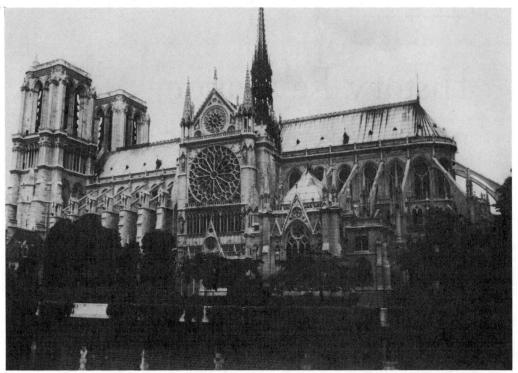

F Cathedral of Notre Dame, Paris. Note especially the system of buttresses and windows. (Photo by Kenneth Lawrence.)

6

History, Revelation, and the Knowledge of God

INTRODUCTION

In Part II of *Exploring Religious Meaning*, a number of cases of religious experiences of individuals and groups were examined, an analysis of some of the characteristic features and elements of religious experience was presented, and an attempt was made to articulate the broad aspects of religious experience, especially through art and architecture.

Part III shifts from the more subjective dimension of personal—individual or group—experience to the more objective side of that which is experienced. That is, in Part III we attempt to characterize what people who have had such experiences have believed to be their object, source, or goal. In Western religious traditions the object, source, or goal of religious experience is often characterized in personal terms, as God. Since some religions do not conceive of the ultimate reality in strictly personal terms, we will ordinarily use the term *the Divine* to indicate that which is sought in religious experience.

Many have argued that the concepts religious persons use to indicate or to characterize the Divine and the relations that humans have to the Divine arise from the experiences of mundane human life—from the interaction of human beings with their natural environment and from the realm of interpersonal relations. Thus, the Divine may be characterized with images derived from the forces or phenomena of nature, like lightning or a storm, or from human relationships or phenomena, such as a king or an all-powerful father. Because human images of the Divine are based on or derived from human experience of nature and social—personal and interpersonal—life, to speak of the Divine is in some sense to speak of the human. Yet, religious persons are convinced that there is a transhuman reality which they encounter, and which is real regardless of the way it is imagined, conceived, or expressed.

In the present section we attempt to examine images and concepts of the Divine as these have been articulated in different cultural settings and periods of history.

Underlying all the concerns of this section is the overarching question, "why should one think of the Divine at all?" Hardly a culture has existed where this question has not been raised. A hymnic statement from the Vedas of early Hinduism expresses what appears to be inherent human awareness of the Divine. At the same time it leaves open the options concerning the way in which that Divine is to be conceived—as personal or impersonal, historical or timeless, active or quiescent, one or many.

> Who truly knows, and who can here declare it?
> Whence It was born, and how this world was fashioned?
>
> .   .   .
>
> Whether he made the world or did not make it,
> He knows whence this creation came, he only
> Who in the highest heaven guards and watches,
> He knows indeed, but then, perhaps, he knows not![1]
>   Rig Veda, Book X, Hymn 129

Three interrelated topics of particular importance to Western religious traditions—Judaism, Christianity, and Islam—are discussed in this chapter. Naturally, the concepts of *history, revelation,* and *faith* are present in other than Western religious traditions. In this section of *Exploring Religious Meaning* these topics are of special importance, for if we are seeking to examine and understand human concepts and experiences of the Divine, then the question of how the Divine is present in human history, how the Divine is revealed, how the Divine is known (by faith or in other ways) becomes crucial.

Every religious tradition contains some understanding of *revelation*. The *meaning* of revelation ranges from some form of religious insight, as experienced by a Taoist in contemplation of nature or by a Hindu in transcendental meditation, to the idea of a special communication from a personal God to human beings, as when, in Jewish, Christian, Islamic belief, God communicates his will to particular individuals in unique space-time events. Judaism, Christianity, and Islam have, in fact, frequently been called "historical" religions because of their belief that God *does* communicate to people in specific historical contexts through specific historical events. Some of the dimensions of this understanding of revelation, and some of the problems it involves, are discussed in Unit 35; *faith*, as discussed in Units 36 and 37, will be seen to be of universal human significance.

[1]As cited in John Noss, *Man's Religions,* 4th ed. (New York: Macmillan, Inc.), p. 97.

The relationship of faith to reason, as discussed by philosophers and theologians for centuries, is still an issue of very great importance. Also, faith as a comprehensive human possibility, a mode of existence that many have believed both undergirds and transcends the rational dimensions of life, is examined. *Faith* in this sense involves belief, at least some minimum of belief, but it means much more than that: It involves commitment, trust, and basic self-acceptance and self-understanding. The connection of faith, as discussed here, with the definition of the term *religion*, explored in the introduction, should be clear and should provide occasions for a reexamination of the definition of *religion*.

UNIT 35   Revelation: General and Special

Is God self-revealing? If so, how can we understand revelation?

Revelation translates the Greek word *apokalypsis* and literally means "an uncovering, a laying bare, making naked." . . . So understood, R[evelation] presupposes (1) that someone or something is hidden and that this someone or something has not been discovered but, rather, disclosed.[2]

We cannot find a developed concept of revelation in the Bible. Although the Bible contains numerous "images and symbols for the disclosure of God's will and purposes,"[3] revelation has developed as a doctrinal concept during the history of Christianity since the writing of the Scripture. Alan Richardson, author of *Christian Apologetics*, interprets revelation in the following passages:

A   The only kind of theory of the knowledge of God which will adequately embrace all the facts of man's experience will be one which recognizes that there are two kinds of revelation or divine disclosure of truth. There is first general revelation, which pertains to the universal religious consciousness of mankind; and there is also special revelation, which is mediated through particular episodes of definite times and places in history. The broad distinction between general and special revelation is that the former is non-historical, in that its content is not communicated to mankind through particular historical situations but is quite independent of the accidents of time and place, whereas the latter is historical, that is, bound up with certain series of historical persons and happenings through which it is communicated to mankind. This is broadly the distinction between biblical (Jewish-Christian) religion and the non-Christian religions.[4]

Special revelation consists of divine confrontation of God and humankind

[2]Van A. Harvey, *A Handbook of Theological Terms* (New York: Macmillan Inc., 1964), p. 207.
[3]Ibid.
[4]Alan Richardson, *Christian Apologetics* (1947: SCM Press, Ltd. and Harper & Row, Publishers, Inc.), p. 117.

through such actual events as the Israelite exodus from Egypt and the life, death, and resurrection of Christ. Whereas general revelation tends to allow that all persons in some way know about God, special revelation means that God is disclosed in a special way to specific persons so that they personally experience God.

Many who hold to a theory of general revelation stress that we have knowledge of God by means of our reasoning capacities. Charles Hartshorne, twentieth-century process philosopher, for example, holds that strict logical analysis presents us with knowledge of God. Richardson would not want to restrict general revelation to rational reflection, as he notes in the following:

B   The theory of general and special revelation, however, does not restrict the general knowledge of God, to which all men have access, by limiting it to knowledge of one type only, namely, the knowledge which comes by rational reflection. It recognizes that there may be knowledge of God through general religious experience, far outside the biblical and Christian frontiers. Furthermore . . . it helps us to see that there may be a genuine knowledge of God that comes through all forms of art and artistic experience— music, poetry, drama, architecture, sculpture, painting.[5]

Thus, while a theory of general revelation may imply that strict logical analysis presents us with the knowledge of God, it also may include experience of God through art or the natural world. The key to a general revelation or knowledge of God, according to Richardson, relates to the moral experience.

C   It is, however, in the moral sphere that the chief evidence of general revelation is found. Even though some might hold that there are certain people who are totally devoid of religious experience, it is indubitable that all people have had moral experience—the experience of knowing that one ought to do this and ought not to do that. Every human being who is not clearly an imbecile has knowledge of right and wrong.[6]

Alan Richardson claims that general revelation has redeeming power for those who experience God through philosophy, art forms, or nature. Other eminent theologians, however, such as Karl Barth and Emil Brunner (highly influential German theologians during post–World War I decades), hold that special revelation alone serves as the vehicle for saving grace. Barth believes that every person is a sinner, totally devoid of any natural capacity to receive God's revelation. For him, God is known by a person only because God makes that knowledge possible. Brunner agrees with Barth on this point but would argue that in every person there remains a capacity for general knowledge about God, even though such knowledge does not redeem a person from sin. Richardson feels that both Barth and Brunner neglect the saving power that comes from knowledge of God revealed outside Christianity.

[5]Ibid., p. 122.
[6]Ibid., p. 124.

Richardson affirms that non-Christian humanists who do good works or have some vision of God are to be considered vehicles of God's general revelation. He is quick to say, however, that Christians who recognize God-given humanist values in non-Christians should claim special revelation as essential for clarifying and correcting general revelation.

Concerning the necessity of special revelation, Richardson writes: "There is indeed a sense in which the noblest insights of the humanist are fulfilled in Christ, but there is also a sense in which they are judged and transcended by Him. . . . Although all that we have said about the necessity and value of general revelation is true, it is also true that apart from faith in Christ there is no undistorted knowledge of God or of truth at all."[7]

Do you think everyone has a religious consciousness?

Why do those, according to Richardson, under general revelation lack knowledge of God?

Could the concepts of general and special revelation as defined by Richardson be meaningful to those of religious traditions other than Christianity?

UNIT 36   Faith and Reason

In the previous unit, the ways in which God may be revealed—in the permanent structure and characteristics of the created world (general revelation) and in unique historical events of self-disclosure (special revelation)—were examined. These categories have been particularly important to Western religious traditions (Judaism, Christianity, Islam). In this unit, the same topics are examined, but from the point of view of the potential receiver of revelation. That is, the question is raised about possible sources or faculties within human beings by which knowledge of God (or revelation) might be experienced. Particularly, we explore the possible relations between faith and reason as two human avenues to the Divine. Again, these concepts have been particularly important in Western religious traditions. Those who stress special revelation probably tend to emphasize faith as a way to know God, and those who affirm the reality and importance of general revelation place a heavy emphasis on reason.

Determining the relationship between faith and reason depends on answering the question, How shall one respond to God's revelation of himself? By faith? By reason? By both faith and reason? Or is there a dimension deeper than either faith or reason?

John Baillie, a Scottish theologian, points to the problem of relating faith and reason by stating that

A   all vital knowledge, all apprehended truth may be regarded as revealed. . . . The knowing mind is active in attending, selecting, and interpreting; but it must attend to, select from, and interpret what is presented to it; and therefore it must be passive as well as active.[8]

[7]Ibid., pp. 129–30.
[8]John Baillie, *The Idea of Revelation* (New York: Columbia University Press, 1956), p. 19.

Here Baillie makes a distinction between the mind's active and passive behavior. When the mind acts, does this mean it reasons? When the mind remains passive, does this mean it lives by faith? Or can faith be considered the active element of man while reason is passive? How do we gain knowledge of the Divine? By naked thought, the unaided exercise of human thinking? Or by receiving direct revelation from God himself? Or does it mislead us to distinguish between faith and reason?

The West has a long history of alternating harmony and disharmony between faith and reason. At times faith has ruled while reason has suffered suppression. At other times reason has reigned over faith. There have been times when reason and revelation have existed together in relative peace.

In the following columns, faith and reason can be seen to have differing emphases:

Faith May Include an Emphasis on	Reason May Include an Emphasis on
revelation	discursive thinking
theology	philosophy
man's will	man's intellect
man's freedom	man's knowledge
trust	logic
decisive affirmation	philosophical speculations
God as personal	God as abstract and impersonal
Divine disclosure	human discovery

Comparisons between the categories suggest why faith and reason have differing roles both in religious understanding and in particular religious traditions. In the West, there have traditionally been four basic ways of relating faith and reason; we shall now examine them.

I. Reason Rejecting Faith

When reason rejects faith, it tends to result in skepticism about God. Reason alone has sought God but in many cases has reached an atheistic (no God) or an agnostic (no knowledge of God) position. Some interpreters who have a thoroughgoing use of reason without the help of faith have concluded that religious affirmations of God or life after death equal faith in goblins, Santa Claus, fairies, and monsters in the night. According to some thinkers, reason seeks evidence for God's existence, but in the absence of evidence for God's existence, atheism becomes obligatory.[9] A similar, though not identical, position has been proposed by A. J. Ayer:

B

We conclude, therefore, that the argument from religious experience is altogether fallacious. The fact that people have religious experiences is interesting from a psychological point of view, but it does not in any way imply that there is such a thing as religious knowledge. . . .

The theist, like the moralist, may believe that his experiences are cognitive experiences, but, unless he can formulate his "knowledge" in propositions that are empirically verifiable, we may be sure he is deceiving himself.[10]

[9]Michael Scriven, *Primary Philosophy* (New York: McGraw-Hill, 1966), p. 103.
[10]A. J. Ayer, *Language, Truth and Logic*, 2nd ed. (New York: Dover, 1946), p. 120.

Ayer refuses to accept any statements about reality as having meaning unless they are grounded in testable sense experiences. Others, such as Aristotle, Leibniz, and Hartshorne, have claimed to have knowledge of God through reason alone.

II. Reason Embracing Faith

A number of interpreters have held the view that reason includes the way of faith. Adherents of this position have seen a common denominator of Divine Truth in both philosophy and the Judeo-Christian tradition. Justin Martyr, a second-century philosopher and Christian martyr, held "that a saving natural knowledge of God was possible through philosophy . . ."[11] He saw a close identity between Christian teachings and much in the best philosophers. He felt Christianity inherited all the truth discerned by Greek philosophers.[12] For Justin, reason and faith represented a common ground.

Justin fathered a tradition that was articulated strongly by Clement and Origen. Clement tended to equate the saving power of philosophy with Jewish law and prophecy. He saw Plato as a Moses talking Attic Greek.[13] Origen, Christianity's earliest systematic theologian, developed a system of theology in which he saw a close proximity between the Word of the Greek philosophers and the Word become flesh, Christ, the incarnation of God. In his classic work, *First Principles*, he relates in creative ways the message of scriptural faith to the teachings of philosophy and reason.

Peter Abelard, Christian philosopher of the twelfth century, refocused the emphasis on a reasoned faith in the Middle Ages. "He held that what had been revealed to the Jews by prophecy had been given to the Greeks by philosophy and that the doctrine of the Trinity, and other Christian truths, had been taught by Heraclitus and Plato. . . ."[14] Abelard's method emphasized doubting as a way to understand faith. He did not intend to make reason primary to faith, but his approach did open the way for more rationalism in theology, culminating in Immanuel Kant's attempt to confine "religion within the limits of reason alone."

III. Faith Rejecting Reason

In reaction to the tendency of reason to suppress faith, some men of faith have tended to negate reason altogether. At times, Tertullian, an early Christian theologian, rejected reason, "denouncing Greek philosophy as the bridal gift of the fallen angels to the daughters of men and the Greek philosophers as the patriarchs of the heretics."[15] Bernard of Clairvaux, a Christian mystic, felt that Abelard threatened the true faith with his rationalism. Doubting reason as a reliable guide to God, Bernard said: "By faith I think of God . . ."[16] Martin Luther, father of the Protes-

[11] Alan Richardson, *Christian Apologetics*, p. 228.
[12] Ibid., p. 229.
[13] Ibid.
[14] Ibid.
[15] Ibid., p. 228.
[16] Bernard of Clairvaux, "Selections from His Sermons," in *The Christian Reader: Inspirational and Devotional Classics*, comp. and ed. Stanley Irving Stuber (New York: Association Press, 1952), p. 106.

tant Reformation, held that no one can enter into a right relationship with God through good works or the power of thought. While reason may help us in practical living, such as making clothes or doing a job, human reasoning falls short in spiritual matters; other power is required here—something given only by God and made known in divine word (See Unit 19).[17] That which God grants, in Luther's understanding, is faith alone, the gift of trust in God's saving strength.

In our own century, the theologian Karl Barth expressed serious apprehensions about reason's ability to point adequately to God: "Knowledge of God is a knowledge completely effected and determined from the side of its object, from the side of God. . . . Our concepts are not adequate to grasp this treasure."[18] We should note, however, that Barth, as well as others who rejected reason in the realm of faith, had to depend upon the expressions of reason to reject reason. Although some voices may justifiably cry out against the excesses of rationalism, no one can be free completely from the philosophy of the times.

IV. Faith Embracing Reason

The classical Christian answer to the conflict between faith and reason finds apt expression in the words of Saint Augustine, Bishop of Hippo in Africa in the fifth century:

C   Understanding is the reward of faith. Therefore seek not to understand that thou mayest believe, but believe that thou mayest understand. . . . We believed that we might know; for if we wished first to know and then to believe, we should not be able to know or to believe. . . . They did not believe because they knew, but they believed in order that they might know.[19]

Here Augustine exhibits an orthodox Christian view of the relationship between faith and reason. Reason comes to creative fruition only as it is guided by faith. Faith orders understanding.

This does not mean that faith supplies factual data of sense experience. Reason still must function to assess and make judgments about facts of knowledge, but the power of reason to function adequately comes from faith. In knowing, "faith supplies the 'clues' or categories of interpretation by which alone the empirical *data* of science and religion can be rightly understood."[20] According to Augustine's approach, every philosophy must follow the lead of a faith principle to give valid meaning to existence. Faith serves as the condition of sound reasoning. In fact, according to Augustine, the man of faith is freed to exercise his reason more responsibly. Faith enables the believer to understand.

[17]*A Compend of Luther's Theology*, ed. Hugh Thomson Kerr, Jr. (Philadelphia: The Westminster Press, 1958), p. 3. © The Westminster Press, 1958.

[18]Karl Barth, *Dogmatics in Outline*, trans. G. T. Thomson (New York: Philosophical Library, 1949), p. 24.

[19]Saint Augustine, "In Joannis Evangelium Tractatus," in Erich Pryzywara, ed., *An Augustine Synthesis* (New York: Harper & Brothers, Publishers, 1958), pp. 58–59.

[20]Richardson, *Christian Apologetics*, p. 230.

Further Considerations

We do not claim that our presentation of the four ways of relating faith and reason solves the problem. For some the whole idea of distinguishing between faith and reason may fracture the knowledge of God. We should point out, therefore, that thinkers in this century have endeavored to overcome the fragmentation of human personality. Not only have some psychologists and psychiatrists begun to view human life as a unified whole instead of a sum of separable facets (for example, intellect, will, emotions) but also theologians have begun to reinterpret faith in a more inclusive way.

John Dillenberger, a contemporary theologian, exhibits an idea of faith that encompasses various dimensions of human response to revelation. He says that faith implies not only belief but also thoughtful discernment and an active imagination. Feeling and thinking require each other. "The great ideas move the heart. The stirrings of the heart transform and create thought."[21] Dillenberger sees faith as more than emotion, doctrine, or trust. Although he allows that faith may include feelings and intellectually defined doctrines, as well as the trust "that one has been found in the divine," he asserts that faith roots deeper than any of its facets.[22] Faith finds its home in the human spirit, including "heart stirrings" and "thought stirrings."

The discussion of faith in the next unit attempts to explore the concept as inclusive in the way that Dillenberger and other recent theologians, Catholic and Protestant, have suggested.

> *Can reason operate apart from faith?*
> *Does faith undermine reason, or enhance the intellectual process?*
> *Does faith enable understanding?*
> *Which of the categories listed on page 111 for faith and reason are most important to you? Least important?*

UNIT 37   The Anatomy of Faith

In the preceding unit, it was emphasized that many contemporary theologians, influenced by twentieth-century concepts of personality as an integrated whole, have attempted to understand the concept of faith as involving more than the cognitive dimension of belief. This unit attempts to develop this view further.

Faith—for many persons one of the most familiar of religious concepts—is also one of the most easily and consistently misunderstood. Paul Tillich comments, "There are few words in the language of religion which cry for as much semantic purging as the word 'faith.' It is continually being confused with belief in something for which there is no evidence, or in something intrinsically unbelievable, or in

---

[21]John Dillenberger, *Contours of Faith: Changing Forms of Christian Thought* (Nashville: Abingdon Press, 1969), p. 84.
[22]Ibid., p. 85.

absurdities or nonsense. It is extremely difficult to remove these distorting connotations from the genuine meaning of faith."[23]

The understanding of faith as belief "in something for which there is no evidence," though common, is a most dangerous form of misunderstanding. It unwittingly pits faith against reason and knowledge. To say that you believe "by faith" in something that is unknown or cannot be rationally proved is to affirm its existence and relevance even though you lack evidence to support your faith. In a day when rational evidence is the hallmark for accepting anything as true, it is obvious that knowledge that can be rationally validated will appear more trustworthy than faith that cannot. Therefore, in an era of expanding "knowledge," an individual with this understanding of faith assumes that he or she is less and less dependent upon faith. As knowledge expands in the life of the individual, its importance tends to overpower and outweigh that of faith—faith is reduced to a wholly subjective and relatively unimportant part of life.

So it would seem that the most common understanding of faith leads to a struggle between knowledge and faith wherein faith is the inevitable loser. Perhaps this understanding has contributed to modern man's relegation of religion to a secondary (or even nonexistent) role in life. In any case, it is evident that the misunderstanding of the nature and meaning of faith has important consequences.

To understand faith as the opposite of knowledge is not only misleading but also unnecessary. Much of the difficulty arises over the tendency to use the words *belief* and *faith* as synonyms. For many persons, to say "I believe in America" means "I have faith in America"—the two expressions are used without recognizable distinction. Yet the words do not mean the same thing. *Faith* connotes "reliance on," "trust in," "commitment to." Having faith means being personally willing to trust or depend on something. On the other hand, believing in something means holding or thinking that it exists, but it does not necessarily mean trust. H. Richard Niebuhr helpfully points up this distinction:

A

The belief that something exists is an experience of a wholly different order from the experience of reliance on it. The faith we speak of . . . is not intellectual assent to the truth of certain propositions, but a personal, practical trusting in, reliance on, counting upon something. So we have faith in democracy not insofar as we believe that democracy exists, but insofar as we rely upon the democratic idea or spirit to maintain itself and to influence the lives of people continuously. We have faith in the people not insofar as we believe in the existence of such a reality as "the people," but insofar as we count upon the character of what we call the people to manifest itself steadfastly in the maintenance of certain values. Faith, in other words, always refers primarily to character and power rather than to existence. Existence is implied and necessarily implied; but there is no direct road from assent to the intellectual proposition that something exists to the act of confidence and reliance upon it. Faith is an active thing, a committing of self to something, an anticipation. It is directed toward something that is also active, that

[23] Paul Tillich, *Systematic Theology* (Chicago: The University of Chicago Press, 1963), III, 130.

has power or is power. . . . Belief as assent to the truth of propositions does not necessarily involve reliance in action on that which is believed, and it refers to propositions rather than, as faith does, to agencies and powers.[24]

Belief should be distinguished from *faith* in our common usage of the terms. Faith may entail belief—that is, the acceptance of something—but it goes beyond acceptance to actual dependence. Conversely, belief may be present without faith—that is, one may believe but not really trust. Such, in fact, is the case with the religious understanding of many persons. They may believe many things—that God exists, that Jesus Christ is Saviour, that certain religious propositions are true—yet they do not act in their daily existence upon what these beliefs imply, and in failing to do so they reveal the inconsistency between their beliefs and their faith. Such inconsistency is easily recognized by others as hypocrisy, although it is seldom recognized by the individual, for the individual thinks that his or her beliefs and faith are the same.

If the distinction between faith and belief is kept in mind, we may return to the relation between faith and knowledge. Although it is true that knowledge is based on specific evidence, it is also true that knowledge relies on (trusts) certain presuppositions. The scientists build their store of knowledge on the assumption that the universe is ultimately orderly and that this order is discoverable. They place faith in that orderliness and work from this presupposition. Faith then lies behind their endeavors. Evidence from the universe and the knowledge built upon it substantiates their initial trust. Religious faith follows a similar pattern. It also operates on an assumption—that the universe has meaning and purpose and that purpose is evident in human experience of life. Theologians then trust this assumption and think, like the scientists, that life provides evidence for the validity of the assumption. The religious experience, abundant throughout man's existence, may not be of the same form as that found in the physical world with which the scientist works, but it is no less valid because of this. Meaning in the universe may call for evidence of a different order or genre than that of function in the universe, but both are legitimate and necessary. In either case, faith is an active element in human experience. Science and religion depend on both faith *and* knowledge, and they do not oppose each other.

A more acute problem may be, instead of opposition between faith and knowledge, a conflict between opposing "faiths." We attach our trust (faith) to many objects in the course of our lives (or even in the course of one day): self, occupation, money, scientific method, distinctive religious formulations, particular political systems, and moral standards, to mention only a few. Each of these demands of us trust and commitment resulting in the exclusion of other alternatives. We find ourselves creatures with many faiths—in Niebuhr's words, "our natural religion is polytheistic."[25] At one moment we pursue and trust one faith and in the next another. On some occasions we find that we must choose between these faiths—one must be more important than another.

For those willing to accept a religious solution to this problem of opposing faiths, Niebuhr offers some useful insights. He points out that all of these faiths are ultimately finite—they are insufficient to carry the weight of full and total commitment.

B

None of these can guarantee meaning to our life in the world save for a time. They are finite in time as in space and make finite claims upon us. . . . None of these beings on which we rely to give content and meaning to our lives is able to supply continuous meaning and value.[26]

When the finitude of these faiths is recognized and accepted, when each one is destroyed or loses effectiveness, we are faced with a failure of meaning or purpose. At that moment we are enabled to place our faith in "the one reality beyond all the many, which is the last power, the infinite source of all particular beings as well as their end. And insofar as our faith, our reliance for meaning and worth, has been attached to this source and enemy of all our gods, we have been able to call this reality God."[27] When all our lesser faiths have been destroyed, we are able to trust in that which stands behind all others—the source of all meaning and purpose—God.

Such an answer is, of course, unacceptable if we affirm other faith commitments as definitive and sufficient or if we define faith as something other than trust. Nevertheless, any solution to the problems of conflicting faiths demands that the object of our faith be clearly identified and that faith be distinguished from belief and from knowledge. If that which can be distinguished from belief and knowledge—faith—can be seen as reliable, it may again be recognized for the role it actually plays in the human experience.

When in this study of religion we define religion as "reliance on a pivotal value," we are speaking of faith—a faith that supersedes and dominates all other claims for attention and action.

[26]Ibid., pp. 120–22.
[27]Ibid., pp. 122–23.

7 _____

Ways of Conceiving
the Divine

INTRODUCTION

The nature of religious experience is often encased in descriptions of rites and rituals, credal formulations and teaching formulas, or theological concepts expressing beliefs and doctrines. Religious experience is, however, too rich and varied to be captured by such manifestations of its presence. Behind these is a primary encounter between the divine and the individual.

The purpose of this chapter is to probe some of the ways persons have sought to talk about this encounter and to examine some of the concepts by which they have sought to characterize the one encountered. Such an encounter is not always easily described in rational terms, as the first unit makes clear. The second and third units present differing cultural views of the Divine. The chapter closes with an examination of "spirit," since this concept is frequently related to the Divine in human experience.

In Part I we explicated an understanding of religion that embraces not only "sacred," or "theistic," views of the Divine but also "secular," or "nontheistic," commitments. Although the following units lean toward theistic conceptions of the Divine, the reader should keep in mind our definition of religion as involving commitment to a supreme or pivotal value which becomes the focus for the whole of life. Thus, even nontheistic religions and secular movements may be seen to involve a concept of the Divine as the ultimate object or source of an individual's or a group's commitment.

UNIT 38 The Holy

Religious experience in any of its many forms is grounded in an encounter with transcendent reality which gives it a sacredness, or holiness, that distinguishes it from other human experiences. Rudolf Otto, in his work *The Idea of the Holy*, speaks of this encounter including a "moment of consciousness or a state of mind" in which one is overwhelmed by an awareness of the Divine. Such an experience gives one a feeling of "awe"—a sense of "astonishment" or "blank wonder." For Otto this encounter with the "wholly-other" lies behind and permeates all other religious consciousness.[1] In essence it is an encounter with the mystery that lies at the core of life. Otto's name for this mysterious reality is the *mysterium tremendum*, which suggests its power and centrality.

A

Let us consider the deepest and most fundamental element in all strong and sincerely felt religious emotion. Faith unto salvation, trust, love—all these are there. But over and above these is an element which may also on occasion, quite apart from them, profoundly affect us and occupy the mind with a well-nigh bewildering strength. Let us follow it up with every effort of sympathy and imaginative intuition whenever it is to be found, in the lives of those around us, in sudden, strong ebullitions [outbursts or manifestations] of personal piety and the frames of mind such ebullitions evince, in the fixed and ordered solemnities of rites and liturgies, and again in the atmosphere that clings to old religious monuments and buildings, to temples and to churches. If we do so we shall find we are dealing with something for which there is only one appropriate expression, "*mysterium tremendum.*" The feeling of it may at times come sweeping like a gentle tide, pervading the mind with a tranquil mood of deepest worship. It may pass over into a more set and lasting attitude of the soul, continuing, as it were, thrillingly vibrant and resonant, until at last it dies away and the soul resumes its "profane," nonreligious mood of everyday experience. It may burst in sudden eruption up from the depth of the soul with spasms and convulsions, or lead to the strangest excitements, to intoxicated frenzy, to transport, and to ecstasy. It has its wild and demonic forms and can sink to almost grisly horror and shuddering. It has its crude barbaric antecedents and early manifestations, and again it may be developed into something beautiful and pure and glorious. It may become the hushed, trembling, and speechless humility of the creature in the presence of—whom or what? In the presence of that which is a *mystery* inexpressible and above all creatures.

Although one confronts that which is finally a mystery in such a religious encounter, Otto suggests that what is encountered here is a distinctively positive reality, even if *mystery* is normally understood to carry negative connotations.

It is again evident at once that here too our attempted formulation by means of a concept is once more a merely negative one. Conceptually *mysterium* denotes merely that which is hidden and esoteric, that which is beyond conception or un-

[1]Rudolf Otto, *The Idea of the Holy* (Oxford: Oxford University Press, 1923), passim. Reprinted by permission. Otto's work is a thorough investigation of the phenomenon of "numinous" encounters with the Divine.

derstanding, extraordinary and unfamiliar. The term does not define the object more positively in its qualitative character. But though what is enunciated in the word is negative, what is meant is something absolutely and intensely positive.[2]

As Otto indicates, such an encounter may have many different aspects—it may take place in a dynamic moment or through a tranquil mood or in any number of other forms. Yet the experience itself—whatever its occasion or form—leaves one with a conviction of the reality and presence of the *mysterium tremendum*—the transcendent, the divine—God.

Otto's suggestive analysis and description of the mystery that lies at the core of all religion helps one conceptualize this central element in religion. But conceptual descriptions, as important as they may be, are only part of such an experience. Whatever its occasion or form, such an experience demands not only recognition but also response—whether positive or negative, expressible or inexpressible. The following items illustrate how persons from differing religious traditions have responded to and described this experience:

I

The first illustration comes from Jewish literature. The Hebrew prophet Isaiah describes the encounter with the *mysterium tremendum* (God) which began and empowered his prophetic career.

B

In the year that King Uzziah died I saw the Lord sitting upon a throne, high and lifted up; and his train filled the temple. Above him stood the seraphim; each had six wings: with two he covered his face, and with two he covered his feet, and with two he flew. And one called to another and said:

> Holy, holy, holy is the Lord of hosts;
> the whole earth is full of his glory.

And the foundations of the thresholds shook at the voice of him who called, and the house was filled with smoke. And I said: Woe is me! For I am lost; for I am a man of unclean lips, and I dwell in the midst of a people of unclean lips; for my eyes have seen the King, the Lord of hosts!

Then flew one of the seraphim to me, having in his hand a burning coal which he had taken with tongs from the altar. And he touched my mouth and said: Behold, this has touched your lips; your guilt is taken away and your sin forgiven. And I heard the voice of the Lord saying, Whom shall I send, and who will go for us? Then I said, Here I am! Send me. (Isaiah 6:1–8, RSV)

II

The second example is taken from Chinese literature and art. Lao-Tzu filled the *Tao Te Ching* with pithy images that suggest how life should properly be lived. Behind these images was an acute consciousness of the Holy, the mystery which underlies life. In Chinese culture the mystery present in all of the universe is symbolized by the world *Tao*. Lao-Tzu often used the symbol in unusual ways to point beyond to the hidden mystery of the Divine found in ordinary life.

[2]Ibid., pp. 12–13.

C   When the highest type of men hear the Tao (truth),
         They practice it diligently.
     When the mediocre type hear the Tao,
         They seem to be aware and yet unaware of it.
     When the lowest type hear the Tao,
         They break into loud laughter,—
     If it were not laughed at, it would not be Tao.

     Therefore there is the established saying:
         "Who understands Tao seems dull of comprehension;
         Who is advanced in Tao seems to slip backwards;
         Who moves on the even Tao (Path) seems to go up and down."

     Superior virtue appears like a hollow (valley);
     Sheer white appears like tarnished;
     Great character appears like insufficient;
     Solid character appears like infirm;
     Pure worth appears like contaminated.
         Great space has no corners;
         Great talent takes long to mature;
         Great music is faintly heard;
         Great Form has no contour;
         And Tao is hidden without a name.
     It is this Tao that is adept at lending (its power) and bringing fullfillment.[3]

Expressions of the divine mystery are certainly not limited to their verbal expressions in poetry or prose. Traditional Chinese art radiates an awareness of the Divine—the *Tao*. In the following passage, Otto Fischer describes this element as it is expressed in Chinese paintings. (see illustration E, p. 122)

D   The spectator who, as it were, immerses himself in them feels behind these waters and clouds and mountains the mysterious breath of the primeval Tao, the pulse of innermost being. Many a mystery lies half-concealed and half-revealed in these pictures. They contain the knowledge of the "nothingness" and the "void," of the "Tao" of heaven and earth, which is also the Tao of the human heart. And so, despite their perpetual agitation, they seem as remotely distant and as profoundly calm as though they drew secret breath at the bottom of the sea.[4]

III

The third and final example reflecting an encounter with the Holy is drawn from the Hindu classic *The Bhagavad Gita*. In the philosophic tradition of Hindu holy men, the Divine is beyond description and grasp, since any human attempt to express it is necessarily a part of the illusory world (see Unit 11). For the majority of Hindus, however, the Divine is often expressed through an array of gods and

[3]From *The Wisdom of China and India*, ed. Lin Yutang (New York: Random House, Inc., 1942), p. 606. Copyright 1942 and renewed 1970 by Random House, Inc. Reprinted by permission of the publisher.

[4]Otto, *Idea of the Holy*, p. 67.

E

Li K'o-Jan
The Poet T'ao Yüan-Ming
(Prague National Gallery. Used by
permission.)

goddesses. Each divine being may have many representatives or embodiments, all expressing the majesty and wonder of the *mysterium tremendum*. In the passage that follows, Krishna, a popular embodiment of one of the three greatest gods of Hinduism, has been asked by his disciple, Arjuna, to reveal himself in all his glory. Krishna grants the request, suggesting that this is indeed a very unusual gift, withheld even from the other gods.

F

Then, O king, when he had spoken these words, Sri Krishna, Master of all yogis, revealed to Arjuna his transcendent, divine Form, speaking from innumerable mouths, seeing with a myriad eyes, of many marvellous aspects, adorned with countless divine ornaments, brandishing all kinds of heavenly weapons, wearing celestial garlands and the raiment of paradise, anointed with perfumes of heavenly fragrance, full of revelations, resplendent, boundless, of ubiquitous everywhere present regard.

Suppose a thousand suns should rise together into the sky: such is the glory of the Shape of Infinite God.

Then the son of Pandu beheld the entire universe, in all its multitudinous diversity, lodged as one being within the body of the God of gods.

Then was Arjuna, that lord of mighty riches, overcome with wonder. His hair stood erect. He bowed low before God in adoration, and clasped his hands, and spoke:

"Ah, my God, I see all gods within your body;
Each in his degree, the multitude of creatures;
See Lord Brahma throned upon the lotus;
See all the sages, and the holy serpents.

Universal Form, I see you without limit,
Infinite of arms, eyes, mouths and bellies—
See, and find no end, midst, or beginning.

Crowned with diadems, you wield the mace and discus,
Shining every way—the eyes shrink from your splendour
Brilliant like the sun: like fire, blazing, boundless.

You are all we know, supreme, beyond man's measure,
This world's sure-set plinth and refuge never shaken,
Guardian of eternal law, life's Soul undying.
Birthless, deathless; yours the strength titanic,
Million-armed, the sun and moon your eyeballs,
Fiery-faced, you blast the world to ashes,

Fill the sky's four corners, span the chasm
Sundering heaven from earth. Superb and awful
Is your Form that makes the three worlds tremble.

Into you, the companies of devas [gods]
Enter with clasped hands, in dread and wonder.
Crying 'Peace,' the Rishis and the Siddhas [disciples]
Sing your praise with hymns of adoration. . . ."[5]

Arjuna, attempting here to express the immensity of this confrontation with the Divine, clearly can only point to the fact that no description will be adequate. The power, majesty, and wonder of the God is simply overwhelming and beyond expression.

In each of these examples, drawn as they are from different religious traditions, the presence and experience of the *mysterium tremendum* is expressed. However, as Otto points out, the best and most poignant descriptions never really do justice to the inexpressible "awe" that humans, aware of their finitude, feel before God.

Is such an experience common to everyone?

Is it necessarily a religious experience? If so, what makes it so? Are there more common experiences in ordinary life that incorporate the same reality and experience? Is the consciousness of the numinous a necessary experience for valid religious encounter, as Otto appears to assume?

[5]Swami Prabhavananda and Christopher Isherwood, trans. *The Song of God: Bhagavad-Gita* (Hollywood: Vedanta Press, 1951), pp. 91–97. Used by the permission of the Vedanta Society of Southern California.

UNIT 39 The Divine Expressed in Religious Texts

In the preceding unit, Rudolf Otto's characterization of the feeling of awe and mystery characteristic of human experience of the Divine was discussed. This experience may be a recurring momentary event in human life. Once statements about the Divine are given textual expression, however, they take on a reality to some extent independent of momentary human experiences. As Paul Ricoeur and other contemporary philosophers have noted, the text takes on life of its own, projecting a reality (which Ricoeur calls the world of the text) *ahead of* its readers or users (many texts concerning the Divine are primarily *used* for liturgical or cultic purposes) that they are invited to enter. Thus textual statements that originally expressed thoughts and feelings about the Divine become the basis for an unending human dialogue; they become both guides and criteria for later thoughts, feelings, and experiences that humans have about that which concerns them ultimately.

In this unit, a number of textually expressed ways of conceiving of God are presented for examination and comparison. These are drawn from different cultures, different religious traditions, and different historical periods. There is some overlap: The passages from the Jewish Scriptures can also be taken as illustrating important dimensions of Christian and Islamic understanding of God, since Christians and Muslims understand the God of the Jewish Scriptures to be their God, too. Additional and similar Christian interpretations of God are represented in selections from the New Testament and from the medieval Christian writer Thomas Aquinas. Although these passages differ in language—the New Testament passages characterize God in very concrete personal ways, whereas the passage by Aquinas uses a more abstract, philosophical approach—most Christians would hold that they both express truths about the God worshiped and believed in by Christians.

From most of the traditions represented in this unit, other and differently expressed statements about the nature and reality of God could be found. There are other traditions, too, from which significant statements might have been taken. The statements included resemble one another in some ways. They also differ rather dramatically. Some are primarily conceptual philosophical expressions; others are more direct, poetic statements growing out of practical life and the experience of worship. But it would be difficult and perhaps false to say that even the most abstractly expressed textual statement about God—for instance Aristotle's—did not grow out of personal experience and deep or intense concern. Since the unit is long and contains a number of texts that lend themselves to analysis and discussion, it is divided into two major sections. The following questions may help you analyze the examples:

> *How do you respond to the different views of God presented here?*
> *Which of the views, if any of them, are most like ways you have heard God spoken of?*
> *How do they differ from, and agree with, each other?*

I

God in the Jewish Scriptures

A

You are the people whom the Lord brought out of Egypt . . . and took for his own possession, as you are to this day. . . . Be careful not to forget the covenant which the Lord your God made with you, and do not make yourself a carved figure of anything which the Lord your God has forbidden. For the Lord your God is a devouring fire, a jealous God. . . . When you have children and grandchildren and grow old in the land, if you then fall into the degrading practice of making any kind of carved figure, doing what is wrong in the eyes of the Lord your God and provoking him to anger . . . the Lord will disperse you among the peoples, and you will be left few in number among the nations to which the Lord will lead you. But if from there you seek the Lord your God, you will find him. . . . When you are in distress and all these things come upon you, you will in days to come turn back to the Lord your God and obey Him. The Lord your God is a merciful god; he will never fail you nor destroy you, nor will he forget the covenant guaranteed by oath with your forefathers.

(Deuteronomy 4:20-32, NEB)

B

Do you not know, have you not heard, were you not told long ago, have
　　you not perceived ever since the world began, that God sits throned
　　　　on the vaulted roof of earth,
　　whose inhabitants are like grasshoppers?

　　He stretches out the skies like a curtain
　　He spreads them out like a tent to live in;
　　He reduces the great to nothing
　　and makes all earth's princes less than nothing.
Scarcely are they planted, scarcely sown, scarcely have they taken root in
　　the earth,
　　before he blows upon them and they wither away,
　　and a whirlwind carries them off like chaff.
　　To whom then will you liken me,
　　whom set up as my equal?
　　asks the Holy One.
Lift up your eyes to the heavens; consider who created it all, led out their
　　host one by one and called them all by their names;
　　through his great might, his might and power,
　　not one is missing.
Why do you complain, O Jacob,
　　and you, Israel, why do you say,
　　"My plight is hidden from the Lord
　　and my cause has passed out of God's notice"?
Do you not know, have you not heard?
The Lord, the everlasting God, creator of the wide world,
　　grows neither weary nor faint;
　　no man can fathom his understanding.
　　He gives vigour to the weary,
　　new strength to the exhausted. (Isaiah 40:21–29 NEB)

C
What shall I bring when I approach the Lord?
How shall I stoop before God on high?
Am I to approach him with whole-offerings or yearling calves?
    Will the Lord accept thousands of rams
    or ten thousand rivers of oil?
    Shall I offer my eldest son for my own wrongdoing,
    my children for my own sin?
God has told you what is good;
    and what is it that the Lord asks of you?
    Only to act justly, to love loyalty,
    to walk wisely before your God. (Micah 6:6–8 NEB)

Aristotle: God as Pure Being, The Unmoved Mover

The view of God held by Aristotle, a Greek philosopher of the fourth century B.C.E., greatly influenced later Western thought. Joined or fused with the Jewish view of God the active Creator, it influenced Jewish, Muslim, and Christian thought.

Aristotle's beginning point is with the world of nature that we observe. He sees natural entities—organisms—as having an innate tendency to develop. An acorn has within itself an innate tendency to grow into a fully developed oak tree, provided its environment is favorable. A newborn human baby will naturally develop into a full-grown human being, capable of self-sustaining life and rational activities. Even the stars and planets seem to move in accordance with a law of their being.

Aristotle was convinced that the motion and development characteristic of things that we observe must have an ultimate source, or cause. This first cause of motion must be perfect and complete in every way. It must not itself be subject to change or development, for otherwise its own development would need an explanation that goes beyond it. He calls this perfect source of motion and development for the whole universe God, or the Unmoved Mover. For Aristotle, God does not create the world; the world is uncreated and exists eternally. God is the source of motion and development in the world, the perfect reality that exists as an object of love and desire, the standard of absolute perfection for all other things. Aristotle characterizes God as follows:

D
The first mover, then, exists of necessity; and insofar as it exists by necessity, its mode of being is good, and it is in this sense a first principle. For the necessary has all these senses—that which is necessary perforce because it is contrary to the natural impulse, that without which the good is impossible, and that which cannot be otherwise but can exist only in a single way.

On such a principle, then, depends the heavens and the world of nature. And it is a life such as the best which we enjoy, and enjoy for but a short time (for it is ever in this state, which we cannot be), since its actuality is also pleasure. (And for this reason are waking, perception, and thinking most pleasant, and hopes and memories are so on account of these.)

What is God's life, his activity, like, according to Aristotle?

And thinking in itself deals with that which is best in itself, and that which is thinking in the fullest sense with that which is best in the fullest sense. And thought thinks on itself because it shares the nature of the object of thought; for it becomes an object of thought in coming into contact with and thinking its objects, so that thought and object of thought are the same. For that which is *capable* of receiving the object of thought, i.e., the essence, is thought. But it is *active* when it *possesses* this object. Therefore, the possession rather than the receptivity is the divine element which thought seems to contain, and the act of contemplation is what is most pleasant and best. If then, God is always in that good state in which we sometimes are, this compels our wonder; and if in a better this compels it yet more. And God *is* in a better state. And life also belongs to God; for the actuality of thought is life, and God is that actuality; and God's self-dependent actuality is life most good and eternal.

We say therefore that God is a living being, eternal, and most good, so that life and duration continuous and eternal belongs to God; for this is God.[6]

> Since, according to Aristotle, to know the world would mean to know change, and thus to change in his knowledge, God does not *know* the world: He knows only his own unchanging mind.

Saint Thomas Aquinas: God as He Who Is

Thomas Aquinas, one of the great theologians and philosophers of medieval Christianity, drew on Christian scripture and tradition, as well as on the philosophical reflections of Christian thinkers like Saint Augustine and on Aristotelian philosophy, in formulating his statements about the nature and reality of God.

E

This name, HE WHO IS, is most properly applied to God, for three reasons:

First, because of its signification. For it does not signify form, but simply existence itself. Hence since the existence of God is His essence itself, which can be said of no other (Q. III, A, 4), it is clear that among other names this one specially denominates God, for everything is denominated by its form.

Secondly, on account of its universality. For all other names are either less universal, or if convertible with it, add something above it at least in idea; hence in a certain way they inform and determine it. Now our intellect cannot know the essence of God itself in this life, as it is in itself, but whatever mode it applies in determining what it understands about God, it falls short of the mode of what God is in Himself. Therefore the less determinate the names are, and the more universal and absolute they are, the more properly are they applied to God. Hence Damascene says (*de. Fid. Orth.* i.) that, HE WHO IS, *is the principal of all names*

[6]Aristotle, *Metaphysics*, Book 12, ch. 7, 1072b, trans. W. D. Ross, from *The Oxford Translations of Aristotle*, Vol. 3, 2nd ed. (Oxford: Oxford University Press, 1928). Used by permission of publisher.

applied to God; for comprehending all in itself, it contains existence itself as an infinite and indeterminate sea of substance. Now by any other name some mode of substance is determined, whereas this name, HE WHO IS, determines no mode of being but is determinate to all; and there-fore it denominates the *infinite ocean of substance.*

Thirdly, from its consignification, for it signifies present existence; and this above all properly applies to God, whose existence knows not past or future, as Augustine says *(De Trin. v.)*[7]

II

The Divine in Navaho Life

Conceptions of the Divine held by the Navaho Indians may seem strange to people not familiar with polytheistic religions. If you are familiar with the gods and goddesses of Greek mythology, or with the stories of creation that appear in early Babylonian or Japanese religions, you may detect similarities to the following account of Navaho belief.

The stories of the Navaho Holy People primarily were oral tradition, but they have been given textual form by students of Navaho life.

F   The universe of The People contains two classes of personal forces. There are the Earth Surface People, living and dead; these are ordinary human beings. Then there are the Holy People. They are not "holy" in the sense of possessing moral sanctity, for often their deeds have a very different odor. They are "holy" in the meaning of "powerful and mysterious," of belonging to the sacred as opposed to the profane world. They travel about on sunbeams, on the rainbow, on the light-nings. They have great powers to aid or to harm Earth Surface People. But it is bet-ter not to call them gods because the word "god" has so many connotations which are inappropriate. The Holy People are not portrayed as all-knowing or even as all-powerful. They certainly are not de-picted as wholly good. While they are supplicated and propitiated, they may also be coerced. Probably coercion is in-deed the dominant note. In general, the relationship between them and the Earth Surface People is very different from what Christians think of as the connection be-tween God and man.

As described in the Navaho origin myth, the Holy People lived first below the surface of the earth. They moved from one lower world to another because of witchcraft practiced by one of them. In the last of the twelve lower worlds the sexes were separated because of a quarrel, and monsters were born from the female Holy People. Finally a great flood drove the Holy People to ascend to the present world through a reed. Natural objects were created. Then came the first death among the Holy People. About this time too, Changing Woman, the principal figure among them, was created. After she reached puberty, she was magically impregnated by the rays of the Sun and by water from a waterfall, and bore twin sons. These Hero Twins journeyed to the house of their father, the Sun, encounter-ing many adventures and slaying most of the monsters. . . .

The Hero Twins—Monster Slayer and Child of the Water (sometimes called Reared-within-the-Earth and Changing Grandchild)—are invoked in almost every Navaho ceremonial. Their adven-tures establish many of the Navaho ideals for young manhood. They serve espe-

[7]Thomas Aquinas, *Summa Theologica*, trans. Fathers of the English Dominican Provinces (London: Burns, Oates & Washbourne, Ltd., 1920), Part 1, QQ I-XXXVI (abridged).

cially as models of conduct in war and can almost be called the Navaho war gods. The Hero Twins slew most of the monsters, but they did not kill all of these potential enemies of mankind. Hunger, Poverty, Old Age, and Dirt survived, for they proved to have a place in human life. The exploits of the Twins, as well as those of other Holy People, define many features of the Navaho landscape as holy places. The lava fields, which are so conspicuous in the Navaho country, are the dried blood of the slain monsters.

Changing Woman, the Sun, and the Hero Twins are four supernatural beings who seem to bulk largest in the religious thought and lore of The People. In the background are First Man and First Woman, who were transformed from two ears of white and yellow corn, and others prominent in the stories of life in the lower worlds. Most of The People believe that First Man created the universe, but another version of the incident, possibly due to Christian influence, pictures a being called *be' gochidi* as the creator of the world. . . .

But of these beings and powers, of whom we have mentioned only a few, Changing Woman alone is consistently well-wishing to the Earth Surface People. The other beings are undependable, even though they may have given mankind many of their prized possessions. The Sun and the Moon demand a human life each day: the Hero Twins are often pitiless; First Man is a witch; Coyote is a trickster.[8]

Śankara: Brahman, The One Eternal Self

Śankara, a Hindu philosopher who lived from approximately 788 to 820, describes God—Brahman—as the *One Reality*—"One without a second." Brahman is that source of the changing world of illusion, whose reality, in contrast to the One reality, is only apparent or illusory, a product of Nescience, a sort of false or mistaken knowledge that is really ignorance.

G

Brahman as the eternal subject (pratyagâtman, the inward Self) is never an object, and . . . the distinction of objects known, knowers, acts of knowledge, etc. . . . is fictitiously created by Nescience.

Of Brahman . . . the two following passages [from the Upanishads] declare that it is incapable of receiving any accretion and is eternally pure, "He is the one God, hidden in all beings, all-pervading, the Self within all beings, watching over all works, dwelling in all beings, the witness, the perceiver, the only one; free from qualities" and "He pervaded all, bright, incorporeal, scatheless, without muscles, pure, untouched by evil". . . .

The Self is not to be known as manifold, qualified by the universe of effects; you are rather to dissolve by true knowledge the universe of effects, which is mere product of Nescience, and to know that one Self, which is the general abode, as uniform.[9]

Jesus: God as Loving Father

H

You have learned that they were told, "Love your neighbor, hate your enemy." But what I tell you is this: Love your enemies and pray for your persecutors; only so can you be children of your heavenly Father, who makes his sun rise on good and bad alike, and sends the rain on the honest and the dishonest. If you

[8]Clyde Kluckhohn and Dorothea Leighton, *The Navaho* (Cambridge, Mass: Harvard University Press, 1946), pp. 122–25.

[9]F. Max Müller, ed., *The Sacred Books of the East*, trans. George Shebaut (Oxford: Clarendon Press, 1890), p. 32.

love only those who love you, what reward can you expect? Surely the taxgatherers do as much as that. And if you greet only your brothers, what is there extraordinary about that? Even the heathen do as much. There must be no limit to your goodness, as your heavenly Father's goodness knows no bounds. . . .

(Matthew 5:43-48, NEB)

For if you forgive others the wrongs they have done, your heavenly Father will also forgive you; but if you do not forgive others, then the wrongs you have done will not be forgiven by your Father. . . .

(Matthew 6:14-15, NEB)

Surely life is more than food, the body more than clothes. Look at the birds of the air; they do not sow and reap and store in barns, yet your heavenly Father feeds them. You are worth more than the birds! Is there a man of you who by anxious thought can add a foot to his height? And why be anxious about clothes? Consider how the lilies grow in the fields; they do not work, they do not spin; and yet, I tell you, even Solomon in all his splendour was not attired like one of these. But if that is how God clothes the grass in the fields, which is there today and tomorrow is thrown on the stove, will he not all the more clothe you? How little faith you have! No, do not ask anxiously, "What are we to eat? What are we to drink? What shall we wear?"

(Matthew 6:26-32, NEB)

Emptiness (Shunyata): The Void in Buddhism

Some forms of Buddhism are often described as being atheistic, since beliefs about a God or gods are not given prominent attention or are even looked upon as idle speculation. But students of Buddhism have noted that even in so-called atheistic forms of Buddhism, there are concepts that have some resemblance to concepts of God in other religious traditions. One such Buddhist concept is that of "the Void." Nancy Ross Wilson has written:

The Buddhist Void is far from being a nihilistic doctrine. The Void is not nothingness or annihilation but the very source of all life. In speaking of this theory as taught in the Buddhism of China and Japan (where it has influenced the creation of a very subtle aesthetics . . .), Hajime Nakamura, the Japanese Buddhist scholar, says:
"Voidness . . . is . . . that which stands right in the middle between affirmation and negation, existence and nonexistence. . . . The void is all-inclusive; having no opposite, there is nothing which it excludes or opposes. It is living void, because all forms come out of it, and whoever realizes the void is filled with life and power and the . . . love of all beings."
This subtle doctrine is, by its very nature—expressed in the term "Void" itself—not a matter that readily lends itself to brief or simple exposition. Perhaps, however, modern science can again be brought to our aid if we remind ourselves that in this century the nonmaterial nature of the universe has been widely accepted since Eddington in *The Nature of the Physical World* presented his two famous tables: one seemingly solid "symbol," the other a mysteriously balanced group of invisible energies and forces. Still, though accepted as scientific fact, such knowledge as the nonsubstantiality of substance plays little part in the living of our everyday lives or the thinking of our everyday thoughts. The early Buddhists, being Indians, perhaps found less difficulty than Westerners in acceptance of the world as maya, or a kind of magical show in which what is seen is both true and not true. Buddhism would say this is not to argue that what is seen is nonexistent, but only that we take it for what it essentially is not.[10]

[10]Nancy Ross Wilson, *Three Ways of Asian Wisdom* (New York: Simon and Schuster, 1968), pp. 121–22.

UNIT 40   Conceptualization of the Divine

The following table may be useful for considering the concept of God found in the texts given both in the preceding unit and elsewhere.

A Framework for Conceptualizing Images and Concepts of the Divine

A DEISTIC VIEWS	C TRANSCENDENT-IMMANENT VIEWS	B PANTHEISTIC VIEWS
1. *Polytheistic deism:* There are many divine beings. They *belong to* the natural order.		3. *Dualistic pantheism:* The natural order is a manifestation or superficial appearance of the One Divine Reality.
	5. There is One Divine Being, who both transcends the natural order as its Creator or source and is present and active in it.	
2. *Dualistic deism:* There is one divine being transcending the natural order as its creator or source, with a relative separation between the divine and the natural.		4. *Materialism:* The basic physical components (matter, energy, etc.) of the natural order are what is ultimately real.

Deistic Positions

In deistic positions, God or the gods are viewed as individual beings. In *polytheistic deism*, the gods are beings, usually possessing extraordinary powers, *within* the universe. They may create and maintain parts of it. They may come into being, may themselves be created or born. Some of them may die; others may be held to be immortal. Polytheistic deism is found in many religious traditions, including the following: popular Hinduism, popular Taoism, the Babylonian and Japanese creation stories (see Unit 85), and the Navaho religion (see the preceding unit). Ordinarily in polytheistic religions, some divine beings are male, others female, some are animals, some are other natural forms such as the sun and moon or the wind.

In *dualistic deism*, the Divine and the world are relatively separate from each other, though the Divine is ultimately the creator, or in some manner the source or sustainer, of the universe. Aristotle's concept of God, discussed in the previous unit, is an expression of dualistic deism. For Aristotle, God does not create the universe, but it is totally dependent on him. A Christian form of dualistic deism became very influential in seventeenth- and eighteenth-century Europe in response to the highly successful scientific work of Isaac Newton. According to this version of deism, God created the universe and allows it to run in accordance with the laws of nature he has established for it. God does not intervene in the natural order by means of miracles or direct presence. He does guarantee reward for the good, however, and punishment for the evil in a future life. Many outstanding intellectual figures of eighteenth century Europe and North America accepted this form of deism, among them Thomas Jefferson, author of the Declaration of Independence and third President of the United States.

Dualistic deism is always *monotheistic*. Many forms of dualistic deism have spoken of the Divine in masculine terms, but this probably was the result of cultural influences, since in the strict sense the Divine would be held to be neither male nor female.

Pantheistic Positions

According to pantheistic positions, the Divine is the *one and only* reality. For *dualistic pantheism*, *everything* is a manifestation of the Divine, but moral, religious, and philosophical discipline and insight are required before this can be realized (in the form of enlightenment) by individuals. For philosophical Hinduism, Brahman is the sole reality. The many gods of Hinduism are merely manifestations of the one Divine Being, which is neither male nor female. The texts in the previous unit from Śankara and concerning the concept of the Void in Buddhism illustrate this position. It is also exemplified in Philosophical Taoism and in the classical Greco-Roman philosophical school known as Stoicism, according to which the Divine Reason or Fire is the source and inner reality of all things.

According to *materialistic pantheism* (sometimes called scientific or philosophical materialism or naturalism) *only* the physical universe—whether conceived of as matter, mass, or energy—is real. The Greco-Roman school of philosophy known as Epicureanism (founded by Epicurus 341–270 B.C.E.), based on the conception of the nature of reality of the earlier Greek philosopher Democritus (460–360 B.C.E.), held that all reality is composed of atoms moving in space. The atoms are eternal. They join by chance collisions to form objects. The objects endure only for a time. Then their atoms separate to become temporary components of other objects. The human soul is composed of atoms and is not immortal. Even the gods are composed of atoms and endure only for a time. A powerful expression was given to Epicureanism in the Latin poem *On the Nature of Things*, by Lucretius (d. 54 B.C.E.). During the nineteenth and twentieth centuries, scientific materialism was widely accepted by educated Europeans. Marxism is one of its many transformations.

Transcendent-Immanent Positions

According to *transcendent-immanent positions*, God is viewed as an individual being both beyond and within the world. This form of theism is found preeminently in Judaism and Christianity and in some schools of philosophical thought. It is monotheistic. Although culturally it has spoken of God primarily in masculine terms, it will generally hold that God is neither male nor female but is the ground, or creator, of sexuality and may at times be symbolized by either, or by neither, masculine or feminine characterizations. (Judaism's long opposition to the polytheistic fertility religious cults of its neighbors in Palestine, which usually had both a male and a female deity who were consorts, may account for the heavily patriarchal language used to describe God in the Jewish Scriptures.)

(1) According to transcendent-immanent positions, God is understood to be the Creator or Source of the created world who transcends it in an ultimate way. The passage from Aquinas in the preceding unit illustrates this. If this had been the only characterization of God given by Aquinas, the Divine would have been understood in a dualistic pantheistic sense. (2) According to transcendent-immanent positions, however, God in *one* aspect is fully present and manifest in the created world. For Judaism, God's wisdom is fully expressed in the Torah, the same wisdom, made explicit, that was/is expressed in the creation and ordering of the created realm. For Christianity, God's wisdom (the second Person of the Trinity, the Wisdom of God in accordance with which the world was/is created) is fully present in the human Jesus. (See the New Testament, Gospel of John, Chapter 1). (3) According to transcendent-immanent views, the Divine is also continuously active in the created world. The Voice or Spirit of God in Judaism makes God's will known to the prophets and to others. For Christians, God as the Holy Spirit (not another Divine Being, but a genuine aspect of the one God) is understood to be present and active in the world, especially within the Christian community, making God's power and purposes known and effective. Various philosophical schools, including Platonism and Neoplatonism, and the twentieth-century philosopher A. N. Whitehead's process philosophy, approximate this view, though Neoplatonism is perhaps closer in some ways to dualistic pantheism.

The preceding chart and discussion are, to some extent, oversimplifications. Nevertheless, they may prove useful in considering both the texts concerning the Divine given in Unit 39, and earlier and later discussions of the Divine—for instance, in the chapter on religious traditions (Chapter 2).

UNIT 41   Spirit

As the other units of this chapter suggest, the human experience of a transcendent reality is not easily expressed. It may take many forms, and any conceptualization of the experience is inadequate and limited. All of our typologies, analogies, and metaphors are means of attempting to express our experience but are insufficient, for they only rarely retain the dynamic vitality of the experience itself.

An attempt to conceptualize this dynamic element has been made through the use of the word *spirit*. When used in connection with the Divine, *spirit* has usually referred to the divine agency that enlivens or empowers life itself. The divine spirit serves as the dynamic interconnection between the transcendent reality and the finite world.

The use of the word *spirit* to denote divine presence is not the only use of the word. In referring to our experience as humans, the word takes on other, though similar, meanings. Modern emphases on scientific descriptions, even in disciplines such as psychology, are primarily dependent on reasoned and reasonable explanations which often make it difficult for us to understand the way *spirit* was used in earlier cultures and is still used among many peoples of the world. Some of that earlier sense of an enlivening force in life is retained in our language, which tends to conserve early usage. The following expressions serve as examples:

> "This is a *spirited horse.*" Here the adjective *spirited* indicates the characteristic "active," "forceful," "resistant to restaint."
>
> "I need some *spirits* of ammonia." Again the word indicates a liquid with the capacity to affect strongly anyone who smells it.
>
> "Will you do it?" "I will try!" "That's the *spirit!*" Here again is a reference to vitality, forcefulness, energetic action, strong intention

These terms reflect an awareness of a force present in human experience that has not been completely rationalized.

Whether *spirit* is used to refer to a divine presence or to the life force present in humanity and the natural world (neither of the meanings necessarily excludes the other), its intent is to point to that which gives vitality or power to life.

Yet persons from all traditions have been conscious that the concept of the spirit goes beyond verbal expression or rational formulation and points beyond itself to the mystery of human–Divine relationships. Consequently, believers have most often resorted to metaphorical modes of expression and thought when speaking of the mystery of spiritual encounter. Biblical examples of Jewish and Christian metaphors are numerous. A few examples illustrate this use:

The Spirit as the "Breath of God"

A   Then the Lord God formed man of dust from the ground, and breathed into his nostrils the breath of life; and man became a living being. (Genesis 2:7, RSV)

The Spirit as a Dove

B   And when Jesus was baptized, he went up immediately from the water, and behold, the heavens were opened and he saw the Spirit of God descending like a dove, and alighting on him.

(Matt. 3:16, RSV)

The Spirit as the Wind

C   When the day of Pentecost had come, they were all together in one place. And suddenly a sound came from heaven like the rush of a mighty wind, and it filled all the house where they were sitting.

(Acts 2:1-2, RSV)

The Spirit as Fire

D

And there appeared to them tongues as of fire, distributed and resting on each one of them. And they were all filled with the Holy Spirit and began to speak in other tongues, as the Spirit gave them utterance. (Acts 2:3-4, RVS)

The metaphorical images here and elsewhere seek to speak of the mysterious power of contact between humans and God. That contact is also understood to bestow on believers new possibilities: "You shall receive power when the Holy Spirit has come upon you "(Acts 1:8). "For the law of the Spirit of life in Christ Jesus has set me free from the law of sin and death" (Romans 8:2).

Even with the limitations of adequately formulating the magnitude of spiritual encounter, each culture seeks to express that reality from its own perspective and experience. Following are four cultural examples illustrating some uses of the concept.

(1) Ancient and Preliterate Thought

Ancient cultures and many present day cultures that do not depend extensively on writing for communication live in a world alive, a world in which objects, events, and other persons have an inherent power. The inner power which impels, dominates, and directs the thought and action of a person is his or her *spirit*. The spirit of a human is often understood to be highly influential in the life of a person or even to come to the person from outside the self. Spirit enters the body and imparts to it identity and the capacity to act. Since spirits come from without the individual, they are thought to be superhuman or divine. In many cultures, they may be either good or evil spirits, as the gods may be either good or evil. There is little question in such cultures about whether or not one has a dominating or enlivening spirit; the question becomes what is the nature of that spirit—good or evil. Since in these cultures all aspects of nature may also be enlivened by spirits, all of reality is dependent on the power and influence of spirits. The particular form of such "spirit power" varies greatly from culture to culture but its presence is seldom doubted. In its varied forms, spirit is the vitality empowering and activating all of life.

(2) Japanese Patterns

Shinto, a native Japanese religion based on nature and ancestor worship, emphasizes the role and function of spirit—known in Shinto as *kami*. From ancient times, *kami* have been understood to be present in all aspects of life and, as Sokyo Ono points out, are generally seen as powers of harmony and blessing:

The Concept of Kami

A

Among the objects or phenomena designated from ancient times as kami are the qualities of growth, fertility, and production; natural phenomena, such as wind and thunder; natural objects, such as the sun, mountains, rivers, trees and rocks; some animals; and ancestral spirits. In the last-named category are the spirits of the

Imperial ancestors, the ancestors of noble families, and in a sense all ancestral spirits. Also regarded as kami are the guardian spirits of the land, occupations, and skills; the spirits of national heroes, men of outstanding deeds or virtues, and those who have contributed to civilization, culture, and human welfare; those who have died for the state or the community; and the pitiable dead. Not only spirits superior to man, but even some that are regarded as pitiable and weak have nonetheless been considered to be kami.

It is true that in many instances there are kami which apparently cannot be distinguished from the deities or spirits of animism or animatism, but in modern Shinto all kami are conceived in a refined sense to be spirits with nobility and authority. The kami-concept today includes the idea of justice, order, and divine favor (blessing), and implies the basic principle that the kami function harmoniously in cooperation with one another and rejoice in the evidence of harmony and cooperation in this world.[11]

(3) Jewish Patterns

An awareness of "spirit power" was present among ancient Jews and their neighbors. The Hebrew word for *spirit*, like the Greek, literally means "breath" or "wind." This elemental use of the term appears repeatedly in the Old Testament and signifies something substantial; the "breath" of life is that entity which, when present, gives life to the body. Elsewhere in the Jewish tradition, the term *spirit* signifies the "soul" or "heart" of a human—that is, something which gives persons their identity and psychic strength. Even though Judaism insisted on a monotheistic faith, its earliest beliefs allowed for supernatural beings (angels and devils) which, though ultimately subservient to God, were influential in human life. These beings were capable of working, at God's discretion, both good and bad in human affairs.

Within this context, however, Jewish thinkers refined and altered their elemental understanding of spirit by elaboration of the concept of "the Spirit of the Lord." Molded by their vision of the one God, the "Spirit of God" signifies the force or power that issues from him, sent into the created order to accomplish his purpose among men. According to Hebrew thought—which Jesus and early Christianity appropriated—the "Spirit of God" had the following significant modes of expression:

B

(a) The Spirit is sent forth by God in the act of creation and in maintaining human life. . . .

(b) Extraordinary endowments of body or leadership of God's people are due to the "invasion" of the Spirit. . . .

(c) Widsom and discernment are especially gifts of the Spirit. . . .

(d) Prophecy is a characteristic mark of the Spirit's presence among men. . . .

We may sum up by saying that the Spirit is the divine Power immanent in human history, but chiefly in Israel's. It is immanent only because it is essentially transcendent, coming forth out of the supernatural life of a God who deals directly with men.[12]

In Hebrew thought, then, the emphasis is on God through his spirit (sometimes present as angelic beings) empowering and vitalizing human life. The im-

---

[11]Sokyo Ono, *Shinto: The KamiWay* (Rutland, Vt. and Tokyo: Charles E. Tuttle Co., 1962), p. 7.

[12]George Johnston, "Spirit," in *A Theological Word Book of the Bible*, ed. Alan Richardson (New York: Macmillan, Inc., 1950), pp. 233–37.

agery is clearly that of the human spirit centered in and directed by the one all-powerful, divine spirit overarching and influencing all of life.

(4) Christian Thought Patterns

Christian thought is clearly grounded in the Jewish precepts just described. Many of the nuances and dimensions of the phrase *Spirit of God* found in Jewish usage were appropriated by early Christians to talk about God's action in human life. Two other elements became important for Christian thinking, however. First, Jesus was seen as God's very presence in the world; therefore, many of the attributes of spirit are used by early Christian writers to characterize the forceful, impressive ministry of Jesus. Jesus' power and authority were identified with the work of the Spirit. He is understood as the very presence of God.

The second element of Christian understanding of the spirit arose from Jesus' teachings concerning the Spirit. In John's gospel, Jesus promises that a "Counselor . . . even the Spirit of Truth" who will dwell in his disciples will be sent by the Father (God) when Jesus is physically gone from their midst (John 14:15–17). The experience of the early church convinced the disciples that God was uniquely with them, guiding and fulfilling their ministry. Remembering this teaching of Jesus, they began to speak of the presence of the "Holy Spirit." For the church, the Holy Spirit came to be understood as the unique presence of the divine spirit of Jesus. Irenaeus, a second-century church father, stated the concept this way:

Know thou that every man is either empty or full. For if he has not the Holy Spirit, he has no knowledge of the Creator; he has not received Jesus Christ the Life; he knows not the Father who is in heaven.[13]

Here the Spirit's role is given prominence equal to that of the Father and the Son, and is made the channel by which humans may come to know God.

In the main, Christians have taken the Spirit for the "whole nature of God."[14] The name *Spirit* defines the nature of God by gathering together in one name the leading attributes of God: power, purity, invisibility, vitality, freedom, love, and so forth. The *Spirit* means God as all-sufficient, almighty, infinite, perfect, the mover of all things. The Spirit for Christians indicates the living action of God in history. That action or movement is understood to take place in a dynamic relationship between God and one's own vitality—spirit.

In what context do you most often use the word spirit? *Does the kami understanding of the Japanese differ from that of the Jewish or Christian traditions? How? Are there similarities between some of the ideas found in Unit 35 and those discussed in this unit?*

[13]Irenaeus, *Fragments XXVI*, quoted in *Handbook of Christian Theology*, eds. Marvin Haverson and Arthur A. Cohen (New York: Meridian Books, Inc., 1958), p. 170.

[14]Richard Sibbes, *The Complete Works of Richard Sibbes, D. D.*, ed. Alexander B. Grosart (Edinburgh: James Nichol, 1863), V, 487.

8 _____

The Problem of Evil

INTRODUCTION

The preceding two chapters have sought to explore concepts and images of the Divine as expressed in scriptures of the world's religious traditions and in theological and philosophical reflections on human religious experience. In this chapter we seek to examine the problem of evil—that is, to discuss and analyze questions related to the experience of a disruptive and destructive force (or forces) encountered by human beings—and to inquire about the relationship between this force and that which is experienced as Divine.

The awareness of evil—the sense that there are personal moral, religious, and philosophical problems about evil—may arise in various ways. The first unit in this chapter discusses the problem of suffering, probing both philosophical and religious answers as to why persons suffer. The second unit focuses on evil as a moral problem that raises questions about the relation of humanity to the Divine.

For some, evil is encountered in interpersonal relationships that assume transcendent significance. For others, evil is perceived as an autonomous force either within or outside the individual and is often personalized in the form of one or more demonic figures. The reader should be aware that the problem of evil is much more acute in the monotheistic religious traditions of the West than in other religious traditions. This is probably at least partly because the Western religious traditions (Judaism, Christianity, and Islam) affirm (1) that everything that exists, even what may be regarded as evil, is *in some sense* the result of the creative activity of one supremely wise, powerful, and good Creator, and (2) that evil is in some sense a reality, not merely an illusion. Thus, the question of how there can be a totally good and powerful Creator who nevertheless *allows* evil to exist has often been a difficult and pressing one for sensitive persons in Western religious traditions. Before investigating the interpretation of evil in non-Western religions, as well as in the Western religions, the reader may want to review the concepts of the Divine discussed in the previous chapter.

(Jacques Bakke)

UNIT 42   Why Suffering?

As both units in this chapter will emphasize, life, for all its good, is often broken, torn, full of pain and sorrow. Albert Outler interprets the way various ancients posed their answers to the question of why humans suffer:

1.   *Ancient popular religions* before Christ pointed to "the careless antics of the sky-gods or the purposeful cruelties of the earth-gods" as the source of evil and thus human suffering.

2. *Platonists* identified evil (suffering) as the privation or corruption of the good (itself identified with being).

3. *Stoics* saw evil and suffering as the result of "unreason and lack of self control."

4. *Epicureans* viewed suffering as evidence of the "blind way of the world from which the wise man withdraws as far as possible."

5. *Buddhism* designated suffering as inherent in self-centered human desire.

What solutions did they propose to the problem of suffering? *Ancient religions* tried to outwit the careless and capricious gods. *Platonists* proposed a mystical escape through philosophical abstraction. *Stoics* believed that reason could order power. *Epicureans* sought serene indifference. *Buddhists* concluded that the cure for suffering is the extinction of self-interested, self-regarding, self-centered desire. The end of suffering is to be reached by extinction of the limited personal self. Those responses to suffering tend "to disengage the divine from the hurly burly of ordinary life and to propose a program of aloofness as the right answer to the problem"[1]

Judeo-Christian answers to suffering do not point to an aloof God. Biblical faith presents God as sovereign over all creation, including good and evil. Suffering has a purpose under God, whether *penal* (punishment for sins) or *pedagogical* (disciplinary correction). The Old Testament emphasizes that God sends suffering as punishment for sin. The sinfulness of Israel was seen to be the cause of national disaster because sin evoked God's wrath. Sin would bring with it suffering both for individuals and for the community.[2]

The biblical character known as Job protested against the view that sufferings were divinely decreed penalties for sins. The Book of Job exhibits Job's suffering as the epitome of anguish and pain, and then struggles with the question of whether this suffering of a righteous man is a true index of justice in the universe. Tradition had pointed to suffering as just punishment for the ungodly. Thus, along with many psalmists, Job focuses the central theological question regarding suffering: Is God just to permit sinners prosperity while the faithful suffer? Job claims innocence before God while his so-called comforters imply otherwise. Elihu, one of Job's counselors, in speaking to Job, connects suffering with transgressions but does intimate that suffering is the means by which, or the context in which, God redeems his own: "He delivers the afflicted by his affliction and opens their ear by adversity."[3] Eliphaz, another adviser, observes that "man is born to trouble as the sparks fly upward,"[4] suggesting that God structures suffering into existence and that no one can escape anguish. Eliphaz does believe, however, that each tyrant will receive just punishment and that good persons can overcome disaster, thus proving God's justice in the long run. Both the prologue and the epilogue of Job present

[1]Albert Outler, *Who Trusts In God, Musings on the Meaning of Providence* (New York: Oxford University Press, 1968), p. 84.

[2]Deuteronomy 31, 32.

[3]Job 36:15 (RSV).

[4]Job 5:7.

suffering as probationary. Job's faithfulness is put to the test. Is his obedience merely self-serving, or does it result from commitment to God? But Job remains a man of his word and then God rewards him, thus corroborating the traditional Old Testament view of ultimate welfare for the righteous and wrath for the unrighteous.[5]

Although most Old Testament writers see suffering as a penalty for transgression, some suggest that suffering has a redeeming purpose (disciplinary, purificatory), as the Psalmist indicates: "It was good for me that I was afflicted, that I might learn thy statutes."[6] Especially in the servant songs of Deutero-Isaiah we do find suffering to be vicarious and redemptive. The Servant, whether corporate or individual, is shown as despised, rejected, "a man of sorrows and acquainted with grief,"[7] even though he is sinless and does not deserve to suffer. The Servant suffers for our sins. His "suffering is neither the result of his own sin nor the chastisement that might lead to his own perfection. . . . The suffering apparently gains for itself a merit that is transferable."[8]

The New Testament does include punitive theories of suffering, although pedagogical and redemptive interpretations are emphasized, especially in connection with Christ's passion. In the New Testament, God is presented more as Father than as judge or King, and from the paternal perspective suffering becomes chiefly pedagogical, corrective, or redemptive. Not only does the Fatherhood of God lend itself to this view of suffering, but also belief in a redeemed future for the faithful fosters courage and hope among the suffering. Paul's affirmation that "all things work together for good to them that love God,"[9] as well as his belief that "the sufferings of this present time are not worthy to be compared with the glory that shall be revealed to us,"[10] expresses a New Testament assurance that suffering will be overcome.[11] This redemptive meaning of suffering focuses in Jesus, who, though sinless, gives Himself for others in order to bring deliverance for sufferers through His atoning death. "For the Son of Man also came not to be served but to serve and to give his life as a ransom for many."[12] Christians claim that the paradox and power of the New Testament faith is that God works through suffering to redeem those who suffer.

Thus, we have considered several answers to the question, "Why suffering?" Which of the answers considered do you think is most viable? Can you think of others?

[5] Alan Richardson, A *Theological Word Book of the Bible*, (New York: Macmillan, Inc., 1959), p. 250.

[6] Psalms 119:71.

[7] Isaiah 53:3.

[8] Richardson, A *Theological Word Book*, p. 251.

[9] Romans 8:28.

[10] Romans 8:18.

[11] Albert C. Knudson, *Basic Issues in Christian Thought* (New York: Abingdon-Cokesbury Press, 1950), pp. 95, 96.

[12] Mark 10:45.

UNIT 43   Concepts of Evil

In his film *The Virgin Spring*, Ingmar Bergman focuses on the presence of evil in a world created by a good God. In Tore's words upon discovering his murdered daughter, Karin, we feel the impact of human anguish over God's silence when persons find themselves confronted by evil. Tore shouts furiously at heaven:

A   You saw it, God. You saw it! The death   You permitted it, and I don't understand
of an innocent child, and my vengeance.   you. [13]

Tore asks questions that many have asked: Is God the source of evil? If so, or if God merely allowed evil even though he had the power to prevent it, how can God be good? For monotheistic religious traditions, such questions have been genuine. Polytheistic religious traditions have found it easier to accept evil as merely a part of things: some divine beings may be evil or indifferent toward humans, others good and compassionate.

Bergman draws no easy lines between good and evil. In *The Virgin Spring*, good and evil intermingle. Karin, Tore's daughter, is raped and murdered on her way to Mass. When the murderers fall into Tore's hands, Tore, a confessing Christian, in turn murders them in a ceremony of pagan revenge, "and proves himself worse than the lecherous murderers of his child."[14] In the end Tore seeks forgiveness: "Yet I now ask you for forgiveness—I do not know of any way to reconcile myself with my own hands. I don't know any other way to live."[15] Thus through prayer Tore is reconciled to God and yet recognizes the reality of a world in which both good and evil are present. As a sign of his renewed faith, he promises to build a church.

On the surface, the ending may seem unrealistic, but if viewed within the context of Bergman's understanding of life as embracing *both* good and evil, the realism obtains, and the film concludes in an open-ended way. Bergman gives no easy answer as to why evil has permeated God's creation. He does not dub God the source of evil, nor does he give any real reason for God's permitting evil. "In fact, Bergman affirms the admixture of good and evil as part of that human condition of which he is so acute an observer. There is no simple dismissal of either element in reality, for maturity consists in realizing that we must expect to find the two mingled: light and dark, authentic and inauthentic, creative and destructive, good and evil."[16] Anthony Schillaci points to a symbol in *Virgin Spring* which graphically expresses the intermingling of good and evil.

B   The envious serving girl, Ingeri, reluc-   journey to Mass, hollows out a loaf of
tantly prepares the lunch for Karin's   bread, greedily wolfing down its contents,

---

[13]Anthony Schillaci, *Movies and Morals* (Notre Dame, Ind.: Fides Publishers, Inc., 1968), p. 102.
[14]*Ibid.*, pp. 98–99.
[15]*Ibid.*, p. 105.
[16]*Ibid.*, p. 101.

and places in it an ugly toad. Later, it is at the precise moment that Karin offers this loaf to the lecherous goatherds that mischief is unleashed and the rape-murder committed. The loaf falls apart and there the toad sits obscenely in the center of the white bread. Like it or not, this is the world as it really is—a good marred by the mystery of evil.[17]

Such mystery is painful for many, as they seek answers to the dilemmas of trusting the God espoused in the religious tradition of their cultures. If God is good and powerful, why does he allow evil? To some, God appears all-powerful but evil in allowing evil. To others, he may seem good but weak, powerless to prevent evil.

Nicholas Berdyaev, a highly original twentieth-century Russian philosopher and lay Christian, posed the problem as follows:

C   The feud between the Creator and the creature which overshadows our whole existence concerns evil and its origin. And the struggle against the Creator is waged not only by those who distort with evil the image of the created world, but also by those who suffer from the evil in it. . . . The good as well as the wicked rebel against God, for they cannot reconcile themselves to the existence of evil. . . . The wicked hate God because He prevents them from doing evil, and the good are ready to hate Him for not preventing the wicked from doing evil and for allowing the existence of evil.[18]

Berdyaev goes on to note that much theology deals poorly with the problem of evil by depending on John Calvin's conclusion "that God has from all eternity predestined some to eternal salvation and others to eternal damnation."[19] Berdyaev then offers his solution to the problem of evil by pointing to German mystical theology. Following the cues given him by Meister Eckhardt and Jacob Boehme, he concludes that the Creator God did not author man's freedom to choose or reject evil, but that freedom comes from the "Nothing out of which God created the world. . . . both God and freedom are manifested out of the *Ungrund*,"[20] the mystical term for the realm of nonbeing, the mysterious abyss that serves as the source of all that is. Freedom has another source beyond the Creator God; it remains rooted in mysterious nothingness. Evil, therefore, emerged when nonbeing consented to God's acts of creation and thus intermingled with being, giving rise to the pain of the mixing and thus the corruption of man.

Berdyaev's thinking and that of the German mystics seem strange to most European and American Christians who do not usually conceive God the Creator as having any source beyond himself.

Many Christians struggling with the logical problem of how evil can exist when everything has been created by a good and all-powerful God have accepted the position that evil comes from a real but inferior power created by God. By recognizing evil as real, Christianity differs from Eastern strategies that deny the

[17]*Ibid.*

[18]Nicholas Berdyaev, *The Destiny of Man*, trans. Natalie Duddington (Glasgow: The University Press, 1954), p. 23.

[19]*Ibid.*, p. 24.

[20]*Ibid.*, p. 25.

basic reality of evil, reducing it to the status of "illusion, mirage, *maya*, giving it only a deceptive appearance of reality within a great all-encompassing monism. . . ."[21] By viewing evil as inferior to God, Christianity seeks to reject any idea of evil as one all-powerful facet of a dual reality vying on equal terms with God in a divided universe. "Thus the Christian maintains neither the monist nor the dualist solution of the problem of evil while holding it [evil] is both subordinate [to God] and perverse."[22]

Roland Frye, an interpreter of theology in literature, presents his understanding of the normative Christian view of evil as follows:

D

Christianity summarizes the source of evil under the symbol of the demonic, and the essence of the demonic is the aspiration to godhead, the attempt to usurp the place of the Creator, followed by assault upon creation in a frenzy of hate which irrevocably dedicates itself to a continuous destruction of life. Satan is thus *the* continuous source of evil. . . . He is not an independent evil being set opposite an equally independent good being, and his fall from heaven comes precisely from his false claim to be just that. . . . In the Christian conception, then, evil is totally subordinate to God: it is good in its created intention, but perverted from its normative goals. In poetic terms, Satan is a perversion of the great, but subordinate, good, which was Lucifer. . . . It is thus basically a lie, carrying at the core of its existence a falsification of its own nature.[23]

E

M. Gustave Doré, illustration for Milton's *Paradise Lost*, Book IX, lns. 99, 100.

[21]Roland Mushat Frye, *God, Man and Satan: Patterns of Christian Thought and Life in Paradise Lost, Pilgrim's Progress and the Great Theologians* (Princeton, N.J.: Princeton University Press, 1960), p. 2. Copyright © 1960 by Princeton University Press. Used by permission.
[22]*Ibid.*
[23]*Ibid.*, pp. 22–23.

According to Frye, in seeking to elevate himself above God, Satan became the symbol of the fall of all humans and the participation in evil of all humanity.

F

M. Gustave Doré, illustration for Dante's *Inferno*, Canto XXXIV, lns. 20, 21.

G

Albrecht Dürer, *The Angel with the Key* (Detail).

Can you think of other ways that the devil has been portrayed?

What is the significance of the various characteristics applied to him in different representations?

The belief that Satan is a powerful demonic being and enemy of God was held by many in the first-century Jewish context in which Christianity originated. Some Christians have interpreted Satan or the devil as *merely* a symbol for the sources of evil within humans that cause them to turn from God and to inflict harm on themselves, the world, and other humans through selfishness, greed, cruelty, and anger. Others have interpreted Satan as a symbol for the power of collective movements, such as extreme nationalism (as in German Nazism) or powerful institutions (as in a cruel system of punishment of offenders against the law, or the racist laws and practices of South Africa's apartheid). Most Christians have probably believed in the transhuman objective reality of Satan—a being originally good, created by God for goodness, but who through misuse of freedom became evil and, as just discussed by Frye, the major source of evil in the universe. Some Christians, including the great seventeenth-century French Catholic mathematician and religious thinker Blaise Pascal, have at times been willing to see their religious opponents, fellow Christians, as instruments in the hands and under the influence of Satan. Pascal accused his Jesuit opponents (members of the Catholic religious order founded by Ignatius Loyola, the Society of Jesus, who were active in political and religious controversy in Pascal's time) of having the mind of, and being the children of, the devil.

During sixteenth-century religious conflicts in Europe, not only some Protestant and Catholic leaders but also some within opposing Protestant groups accused their opponents of being instruments of Satan. Other Christians cautioned that, no matter how intense differences of belief and opinion may be, attributing one's opponents' motives and conduct to the devil's influence is not compatible with the New Testament commandment for Christians to love one another.

Since the emergence of modern psychotherapy, there has been a tendency to understand "demonic possession" as a prescientific age's way of describing emotional or behavioral ("mental") disturbances. However, in a recent study called *People of the Lie*, M. Scott Peck, a psychoanalyst and lay Christian, has argued that there are genuine instances of persons falling under the influence of demonic— objective and external transhuman—powers distinct from ordinary emotional disturbances such as neuroses and psychoses that can be medically treated. According to Peck, there are people who actually become evil because of having allowed themselves to become possessed by evil powers. Peck is cautious rather than sensational in the development of his theory and cautions against the tendency to understand "demonic" forces as they are often represented in anthropomorphically popular and classical art and literature, or in cartoons and comic strips.[27] Others warn against the theory itself as tending to produce irresponsible charges against one's

[26]M. Scott Peck, M.D., *People of the Lie: The Hope for Healing Human Evil* (New York: Simon and Schuster, Inc., 1983).

opponents or to lead neurotic persons to see themselves as under demonic attack when their disorders may actually be better dealt with if seen as produced by emotional or physical disturbances.

Instead of seeing evil, as Berdyaev did, as deriving from a freedom prior to God, most Christians have understood evil as arising through a misuse of something good—the ability to make free decisions. In an influential work called *On the Free Choice of the Will*, the fourth century North African bishop, Augustine, argued that free will is a part of human nature as humans were created by God. It is a necessary part of human nature, for without free choice, humans could neither be good nor respond to God and their fellow humans in the free choice of unselfish love. But free choice of will has been misused. In fact, Augustine was convinced that all humans misuse it because human nature has fallen away from its original goodness and become evil—selfish and self-centered. Thus, for Augustine, the problem of the existence of evil—how or why there is evil in a world created by a good and all-powerful God—ceases to be a logical problem and becomes instead a practical problem: How can humans regain their original freedom to use their capacity of free choice or free will in ways that will bring good rather than evil? This is perhaps the question that the character Tore in Bergman's film finally found himself asking. Various answers to this question, and various other ways of responding to the problem of evil, will be explored in later units of this book, especially in the chapters on sin and guilt, and salvation and redemption (Chapters 11 and 13).

9

Understanding the Self

INTRODUCTION

In the two preceding parts of the book, the varieties of human religious experience and of conceptions of the Divine or ultimate reality were explored. In this section and the next, attention will be focused on human existence and its religious dimensions. This section deals with the nature of human existence and the meaning of individual selfhood as viewed from different religious-cultural points of view. In the next section, the social dimension of human existence—the interrelationship of the self with other selves, the social solidarity of human existence—will be examined.

Human beings are, as Aristotle and other social philosophers have suggested, social animals. In a very direct and literal sense, we have to *learn* to be human, and each society develops its own models and images of what human beings should be like. Nevertheless, human beings, at least in most societies, tend to develop a sense of individuality. In some societies—including Western societies during the modern period—great emphasis has been placed on the uniqueness, the irreplaceable value, of each individual. Even in societies in which the individual's sense of unique identity is muted (as in most societies until the modern period, and as in the kibbutzim of contemporary Israel, where the individual sees everything, or attempts to see everything, through the eyes of the group), the importance of the individual, even if only as a part of the group, has been recognized.

What does it mean to be a person, to be (or have) a self? Throughout the history of human civilizations this question has frequently been raised. In myths of origin, from those of Babylon and Assyria to those of Japan or the Navaho Indians, in philosophical and scientific speculation, from Gautama Buddha and Socrates to twentieth-century existentialists like Martin Heidegger or behaviorists like B. F. Skinner, and in religious literature, questions about the nature and characteristics of human existence have been posed. In our own time, as in many others, these questions have been of deep concern, sometimes painfully so, to individuals searching for meaning in life. Some answers to the questions will be discussed in this chapter.

Attitudes and ideas about the meaning of human existence—what it means to be human, what it means to be a self in isolation from or in relation to other selves—have frequently become ingrained in a culture and its religions. These attitudes and ideas are transmitted to the young through cultural practices and institutions, often without conscious intent. They become such a pervasive feature of the culture that people are scarcely aware of them; they seem as natural a part of the lifescape as the air or the topography. In times of cultural crisis, people become aware of them in especially sharp ways, when critical attention is directed at their possible inadequacies or biases. One characteristic of our own time is that social unrest and expanding contacts of many different cultural traditions with one another have caused many people to question traditional assumptions about the nature of human existence and the meaning of individuality.

UNIT 44   The Nature of Humanity

A hauntingly recurrent theme in human history has been inquiry into humanity's nature, essence, and uniqueness. The modern behavioral sciences of sociology and psychology often provide astounding insights into elements of human nature—yet they fail to give a complete definition. Perhaps this only suggests that the complexity and variety of human nature may not accommodate itself to a rational definition. Even if this is true, human beings continue to seek explanations of themselves.

Definitions of humanity offered through history are myriad. Erich Fromm and Ramon Xirau provide a convenient set of categories describing human attributes—"reason, the capacity for production, the creation of social organization, and the capacity for symbol making."[1] To these attributes or potentialities may be added many others, such as moral systems, propensity for religious affirmations, and as the insights of modern philosophy and psychology have taught us, the fact that humanity is constantly becoming—modifying, changing. Attributes, insights, beliefs, and a host of other elements all help distinguish the species.

Following are representative statements concerning the nature of humanity. Each in its own way, without attempting to be inclusive, expresses a particular understanding of what it means to be human.

[1] Erich Fromm and Ramon Xirau, *The Nature of Man* (New York: Macmillan, Inc., 1968), p. 6. Copyright © 1968 by Macmillan, Inc. Used by permission.

Blaise Pascal's often-quoted characterization of man as a "thinking reed" exemplifies the Western philosophical tradition that defines human nature by the ability to reason.

A

Man is but a reed, the most feeble thing in nature; but he is a thinking reed. The entire universe need not arm itself to crush him. A vapour, a drop of water suffices to kill him. But, if the universe were to crush him, man would still be more noble than that which killed him, because he knows that he dies and the advantage which the universe has over him; the universe knows nothing of this.

All our dignity consists, then, in thought. By it we must elevate ourselves, and not by space and time which we cannot fill. Let us endeavour, then, to think well; this is the principle of morality.[2]

Fromm and Xirau, summarizing variant positions, maintain that human self-awareness incorporates, yet transcends, reason, becoming one's essential nature—a position hinted at in Pascal's statement.

B

It can be stated that there is a significant consensus among those who have examined the nature of man. It is believed that man has to be looked upon in all his concreteness as a physical being placed in a specific physical and social world with all the limitations and weaknesses that follow from this aspect of his existence. At the same time he is the only creature in whom life has become aware of itself, who has an ever-increasing awareness of himself and the world around him, and who has the possibilities for the development of new capacities, material and spiritual, which make his life an open road with a determinable end. As Pascal said, if man is the weakest of all beings, if he is nothing but a "reed," he is also the center of the universe, because he is a "thinking reed."[3]

Erich Fromm, working from modern psychological and philosophical insights, also suggests that the ability to transcend one's animal nature creates for humans conflicts and questions that constantly lead them to seek answers. The essence of human nature, then, is to be always becoming—life is a never-ending process of better answers to old and new questions caused by our unique situation of not being merely animals.

C

He [Fromm] sees the essence, or nature, of man in certain contradictions in human—as against animal—existence. Man is an animal, but without having sufficient instincts to direct his actions. He not only has intelligence—as has the animal—but also self-awareness; yet he has not the power to escape the dictates of his nature. He is a "freak of nature," being in nature and at the same time transcending it. These contradictions create conflict and fright, a disequilibrium which man must try to solve in order to achieve a better equilibrium. But having reached this, new contradictions emerge and thus again necessitate the search for a new equilibrium, and so forth. In other words, the questions, not the answers, are man's "essence." The answers, trying to solve the dichotomies,

[2]Blaise Pascal, *Pensées* (New York: E. P. Dutton and Co., Inc., n. d.), paragraph 347. Pascal was a seventeenth-century mathematician, physicist, and theologian whose influence on French Catholicism was considerable.

[3]Fromm and Xirau, *The Nature of Man*, p. 6.

lead to various manifestations of human nature. The dichotomies and the resulting disequilibrium are an ineradicable part of man *qua* man; the various kinds of solutions of these contradictions depend on socio-economic, cultural and psychic factors; however, they are by no means arbitrary and indefinite. There is a limited number of answers which have either been reached or anticipated in human history. These answers, while determined by historical circumstances, differ at the same time in terms of solutions, differ in terms of their adequacy to enhance human vitality, strength, joy, and courage. The fact that the solutions depend on many factors does not exclude that human insight and will can work towards attempting to reach better rather than worse solutions.[4]

A different religious insight into the nature of life is provided by the following Hindu affirmation, which stresses that humanity is dependent upon the Divine—the Lord—found within the Self. To discover Self in all its magnificence is to discover the Divine.

D

Lords! Inspiration of sacrifice! May our ears hear the good. May we serve Him with the whole strength of our body. May we, all our life, carry out His will.

Peace, peace, and peace be everywhere.

Welcome to the Lord! . . .

There is nothing that is not Spirit. The personal Self is the impersonal Spirit. It has four conditions.

First comes the material condition—common to all—perception turned outward, seven agents, nineteen agencies, wherein the Self enjoys coarse matter. This is known as the waking condition.

The second is the mental condition, perception turned inward, seven agents, nineteen agencies, wherein the Self enjoys subtle matter. This is known as the dreaming condition.

In deep sleep man feels no desire, creates no dream. This undreaming sleep is the third condition, the intellectual condition.

Because of his union with the Self and his unbroken knowledge of it, he is filled with joy, he knows his joy; his mind is illuminated.

The Self is the lord of all: inhabitant of the hearts of all. He is the source of all; creator and dissolver of beings. There is nothing He does not know.

He is not knowable by perception, turned inward or outward, nor by both combined.

He is neither that which is known nor that which is not known, nor is He the sum of all that might be known. He cannot be seen, grasped, bargained with. He is undefinable, unthinkable, indescribable.

The only proof of His existence is union with Him. The world disappears in Him.

He is the peaceful, the good, the one without a second. This is the fourth condition of the Self—the most worthy of all. . . . He is whole; beyond bargain. The world disappears in Him. He is the good; the one without a second.[5]

Mandookya Upanishad

The following Hebrew psalm indicates wonder at the ability and place of humanity, but sees this as the gift of God, on whom humanity is totally dependent. Humanity is "next to" God, but only because God so blesses it.

[4]*Ibid.*, pp. 8–9.

[5]*The Ten Principle Upanishads*, trans. Shree Purohit Swami and W. B. Yeats (London: Faber & Faber, Ltd., 1937). Reprinted by permission of M. B. Yeats, Benares University, Faber & Faber, and Macmillan, Inc.

E

O Lord, our Lord
   how majestic is thy name in
   all the earth!

Thou whose glory above the
   heaven is chanted by the
   mouth of babes and infants,
thou hast founded a bulwark
   because of thy foes, to still
   the enemy and the avenger.

When I look at thy heavens, the
   work of thy fingers, the moon
   and the stars which thou has
   established;
what is man that thou art mindful
   of him, and the son of man that
   thou dost care for him?

Yet thou hast made him little
   less than God and dost crown
   him with glory and honor.
Thou hast given him dominion
   over the works of thy hands;
   thou hast put all things under
   his feet,
all sheep and oxen, and also
   the beasts of the field,
the birds of the air, and the
   fish of the sea, whatever passes
   along the paths of the sea.

O Lord, our Lord,
   how majestic is thy name in
   all the earth! (Psalm 8, RSV)

The idea that human uniqueness and meaning are found through creation in the "image of God" characterizes the Hebrew-Christian tradition. Even here, however, the image may be expressed through various emphases, as shown by Augustine, a fifth-century theologian, who stressed "obedience," and Paul Ramsey, a modern ethicist, who describes its character as "love."

F

Now, as God also can be known by the worthy, only intellectually . . . there was danger lest the human mind, from being reckoned among invisible and immaterial things, should be thought to be of *the same* nature with Him who created it, and so should fall away by pride from Him to whom it should be united by love. For the mind becomes like God, to the extent vouchsafed by its subjection of itself to Him for information and enlightenment. And if it obtains the greatest nearness by that subjection which produces likeness, it must be far removed from Him by that presumption which would make the likeness greater.[6]

G

Every discussion of the "image of God" among Christians should then be this: This term cannot be defined by probing deep into the nature of man or by employing some sub-Christian sources of insight into what it means to be man. This term, like all other "Christian categories," can be defined only derivatively by decisive reference to the basic "primitive idea" in Christian ethics, i.e., the idea of Christian love which itself in turn can be adequately defined only by indicating Christ Jesus. Jesus' pure humility and prompt obedience to God and his actions expressing pure and instant love for neighbor: these were in fact the same thing, the same image, the very image of God.

    Standing wholly within the relationship of imaging God's will, "with unveiled face, reflecting as a mirror the glory of God," and fully obedient love: these are in reality the same. There is no obedience, no response to God, there are no religious duties beyond this: Thou *shalt* love; and love fulfills every legitimate obedience. Existence within the image of God is the same thing as existence

<hr />

[6]St. Augustine, "The Morals of the Catholic Church," in *Basic Writings of Saint Augustine*, ed. Whitney J. Oates (New York: Random House, 1948), I, 329–30.

for another. Hence he [Kierkegaard] who wrote that "only when God has infinitely become the eternal and omnipresent object of worship, and man always a worshipper, do they resemble one another," also said with equal appropriateness that "we can resemble God only in loving."[7]

Are there other definitions of humanity that are more meaningful to you?

Is it important or enlightening to discuss the nature of humanity?

Why is the nature of humanity an essential religious topic?

How do you define humanity?

UNIT 45　On the Meaning of "Person"

The preceding unit inquired into the nature of humanity—what it means to be human. The present unit continues the inquiry by investigating personhood—what it means to be a particular person.

Every person is in a constant state of becoming, an ever-developing flux of growth and change. There may be arrests and attempts at crystallization that inhibit or thwart growth, but the process continues. Gordon W. Allport described the development of personality in a broad sense as a process, normally ever in flux. One of his best-known writings is entitled *Becoming, Foundations for a Psychology of Personality*.

Erik Erikson has had significant influence on the thought of our time through his writings, which describe a model of the development of identity throughout the human life cycle. Each stage of development presents us with new crises of identity to be resolved through our experience, thus allowing our developing personality to emerge into a new and more complex level. Again, negative resolution of identity crises can stand in the way of reaching full possibilities of human potential. Erikson's model bears certain similarities to ideas of Allport in that he conceives of the person growing, developing, and learning up until the moment of death. In Erikson's model, achieving ego integrity as opposed to experiencing despair in old age is one of the most important possibilities for personality potential.

Generally, in models of human personality, there is some implicit, if not explicit, goal or highest potential. One might say that most human beings seek the attainment of some form of mature personhood or, as Sigmund Freud put it, seek to achieve their own *ego ideal*. From a psychological perspective, religions provide content for the ego ideal—for the goals we accept, establish, hope for, and seek, and for that which we hope to become.

Specifically, the materials that follow exemplify aspects of what it means to be a person—to find a personal identity.

The search for identity on the part of black people continues to be an agoniz-

[7]Paul Ramsey, *Basic Christian Ethics* (New York: Charles Scribner's Sons, 1950), p. 259. Used by permission.

ing phenomenon of our day. These two very different poems reflect some of the important factors in the process. The first of these, by Langston Hughes, exhibits the depth of experience and identification with the earth, which became a part of the perspective of many black persons who worked the land in the old American South. The poet expresses an abiding sense of being a part of the flow of history as he speaks:

A
I've known rivers:
I've known rivers ancient as the world and older than the flow of human
    blood in human veins.

My soul has grown deep like the rivers.

I bathed in the Euphrates when dawns were young.
I built my hut near the Congo and it lulled me to sleep.
I looked upon the Nile and raised the pyramids above it.
I heard the singing of the Mississippi when Abe Lincoln went down to New
    Orleans, and I've seen its muddy bosom turn all golden in the sunset.

I've known rivers:
Ancient, dusky rivers.

My soul has grown deep like the rivers.[8]

In her poem "Status Symbol," Mari Evans speaks of personal identification in an urban world.

B

i	prayer meetings . . .
Have Arrived	today
i	They hired me
am the	it
New Negro	is a status
i	job . . .
am the result of	along
President Lincoln	with my papers
World War I	They
and Paris	gave me my
the Red Ball Express	Status Symbol
white drinking fountains	the
sitdowns and	key
sit-ins	to the
Federal Troops	White . . . Locked . . .
Marches on Washington	John[9]
and	

[8]Copyright 1926 by Alfred A. Knopf, Inc., renewed 1954 by Langston Hughes. "The Negro Speaks of Rivers," from *Selected Poems* by Langston Hughes. Reprinted by permission of the publisher.
[9]Mari Evans, "Status Symbol," *I Am A Black Woman* (New York: William Morrow & Co., Inc., 1970). Used by permission of the author.

During World War II in Germany, Dietrich Bonhoeffer, a leader of the underground church movement, was arrested and eventually killed because he participated in a plot to stop Hitler. While he was in prison, he wrote this questing poem:

C

Who am I? They often tell me
I stepped from my cell's confinement
calmly, cheerfully, firmly,
like a Squire from his country house.

Who am I? They often tell me
I used to speak to my warders
freely and friendly and clearly,
as though it were mine to command.

Who am I? They also tell me
I bore the days of misfortune
equably, smilingly, proudly,
like one accustomed to win.

Am I then really that which other men tell of?
Or am I only what I know of myself?

Restless and longing and sick, like a bird in a cage,
struggling for breath, as though hands were compressing my throat,
yearning for colours, for flowers, for the voices of birds,

thirsting for words of kindness, for neighbourliness,
tossing in expectation of great events,
powerlessly trembling for friends at an infinite distance,
weary and empty at praying, at thinking, at making,
faint, and ready to say farewell to it all.

Who am I? This or the Other?
Am I one person to-day and to-morrow another?
Am I both at once? A hypocrite before others,
and before myself a contemptible woebegone weakling?
Or is something within me still like a beaten army
fleeing in disorder from victory already achieved?

Who am I? They mock me, these lonely questions of mine.
Whoever I am, Thou knowest, O God, I am thine![10]

As has already been illustrated, our contemporary scene is replete with examples of the human search for identity, for the establishment of personhood. What does it mean to be a person? What is a mature person? How does one's religion

[10]Dietrich Bonhoeffer, *The Cost of Discipleship*, trans. J. B. Leishman (New York: Macmillan, Inc., 1959), p. 18. Reprinted by permission of Macmillan, Inc., and SCM Press Ltd.

contribute to and shape the nature of individuality? Paul Tournier, in his book *The Meaning of Persons* elaborates on this subject within the context of a Christian perspective. (See also Carl R. Rogers, *On Becoming a Person.*)

D

Claude Bernard used to describe life as a conflict between the organism and its environment. And it is precisely because the world is relative, imperfect, incomplete like ourselves—that new life is always springing up amidst the resultant conflicts. A completely satisfied man would be a fossil. Dissatisfaction maintains the constant movement of life, like an unending search. "Men seek the chase, and not the quarry," wrote Pascal. The Absolute is in this search itself. The Absolute is not of the order of things, not even absolute, perfect things; it is of the order of persons, and of their revolt against the imperfection of things. . . .

The person is something very different from a nice, round fully-inflated balloon. Rather is it an imponderable, an inner experience which can take place in sickness as well as in health. It is a germ that develops. What is a grain of wheat? You have not defined it when you have weighed it, measured it, and submitted it to chemical analysis and microscopic examination. It contains a whole plant

which you cannot yet see. What is a silkworm? You cannot define it without seeing in advance all its metamorphosis. What is a child? You cannot describe him without thinking of the whole life of the man, with all its unknowns, for which he is preparing. . . .

We must resist the temptation to give a doctrinaire answer to the question with which we began this book: "Who am I?" We must give up the idea that knowing the person means compiling a precise and exhaustive inventory of it. There is always some mystery remaining, arising from the very fact that the person is alive. We can never know what new upsurge of life may transfigure it tomorrow. . . .

It is a mysterious spiritual reality, mysteriously linked to God, mysteriously linked with our fellows. We are aware of these links at those privileged moments when there springs up a fresh current of life, bursting the fatal fetters of the personage, asserting its freedom and breaking out into love.[11]

UNIT 46   Dimensions of the Self and Religion

When we inquire into the religious experience of an individual person, such as those discussed in the previous unit, we often discover that experience may reflect particular emphases. The religious experience of some individuals may be highly intellectualized, dependent on or expressed according to highly theoretical concepts. The experiences of others may be primarily a matter of feeling, emotion, affections. For centuries, persons who have paused to consider such questions have described what they considered ideal. Among the elements identified as particularly significant for religion have been emotional involvement, firm trust and belief, and a life of actions based upon these. A number of theologians and psychologists of religion in the Western world have emphasized the need for balance between these primary facets of religious experience.

[11]From pp. 230–32, 232–34 in *The Meaning of Persons* by Paul Tournier, translated from the French by Edwin Hudson. (Harper & Row, Publishers, Inc.)

Not realizing the extent to which his emotional (affective) and intellectual (cognitive) experiences in religion would lead to action (cognitive), the Englishman John Wesley became the founder of a reform movement in the English Church which eventually would be known as *Methodism*. In the first example to follow, Wesley writes of the event that led him to a deeper religious experience and clarification of his spiritual life. The other quotations indicate Wesley's awareness of the role of one's intellect and the necessity for religious experience to manifest itself in action.

A

In the evening I went very unwillingly to a society in Aldersgate Street, where one was reading Luther's preface to the *Epistle to the Romans*. About a quarter of nine, while he was describing the change which God works in the heart through faith in Christ, I felt my heart strangely warmed. I felt I did trust in Christ, Christ alone for my salvation; and an assurance was given me that He had taken away *my* sins, *even* mine, and saved *me* from the law of sin and death.[12]

. . . We join with you, then, in desiring a religion founded on reason and every way agreeable thereto. But one question remains to be asked, "What do you mean by *reason?*" I suppose you mean the eternal reason, or the nature of things: the nature of God and the nature of man, with relations necessarily subsisting between them. Why, this is the very religion *we* preach: a religion founded on, and every way agreeable to, eternal reason, to the essential nature of things. . . .[13]

Do you show your love by your works? While you have time, as you have opportunity, do you in fact "do good to all men" (Galatians 6:10), neighbors or strangers, friends or enemies, good or bad? Do you do them all the good you can, endeavoring to supply all their wants, assisting them both in body and soul to the uttermost of your power?[14]

. . . This religion we long to see established in the world: a religion of love and joy and peace, having its seat in the inmost soul, but ever showing itself by its fruits, continually springing forth not only in all innocence—for love worketh no ill to his neighbor—but likewise in every kind of beneficence, spreading virtue and happiness all around it.[15]

W. C. Bower, a twentieth-century philosopher of religious education, conceived of creative religion as dynamically reconstructive in nature and believed that this quality is achieved when emotion, belief, and action are integrated.

Religion as Emotional Experience (Affective)

Bower maintains that religion is essentially an emotional experience. The emotional manifestations of religion have been of a wide-ranging character. They have included a sense of dependence upon some power beyond the human. They also have included what Bower calls "crasser forms" of emotional seizures which

---

[12]John Wesley, *Journal*, ed. Nehemiah Curnock (London: The Epworth Press, 1938), I, pp. 475–76.

[13]From *John Wesley* by Albert C. Outler, p. 394. Copyright © 1964 by Oxford University Press, Inc. Reprinted by permission.

[14]*Ibid.*, p. 99.

[15]*Ibid.*, p. 386.

may be characterized as both irrational and primitive. Yet emotional involvement is essential to any real participation in religion.[16]

Religion as Rational Belief (Cognitive)

Bower emphasizes the point that religion has always been concerned with ideas and beliefs. From religious concepts and beliefs, the great creeds have sprung. They have served to clarify thought as well as provide legitimization for functioning ideas and for regulation of the beliefs of a religious community.[17]

Integration of the Cognitive and Affective in the Seeking of Ends (Conative)

The cognitive and affective aspects of religion lead to a more central core. For Bower, this core lies in the conative or end-seeking aspect which centers concern upon the ultimate values in life. Thought in religion arises as meaning and serves as a direction-giving factor. Emotion gives to it warmth and vibrancy. Bower insists that it is an error to mistake either of these basic and important factors for religion itself, in its fullest sense. They are only aspects of the phenomenon. The fundamental and basic character of religion is active when *all* the aspects of religion are directed into endseeking, integrated activity. These ends are concerned with ultimate values in human experience.[18]

UNIT 47   Views of Being Human, East and West

Just as one's religious experience will be shaped by the particular nature of one's encounter with religion and its subsequent expressions in life, so is it molded by views of humanity inherent in the culture of which one may be a part. Eastern and Western cultures view humanity from distinctively different perspectives. As a result, their views of the value and place of humanity in the scheme of the universe contrast rather dramatically, as the following selections indicate.

East: Human Beings as One Species Among Many Natural Beings

A   Painters took nature as their subject, and before assuming brush and silk would go out to nature, lose themselves in it, and become one with it. They would sit for half a day or fourteen years before making a stroke. The Chinese word for landscape painting is composed of the radicals for mountain and water, one of which

[16]W. C. Bower, *Religion and the Good Life* (Nashville: The Abingdon Press, 1933), p. 44.
[17]*Ibid.*, p. 42.
[18]*Ibid.*, p. 51.

B   Landscape by K'un-ts'an (Reproduced with the permission of the Museum fuer Ostasiatische Kunst Berlin, Staatliche Museen Preussicher Kulturbesitz.)

C

suggests vastness and solitude, the other pliability, endurance, and continuous movement. *Man's part in that vastness is small, so we have to look closely for him in the paintings if we find him at all.*[19]

We love natural truth; our philosophers were convinced that human desire has grown beyond bounds; man's eagerness to grasp the object of his desire gives rise to much unnatural and untruthful behaviour. *Man, we think, is no higher in the scale of things than any other kind of matter that comes into being*; rather, he has tended to falsify his original nature, and for that reason we prefer those things that live by instinct or natural compulsion; they are at least true to the purpose for which they were created. We paint figures occasionally, but not so much as you do in the West.[20]

West: Human Beings as God's Creation, an Exalted View of Humanity

D

When I look at thy heavens, the work of thy fingers,
the moon and the stars which thou hast established:
what is man that thou art mindful of him,
   and the son of man that thou dost care for him?

   Yet thou hast made him little less than God,
     and dost crown him with glory and honor.

[19]Excerpt from p. 186 in *The Religions of Man* (hardcover ed.) by Huston Smith (New York: Harper & Row, 1958). Used by permission of the publisher.

[20]Chiang Yee, *The Chinese Eye: An Interpretation of Chinese Painting* (Bloomington: Indiana University Press, 1964), pp. 9–10. All rights reserved, Midland Book ed., 1964, by arrangement with W. W. Norton and Co., Inc. and Methuen & Company Ltd.

Thou hast given him dominion over the works of thy hands;
thou has put all things under his feet,

all sheep and oxen,
and also the beasts of the field,
the birds of the air, and the fish of the sea,
whatever passes along the paths of the sea.

Psalms 8:3–8 (RSV)

E

Apoxyomenos (Scraper). Roman marble copy, probably after a bronze original of c. 330 B.C. by Lysippus. (Reprinted by permission of the Vatican Museums, Vatican City.)

Examine carefully the photographs of the Oriental painting and the Western sculpture. What does comparison of the differences between these symbolic, artistic representations show about the differences between Eastern and Western views of humanity?

10 _____

Freedom and the Self

INTRODUCTION

Some would say that humanity is unique—that human beings are distinguished from other animals because of a freedom to decide, to make choices. Some have said that humanity is altogether free, unfettered, by the determinants and continuous circumstances that limit individual and personal freedom. Others, inclined toward determinism, espouse the view that humans possess little personal freedom because of the many biological, environmental, social, and cultural factors that work together to determine actions, one's very life. If total freedom is seen as one pole of a continuum of thought and determinism as the other, some have taken a stance more toward the center, which maintains that humanity does possess some freedom and that freedom lies in what one is able to do with the determinants that have been bequeathed. Theologically, the question has most often been phrased in terms of freedom, predestination, or freedom within limits: Which offers the best explanation of this aspect of human experience?

The units in this chapter are centered on variant conceptions of personal freedom of action and responsibility. The chapter does not purport to be exhaustive on the subject; rather, the units are designed to assist the reader in considering questions regarding this important aspect of any religion. These questions include problems of defining freedom, freedom and decision making, responsibility and freedom, and conceptions of the nature of humanity as they affect understandings of freedom. Although the units of this chapter concentrate on discussion of the questions of freedom and responsibility in Western religions, the issue is no less complex or relevant to other religious traditions. Their answers have also been varied. Indeed, one can immediately see that the way a particular religion answers this important question determines its outlook on a rather wide range of other areas of religious life.

UNIT 48   Responsible Freedom

To be human means to be responsible. The word *responsible* suggests being able to give an answer, being able to respond genuinely to others, being able to take responsibility, to live responsibly with others. In another sense, *responsibility* and *freedom* are equivalent concepts. One must be free to be responsible. At the same time one must use this freedom responsibly. To be mature means to be able to take responsibility for oneself and one's actions, for one's world, affirmatively and actively.

All of the philosophers who have been called existentialists would accept such a statement, for one of the hallmarks of existentialist thought is the emphasis it has put on human responsibility. Responsibility, for the existentialists, is the very essence of being human. To be human means to be able to respond to the challenges of one's surroundings; it means being able to give meaning to one's life through authentic decision and honesty toward oneself. Most of all, it means being able to respond not just superficially but on a deep personal level of commitment to other persons—sometimes in cooperation, sometimes in opposition, but always with a recognition of the genuinely human freedom of the personality of the other, even when the other must be opposed in the interest of human freedom. Even when trying to escape responsibility, one cannot evade it, for there is no one who can take our responsibility from or for us. This emphasis is characteristic of the religious existentialists—of the Protestants Kierkegaard, Barth, and Tillich, the Catholic Gabriel Marcel, and the Jewish philosopher Martin Buber, who defined humans by the capacity to enter the deeply personal I-Thou relationship. A similar emphasis on personal responsibility is found in Theravada Buddhism's insistence that one is totally responsible for one's own progress to enlightenment. This emphasis on personal responsibility is also characteristic of existentialists who ordinarily have been thought of as nonreligious or antireligious. In *Being and Nothingness*, Jean-Paul Sartre, a French philosopher, wrote:

A   The essential consequence of our earlier remarks is that man being condemned to be free carries the weight of the whole world on his shoulders; he is responsible for the world and for himself as a way of being. We are taking the word "responsibility" in its ordinary sense as "consciousness (of) being the incontestable author of an event or of an object." In this sense the responsibility of the for-itself is overwhelming since he is the one by whom it happens that there is a world; since he is also the one who makes himself be, then whatever may be the situation in which he finds himself, the for-itself must wholly assume this situation with its peculiar coefficient of adversity, even though it be insupportable. He must assume the situation with the proud consciousness of being the author of it, for the very worst disadvantages or the worst threats which can endanger my person have meaning only in and through my project; and it is on the ground of the engagement which I am that they appear. It is therefore senseless to think of complaining since nothing foreign has decided what we feel, what we live, or what we are. . . . Thus there are no *accidents* in a life; a community event which suddenly bursts forth and involves me in it does not come from the outside. If I am mobilized in a war, this war is *my* war; it is in my image and I deserve it. I deserve it first because I could always get out of it by suicide or by desertion; these ultimate possibles are those which must always be present for us when there is a question of

envisaging a situation. For lack of getting out of it, I have chosen it. This can be due to inertia, to cowardice in the face of public opinion, or because I prefer certain other values to the value of the refusal to join in the war (the good opinion of my relatives, the honor of my family, etc.). Anyway you look at it, it is a matter of choice. This choice will be repeated later on again and again without a break until the end of the war. Therefore we must agree with the statement by J. Romains, "In war there are no innocent victims." If therefore I have preferred war to death or to dishonor, everything takes place as if I bore the entire responsibility for this war. Of course others have declared it, and one might be tempted perhaps to consider me as a simple accomplice. But this notion of complicity has only a juridical sense, and it does not hold here. For it depends on me that for me and by me this war should not exist, and I have decided that it does exist.[1]

Sartre states the case for personal responsibility in an extreme form which may be most difficult to appropriate in modern society, in which economic, political, and cultural interdependence constantly becomes more evident and influential in determining the roles of individual responsibility. For how much of our world are we responsible? For all of it, as Sartre maintains? What can personal responsibility actually and concretely mean in the highly mechanized, rationalized world that most of us live in—a world in which people very often never encounter the concrete consequences of their acts, since these acts are only links in the infinite chain of events that we call modern industrial society?

The contemporary American poet James Dickey has attempted to explore several aspects of this problem in his comment about one of his poems:

B

The protagonist of "The Firebombing" is a suburban householder bowed down with making payments, keeping track of his children's toys, getting his sons to scout meetings, mowing the lawn, and all those inconsequential things we do: these things are our lives. He can hardly believe his is the same person who got into the night aircraft and took off with napalm bombs on bomb shackles under

the wings. This memory produces an extremely complex state of mind. He's now a householder, and he realizes with a shock that he's burned up women and children with napalm in his God-like phase. He's wondering how it felt for those people, but he can't really imagine it. They were Japanese, about as foreign to him and his origins as anything could possibly be. But most importantly he

---

[1]Jean-Paul Sartre, *Being and Nothingness*, trans. Hazel E. Barnes (New York: Philosophical Library, 1956), pp. 553–54. Copyright © 1956 by Philosophical Library, Inc.

can't imagine the result of the mission because he never saw it.

In aerial warfare you can't contemplate the results of your destruction, especially at night, because they are hidden from you by distance and darkness. All you see is a flash of fire and, depending on your altitude, you don't even see that sometimes. You have a terrifying detachment from the result of what you are doing. If you had gone down there and seen your destruction of these people, then you would be able to feel guilt, easily. But it's in the nature of the operational function you're performing that you can't do this, even if you want to. This detachment produces a peculiar state of mind. The protagonist feels that his inability to imagine one of his victims knocking at his door with his ears burned off, his inability to imagine anybody knocking at his door except his neighbor coming over to borrow the lawn mower, is a kind of judgment on him—and it is. He is realistic about it, though, and says that there is nothing he can do; and there isn't. Maybe that's the worst sentence of all, to be deprived of feeling what a human being ought to be entitled to feel.[2]

Contrast what Sartre says about responsibility in the modern world with what Dickey says about it. Is the existentialist emphasis that a person should take full responsibility for all his actions and their consequences a reaction (a response) to the loss of the feeling of concrete responsibility that Dickey describes?

You may want to read "The Firebombing." It can be found in Dickey's book of poems *Buckdancer's Choice*.[3] The following units of this chapter explore some ways in which religious traditions have dealt with the questions raised here.

UNIT 49 A Jewish Conception of Human Freedom

Judaism has emphasized the greatness of God—the holiness, wisdom, goodness, and power of the God who is seen as the one God, the Creator of all things, beside whom there are no other gods. With this emphasis on the greatness of God, Judaism has also emphasized the dignity and potential greatness of humanity. Human beings are seen as dependent on God, as receiving being and life and all things necessary to life as gifts from God. However, they are seen also as potentially cocreators with God. Humans should show reverence to God but not sacrifice their own talents or lose their possibilities for creative initiative in blind submission: It is God's will that humanity develop creative potentialities to their fullest in accordance with the commandment that God be loved with all one's heart, soul, and strength (Deuteronomy 6:5) and that one love one's neighbor, all fellow human beings.

This double aspect of the human relationship to God in Judaism is well illustrated in a number of places in the Jewish Scriptures. In the book of Genesis, for instance, Abraham (the patriarch of Judaism) is praised because of his faithful

[2]From *Self-Interviews* by James Dickey, pp. 138–39. Copyright © 1970 by James Dickey. Reprinted by permission of Doubleday and Co., Inc.

[3]James Dickey, "The Firebombing," *Buckdancer's Choice* (Middletown, Connecticut: Wesleyan University Press, 1964, 1965), pp. 11–20.

obedience to God. Certainly there is no lack of reverence for God on Abraham's part. Nevertheless, it is shown as entirely proper that Abraham should attempt to persuade God to change his mind about destroying the wicked cities of Sodom and Gomorrah. Abraham succeeds in getting God to agree to spare the wicked cities, provided some good people can be found in them (see Unit 90). In the same way, Moses is pictured as persuading God to change his mind about destroying the Hebrews who have worshiped a golden calf, thereby showing their lack of faith in God after he has just delivered them from slavery in Egypt (Exodus 32). In both cases, God is pictured as taking counsel and accepting the suggestions of his faithful servants, his obedient and loyal friends.

The same point is made in story form in the Talmud:[4]

A

Rabbi Eliezer disagreed with some other rabbis about a point of law and, unable to convince them, said, "If the law is as I think it is, then this tree shall let me know." Immediately the tree jumped a hundred yards, but the other rabbis said: "One does not prove anything from a tree." Rabbi Eliezer then appealed to a brook, which immediately began to flow upstream, but his colleagues replied: "One does not prove anything from a brook." Rabbi Eliezer said: "If the law is as I think, then the walls of this house will tell." And the walls began to fall. Rabbi Joshua reprimanded the walls: "If scholars argue a point of law, what business have you to fall?" Then the walls stopped midway: to show their respect for Rabbi Joshua, they did not fall further; and in deference to Rabbi Eliezer they did not straighten up. Then Rabbi Eliezer appealed to heaven, and a voice said: "What have you against Rabbi Eliezer? The law is as he says." Rabbi Joshua, however, replied: "It is written in the Bible (Deuteronomy 30:12): It is not in heaven. What does this mean?" Rabbi Jirmijahu said: "The Torah has been given on Mount Sinai, so we no longer pay attention to voices, for on Mount Sinai already thou hast written into the Torah to decide according to the majority." Some time after this dispute, Rabbi Nathan met Elijah, the prophet, and asked him what the Holy One, blessed be His Name, had done in that hour. And Elijah replied: "God smiled and said: My children have won against me, my children have won."[5]

According to Judaism, a full illumination of true humanity can be attained when humans gain this perspective of their relationship to the holy, one God. In the light of this distinctive Jewish understanding of freedom—an interaction with the sovereign God, even to the point of questioning and influencing God's actions— Jewish imagery of the value and place of humanity is greatly enhanced. It has significantly affected Western understandings of humanity.

How does the Jewish understanding of humanity resemble or differ from attitudes found in other religious traditions?

[4]The Talmud is a collection, or collection of collections, of commentaries on the body of law revealed in the Jewish Scriptures. It developed over a period of centuries and was handed down as oral tradition before being put in written form.

[5]An adaptation of a story from The Talmud, Baba Mezia 596, cited by Erich Fromm in *Psychoanalysis and Religion*, p. 45, 1950 (New Haven, CT: Yale University Press).

UNIT 50   Concepts of Christian Freedom and the Dilemmas of Decision Making

The human capacity to make a decision is possibly one factor that distinguishes humans from other animals. Is this ability unique? Many would say yes.

In rural societies of the past, persons lived by the rhythm of nature and often could make many decisions without too much stress. The beat of life was more or less constant. In the urban societies of today, however, some would say that we suffer from "decision stress."

A

Many individuals trapped in dull or slowly changing environments yearn to break out into new jobs or roles that require them to make faster and more complex decisions. But among the people of the future, the problem is reversed. "Decisions, decisions . . ." they mutter as they race anxiously from task to task. The reason they feel harried and upset is that transience, novelty and diversity pose contradictory demands and thus place them in an excruciating double bind. . . .

The rapid injection of novelty into the environment upsets the delicate balance of "programmed" and "non-programmed" decisions in our organizations and our private lives.[6]

Alvin Toffler here helps us understand the pressures of the future that are upon us, pressures that demand that we make countless decisions. This is what he calls "future shock." In this situation, how shall we decide freely without becoming frenzied? What guidelines for understanding the nature of our freedom should we follow? In the sections that follow, we shall consider how some Christian theologians, ancient and modern, have interpreted freedom and what it means to decide.

Concerning Free Will

Pelagius, a British monk who came to Rome late in the fourth century, maintained that man is created free to choose good or evil and that he always has that freedom. He stated:

B

We have implanted in us by God a possibility for acting in both directions. It resembles, as I may say, a root which is most abundant in its produce of fruit. It yields and produces diversely according to man's will; and is capable, at the cultivator's own choice, of either shedding a beautiful bloom of virtues, or of bristling with the thorny thicket of vices. . . . But that we really do a good thing, or speak a good word, or think a good thought, proceeds from our own selves. . . . Nothing good, nothing evil, on account of which we are deemed either laudable or blameworthy, is born with us, but is done by us: for we are born not fully developed, but with a capacity for either conduct; we are formed naturally without either virtue or vice. . . .[7]

[6]Alvin Toffler, *Future Shock* (New York: Random House, Inc., 1970), p. 355.
[7]Paul Lehmann, "The Anti-Pelagian Writings," in A *Companion to the Study of St. Augustine,* ed. Roy Battenhouse (New York: Oxford University Press, 1955), p. 208.

Concerning the "Unfree" Will

Augustine, Christian Bishop of Hippo in North Africa during the fifth century, vehemently rejected Pelagius' position. Augustine felt that Pelagius neglected the grace of God in human actions, and held that although humanity (Adam) originally had freedom to sin, or not to sin, persons because of their pride sinned by choosing themselves over God and therefore lost their freedom to choose between the alternatives of good and evil. Since this original choice, according to Augustine, individuals have no freedom of their own to choose good or evil—they only choose the evil. Humanity's only hope of freedom to choose goodness depends upon God's grace—his willingness to restore human ability to do good. This restoration emphasizes for Augustine humanity's dependence on God for any ability to do good. John Calvin, the sisteenth-century Protestant reformer, agreed with Augustine, as the following statement indicates:

C   The will, therefore, is so bound by the slavery of sin, that it cannot excite itself, much less devote itself to any thing good. . . . We must . . . observe this point of distinction, that man, having been corrupted by his fall, sins voluntarily, not with reluctance or constraint; with the strongest propensity of disposition, not with violent coercion; with the bias of his own passions, and not with external compulsion: yet such is the pravity of his nature, that he cannot be excited and biased to any thing but what is evil. If this be true, there is no impropriety in affirming, that he is under a necessity of sinning. . . .

Man is so enslaved by sin, as to be of his own nature incapable of an effort, or even an inspiration, toward that which is good.[8]

Concerning Freedom in a New Context

The position of Pelagius and Augustine have often been seen as the poles of a continuum on the question of freedom. Christian thinkers have often agreed upon, or argued for, one or the other, or some position of compromise between the two poles. A modern theologian, Carl Michalson, wishing to move beyond these age-old arguments, emphasizes what he considers to be the creation of a new context for freedom through Christian faith. Christians make choices with a new sense of freedom, since they are not limited by their previous conditions and can now decide within the context of a new destiny. Michalson further explains:

D   The distinctive dimension of Christian freedom, however, is not the freedom with which one chooses, not even when that choice is a destiny-determining choice. Christian freedom is the freedom one experiences when the entire volitional facility of the human spirit is mobilized at the new and unanticipated level of the history invoked by Jesus of Nazareth. The new age initiated in Jesus has to do mainly with the issue of human freedom because it sets up the conditions which force upon the past the very possibility of a new authenticity.

Let me test the sense of the Christian meaning of freedom through a series of illustrations. The Japanese daughter of a Samurai was once sent to a mission school where she was given a plot of ground a yard square with which to do

[8]John Calvin, *A Compend of the Institutes of Christian Religion*, Hugh Thomson Kerr, Jr. (Philadelphia: Presbyterian Board of Education, 1939), pp. 49, 51.

entirely as she chose. It was called a "do as you please" garden. She planted it according to her own design and afterward exclaimed it was the first time in her life she had known what it meant to be free. Christian freedom is like that, to be sure, but it is more.

Radhakrishnan, the Indian philosopher and statesman, has likened freedom to being dealt a hand of cards and being allowed to play out the game, but strictly within the limits of the cards in hand. Christian freedom also includes this sense of a certain latitude within prescribed limits.

Pascal's analogy of the wager comes even closer to what Christians mean by freedom. It recapitulates the others but adds still another element. The coin is tossed. One is free to do as he pleases with his decision. But he can only choose "heads" or "tails"; he must play out the game within those limits. What is added by Pascal, however, is urgency. One *must* call out before the coin has fallen. That is to say, man is not free not to choose. He is not free to filibuster with destiny beyond the deadline for authentic resolution. The Roumanian playwright Ionesco has recently called our attention to a new metaphor for freedom emerging from the space age. In outer space one has a sense of weightlessness which he experiences as a sense of infinite possibility. Nothing holds him down. Yet there is no place from which to brace oneself, from which to launch this sense of infinite possibility.[9]

A Christian is given a sense of being freed to be, even though this is freedom within limits. One also recognizes the imperative nature of choice—one must choose.

Michalson continues with a discussion of the content of Christian freedom. He notes four realms that predominate in the Christian's deliverance from the old age:

1. *Freedom from the world*—Here Michalson refers to the fact that a free Christian can live in the world, fulfilling responsibility for the world, but is not of the world. The world does not rule the Christian, but instead God rules the Christian who serves in the world.

2. *Freedom from the law*—This freedom does not mean license for one selfishly to do as he pleases. Rather, it pertains to the freedom from religious legalism, freedom from oppressive religious requirements that have no ultimate significance. This is the freedom that demands that man take responsibility for his own ethical decisions instead of depending merely on rules that short-circuit mature love. Freedom from the law is the freedom to love creatively.

3. *Freedom from sin*—This refers not merely to freedom from sin as rebellion against God, but more specifically to freedom from refusing to accept Jesus of Nazareth as the source of new life. In moving from the old age to the new age the Christian comes up to date. Christ as the ruler of the new age frees the Christian from the sin of turning history into mere pastness. In the new age the Christian can appropriate new modes of life that may better provide authentic freedom for all men.

4. *Freedom from death*—The Christian affirms faith in the resurrection of Jesus as the sign of the new age. He is free from death, not in the sense that he will not die, but in the sense that when death comes, God will be then as He is now—"all in all." Trusting that God will be God in the death of each man frees the Christian from anxiety about the future and thus enables him to live responsibly in the present.[10]

[9]Reprinted by permission of Charles Scribner's Sons from *World Theology*, pages 168–69, by Carl Michalson. Copyright © 1967 Carl Michalson.

[10]*Ibid*. This notation of the realms summarizes Michalson, pp. 171–78.

As the examples show, freedom has been understood in a variety of ways by Christian theologians. It has been defined in still other ways by philosophers and by other cultures where the stress on individual freedom has not been as significant as it has been in Western Christianity.

In the light of these interpretations of freedom, what does it mean to decide?

Do you agree or disagree with Pelagius that we are born without either virtue or vice and can choose between the alternatives of doing good or evil? Why?

Do you agree or disagree with Augustine's understanding that we have no real freedom in doing good or evil? Why?

If there are elements of truth in both positions, what resolution would you propose to rectify the seeming contradictions found between the two positions?

11

Sin and Guilt

INTRODUCTION

Most religions have provided some direction to adherents regarding what is considered "right" or appropriate behavior in one's basic attitudes toward life as well as in social relationships. Failure to live by standards established by such directions often produces feelings of guilt or shame in the adherents, and these feelings play a decisive role in personal direction and control.

Religions thus inculcate in persons the sense of what is appropriate or right and what is wrong. In the Western world, this process has frequently been referred to as the development of "conscience." *Guilt* is understood to be a primary motivational factor in the attitudinal and behavioral functioning of the individual. Students of Oriental religion and culture have sometimes referred to *shame*, as differentiated from guilt in the Western connotation, as the underlying motivation or controller of appropriate behavior. Several of the units in this chapter are designed to explore briefly the concepts of shame and guilt in Oriental and Western contexts. Attention is also given to the concept of sin as developed within the Judeo-Christian heritage.

UNIT 51   Roles of Shame and Guilt

A pompously, pretentiously dressed individual—possibly portrayed by the actor Oliver Hardy—through no fault of his own, slips on a banana peel and careens into a mud puddle. He looks quickly and furtively around and is relieved that no one has seen his fall.

A woman sends a large check to a bank, explaining that years ago a teller had given her twenty dollars too much. Though no one else has ever known about this, she explains that over the years she has come to feel increasingly guilty and is now returning the original sum with the correctly calculated interest.

The two incidents just described illustrate the contrasting attitudes of shame and guilt as discussed by Ruth Benedict in the passage that follows. The man who would have been ashamed if others had seen his disgrace, since no one did see, felt relief, not shame. The woman was burdened by guilt, even though no one else knew she had accepted the money knowing it to be too much. Her guilt could be relieved only by confession (even if she remained anonymous) and restitution.

At the time of writing *The Chrysanthemum and the Sword*, Ruth Benedict believed that Western societies relied heavily on guilt feelings, perhaps as a part of their Puritan heritage, and less on the sense of shame to regulate behavior. Some recent observers have suggested that perhaps a shift has occurred, and that there is more tendency now than formerly for many in Western societies to be shame-oriented rather than guilt-oriented. As you read Benedict's discussion of shame and guilt, ask yourself whether the distinction between the two attitudes and the corresponding contrast between Western and Eastern orientations are as clear as she found them to be.

A

In anthropological studies of different cultures the distinction between those which rely heavily on shame and those that rely heavily on guilt is an important one. A society that inculcates absolute standards of morality and relies on men's developing a conscience is a guilt culture by definition, but a man in such a society may, as in the United States, suffer in addition from shame when he accuses himself of gaucheries which are in no way sins. He may be exceedingly chagrined about not dressing appropriately for the occasion or about a slip of the tongue. In a culture where shame is a major sanction, people are chagrined about acts which we expect people to feel guilty about. This chagrin can be very intense and it cannot be relieved, as guilt can be, by confession and atonement. A man who has sinned can get relief by unburdening himself. This device of confession is used in our secular therapy and by many religious groups which have otherwise little in common. We know it brings relief. Where shame is the major sanction, a man does not experience relief when he makes his fault public even to a confessor. So long as his bad behavior does not "get out into the world" he need not be troubled and confession appears to him merely a way of courting trouble. Shame cultures therefore do not provide for confessions, even to the gods. They have ceremonies for good luck rather than for expiation.

True shame cultures rely on external sanctions for good behavior, not, as true guilt cultures do, on an internalized conviction of sin. Shame is a reaction to other people's criticism. A man is shamed either by being openly ridiculed and rejected or by fantasying to himself that he has been made ridiculous. In either case it is a potent sanction. But it requires an audience or at least a man's fantasy of an audience. Guilt does not. In a nation where honor means living up to one's own picture of oneself, a man may suffer from guilt though no man knows of his misdeed and a man's feeling of guilt may actually be relieved by confessing his sin.

The early Puritans who settled in the United States tried to base their whole morality on guilt and all psychiatrists know what trouble contemporary Americans have with their consciences. But shame is an increasingly heavy burden in the United States and guilt is less extremely felt than in earlier generations. In the United States this is interpreted as a relaxation of morals. There is much truth in this, but that is because we do not expect shame to do the heavy work of morality. We do not harness the acute personal chagrin which accompanies shame to our fundamental system of morality.

The Japanese do. A failure to follow their explicit signposts of good behavior, a failure to balance obligations or to foresee contingencies is a shame *(hajj)*. Shame, they say, is the root of virtue. A man who is sensitive to it will carry out all the rules of good behavior. "A man who knows shame" is sometimes translated "virtuous man," sometimes "man of honor." Shame has the same place of authority in Japanese ethics that "a clear conscience," "being right with God," and the avoidance of sin have in Western ethics. Logically enough, therefore, a man will not be punished in the afterlife. The Japanese—except for priests who know the Indian sutras—are quite unacquainted with the idea of reincarnation dependent upon one's merit in his life, and—except for some well-instructed Christian converts—they do not recognize post-death reward and punishment or a heaven and a hell.[1]

UNIT 52   Guilt and Religious Experience

The concept of guilt in Western religions has many dimensions. It has been held by the majority of Christians that in some sense the death of Jesus made it possible for the guilt of sinful humans—at least those who turned to Christ for forgiveness—to be removed. Guilt within early Judaism (as will be illustrated by the discussion that follows) was treated as an objective contamination (resulting in a kind of decay, rot, or infection). Medieval Christianity also saw guilt as something objective. Anselm of Canterbury (1033–1109 C.E.) understood human guilt on the analogy of a debt owed, but since the debt owed to God—the result of human sinful disobedience—is infinite, only God, not humans, can cancel it.

Johannes Pedersen, a modern biblical scholar, describes the ancient Jewish (or Hebrew) understanding of guilt as follows:

A   It follows from the psychological conception of the Israelites that a man is responsible for all his actions: Every action must exercise its effect, also in the soul of the person who acts. . . . The decisive thing is what is the relation of the action to the acting soul: does it arise in the central will of the soul, or does it merely lie in the periphery of the soul? If the latter is the case, then it can be wiped out and be removed before it gains ground. . . . But if an infringement upon the law of righteousness is more deeply seated in the soul, then it is not to be removed. Sin implies guilt. . . . How the latter acts, we see most clearly when we consider the strongest form of the breach of peace, viz. unrighteous manslaughter.[2]

Like a consuming poison, guilt works recompense for the violated family by destroying the unregenerate soul and thus rids the Jewish community of a danger.

[1]Ruth Benedict, *The Chrysanthemum and the Sword: Patterns of Japanese Culture* (Boston: Houghton Mifflin Co., 1946), pp. 222–24. Used by permission of publisher.

[2]Johannes Pedersen, *Israel, Its Life and Culture* (London: Oxford University Press, 1926), Vols. I–II, p. 419.

This is in accordance with the fundamental Jewish law of the soul. In Israel's conception of psychic life, guilt produces misfortune and righteousness undergirds happiness.

Pedersen concludes his discussion of the way guilt functions in Judaism in the following:

The various examples of guilt breaking out in misfortune are in no wise isolated. Righteousness must carry happiness, because happiness is created in the soul, and the righteous is the soul possessed of the power to create. Violence is falsehood and delusion, and all sin is in reality weakness.

Whereas "justify" means to give vitality, to make strong, so also "unjustify" means to weaken, to rob of the power to self-maintenance.[3]

> But the wicked are like the tossing sea; for it cannot rest, and its waters toss up mire and dirt. There is no peace, says my God, for the wicked. (Isaiah 57:20–21, RSV)

What would be the implications of this religious and societal attitude for the formation of conscience in the young?

Keep such a question in mind when considering the ideas introduced in the material that follows.

In the Judaism of the period of the prophets (750 B.C.E. and afterwards; this movement is especially clear in the writings of Hosea, Isaiah, Jeremiah, and Ezekiel), emphasis began to be placed on the subjective or psychological elements of guilt. Guilt began to be treated as resulting from, and expressing itself in, wrong or rebellious attitudes that needed to be changed rather than as a contamination that could not be removed (as in early Judaism) or a debt that could be paid or cancelled only by God (as in Medieval Christianity). Psychological and subjective aspects of guilt have been emphasized in Christianity from the New Testament period to the present. It was an important emphasis in the writings of Augustine of Hippo (354–430) and in those of more recent writers, including Søren Kierkegaard (1819–1855). John G. McKenzie, an English psychotherapist and adherent of Christianity, in discussing the role of guilt and conscience in personality formation, draws both on the traditions within Judaism and Christianity that have emphasized the subjective and psychological character of guilt and on modern psychological models of personality development. Note his distinction between neurotic (false) and genuine guilt, and his insistence on the need for distinguishing between a socially created and immature conscience (Freud's concept of superego), often functioning on the level of taboos and neurotic guilt, and a mature conscience able to be self-governing in accordance with the authentic needs of (and duties to) the self and others.

B

As the child becomes more integrated, he becomes aware of his feelings and behaviour, he is aware of his aggressive feelings and also of his anxiety-feelings. How much anxiety he will experience will depend very largely on the reactions of

[3]*Ibid.*, p. 428.

adults, especially that of the mother. If she is wholly intolerant of these ambivalent tendencies and the child acquires more fear than love, anxiety-feelings are likely to be repressed, and we are likely to get "tantrums" accompanied by psychosomatic symptoms. If, on the other hand, the mother is patient and always ready to receive gestures of sorrow or regret, then the child will tend to have a healthy anxiety regarding its ambivalent tendencies, and the moral development will be natural. In other words the child accepts the responsibility for its feelings however dim that sense of responsibility may be. . . .

For a true sense of guilt-feelings we have to wait for the growth of the conscience; it is then that the real moral element is experienced. That undoubtedly begins with self-consciousness. Up to between two or three years of age the child tends to speak of himself in the third person. Challenged by his mother for breaking a cup, he will answer "John did it." The day comes when "John" and "I" become one. On that day the "Super-ego" is born, or rather the child becomes aware of it. . . . It is part of the equipment of a potential personality; and its function is to conserve the moral integration of the person. . . .

The child's morality begins with the realization of the approvals and disapprovals of parents and teachers. . . . The barriers or prohibitions come from within the child, and pull the child up sharp.

Parents and teachers cannot always be with the child. Hence nature provides the mind with an innate process of introjecting or internalizing the commands and prohibitions of parents and teachers. . . .

Now, many people never outgrow this infantile Super-ego. Unconsciously they strive to obey the prohibitions and conform to the commands. Inwardly they rebel against its rigidity and compulsions; and they may develop . . . a perfectionist character-trend, or a dynamic trend to restrict their lives within narrow limits. The least deviation from perfection and they are full of guilty-feelings, recriminations, and yet at the same time a raging hostility has to be kept repressed, or projected.

Thus we come, again, up against the ambivalence which lies at the root of the origin of guilt-feelings. I would not say that the child or the adult wants to comply with the Super-ego, but he or she fears the guilt-feelings. He or she is afraid of freedom; they are afraid lest the impulses prove too strong for the Ego to control. Hence unconsciously they cling to the authoritative conscience. . . .

The problem of moral growth is simply the problem of growing up. . . . We have to pass from Super-ego control to conscience-control. . . . It is doubtful whether the Super-ego ever withers away entirely; but with the development of the adult or positive conscience it performs a different role. Instead of repressing through the guilt-sense an offending line of behaviour, it pulls us up, compels us to reflect upon what we are tempted to do; and then exercises control through reason rather than through feeling. If we cross the "barrier" and fall then there is a consciousness of objective guilt, but instead of morbid guilt-feelings with all their threats there is sincere contrition, . . . that is to say, there is sorrow for the guilty behaviour and a turning away from such behaviour. . . . It is the passing from the "borrowed morality" of the Super-ego to the free morality of conscience where *oughts*, *commands* and *prohibitions* have become moral guides and not moral policemen. We accept these not in virtue of external authority, but because we *see* they are true . . .[4]

Finally, how does one move to what many religious persons call *mature responsibility*? McKenzie says that

the sense of responsibility cannot be explained either by the child's fear of the reproaches of the parents or teachers, or the fear of consequences. The sense of

[4]From *Guilt: Its Meaning and Significance* by John G. McKenzie. Copyright © 1962 by Abingdon Press. pp. 32, 34, 35, 40, 48, 49.

ought belongs to the nature of things. That does not mean that the moral principles we teach the child or the ethical ideals we keep in front of his growing mind are necessarily justified. Depth-psychology may be able to explain the content of the ought, but it cannot account for our being "ethical animals." Dogs have "Super-ego" insofar as they obey their masters; but they have no conscience, no sense of ought. On the other hand, depth-psychology has a right to demand that the moral principles and ethical ideals taught shall be consistent with what we know of the law of the development of moral personality. We need to know what human nature is; so that we are not trying to make it what it was never meant to become.[5]

Do you distinguish between types of guilt–for example, healthy and unhealthy guilt?

Do religions play a constructive role in society in terms of providing some content for the conscience?

Do you agree with McKenzie that "appropriate" or "healthy" guilt experiences are necessary for persons to live in a social context?

UNIT 53   Judeo-Christian Concepts of Sin

A central emphasis in the Judeo-Christian tradition has been the broken relationship between God and humankind denoted by the word *sin*: Most Christians have connected the concept of sin with disobedience to the commandments or law(s) of God. The Ten Commandments given by God to the descendants of Israel (see Exodus 20) have often been taken as a prototype of God's commandments; they have been felt to contain, in broad outline, an indication of the conduct God desires and forbids. Primarily, God's will has been interpreted to include exclusive devotion to God and justice and love toward one's fellow humans. Christianity, departing from Judaism, has laid great stress on *original sin*, an attitude involving self-will and self-indulgence held to be characteristic of *all* fallen humanity. This attitude has been held to precede and to cause specific acts of sinfulness. Thus, Medieval Christianity stressed as the Seven Deadly Sins seven dispositions or character traits—pride, covetousness, lust, envy, gluttony, anger, and sloth—which as particular manifestations of the underlying original sin (an attitude or disposition rather than an act) are motivating causes of sinful acts both in the unredeemed and in Christians who have fallen away from the restored innocence given them by baptism and have let sin increasingly regain control of their lives.

In the following passage, the author of the biblical book of Genesis gives an account of the fall of Adam and Eve, which many Christians and Jews have taken to symbolize the fall of all humans.

A   Now the serpent was more subtle than any other wild creature that the Lord God had made. He said to the woman, "Did God say, 'You shall not eat of any tree of the garden'?" And the woman said to the serpent, "We may eat of the fruit of the trees of the garden; but God said, 'You shall not eat of the fruit of the tree which

[5]*Ibid.*, p. 175.

is in the midst of the garden, neither shall you touch it, lest you die.' " But the serpent said to the woman, "You will not die. For God knows that when you eat of it your eyes will be opened, and you will be like God, knowing good and evil." So when the woman saw that the tree was good for food, and that it was a delight to the eyes, and that the tree was to be desired to make one wise, she took of its fruit and ate; and she also gave some to her husband, and he ate. Then the eyes of both were opened, and they knew that they were naked; and they sewed fig leaves together and made themselves aprons. And they heard the sound of the Lord God walking in the garden in the cool of the day, and the man and his wife hid themselves from the presence of the Lord God among the trees of the garden. But the Lord God called to the man, and said to him, "Where are you?" And he said, "I heard the sound of thee in the garden, and I was afraid, because I was naked; and I hid myself." He said, "Who told you that you were naked? Have you eaten of the tree of which I commanded you not to eat?" The man said, "The woman whom thou gavest to be with me, she gave me fruit of the tree, and I ate." Then the Lord God said to the woman, "What is this that you have done?" The woman said, "The serpent beguiled me, and I ate." (Genesis 3:1–13 RSV)

This passage describes actual disobedience but also—and more important—the desire to be like God or to be God, a wish that causes separation of humanity and God. Reinhold Niebuhr, a contemporary theologian, expands upon this interpretation.

B

Since Augustine it has been the consistent view of Christian orthodoxy that the basic sin of man was his pride. In this view Christian thought agreed with the conception of the Greek tragedies, which regarded *hybris* as man's most flagrant fault and one which was invariably followed by punishment or *nemesis*. The basic sign of pride does not mean some conscious bit of exaggerated self-esteem, but the general inclination of all men to overestimate their virtues, powers, and achievements. Augustine defined sin as the "perverse desire of height," or as man's regarding himself as his own end, instead of realizing that he is but a part of a total scheme of means and ends.[6]

Although Niebuhr stresses sin as pride, he also finds another basic mode of human sinfulness in sloth or self-indulgence. Harvey Cox, another contemporary theologian, offers yet another explanation of sin—one which contrasts with the broadly accepted concept of sin as pride but to some extent resembles Niebuhr's concept of sin as sloth.

C

Man-as-sinner has usually been pictured by religious writers as man-the-insurrectionary, the proud heaven-storming rebel who has not learned to be content with his lot. Refined and escalated in literature, this image blossoms in the heroic Satans and Lucifers of Goethe and Milton. No wonder we find sin so interesting and sinners more attractive than saints. No wonder we secretly admire Lucifer while our orthodox doctrine condemns him to the lake of fire. This misleading view of sin as pride and rebelliousness has given the very word sin an intriguing lustre: a naked Eve with moist bedroom eyes guiltily tasting the forbidden apple; a slithery, clearly phallic, serpent; man defying the petty conventions

[6]Reinhold Niebuhr, "Sin," in *A Handbook of Christian Theology*, ed. Marvin Halverson and Arthur A. Cohen (New York: World Publishing Company, 1958), p. 348.

imposed on him by small-minded people. In these terms why shouldn't we be in favor of sin? The only trouble is this mish-mash of sex and self-affirmation images has almost nothing to do with the biblical idea of sin. It is basically a Greek, or more precisely, promethean notion larded with remnants of medieval folk piety, Victorian antisexuality, and the bourgeois obsession with orderliness.[7]

. . . Apathy is the key form of sin in today's world. . . . For Adam and Eve, apathy meant letting a snake tell them what to do. It meant abdicating what the theologians have called *gubernatio mundi*, the exercise of dominion and control over the world. For us it means allowing others to dictate the identities with which we live out our lives.[8]

. . . I believe a careful examination of the biblical sources will indicate that man's most debilitating proclivity is *not* his pride. It is *not* his attempt to be more than man . . . it is his sloth, his unwillingness to be everything man was intended to be.[9]

Is it necessary to have a concept of sin or wrongdoing in a religion? If so, why is it necessary? If not, how can broken human relationships be explained?

What does Niebuhr mean by sin as pride?

Which of the explanations of sin presented here do you find most appropriate?

---

[7]Harvey Cox, *On Not Leaving It to the Snake* (New York: Macmillan, Inc., 1964), pp. xi–xii. Copyright © 1964, 1965, 1967 by Harvey G. Cox. Used by permission.

[8]*Ibid.*, p. xviii.

[9]*Ibid.*, p. xi.

12 _____

Death and the Self

INTRODUCTION

In every society, in every period of human history, individuals and groups of human beings have been preoccupied with the experience and meaning of death. It is a custom among some Christian groups for individuals to remind each other on Ash Wednesday each year: "Recall, O man, thou art mortal. Dust thou art, and to dust thou shalt return." There is hardly any reality of which human beings in their long history have been more aware than the fact, the inevitability, of death. Death, its meaning, its mystery, and the uncertainty or promise of what may come after death have been subjects of wide-ranging speculation and deepest interest.

A student wrote in a journal entry:

Why are some people so sure they will find the answers to life when they die? I asked one person why she was sure. She said, "Because Jesus said so in the Bible." Faith is their answer. Faith is not my answer. I have heard people witness of God's part in their lives, and how they could feel his presence. But I haven't felt Him directly in my life. I have experienced the love of people. I guess that's how He works. God is very vague to me. I guess that is why I'm not sure I'll find the "whys" of life when I die. I don't have any idea of what is after death, as some people think they do. Perhaps that is why death scares me. I talked to a girl one time who believes there is nothing after death. I can't believe that either. I can't imagine a nothing. I can't feature a complete end to everything.

The ambiguity of feelings toward life and death expressed in this statement is not an uncommon human experience. The reality of death is recognized while there is little assurance of an afterlife; nevertheless, there is still the hope and anticipation of continuance. Religions have usually embraced a more positive stance toward death and its consequences.

Every religious tradition has interpreted the meaning of death to its adherents. Most religious traditions have contained teachings about the meaning of existence beyond the present one, in the continuity of future generations, in an afterlife, in a succession of rebirths, or in a restored or resurrected, totally renewed existence.

This chapter explores the phenomenon of death as a fundamental human experience. Basic human attitudes toward it are examined. Examples of various religious interpretations of death as well as of an afterlife are also explored.

UNIT 54   How It Feels to Die

The reality of death has always intrigued humanity, and the event itself has been surrounded in all cultures by ritual preparation, elaborate burial practices, and stylized grief formulas. Accounts of death and descriptions of the experience of both death and anticipated afterlife have been numerous throughout history; for example, the ancient Tibetan *Book of the Dead* contains elaborate descriptions of the patterns of death and methods for contacting the dead.

Attention has more recently been focused on "near-death" experiences as the advances of modern medicine have made the phenomenon of "clinical death" more common. Accounts of such experiences have become popular reading, and the frequency of the phenomenon has opened discussions of life after death among psychologists and medical professions in ways unanticipated a few years ago. Accounts of such experiences inevitably raise anew images and questions that have been an integral part of religious traditions for all of human history. The following account of such an episode contains many features that have been reported by others who have had similar experiences: enhanced awareness, a sense of detachment, euphoria, dying by stages and from the extremities, an encounter with *something* greater than life.

A little more than 24 hours ago, as I write this, I learned what it is like to die.

By nearly every clinical standard an arresting of life did occur. The cause of my "death" was a condition known to doctors as anaphylactic shock. This is a rapid failure of vital functions induced by an acute allergic reaction to an alien protein introduced into the tissues—as, for example, the extreme reaction that sometimes occurs when a person has been stung by a bee.

In my case, the alien substance was penicillin. For most people, a dosage of this drug, properly administered, does the job expected of it. For me, with long-dormant allergic factors lurking in my system, the dosage could hardly have been more hostile had it been spat from the fangs of a cobra. . . .

The allergic onslaught was massive and swift. At the last possible moment it was neutralized and reversed by specific counteragents. Had I reached the doctor a minute or two later, or had there not been a supply of the counteragents on hand, I could not have survived. A busy telephone line, a low battery in the car, a misplaced ignition key, a blocked street—any number of things could have made the difference.

Slumped upon a chair in . . . [the Doctor's] residential consulting room, I was slipping across the honed edge of death. For a period of some minutes there had been no pulse, no blood pressure, no pronounced stirring of the heart. My eyes, I have been told, were glazed. My limbs were flaccid, my face swollen and ashen. In the last extreme seconds, only *awareness* remained of the vital functions. As the crisis deepened, I was acutely, almost electrically, aware of things around me and then, when this awareness receded, of things *within* me. I was an enthralled eyewitness and mind witness to my own rapidly advancing demise.

It was a turbulent experience but not at all terrifying—and it had its moments, as I recall them now, of pure black humor. At the end I gazed into something that I believe to be life's supreme mystery. . . .

The nasal irritation had come upon me earlier in the week. I thought it was a cold. But it dragged on, with none of the other, droopy symptoms of a cold, and on Saturday morning I awoke with a raw and scratchy throat. I suspected that this could be a strep infection, and made a mental note to give the Doctor a call later in the day.

Then I looked in the medicine cabinet for some throat lozenges. My eyes fell upon a bottle containing a dozen or so penicillin tablets left over from a pediatrician's prescription for my two small children. The bottle still had its factory label, which recommended a dosage of two tablets four times a day. So why bother the Doctor on her weekend? Although I was aware that self-prescription was poor business for the layman, I took two tablets and noted the time. It was 7:03 a.m.

During the next half-hour or so, I went through the morning routine of feeding the dog and putting her into the fenced-in backyard and brewing the cof-

fee. While listening to news broadcasts, I became aware of a prickly itching sensation on my ankles and legs. It spread rapidly to the wrists and palms, then across the shoulders, lower back and chest. With a cup of coffee for myself and a wake-up one for my wife, I started up the stairs. The itching was taking fire. Halfway up, I set the cups and saucers on the step ahead and went into a frenzy of scratching. I could see coin-size white blotches rising on the backs of my hands. I remembered that long-forgotten reaction to the first penicillin. . . .

I became increasingly aware of a thickening and stiffening of the facial features, and a wheezing of the breath. Turning to the mirror, I scarcely recognized the swollen, crimson-splashed face that stared back at me.

My wife called the Doctor and told her about the penicillin and the reaction, listened a moment, said, "All right, we'll do our best," and hung up.

"The Doctor said we must come at once," she said quietly. . . .

Then I was inside the car, lying on my back across the middle row of seats. The car was bumping along and I heard the clatter of the engine. Behind me, in the third row, my 5-year-old daughter was prattling. My 7-year-old son was commanding her to be quiet. I remember thinking what a nice ad it would make: *A Volkswagen bus is a handy family car to die in.*

We had stopped. As the door spilled open and my wife started tugging me out, I saw a flash of color at the head of the walkway, atop the steps at the patients' side entrance to the big cream stucco house. It was the Doctor in her red-and-blue-plaid dressing robe, looking decidedly unprofessional against the backlight of the morning glare. She was standing in the doorway, leaning out.

As my wife pulled me to my feet, the Doctor, from a distance of 15 or so yards, sized up my condition. She could see the un-coordinated rolling of my eyes, the death pallor of my face, the wobble of my legs. These indications told her that the shock was far advanced and that I might pass out before I could reach the consultation room. For her to try to drag my 200-pound bulk up the five steps and inside would be a futility. So she went back to retrieve the setup in case she had to perform the treatment on the sidewalk.

Momentarily rejuvenated by the rest during the car trip, I was able to make it up the walk. Supported by my wife, I climbed the steps, crossed through the waiting lounge into the consultation room and sank into a green leather-covered armchair. . . .

The hour was 8. Nine minutes had elapsed since my wife's call to the Doctor. I was approximately three minutes away from my confrontation with death.

"Poor Doctor," I said, through a swollen smile, "what an hour for friends to drop in." . . .

For me, a kind of euphoria was setting in. It was marked by exaggerated good humor, a sense of detachment and, I noted even as I experienced it, a hyper-alertness which seemed to furnish me with superior logic and reason. . . .

Then, from far away, as though on some disembodied arm, I felt the tickle of the hypodermic and a tightening little knot as the solution of adrenalin flowed into the muscle. And I observed, but thought it curious that I did not feel, that the Doctor was taking my pulse.

As I was to learn subsequently, her emergency treatment was based on a strategic concept, with allowance for tactical variations as the need might arise.

The adrenalin had to go in first, to start my heart which now was all but dormant. . . .

Now the strategy would proceed to its second phase. When an allergic reaction has set in, a chemical called histamine is excessively generated within the body, causing an increase in the permeability of cells throughout the body. This produces the effects commonly associated with allergy—a rash, an asthmatic swelling of the respiratory passages or a fit of sneezing. In acute cases the overproduction of histamine is enormous. The blood's serum and lymph spill through capillary walls in a floodtide and the blood itself tends to pile up in pools rather than return to the heart. This is the swift chain-reacting characteristic of anaphylactic shock, and it has any number of destructive side effects. The condition can still be reversed until, with cell and tissue death, the shock enters its so-called stagnant stage. Then the body must die.

To buy a little time by attacking the histamine, the Doctor sponged my upper right arm and injected the high-potency antihistamine, Chlor-Trimeton.

In a military sense the injection of adrenalin and antihistamine had been tactical and defensive. Now it was time for the all-out assault with the Neutrapen. In reserve was the cortisone, which might tip the balance in any close engagement. But the Neutrapen was the big one, a mechanism of strategic overkill aimed squarely at the penicillin. It was the ultimate weapon on which the war within my system could be won or lost.

Dimly now, for my external awareness was receding, I saw the Doctor probing for a vein in the crook of my left arm—for years the despair of blood samplers who have tried there first, give up and switched over to the big vein in my right arm.

"Try the right arm, Doctor," I said. "No one can ever find the vein in the left."

"Perhaps God has pointed the way," she said. She had hit the left's elusive vein on the very first try. The dosage went in, 800,000 units of Neutrapen—all she had on hand—to seek and destroy the 500,000 units of penicillin. Now it was up to the bloodstream to deliver.

But at that moment, the Doctor later said, there was no pulse, no discernible pressure, movement or flow of blood. The adrenalin, lost in a limbo of its own, had not taken effect.

Suddenly I knew.

"*Am I dying, Doctor? Is it now?*"

No reply, or rather, none that I could hear.

"*Tell me truly. Am I dying now?*"

"Now, we aren't going to let you," she said, though I did not hear her.

"*Listen, I want to tell you just how it*

is, describe it to you . . . please write it down . . ."

External awareness had slipped away—I heard, saw nothing. I sagged forward as my wife held my head to keep me from pitching from the chair. To the Doctor I had reached clinical death. But for me there was a surge of internal awareness—magnified, finely focused, brilliant.

It is a progressive thing, this death. You feel the toes going first, then the feet, cell by cell, death churning them like waves washing the sands. Now the legs, the cells winking out. Closer now, and the visibility is better. Hands, arms, abdomen and chest, each cell flaring into a supernova, then gone. There is order and system in death, as in all that is life. I must try to control the progression, to save the brain for last so that it may know. Now the neck. The lower jaw. The teeth. How strange to feel one's teeth die, one by one, cell igniting cell, galaxies of cells dying in brilliance.

Now, in retrospect, I grope for this other thing. There was *something* else, something that I felt or experienced or beheld at the very last instant. What was it? I knew it so well when it was there, opening before me, something more beautiful, more gentle, more loving than the mind or imagination of living creature could ever conceive.

But it is gone.

The thunderclap of adrenalin into the heart, reverberations through all the grottoes and canyons and cliffs and peaks of the body. Sprays of sleet, gale-driven against my nakedness, stinging, slashing. Then blurs of motion, sounds of voices.

It is only three or four minutes since I first settled into the green leather chair. The Doctor is at my right side, feeling my pulse as I stir from the coma. Her husband, the surgeon, in his blue terry-cloth dressing robe, has appeared from somewhere and is at my left, holding the other pulse. As I was to learn, in the moments of extremity, as my eyes rolled back in my head, she had run to a hall doorway and shouted for her husband, a tall and powerful man, to come down. She wanted him to do a heart massage. Then she started to prepare the long intracardiac needle. As he entered, however, the earlier dosage of adrenalin took effect.

"Well," he is saying, "we're getting a good pulse now. Good and strong."

The ambulance moves, sunlight through the windows, glimpses of trees in chartreuse bud. An oxygen cup is placed over my nose and mouth. I suck hungrily at the odorless nothingness.

Now the bump-bump-bump of potholes, the honk-honk-honk of the ambulance horn as traffic is encountered. The good sounds, sounds of life and the living.

"No siren?" my wife asks.

"We don't have one," says the woman in white.

Inside the oxygen mask I raise my voice in a wild howl. The woman in white takes alarm, but my wife gets the message. She smiles and blinks back the tears.

"He's supplying the siren," she says.[1,2]

What is your reaction to such descriptions? Do you think the content of the experience was real or the product of hallucination?

To what extent, if any, have Mr. Snell's own background, insights, and sensitivity contributed to this account of his experience?

[1]David Snell, "How It Feels to Die," *Life*, May 26, 1967, pp. 38–40, 42, 44, 49. © 1967 Time Inc. Used with permission.

[2]Experiences similar to Mr. Snell's, in which there are discernible patterns in the near-death process, are described and analyzed in Elisabeth Kübler-Ross's *On Death and Dying* (New York: Macmillan, Inc., 1969), Raymond Moody's *Life after Life* (New York: Bantam Books, Inc., 1975), and Craig R. Lundahl's A *Collection of Near-Death Research Readings* (Chicago: Nelson-Hall Publishers, 1982). These works themselves have been analyzed and discussed in such works as Hans Küng's *Eternal Life?* (Garden City, New York: Doubleday & Co., Inc., 1984).

Compare and contrast Mr. Snell's experience of the mysterious "something else" with: (1) Gautama's comments concerning Nirvana, Unit 21; (2) Zen enlightenment, Unit 28; (3) mystical experience of God, Unit 28.

UNIT 55 Attitudes toward Death

Life, in all its aspects, has been greatly modified by the scientific and technological developments of the past century, particularly in the West. This is most obvious in the health care field, where startling innovations have greatly lengthened our life span and increased our control over disease. Such advances are seldom without their prices, however. One of these has been the need to modify and change the patterns by which we deal with death. Death now usually occurs in a hospital or nursing home, often in an impersonal intensive care unit. Family, patients, and friends are often cut off from each other. The traditional grief processes are interrupted and sometimes eliminated. The medical community, to a large degree, takes death as a sign of failure, since the goal of medicine is to sustain life. The result is the establishment of patterns of behavior that remove us from the death process.

In the last several years, persons working with the dying have come to recognize that these changing patterns have turned us into a society that denies the reality of death, creating for itself enormous psychological, emotional, and religious problems. This recognition has led to an immense amount of investigation and writing on death, with workshops and seminars for health professionals, social workers, chaplains, pastors, and laity attempting to face openly the problems arising out of the changing patterns.

There has arisen among some of the professionals who work with the dying a renewed consciousness that society as a whole needs to admit the reality of death and to accept it as a part of life. The awareness of death may indeed mean the growth and expansion of meaning for life as we live it each day.

Dr. Kübler-Ross, after extensive study of dying persons, suggests that there are five stages through which dying patients and their loved ones normally pass:

A

1. *Denial*—"No, not me." This is a typical reaction when a patient learns that he or she is terminally ill. Denial, says Doctor Ross, is important and necessary. It helps cushion the impact of the patient's awareness that death is inevitable.

2. *Rage and anger*—"Why me?" The patient resents the fact that others will remain healthy and alive while he or she must die. God is a special target for anger, since He is regarded as imposing, arbitrarily, the death sentence. To those who are shocked at her claim that such anger is not only permissible but inevitable, Doctor Ross replies succinctly, "God can take it."

3. *Bargaining*—"Yes me, but . . ." Patients accept the fact of death but strike bargains for more time. Mostly they bargain with God—"even among people who never talked with God before." They promise to be good or to do something in exchange for another week or month or year of life. Notes Doctor Ross: "What they promise is totally irrelevant, because they don't keep their promises anyway."

4. *Depression*—"Yes, me." First, the

person mourns past losses, things not done, wrongs committed. But then he or she enters a state of "preparatory grief," getting ready for the arrival of death. The patient grows quiet, doesn't want visitors. "When a dying patient doesn't want to see you any more," says Doctor Ross, "this is a sign he has finished his unfinished business with you, and it is a blessing. He can now let go peacefully."

5. *Acceptance*—"My time is very close now and it's all right." Doctor Ross describes this final stage as "not a happy stage, but neither is it unhappy. It's devoid of feelings but it's not resignation, it's really a victory."

These stages provide a very useful guide to understanding the different phases that dying patients may go through. They are not absolute; not everyone goes through every stage, in this exact sequence, at some predictable pace. But this paradigm can, if used in a flexible, insight-producing way, be a valuable tool in understanding why a patient may be behaving as he does.[3]

Dr. Ross has also pointed out that the bereaved normally go through these same stages. How well one handles this grief work, whether before or after the death of a loved one, depends upon a number of factors, including personality, training, emotional stability, and religious faith. Healthy grief work is necessary for the person to achieve the position in which he or she can accept and find meaning in death.

The title of one of Dr. Ross's books, *Death: The Final Stage of Growth*, expresses her conviction that the acceptance of our own death and that of loved ones is ultimately a growing experience wherein we come to recognize the importance of each day of our lives. Growth here means awareness of ourselves and our situation, acceptance of ourselves and others, embracing our own value structures and not merely those of other people, and willingness to share ourselves and our insights with other persons. Out of this, life becomes meaningful just when it seems to have lost all meaning.

B

Dying is something we human beings do continuously, not just at the end of our physical lives on this earth. The stages of dying that I have described apply equally to any significant change (e.g., retirement, moving to a new city, changing jobs, divorce) in a person's life, and change is a regular occurrence in human existence. If you can face and understand your ultimate death, perhaps you can learn to face and deal productively with each change that presents itself in your life. Through a willingness to risk the unknown, to venture forth into unfamiliar territory, you can undertake the search for your own self—the ultimate goal of growth. Through reaching out and committing yourself to dialogue with fellow human beings, you can begin to transcend your individual existence, becoming at one with yourself *and* others. And through a lifetime of such commitment, you can face your final end with peace and joy, knowing that you have lived your life well.[4]

C

It is the denial of death that is partially responsible for people living empty, purposeless lives; for when you live as if you'll live forever, it becomes too easy to

[3]Summarized by Hans O. Mauksch, "The Organizational Context of Dying," in Elisabeth Kübler-Ross, *Death: The Final Stage of Growth* (Englewood Cliffs, N.J.: Prentice-Hall, Inc., 1975), p. 10. Used by permission.
[4]Elisabeth Kübler-Ross, *Death: The Final Stage of Growth*, p. 145.

postpone the things you know that you must do. You live your life in preparation for tomorrow or in remembrance of yesterday, and meanwhile, each today is lost. In contrast, when you fully under- stand that each day you awaken could be the last you have, you take the time *that day* to grow, to become more of who you really are, to reach out to other human beings.[5]

Insights such as these into the meaning of everyday life and the function of death in life have historically been taught by the various religious traditions. As modern society has placed less emphasis upon religious foundations for meaning and purpose in life, these insights and the patterns of behavior they cultivate have often been abandoned—now to be rediscovered by psychologists and others who deal with the difficulties that abandonment creates.

The phenomenon of detachment from death and the inability to deal constructively with it is not limited to modern industrial societies. Yet it seems to be most acute in the societies in which medical advances and death patterns have removed family members and friends from the actual death event. In recent years, attempts to counteract this disengagement have arisen in renewed education about death and in such movements as hospice groups, which provide homelike alternatives to hospital deaths for terminally ill patients.

What is your attitude toward death? How have your experiences with death shaped that understanding?

Do you think that the death of the person closest to you could bring growth to your life?

Is Kubler-Ross correct when she says that acceptance of death can mean acceptance of life, making it more meaningful?

UNIT 56   Death and the Afterlife: Cultural Perspectives

Responses to and treatment of death vary among cultures, as evidenced in the following descriptions. Belief in an afterlife has been almost universal among religious traditions and is often an important feature of cultural attitudes toward death. Although the following examples are drawn from several cultures and their religious traditions, it should be noted that philosophical systems that incorporate monism and pantheism also display a belief in forms of immortality.

Judaism

A

As Judaism firmly believes in the God-given soul, bestowed pure on every man, it also maintains a firm faith in *Olam Haba*, the world to come. This is not the same as the time of the Messiah, or the Resurrection. It is the sheltering of souls in God's eternal dwelling forever. There they will share the joys of their closeness to the divine glory.

Again, Maimonides [a Jewish philosopher] warns against the formulation of any picture. As we do not know God, we know not what He has in store for us. But Judaism does not devote ex-

[5]*Ibid.*, p. 164.

cessive thought to the question of the "salvation" of souls. "All of Israel will have a share in the world to come." "All the righteous of the peoples of the world have a share in it."[6]

As Trepp suggests, the expectation of a Messiah who would right the evils of the world and of a resurrected state in which good would be triumphant have historically been prominent features of Jewish belief (See Unit 57). Yet many modern Jews reject concepts of an afterlife, believing that the present life is a sufficient field of encounter with God, and there is no necessity for continuation. Jewish tradition does not stress doctrinal agreement over such questions.

Christianity

B

In the light of the Christian gospel death appears both as the penalty of sin and as the means of salvation. As the penalty of sin it brings estrangement from God. Not spatial separation from Him . . . but spiritual and moral remoteness from God which makes the sinner's inability to escape from God a torment. . . .

The death of Christ, the second Adam, transforms death, sin's penalty, into a means of deliverance from its guilt and power. Because Christ "has tasted death for every man," He has made death the gateway into eternal life. The crucified Son of God has drawn the sting of death—which is sin. The believer must still undergo "natural" death, but he has been delivered from "the second death" of final estrangement from God. He lives in newness of life, because by the saving grace of God in Christ *he has learned how to die.*[7]

C

The wheel is one of the symbols used in Hindu religion and represents the cyclical nature of existence. This is one of a number on the temple of Surya, Konarak, India. (Reproduced with permission of the Hamlyn Group.)

[6]Leo Trepp, *Judaism: Development and Life* (Belmont, Calif., Dickenson Publishing Co., Inc., 1966), p. 135.

[7]H. F. Lovell Cocks, "Death," in *A Handbook of Christian Theology*, ed. Marvin Halverson and Author A. Cohen (New York: World Publishing Co., 1958), p. 73.

Hinduism

The Hindu believes in *samsara*, that the present life is the result of his previous existences boud by the law of Karma. The law is based on the causal relationship in that what one does in the present form of existence determines what one will be in the next form of existence. This endless cycle of birth, growth, decay, and death will not be broken until one experiences *moksha*—release from samsara. Thus, to one who believes in reincarnation, death is just another phase in the endless cycle of rebirths. "Death is the separation of the soul [Atman] from the physical body; it becomes a starting point for a new life with fresh opportunities. It opens the door for higher forms of life; it is a gateway to fuller life."[8] (See Unit 11)

Taoism

D   Since man is an aspect of Tao, death is but another incident in the eternal movements of nature. It is told of Chuang Tzu that he sang and beat time on a wooden bowl, when his wife lay dead. Reproached for this apparent callousness, he replied that her death was but a change into a new aspect, as fall merges into winter, as a leaf drops from a tree to become leaf mold. For him to grieve over her death would be to show himself ignorant of Tao. In original Taoism, therefore, there is no positive view of life after death, but only the idea of changing into a new aspect of the monistic principle of Tao.[9] (See Unit 13)

Shinto

E   Since one's kami nature will survive death, a man desires to be worthy of being remembered with approbation by his descendants. Therefore it is preferable to die than to fail in duty to one's family or nation. The famous kamikaze pilots of World War II acted on this princi-ple. . . . A kamikaze pilot, by his brave but suicidal action in the national cause, exemplified the height of loyalty to the emperor and his people. He then became an illustrious ancestor, joining the eight hundred myriads of kami beings in the spirit world.[10]

Which, if any, of these views is most similar to yours?
What elements in these passages do you find attractive?
What are the similarities and differences between these views?
What is your own understanding of death or the afterlife?

UNIT 57   Resurrection and Monotheistic Faith

In Western cultures the reality of death and the emphasis upon hope have often been accompanied by the belief in a resurrection of the dead. Resurrection is an ancient concept shared by several Near Eastern religions—among them Judaism

[8]Frederick H. Holck, ed., *Death and Eastern Thought* (Nashville: Abingdon Press, 1974), p. 194.

[9]Bradley, *A Guide to The World's Religions*, p. 138.

[10]*Ibid.*, p. 154. *Kami* is a Shinto word denoting the spiritual force in all things (See Unit 41).

F

(*Jacques Bakke*)

and Christianity. In Egypt, Mesopotamia, and Canaan, the seasonal cycle of nature became the basis for religious affirmations of an interconnection between the annual dying and rising of the gods and the natural productivity of the land. The idea of rising from the dead was, then, part of the common culture that surrounded Israel from its earliest days. It is not surprising to find Hebrew Scriptures, depending upon an utter confidence in the sovereignty of God, referring to dying and rising by God's power (I Samuel 2:6; Deuteronomy 32:39). The story of Elijah's restoring the life of a widow's son goes further to imply a conception of resurrection, although it is not very clearly developed (I Kings 17:17–24).

The Hebrew idea of resurrection and restoration is most vividly portrayed in the writings of the prophets. Grounding their ideas on God's covenantal promises to sustain and not desert Israel—especially the promise made to uphold David's household—the prophets, often faced with difficulty and discouragement, saw the only hope of fulfillment of these promises to lie in a great day of restoration and renewal. "In that day, I will raise up the booth of David that is fallen and repair its breaches, and raise up its ruins, and rebuild it as in the days of old" (Amos 9:11, RSV).

Ezekiel's valley of dry bones (31:1–14) carries the symbolism to the point of restoring dead Israel. From the threat of death and complete extinction, the prophet constantly looks to the day of restoration. In the prophetic treatment, the concept generally remains that of anticipated communal resurrection of Israel as a faithful and blessed community of God.

After the Israelite exile to Babylon, the concept of resurrection began to change in that the communal restitution now was joined to a belief in resurrection of the individual. The books of Daniel and The Maccabees, written in times of national crisis when extinction of the community was a clear possibility, contain affirmations of individual resurrection within a communal hope. Here also the concept of a great day of renewal, when all Israel's enemies would be overcome and Israel would be restored, was joined with the idea of last day of judgment, when each individual would be judged on the basis of his faithfulness or unfaithfulness to God. How much this latter concept can be credited to the influence of Persian religion is a debatable question. It is clear that Persian Zoroastrianism did contain the basic concept of a final great battle of good and evil wherein good would triumph and there would be a general resurrection of the dead. Israelite elaboration of similar concepts came to full fruition in the period after the exile and lengthy contact with the Persian community.

> At that moment Michael shall appear,
> Michael the great captain,
> who stands guard over your fellow-countrymen;
> and there will be a time of distress
> such as has never been . . .
> But at that moment your people will be delivered,
> every one who is written in the book:
> many of those who sleep in the dust of the earth will wake,
> some to everlasting life

and some to the reproach of eternal abhorrence.
The wise leaders shall shine
like the bright vault of heaven,
and those who have guided the people in the true path
shall be like the stars for ever and ever.

Daniel 12:1–3 (NEB)

By the New Testament period, resurrection of both the individual and the community was accepted broadly within the Hebrew community, although not necessarily embraced by all Jews. The attempt of the Sadducees (one of the religious parties that rejected resurrection) to trap Jesus over a question about resurrection illustrates that the concept was disputed belief during the time of Jesus (Mark 12:18–27).

In Hebrew thought, the body meant the whole person, for no distinction was made between physical body and spiritual soul. Resurrection, then, was a resurrection of the entire person. Unlike the Greek concept of an immortal soul which continued after the death of the physical body, the Hebrew understanding envisioned a renewal—a new beginning—for the person. Immortality was, therefore, not a part of original Hebrew belief. Resurrection did not represent a continuation of life, but a renewal made possible only through the grace of God and dependent upon his initiation and his sovereignty.

Christianity, arising in the Hebrew milieu, appropriated belief in both individual and communal resurrection. In Christianity these beliefs formed the background for early church emphasis on the second coming of Christ and became a prominent part of Christian eschatology, as expressed, for example, in the Revelation to John.

However, Christianity did not simply adopt the ancient ideas. The Christian testimony and affirmation that the man Jesus had been resurrected carried the concept to a new and unique dimension. Christianity did not apply resurrection to the distant future but declared that it was now present in history itself. God's sovereignty over life *and* death was evident within historical life as a dynamically different testimony to God's love. The death and then the resurrection became the climactic act in the drama of Jesus' revelation of God's love and power. It served as the central sign of God's power over man's sin and over the demons and powers of the universe. Jesus' exaltation, through resurrection, as the Lord of life came to symbolize the new life of a Christian believer. "So you must consider yourselves dead to sin and alive to God in Christ Jesus" (Romans 6:1, RSV). In this central act the Christian saw God's ultimate sovereignty, his gracious love of humankind, and humanity's dependence upon his grace. Belief in this unique act carried a new realization of one's own relationship to God and dependence on the love revealed in Jesus' life, death, and resurrection. For the Christian, the concept of resurrection was no longer limited to that which had been accepted among the Jews but was significantly and decisively expanded. It now constituted a new revelation of God's love and therefore became a unique event. Resurrection of Jesus, then, was and is a central precept of ancient and modern Christian belief; it gave new understanding of God and became the basis of Christian trust (faith) in him.

Christianity has also conceptualized Jesus' resurrection as testimony to the reality of the more ancient concepts of resurrection. Jesus' resurrection—an example of God's might, power, and inexhaustible love—has become the touchstone of belief in personal and communal resurrection appropriated from the Jewish culture. (It is interesting that modern Judaism has, to a large degree, rejected the belief in individual resurrection, although the messianic expectation of communal renewal is still widely accepted.) The ancient concepts and the new understanding of resurrection as revealed in Jesus, though distinguishable in Christianity, are closely related. They have occasionally been confused with each other, causing variant understandings to arise.

Why do Christians insist that belief in resurrection is necessary to Christian faith?

For further comments on resurrection see Paul's commentary in I Corinthians 15 and I Thessalonians 4.

13 _____

Salvation and Redemption

INTRODUCTION

Heaven, Nirvana, enlightenment, wholeness, self-actualization, absorption into the ultimate, concord, reconciliation between humans and God—these and many other terms refer to the ultimate goal, or destiny, of human beings as proclaimed in the various religious traditions. The term *salvation* itself is closely identified with the Christian religious tradition. It connotes a process or event or state of healing or health, fulfillment, and wholeness. But every religion has a concept, or concepts, of wholeness and fulfillment, and most religions stress the need to arrive at this state from a state of brokenness or lack or separation.

In this chapter, the concepts of salvation and redemption are examined. The terms take on rich meaning and variety of use not only among different religious traditions but also within the same tradition. Some aspects of this richness and diversity are dealt with in the units that follow. These units explore (1) the meaning of the concept *salvation*, (2) a concept of salvation that is identified with God's grace or divine action, and (3) varied expressions, both religious and secular, of the vision of the transition from the present "broken" age or world to a new and transformed age or world, a vision that often expresses most fully what *salvation* means to groups or individuals.

UNIT 58   Salvation

Salvation is a key term in Christian religious traditions. It has a variety of meanings that have partly depended on particular theological perspectives and specific historical settings. Because of its key role in dominantly Christian societies, it has sometimes been transferred to secular or nonreligious contexts. Whatever the interpretation, however, the concept signifies movement from one state or condition of being—a bad, deficient, inadequate, or "lost" state—to another—a good, fulfilled, adequate, or "saved" state. This movement may be interpreted as something that suddenly grasps one. It may mean an unfolding and developing process, a growth into the new life, a developing insight or change of character. Whatever the process, salvation implies the belief that something is wrong in the present natural state of human life, that existence has gone askew. Human beings are in a "fallen" or "sinful" state and need restoration to a redeemed or God- or reality-centered state.

Redemption, or restoration, depends upon some activity, process, event, or agent that can reorient one's existence. For the Christian, the agent is God's love in Jesus Christ and the process or event of salvation involves belief and trust in God's mercy given in Christ. Salvation, in this case, means being saved from a destructive self-centeredness through repentance and faith in Jesus Christ.

A

> It [the gift of Jesus] is the saving power of God for everyone who has faith . . . because here is revealed God's way of righting the wrong, a way that starts from faith and ends in faith.   (Romans 1:16–17, NEB)

The concept itself is not, however, limited to Christianity, but is found in one form or another in other religions, as the following example illustrates.

B

The transcendental vibration established by the chanting of Hare Krishna, Hare Krishna, Krishna Krishna, Hare Hare/ Hare Rāma, Hare Rāma, Rāma Rāma, Hare Hare is the sublime method for reviving our transcendental consciousness. As living spiritual souls, we are all originally Krishna conscious entities, but due to our association with matter from time immemorial, our consciousness is now adulterated by the material atmosphere. The material atmosphere, in which we are now living, is called *māyā*, or illusion. *Māyā* means that which is not. And what is this illusion? The illusion is that we are all trying to be lords of material nature, while actually we are under the grip of her stringent laws. . . . We are trying to exploit the resources of material nature, but actually we are becoming more and more entangled in her complexities. Therefore, although we are engaged in a hard struggle to conquer nature, we are ever more dependent on her. This illustory struggle against nature can be stopped at once by revival of our eternal Krishna consciousness.

Hare Krishna, Hare Krishna, Krishna Krishna, Hare Hare is the transcendental process for reviving this original pure consciousness. By chanting this transcendental vibration, we can cleanse away all misgivings within our hearts. The basic principle of all such misgivings is the false consciousness that I am the lord of all I survey.[1]

[1]A. C. Bhaktvedanta Swami Prabhupada, *On Chanting the Hare Krishna Mantra* (Boston: Iskcon Press, n.d.), p. 5.

Every religion has a concept, or concepts, of salvation. For the Hindu, the movement from *maya* (illusion) to *moksha* (release from the cycle of rebirths), and for the Buddhist, the movement from bondage to destructive desire to Nirvana signify salvation, or fulfillment. Concepts of salvation appear even in secular movements and ideologies. The Marxist concept of a classless society in which there will be no oppression and in which there will be equality, material plenty, and freedom for all is a concept of salvation. In Nazi Germany the concept of the thousand-year reich in which the Aryan master race would rule the world was a concept of salvation.

> *Do you believe that every individual has, or needs, some concept of salvation in order for life to make sense?*

UNIT 59   Grace as Divine Acceptance

The *religious* concept of salvation depends generally on action on behalf of an individual or society by God (or the gods). In the Christian tradition this action is denoted by the word *grace*. It is a central concept characteristic of the tradition. The basic idea is also found in other, but not in all, religions.

For some in the Christian community, grace is understood in an objective sense, primarily signifying the beneficence of God toward the natural order—including humanity—which he has created. This view has been preserved and transmitted within the Roman Catholic tradition, in which grace has often referred to a supernatural substance bestowed upon the believer to supplement and complete his natural being.

The term *grace (charis)* was used by common people in Greek times at the beginning of letters to mean simply "Hi! I hope you are well." Paul took the word and infused it with new meaning. For Paul, man stands in court before God indicted for disobedience and guilty as charged. But God, even though He is judge, does not act in wrath, but through Jesus His Son offers forgiveness to those who throw themselves upon the mercy of the court. This unmerited, undeserved willingness of God to treat men as innocent even though guilty he terms "grace."

On the other hand, some understand grace in a subjective sense. As Hegel points out, a new awareness and concern arose in Europe, and especially Germany, in the late medieval period—the internalization both of guilt and of grace.

This development set the stage for the modern Protestant exploration of the meaning of grace. Paul Tillich, in one of the most famous Christian sermons of the twentieth century, explores the idea of grace as inner experience.

A   Sin and grace are bound to each other. We do not even have a knowledge of sin unless we have already experienced the unity of life, which is grace. And conversely, we could not grasp the meaning of grace without having experienced the separation of life, which is sin. Grace is just as difficult to describe as sin. For some people, grace is the willingness of a divine king and father to forgive ever and again the foolishness and weakness of his subjects and children. We must reject such a concept of grace; for it is a merely childish destruction of human dignity. For others, grace is a magic power in the dark places of the soul, but a power without any significance for practical life, a quickly vanishing and useless idea. For others, grace is the benevolence that we may find beside the cruelty and destructiveness in life. But then, it does not matter whether we say "life goes on," or whether we say "there is grace in life"; if grace means no more than this, the word should, and will disappear. For other people, grace indicates the gifts that one has received from nature or society, and the power to do good things with the help of these gifts. But grace is more than gifts. In grace something is overcome; grace occurs "in spite of" something; grace occurs in spite of separation and estrangement. Grace is the reunion of life with life, the reconciliation of the self with itself. Grace is the acceptance of that which is rejected. Grace transforms fate into a meaningful destiny; it changes guilt into confidence and courage. There is something triumphant in the word "grace": in spite of the abounding of sin grace abounds much more. . . .

"Where sin abounded, grace did much more abound," says Paul in the same letter in which he describes the unimaginable power of separation and self-destruction within society and the individual soul. He does not say these words because sentimental interests demand a happy ending for everything tragic. He says them because they describe the most overwhelming and determining experience of his life. In the picture of Jesus as the Christ, which appeared to him at the

moment of his greatest separation from other men, from himself and God, he found himself accepted in spite of his being rejected. And when he found that he was accepted, he was able to accept himself and to be reconciled to others. The moment in which grace struck him and overwhelmed him, he was reunited with that to which he belonged, and from which he was estranged in utter strangeness. Do we know what it means to be struck by grace? It does *not* mean that we suddenly believe that God exists, or that Jesus is the Saviour, or that the Bible contains the truth. To believe that something *is*, is almost contrary to the meaning of grace. Furthermore, grace does not mean simply that we are making progress in our moral self-control, in our fight against society. Moral progress may be a fruit of grace, but it is not grace itself, and it can even prevent us from receiving grace. For there is too often a graceless acceptance of Christian doctrines and a graceless battle against the structures of evil in our personalities. Such a graceless relation to God may lead us by necessity either to arrogance or to despair. It would be better to refuse God and the Christ and the Bible than to accept Them without grace. For if we accept without grace, we do so in the state of separation, and can only succeed in deepening the separation. We cannot transform our lives, unless we allow them to be transformed by that stroke of grace. It happens; or it does not happen. And certainly it does *not* happen so long as we think in our self-complacency, that we have no need of it. Grace strikes us when we are in great pain and restlessness. It strikes us when we walk through the dark valley of a meaningless and empty life. It strikes us when we feel that our separation is deeper than usual, because we have violated another life, a life which we loved, or from which we were estranged. It strikes us when our disgust for our own being, our indifference, our weakness, our hostility, and our lack of direction and composure have become intolerable to us. It strikes us when, year after year, the longed-for perfection of life does not appear, when the old compulsions reign within us as they have for decades, when despair destroys all joy and courage. Sometimes at that moment a wave of light breaks into our darkness, and it is as though a voice were saying: "You are accepted. *You are accepted*, accepted by that which is greater than you, and the name of which you do not know. Do not ask for the name now; perhaps you will find it later. Do not try to do anything now; perhaps later you will do much. Do not seek for anything; do not perform anything; do not intend anything. *Simply accept the fact that you are accepted!*" If that happens to us, we experience grace. After such an experience we may not be better than before, and we may not believe more than before. But everything is transformed. In the moment grace conquers sin, and reconciliation bridges the gulf of estrangement. And nothing is demanded of this experience, no religious or moral or intellectual presupposition, nothing but *acceptance*.

In the light of this grace we perceive the power of grace in our relation to others and to ourselves. We experience the grace of being able to look frankly into the eyes of another, the miraculous grace of understanding each other's words. We understand not merely the literal meaning of the words, but also that which lies behind them, even then there is a longing to break through the walls of separation.

We experience the grace of being able to accept the life of another, even if it be hostile and harmful to us, for, through grace, we know that it belongs to the same Ground to which we belong, and by which we have been accepted. We experience the grace which is able to overcome the tragic separation of the sexes, of the generations, of the nations, of the races, and even the utter strangeness between man and nature. Sometimes grace appears in all these separations to reunite us with those to whom we belong. For life belongs to life.

And in the light of this grace we perceive the power of grace in our relation to ourselves. We experience moments in which we accept ourselves, because we feel that we have been accepted by that which is greater than we. If only more such moments were given to us! For it is such moments that make us love our life, that make us accept ourselves, not in our goodness and self-complacency, but in our certainty of the eternal meaning of our life. We cannot compel anyone to accept himself. But sometimes it happens that we receive the power to say "yes" to ourselves, that peace enters into us and makes us whole, that self-hate and self-contempt disappear, and that our self is reunited with itself. Then we can say that grace has come upon us.[2]

B

"What shall I render unto the Lord," that, whilst my memory recalls these things, my soul is not affrighted at them? I will love Thee, O Lord, and thank Thee, and confess unto Thy name; because Thou has forgiven me these so great and heinous deeds of mine. To Thy grace I ascribe it, and to Thy mercy, that Thou has melted away my sins as it were ice. To Thy grace I ascribe also whatsoever I have not done of evil; for what might I not have done, who even loved a sin for its own sake? Yea, all I confess to have been forgiven me; both what evils I committed by my own wilfulness, and what by Thy guidance I committed not.[3]

---

[2]Excerpts from *The Shaking of the Foundations*, pp. 155–56, and 160–63, by Paul Tillich are reprinted with the permission of Charles Scribner's Sons. Copyright 1948 Charles Scribner's Sons.

[3]Saint Augustine, "The Morals of the Catholic Church," in *Basic Writings of St. Augustine*, Vol. I, ed. Whitney J. Oates (New York: Random House, Inc., 1948).

Objective and subjective understandings of what God's grace is and how it brings salvation to humans are usually combined in Christian traditions. Grace is usually thought of as something real (objective) that God bestows on humans either directly or through agencies he has created (the church, preaching, the sacraments). It is also usually held to be accompanied by a personal (subjective) awareness on the recipient's part. Some Christian traditions (Roman Catholic, for example, and some Protestant) have stressed the need for human cooperative response to God's grace (even if God has in some sense previously provided grace to enable the response). Others (especially Lutheran and Calvinist traditions) have insisted that God's grace *and* human response to it are entirely a gift from God and that it is misleading to speak of the cooperation of those who can only passively receive. Whatever a particular Christian's definition of grace, it represents the power of God acting within life, transforming the life of the believer.

A similar concept of the graciousness of the Divine is found in those forms of Hinduism that stress reliance on the gods Vishnu and Shiva for assistance in attaining release from reincarnation. For the Mahayana Buddhist, the role of the *Bodhisattva* suggests a form of gracious love benefiting the believer in the journey toward Nirvana. Muslim and Jewish tradition incorporate similar concepts whereby salvation is dependent on God's gracious love. Even in polytheistic religions, there is frequently a concept of grace as the special unbidden, unmerited state bestowed on some human individual or group by a god or goddess. A kind of grace, or healing and restoring power, may be conferred by the impersonal (divine) nature of things. This is exemplified in some of the Greek tragedies, as when Oedipus, after having suffered terribly in expiation of a fate-ordained violation of the order of nature by murdering his father and marrying his mother, became a source of blessing (grace) to those among whom he resided.

UNIT 60   Eschatology: The Coming Fulfillment

The supreme vision of what salvation—health, wholeness, fulfillment, well-being—means in a religious or secular tradition may often be seen in its *eschatology*. The term *eschatology* literally means "a study of last things" and in Christian tradition includes doctrines dealing with the end of history—both the termination and transformation of history as we know it. Among Christian groups, eschatology includes interpretation of such concepts as the second coming of Christ, resurrection of the dead, immortality of the soul, final judgment, and Heaven and Hell.

For some, Christian eschatology may be focused primarily on the destiny of individuals (the soul, what happens after death). Ordinarily, however, eschatology for Christians is centered not only on the ultimate fate of individuals in relation to good and evil and God's ultimate power, but also on the ultimate destiny of the whole human race and of the cosmos. Thus, Christian eschatology reflects the earlier tradition of Jewish apocalyptic which, especially from about 170 B.C.E. until the second destruction of Jerusalem by the Romans in 135 C.E., was expressed in *apocalyptic* works. *Apocalypse* means revelation, and *apocalyptic* writings of Judaism depicted in highly symbolic form the present as a time in which the dominant forces of evil were about to be defeated by the power of God. The struggle was foreseen as bitter and intense, frequently involving terrible suffering of humans, both evil and good (those who remained faithful to God in spite of terrible persecution). The results of the struggle would be a complete, decisive, and final triumph of God and the forces of good, a cosmological victory which would result in the transition from the old evil order of things in our world to a new and perfect realm under God's justice. Salvation would be finally real: The faithful would be vindicated and the evil judged and rendered powerless and ineffectual.

While such an understanding of eschatology is familiar in Christian, Jewish, and Islamic traditions, it is by no means the only pattern. In the selections that follow, eschatological concepts, both religious and secular, of what complete salvation will mean and beliefs about how it will come about, are presented.

I

A   The Communist Internationale

Arise, you wretched and downtrodden
Hungry, enslaved masses of the earth.
Our outraged spirits cry out:
We are ready to fight to the end
To destroy the world ruled by violence.
We will build a new world,
Our world of freedom.
Those who are nothing
    will inherit the earth.

The eschatology of communism is articulated clearly in the words of the Communist Internationale and in the statement by Lenin that follows. According to Marxist communism, vigorous struggle is underway between the forces of the "workers" and the "capitalists," a struggle within history with an anticipated completion within history. The success of the struggle against "the capitalist yoke" and the "world ruled by violence" is already apparent, with the final victory of the horizon. The vision of the "new world, a world of freedom" in which "those who have nothing will inherit the earth" is a bright hope to which the adherents of this veiw look with eager longing. True to the eschatological perspective, the affirmation is also a challenge to renewed action and dedication.

In the words of V. I. Lenin:

B   Now the workers, who are still faithful to   yoke, call themselves Communists. This
the cause of throwing off the capitalist   union of Communists is growing all over

the world, and, in a number of countries, Soviet power has already won. Not long from now, we will see the victory of Communism everywhere. We will see the establishment of a worldwide Federated Republic of the Soviets.[4]

(*Jacques Bakke*)

II

The civil rights movement in the United States drew upon three powerful sources for its strength and impetus: the affirmations of the Constitution and of the Jewish and Christian faiths concerning the rights and dignity of individuals. Martin Luther King, committed to nonviolent love, was aware that he was involved in a life-and-death struggle.

Yet the sense of imminent victory and the vision of a day of fulfillment implicit in the eschatological perspective are apparent in the statement that follows. This sense of approaching triumph was even more intense when the speech was

[4]"The Russian Revolution," produced by Leroy Pakins, Columbia Records, Inc., © 1967, CBS Legacy Collection.

delivered at the civil rights march on Washington in August 1963. Approximately 200,000 persons gathered on the Mall between the Washington Monument and the Lincoln Memorial to demonstrate peacefully in support of pending civil rights legislation. To the outside observer, it seemed that there were many people involved, but the event was nothing extraordinary. To the person inside the civil rights movement, however, it was a tremendous sign of the strength of the movement and its fast-approaching victory.

C

I say to you today, my friends, even though we face the difficulties of today and tomorrow, I still have a dream. It is a dream deeply rooted in the American dream.

I have a dream that one day this nation will rise up and live out the true meaning of its creed: "We hold these truths to be self-evident; that all men are created equal."

I have a dream that one day on the red hills of Georgia the sons of former slaves and the sons of former slaveowners will be able to sit down together at the table of brotherhood.

I have a dream that one day even the state of Mississippi, a state sweltering with the heat of injustice, sweltering with the heat of oppression, will be transformed into an oasis of freedom and justice.

I have a dream that my four little children will one day live in a nation where they will not be judged by the color of their skin but by the content of their character.

I have a dream today.

I have a dream that one day, down in Alabama, with its vicious racists, with its Governor having his lips dripping with the words of interposition and nullification, one day right there in Alabama little black boys and little black girls will be able to join hands with little white boys and white girls as sisters and brothers.

I have a dream today.

I have a dream that one day every valley shall be exalted, every hill and mountain shall be made low, the rough places will be made plain, and the crooked places will be made straight, and the glory of the Lord shall be revealed, and all flesh shall see it together.

This is our hope. This is the faith with which I return to the South. With this faith we will be able to hew out of this mountain of despair a stone of hope. With this faith we will be able to transform the jangling discords of our nation into a beautiful symphony of brotherhood. With this faith we will be able to work together, to pray together, to struggle together, to go to jail together, to stand up for freedom together, knowing that we will be free one day. . . .

Let freedom ring from every hill and molehill of Mississippi. From every mountainside, let freedom ring. And when this happens—when we let freedom ring, when we let it ring from every village and every hamlet, from every state and every city, we will be able to speed up that day when all of God's children, black men and white men, Jews and Gentiles, Protestants and Catholics, will be able to join hands and sing in the words of the old Negro spiritual, "Free at last! free at last! thank God almighty, we are free at last!"[5]

III

During the mid- and late 1960s, many Americans, especially the young, became convinced that their society was dominated by oppressive political and economic

[5]Martin Luther King, Jr., "I Have A Dream" from *Selected Speeches from American History*, ed. by Robert T. Oliver and Eugene E. White (Boston: Allyn and Bacon, Inc., 1966), pp. 293–94. Reprinted by permission of Joan Daves. Copyright © 1963 by Martin Luther King, Jr.

power. They protested America's prosecution of a war in Vietnam, the continued denial of equal rights to Americans, especially blacks, and attitudes of thoughtless greed on the part of large corporations, resulting in pollution of the environment. Some became convinced that America could be saved by a transformation of consciousness, changing attitudes of selfishness, aggression, and greed to those of peacefulness and love. This notion was expressed in a book that quickly became a best-seller, *The Greening of America*, written by a Yale law school professor.[6] It probably found its most popular and effective expression in the words and music of a successful folk-rock musical called *Hair*, which was later made into a powerful film, dramatizing protest against the Vietnam War, racial discrimination, and subordination of the individual, especially the young, to harsh and puritanical moral and economic restrictions by an uncaring older-generation establishment. The song "Aquarius" captures what many of the young involved in "the movement" of the sixties believed and shows how, often indiscriminately, sources of salvation were sought—in reinterpretations of traditional religious figures (Jesus, Gautama) and their teachings, in commonly rejected sources of spiritual insight (astrology), in drugs and rock music and free sexual expression as sources of consciousness transformation. In the eyes of many of the younger and some of the older generation of that time period, institutionalized religion, especially Christianity and Judaism, had failed to protest the wrongs of society, indeed frequently had given moral support to war and racial injustice. "Aquarius" thus brought to bear a semireligious world view—astrology—in support of longed-for social and individual experiences.

D

When the moon is in the seventh house,
   and Jupiter aligns with Mars,
Then peace will guide the planets
   and love will steer the stars.

This is the dawning of the Age of Aquarius,
The Age of Aquarius, Aquarius, Aquarius.

Harmony and Understanding,
   sympathy and trust abounding,
No more falsehoods or derisions,
   golden living dreams of visions,
Mystic crystal revelation
   and the mind's true liberation,
Aquarius, Aquarius.

When the moon is in the seventh house
   and Jupiter aligns with Mars,
Then peace will guide the planets
   and love will steer the stars.

This is the dawning of the Age of Aquarius,
The Age of Aquarius, Aquarius, Aquarius
   Aquarius, Aquarius, Aquarius.[7]

[6]Charles A. Reich, *The Greening of America* (New York: Random House, Inc., 1970).
[7]"Aquarius" © 1966, 1967, 1968 James Rado, Gerome Ragni, Galt MacDermot, Nat Shapiro, and United Artists Music Co., Inc. All rights administered by United Artists Music Co. Inc. Used by permission.

IV

For Jeremiah, like the prophets before him and the apocalyptic thinkers who came afterward, history was the arena in which God was at work. The purpose of his activity was the creation of a redeemed, responsive people. Yet Jeremiah believed that the history of the Hebrew nation had become the history of a continuing conflict between God and many within the Jewish covenant people. This could not continue. Jeremiah had spent his life delivering, though reluctantly and sometimes almost bitterly, the word from God concerning his judgment. He told the people of Judah that God's judgment was against them. He prophesied an invasion of Judah from the North. Few believed him because the King of Judah had surrounded himself with false prophets of optimism who said that all was well with God's people.

Suddenly, after the destruction of Jerusalem in 598 B.C.E. and before its devastation in 587 B.C.E. by the Babylonians, everybody believed. And just as suddenly the word of God changed from doom to hope. Jeremiah announced God's decision to fulfill his ancient purpose in the times to come. The "old" covenant would be perfected by a "new" covenant written within the heart, and God's purpose behind the old would become a reality in the new—"I will be their God, and they shall be my people." The struggle between faithful God and unfaithful people, which had infected the life of man and nature, would be resolved, and the Jewish nation would fully become that which God had intended: the faithful wife of a compassionate "husband."

E Behold, the days are coming, says the Lord, when I will sow the house of Israel and the house of Judah with the seed of man and the seed of beast. And it shall come to pass that as I have watched over them to pluck up and break down, to overthrow, destroy, and bring evil, so I will watch over them to build and to plant, says the Lord.

In those days they shall no longer say: "The fathers have eaten sour grapes, and the children's teeth are set on edge." But everyone shall die for his own sin; each man who eats sour grapes, his teeth shall be set on edge.

Behold, the days are coming, says the Lord, when I will make a new covenant with the house of Israel and the house of Judah, not like the covenant which I made with their fathers when I took them by the hand to bring them out of the land of Egypt, my covenant which they broke, though I was their husband, says the Lord. But this is the covenant which I will make with the house of Israel after those days, says the Lord: I will put my law within them, and I will write it upon their hearts; and I will be their God, and they shall be my people. And no longer shall each man teach his neighbor and each his brother, saying "Know the Lord," for they shall all know me, from the least of them to the greatest, says the Lord; for I will forgive their iniquity, and I will remember their sin no more. (Jeremiah 31:27–34, RSV)

V

The following passage from the Koran is an example of one of the most common types of eschatology, one which looks for an end to the present existence and something totally new in the times to come.

Mohammed clearly announced the coming of a day of judgment by Allah, when the earth and all creation would be shaken and Allah would come on his Throne. The judgment would follow, each man being rewarded or punished in accord with his actions in this world.

Mohammed had declared in pronouncements found elsewhere in Muslim Scriptures that this life is a time of testing, when man must choose between submission to Allah and the doing of his will, and following the way of Satan, the rebel against the All-Merciful. This struggle between the forces of good and evil, of righteousness and sin, inevitably and unalterably will end with the assertion of Allah's sovereignty and power. The wise man chooses and lives by the will of Allah, and lives this life in awareness of the new life to come.

F

So, when the Trumpet is blown with a single blast
and the earth and the mountains are lifted up and crushed with a single
    blow,
then, on that day, the Terror shall come to pass,
and heaven shall split, for upon that day it shall be very frail,
and the angels shall stand upon its borders,
and upon that day eight shall carry above them
the Throne of the Lord.
On that day you shall be exposed, not one secret of yours concealed.
Then as for him who is given his book in his right hand,
he shall say, "Here, take and read my book!
Certainly I thought that I should encounter my reckoning." So he
        shall be in a pleasing life
        in a lofty Garden,
        its clusters nigh to gather.
"Eat and drink with wholesome appetite for that
you did long ago, in the days gone by."

But as for him who is given his book in his left hand,
he shall say, "Would that I had not been given my book and not known
    my reckoning! Would it had been the end!
        My wealth has not availed me,
        my authority is gone from me."
Take him, and fetter him, and then roast him
in Hell, then in a chain of seventy cubits' length
insert him! Behold, he never believed in God
the All-mighty, and he never urged the feeding
of the needy; therefore he today has not here
one loyal friend, neither any food saving foul pus,
that none excepting the sinners eat.[8]

The Koran, Sura LXIX

[8]Reprinted with permission of Macmillan, Inc., from *The Koran Interpreted* by Arthur J. Arberry, Sura LXIX, verses 13–37. © George Allen & Unwin, Ltd. 1955.

VI

Written some 500 years before the ministry of Mohammed, the following passage likewise looks forward to the complete and final end of this world and the coming of a new, splendid creation. But although Mohammed may have envisioned a complete reordering of this creation, the author of the Revelation to John thought it beyond renovation.

This work articulates apocalyptic eschatology at its fullest. The author saw in the historical events just before and during his time the implementation in human experience of the cosmic, age-old plan and purpose of God. Men and nations were caught up in the pervasive struggle between God and Satan, Christ and Anti-Christ, the saints and the wicked. Convinced that God had revealed to him the secrets of his purpose and activity, he interpreted for his fellow Christians the hidden, "real" meaning of what appeared to be ordinary, worldly events. And then would come the end—very shortly.

The portrayal of the end of the present heaven and earth is bluntly stated, followed by the resurrection and the judgment. But the author quickly passes to his real interest—the glorious new existence which is to come. In the new heaven and the new earth, the "sea"—which in Jewish literature had come to stand for all that threatens human life—would be no more. The covenant promise to ancient Israel would be fulfilled, not within but beyond history. God—the beginning and the end of all things—would make it so.

G
Then I saw a great white throne
and him who sat upon it;
from his presence earth and sky fled away,
    and no place was found for them.
And I saw the dead, great and small,
    standing before the throne,
and books were opened.
Also another book was opened,
    which is the book of life.
And the dead were judged by what was written
in the books, by what they had done.
And the sea gave up the dead in it, Death and
Hades gave up the dead in them, and all were
judged by what they had done.
Then Death and Hades were thrown into the
lake of fire. This is the second death,
the lake of fire; and if any one's name was
not found written in the book of life, he
was thrown into the lake of fire.
Then I saw a new heaven and a new earth;
for the first heaven and the first earth
    had passed away,
and the sea was no more.

And I saw the holy city, new Jerusalem,
coming down out of heaven from God,
    prepared as a bride adorned for her husband;
and I heard a great voice from the throne saying,
    "Behold, the dwelling of God is with men.
    He will dwell with them,
    and they shall be his people,
    and God himself will be with them;
    he will wipe away every tear from their eyes,
    and death shall be no more.
    neither shall there be mourning nor crying
        nor pain any more,
    for the former things have passed away." . . .
And he said to me,
    "It is done!
    I am the Alpha and the Omega,
        the beginning and the end."
The Revelation to John 20:11–21:4, 6 (RSV)

Some Christian religious groups have almost completely ignored eschatological elements in the earlier Christian traditions; other groups—for instance, the Jehovah's Witnesses—have made them their dominant concern. Why do some religious traditions emphasize eschatological salvation as a universal, cosmic event whereas others do not?

In traditions emphasizing mystical religion, eschatology often takes the form of inner subjective fulfillment, union or communion with the Divine, rather than looking to a fulfilling future historical state. What forms of eschatology—visions of a fulfilled or perfected state of being involving all, or most, humans and the future world—other than those presented in the unit above, can you think of?

14 _____

The Religious Matrix
of Interpersonal Relations

INTRODUCTION

In the preceding section, we have examined the self and the dimensions of religion that affect its sense of identity, its selfhood. Now we move to a discussion of the sociocultural setting that profoundly affects the way persons define what selfhood means. The social setting of the self is all important both for the sense of personal identity and for the religious dimensions of the self's experiences.

A moral code, or competing codes of morality, and a definition, or definitions, of truth, competing scientific systems, and competing systems of religious belief and practice will be offered to the individual by society, by the culture that the individual participates in, inherits, belongs to, or inhabits.

Religion—every religion, even the religion of a tiny minority—is a social phenomenon. And culture is a social product. Religion is a part of culture. Some anthropologists have defined culture as "the social heritage . . . the sum of the historical achievements of human social life transmitted in the form of a tradition."[1] According to this definition, the term *culture* would refer to the things a society teaches the individuals who are members of that society. Culture then would be something already existing that individuals absorb or passively acquire.

Other students of human behavior have questioned this definition of culture. The anthropologist David Bidney holds that humans are active creators and transformers of culture.[2] And the sociologists Peter Berger and Thomas Luckmann write,

[1]David Bidney, *Theoretical Anthropology* (New York: Columbia University Press, 1953), p. 25.
[2]*Ibid.*

"Society is a human product. Society is an objective reality. Man is a social product."[3] Berger and Luckmann emphasize here that humans are created by their societies and the cultures of those societies but that ultimately the societies and cultures are created by actual, specific, individual human beings interacting with other human beings. According to this view, culture is not just something handed down from generation to generation: each person, in interaction with other persons—in interaction with the whole of society during that person's life's span—creates culture by acquiring and transforming it.

To see the connectedness of selves in society is not sufficient. We need to analyze various ways in which religious commitment enters the process of individual and group interaction. In the present section, we consider general dimensions of individual and group, and of group and group, interaction. Ethical dimensions of the web of interpersonal relations are presented. Also, the role of religion in promoting social stability and as an agent of social change and as affected by social change is examined.

Our concern in this chapter is to explore the context in which the self relates to other selves. Every self finds itself defined in interpersonal relationships with other selves. One is neither born nor lives in a vacuum. Most of daily living consists of interpersonal relationships with others, so the interaction between individuals is a most significant element in our understanding of ourselves and the society, or societies, in which we live. The units in this chapter focus on ethical issues that arise as a person relates to others—primarily on the way the individual relates to other individuals. The discussion of ethical issues involving relationships between groups will be considered in the next chapter.

The first unit deals with the tension or dynamic interplay that exists between an individual and his or her community. We then turn to an exploration of love and duty as two approaches to personal involvement in a community. Finally, we examine the connection between particular actions and the motivations for those actions.

The phrase *religious matrix* in the title of this chapter refers to the creative power of religion to give meaning to relationships between the self and others.

UNIT 61   The Individual and the Community

In the modern world the desire to preserve individual identity is seldom exactly and delicately balanced with the concurrent necessity to participate in corporate life. Each changing moment tilts the balance one way or the other, and many feel that life results in a frightening and often disorienting seesaw as we try to be ourselves in an increasingly complex world. Historically, humans seeking to escape such disorientation have emphasized one aspect of identity over the other. An emphasis on

[3]Peter L. Berger and Thomas Luckmann, *The Social Construction of Reality* (Garden City, N.Y.: Doubleday & Co., Inc., 1966), p. 58.

either pole reflects a particular understanding of the human role in the natural order. These interpretations of humanity in turn reflect religious beliefs or perceptions that are often illustrated in secular and religious literature.

William Ernest Henley, writing in the late nineteenth century, reflects the extreme individualism of the period, the roots of which reach back at least into the eighteenth century.

A Out of the night that covers me,
　　Black as the Pit from pole to pole,
I thank whatever gods may be
　　For my unconquerable soul.

In the fell clutch of circumstance
　　I have not winced nor cried aloud.
Under the bludgeonings of chance
　　My head is bloody, but unbowed.

Beyond this place of wrath and tears
　　Looms but the Horror of the shade,
And yet the menace of the years
　　Finds, and shall find, me unafraid.

It matters not how strait the gate,
　　How charged with punishments the scroll,
I am the master of my fate;
　　I am the captain of my soul.[4]

Henley's poem emphasizes the individual's capability to determine his or her life. Little room is left for the influence of other persons and society, or for any Divine influence on life events. For Henley, the "gods," if there be any, clearly have no final or pervasive control over life or the future: It is the individual who determines his or her own fate.

B Some thirty inches from my nose
The frontier of my Person goes,
And all the untilled air between
Is private *pagus* or demesne.
Stranger, unless with bedroom eyes,
I beckon you to fraternize,
Beware of rudely crossing it:
I have no gun, but I can spit.[5]

In this brief poem, W.H. Auden also stresses the need to be an individual—everyone must have one's own space, one's own being. Yet he recognizes the

[4]William Ernest Henley, "Invictus," in *Poems* (New York: Charles Scribner's Sons, 1919), p. 119.
[5]W. H. Auden, "Thanksgiving for a Habitat," in *About The House* (New York: Random House, Inc., 1963), p. 4. Copyright © 1965. Reprinted by permission of Random House, Inc.

concurrent reality: No individual is alone, an island unto himself or herself. An individual is always part of some community. While one may be responsible for maintaining personal identity in the context of a community, one can never escape the reality of the social character of human existence.

This social nature of humanity has led many to understand the interests, goals, and purposes of the community to supersede those of the individual. Personal fulfillment in life does not necessarily depend on what accrues to one, but rather on one's contribution to the community. This interpretation led Mo-ti, an early Chinese moral philosopher, to insist that the needs of a community overarch and encompass those of an individual:

C   Mo-ti said: The purpose of the magnanimous is to be found in procuring benefits for the world and eliminating its calamities.

But what are the benefits of the world and what its calamities?

Mo-ti said: Mutual attacks among states, mutual usurpation among houses, mutual injuries among individuals; the lack of grace and loyalty between ruler and ruled, the lack of affection and filial piety between father and son, the lack of harmony between elder and younger brothers—these are the major calamities in the world.

But whence did these calamities arise, out of mutual love?

Mo-ti said: They arise out of want of mutual love. At present feudal lords have learned only to love their own states and not those of others. Therefore they do not scruple about attacking other states. The heads of houses have learned only to love their own houses and not those of others. Therefore they do not scruple about usurping other houses. And individuals have learned only to love themselves and not others. . . . Therefore all the calamities, strifes, complaints, and hatred in the world have arisen out of the want of mutual love. . . .

But what is the way of universal love and mutual aid?

Mo-ti said: It is to regard the state of others as one's own, the houses of others as one's own, the persons of others as one's self. When feudal lords love one another there will be no more war; when heads of houses love one another there will be no more mutual usurpation; when individuals love one another there will be no more mutual injury.[6]

The ideal of social responsibility noted in Mo-ti's comments incorporates a consciousness of the self that in reality becomes the basis for relationships in the community. One does not lose one's identity in the community, but the needs of others are as important as, if not more important than, one's own needs. Reinhold Niebuhr, a twentieth-century American Christian theologian, goes a step further when he maintains that love of one's fellow humans is a basic law of humanity demanded by the social character of human existence:

D   [Another] source of religious vitality is derived from the social character of human existence; from the fact that men cannot be themselves or fulfill themselves within themselves, but only in an affectionate and responsible relation to their fellows. It is this fact, rather than the fiat of any scripture, which makes the law of love the basic law for man. The law is not of purely religious origin, and indeed it is not necessary to be religious to ascertain its validity.[7]

[6]Mo-ti, "Universal Love II," trans. Y. P. Mie, in *The Wisdom of China and India*, ed. Lin Yutang (New York: Random House, Inc., 1942), pp. 794–95.
[7]Reinhold Niebuhr, "The Religious Situation in America," in *Religion and Contemporary Society*, ed. Harold Stahmer (New York: Macmillan, Inc., 1963), p. 146.

Niebuhr's suggestion assumes that an individual *only* lives purposefully and completely in interaction with others.

The contrast between positions as diverse as those of Henley and Niebuhr is obvious. Most major religious traditions agree with the insights of Mo-ti and Niebuhr that the needs of others (the community) take precedence over the wants and needs of the individual, and that an individual cannot find fulfillment solely in the self.

> *Is it possible to achieve a meaningful balance between the individual and the society? Is it necessary to achieve such a balance? Why?*
>
> *Which of the positions is closer to your own understanding? Why?*
>
> *What value is there in each of the positions?*

UNIT 62   Love and Duty

Although, as the previous unit suggests, there are persons whose self-image is uniquely individualistic and perhaps antisocial, most persons find genuine fulfillment in their social contact and dependence. The modes or forms of involvement with others are multitudinous, but there are discernible patterns of response that tell us much about basic life attitudes and assumptions (both conscious and unconscious).

Among the many ways persons relate to others and society, two patterns are central: love and duty. In every culture, feelings of affection (love) and a sense of responsibility (duty) motivate responses of persons to others. Love and duty often complement and support each other in daily life, but they may also be a cause of anxiety and conflict. Many times one must balance the demands of affection and responsibility, occasionally selecting one over the other. This process is often unconscious, yet it reflects basic personal assumptions about the nature of life.

Love by its very nature expresses the content of a relationship between two individuals; consequently, ⌐it is often understood to express a social attitude that begins with the individual. While it may not be limited to one individual and may incorporate many or a group, it usually begins with the concern of one for another.⌐ In love one begins with the self and moves toward the other—love bridges the gap between. In this movement, the individual will and its encounter, assessment, and acceptance or rejection of another is primary to all other considerations.

Duty, on the other hand, begins with the sense of responsibility for or to the other. It is the other, often the corporate group itself, which defines one's duties or responsibilities. By performing one's duties, one finds fulfillment as a part of the larger whole; therefore society—expressed in the family, village, caste, or modern industrial society—is the central focus of life. ⌐Persons achieve significance as they perform their duties within the larger community.

The contrast between the approach of love based on individual affection and that of duty based on social responsibility is obvious. They are both present in daily personal life and in all cultures. Sometimes they are delicately balanced and sometimes one dominates the other. Preliterate and Eastern cultures, with their emphasis on society and the family as the primary unit of human life, often stress responsibility or duty to the society before personal affection. In contrast to this understanding, modern Western culture, grounded in an early belief in a personal God and his relationship to individuals, emphasizes personal relationships and accomplishments as primary and tends to idealize love as the central pattern of human relationships. Illustrations of both positions and their interconnection abound in the literature of both East and West.

Love

Charlie Brown's incredulous response to a love that continues to offer itself even to the unloving suggests one of the deepest insights into the unlimited nature of love.

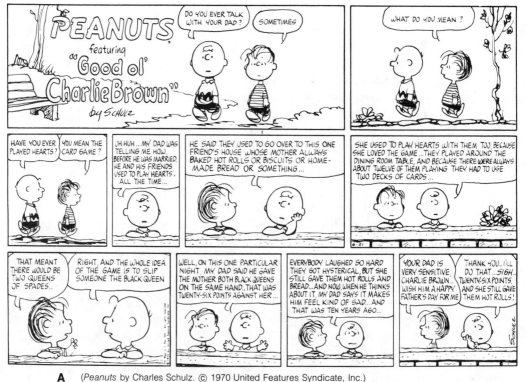

A   (*Peanuts* by Charles Schulz. © 1970 United Features Syndicate, Inc.)

In Mahayana Buddhism (see Unit 12), the ideal human is a *Bodhisattva*— one who has come close to Nirvana yet delays entrance into that state in order compassionately (lovingly) to lead others toward it. This compassion is overwhelming and all-consuming.

B A Bodhisattva resolves: *I take upon myself the burden of suffering*, I am resolved to do so, I will endure it. . . . *I have made the vow to save all beings.* All beings I must set free. The whole world of living beings I must rescue, from the terrors of birth, of old age, of sickness, of death and rebirth, of all kinds of moral offence, of all states of woe, of the whole cycle of birth-and-death, of the jungle of false views, of the loss of wholesome dharmas, of the concomitants of ignorance,—from all these terrors I must rescue all beings. . . . And I must not cheat all beings out of my store of merit. I am resolved to abide in each single state of woe for numberless aeons; and so I will help all beings to freedom, in all the states of woe that may be found in any world system whatsoever.

Sikshasamuccaya, 280–81
(Vajradhvaja Sutra)

In his play *J.B.*, Archibald MacLeish retells the Biblical story of Job in a modern setting. J.B. (Job) had been blessed, as he believed, by God with a large, happy family and material wealth. Through a series of calamities, J.B. finds himself stripped of his children, his material possessions, and his wife's love. All that he has known has been destroyed, and his town has been devastated (perhaps in a nuclear attack). Tempted to renounce God and his goodness and puzzled as to the meaning of life, J.B. remains faithful to his belief that God's love is still present, even if incomprehensible. The play closes with J.B. and his wife, Sarah, speaking of the imperishable nature of love, which, in the midst of disaster, transcends all suffering and forms the basis of creative interpersonal relationships.

C J.B.:   You left me, Sarah.
SARAH: Yes, I left you.
I thought there was a way away.
Out of the world. Out of the world.
Water under bridges opens
Closing and the companion stars
Still float there afterwards. I thought the door
Opened into closing water.
J.B.:   Sarah!
SARAH: Oh, I never could.
I never could. Even this—
Even the green leaf on the branch—could stop me.
J.B.:   Why have you come back again?
SARAH: [Kneels c. She has found a stub of candle in her pocket.]
Because I love you.
J.B.:   Because you love me!
The one thing certain in this hurtful world
Is love's inevitable heartbreak.
What's the future but the past to come
Over and over, love and loss,
What's loved most lost most.
[Sarah has moved into the rubble of the ring. She kneels, setting things to rights.
Her mind is on her task, not on J.B.'s words.]
SARAH: I know that, Job.
J.B.:   Nothing is certain but the loss of love.
And yet . . . you say you love me!

SARAH: Yes.
J.B.:   The stones in those dead streets would crack
           With terrible indecent laughter
           Hearing *you* and *me* say love!
SARAH: I have no light to light the candle.
J.B.:   [Violently]
           You have our love to light it with!
           Blow on the coal of the heart, poor Sarah.
SARAH: Blow on the coal of the heart . . .?
J.B.:   The candles in churches are out.
           The lights have gone out in the sky!
SARAH: The candles in churches are out.
           The lights have gone out in the sky.
           Blow on the coal of the heart
           And we'll see by and by. . . .
                         we'll see where we are.
           We'll know. We'll know.
J.B.:   [Slowly, with difficulty, the hard words said at last.]
                         We can never *know*.
           He answered me like the stillness of a star
           That silences us asking.
                         No, Sarah, no:
           [Kneels beside her.]
           We *are* and that is all our answer.
           We are and what we are can suffer.
           But . . .
                   what suffers loves.
                            And love
           Will live its suffering again,
           Risk its own defeat again,
           Endure the loss of everything again
           And yet again and yet again
           In doubt, in dread, in ignorance, unanswered,
           Over and over, with the dark before,
           The dark behind it . . . and still live . . . still love.
           [J.B. strikes match, touches Sarah's cheek with his hand.]
                   THE PLAY IS ENDED[8]

Duty

India's ancient caste system was founded on the principle that each person
finds a productive place within society by performing the proper duties of one's
caste. To break caste is to destroy self and society. (Modern developments have
modified the rigidity of the caste system somewhat, but ancient concepts are slow to
change and it is still highly influential.) The following passage is taken from the
Puranas (c.350):

[8]Archibald MacLeish, *J.B.: A Play in Verse* (New York: Samuel French, Inc., 1958). Used by
permission of Houghton Mifflin Company, publisher.

D

He best worships Vishnu who observes the duties laid down by scripture for every caste and condition of life; there is no other mode. . . .

The Brahmana *(member of priestly caste)* must advance the well-being of all and do injury to none—for the greatest wealth of a Brahmana consists in cherishing kind feelings towards all. He must consider with an equal eye the jewel and stone belonging to another. . . .

The duties of the Kshatriya *[member of warrior caste]* consist in making gifts to the Brahmanas at pleasure, in worshiping Vishnu with various sacrifices and receiving instruction from the preceptor. His principal sources of maintenance are arms and protection of the earth. But his greatest duty consists in guarding the earth. By protecting the earth a king attains his objects, for he gets a share of the merit of all sacrifices. If a king, by maintaining the order of caste, represses the wicked, supports the pious, he proceeds to whatever region he desires.

The Father of Creation has assigned to the Vaisyas *[members of the merchant caste]*, for their maintenance, the feeding of the cattle, commerce, and agriculture. Study, sacrifice, and gift are also within the duties of the Vaisyas: besides these, they may also observe the other fixed and occasional rites.

The Sudra *[member of the servant caste]* must maintain himself by attending upon the three higher castes, or by the profits of trade, or the earnings of mechanical labour. He may also make gifts, offer the sacrifices in which food is presented, and he may also make obsequial offerings.

Besides these, the four castes have their other duties, namely—the acquisition of wealth for the support of servants, cohabitation with their wives for the sake of children, kindness towards all creatures, patience, humility, truth, purity, contentment, decorum of manners, gentleness of speech, friendliness, freedom from envy or avarice and the habit of vilifying. These also constitute the duties of every condition of life.[9]

Traditional Chinese culture has been built on the principle of "filial piety" (respect, honor, and obedience to one's family and ancestors). One lives fully and completely when one performs all of one's proper duties to family and society. The principle of *shu*, or reciprocity, spelled out by Confucius, formed the basis of these proper relationships.

E

Tzu-kung asked, saying, "Is there one word which may serve as a rule of practice for all one's life?" The Master said, "Is not Reciprocity [shu] such a word? What you do not want done to yourself, do not do to others.[10]

Confucius made this principle the basis of the widely known "Five Relationships." In each set of relationships, one's duty or responsibility to the other is central to a proper and fulfilling life.

F

Kindness in the father, filial piety in the
    son
Gentility in the eldest brother, humility
    and respect in the younger
Righteous behavior in the husband,
    obedience in the wife

---

[9]Excerpts from *The Vishnu Purana*, trans. H. H. Wilson, ed. M. N. Dutt (Calcutta, 1894), as cited in Lewis Browne, *The World's Great Scriptures* (New York: Macmillan, Inc., 1946), pp. 121–22.

[10]Robert Ballou, *The Bible of the World* (New York: The Viking Press, 1939), p. 413.

> Humane consideration in elders,
> deference in juniors
> Benevolence in ruler, loyalty in
> ministers and subjects.[11]

The same sense of duty to family and society carried over from China to Japan, where it became incorporated in the ethical code of the Japanese warrior-knight. Known as the *Bushido Code*, it incorporates many virtues, all derivative of proper performance of duty. The following is an analysis of the code by a Christian missionary:

G

1. Loyalty.
   This was due first of all to the Emperor and under him to the lord whom one more immediately serves. One of the most familiar proverbs says, "A loyal retainer does not serve two lords."

2. Gratitude.
   It may surprise some to hear that this is a Japanese characteristic, but the Christian doctrine that the spring of a right life is not duty, but gratitude, is one that is readily appreciated by the Japanese.

3. Courage.
   Life itself is to be surrendered gladly in the service of the lord. An American cannot fail to be touched by the noble words of a young warrior of ancient times to the effect that he wanted to die in battle for his lord and feared nothing so much as dying in bed before he had a chance to sacrifice his life for the object of his devotion.

4. Justice.
   This means not allowing any selfishness to stand in the way of one's duty.

5. Truthfulness.
   A knight scorns to tell a lie in order to avoid harm or hurt to himself.

6. Politeness.
   It is the mark of a strong man to be polite in all circumstances, even to an enemy.

7. Reserve.
   No matter how deeply one is moved, feeling should not be shown.

8. Honor.
   Death is preferable to disgrace. The knight always carried two swords, a long one to fight his foes, a short one to turn upon his own body in case of blunder or defeat.[12]

Is it correct to say that love essentially emphasizes an individual approach to one's understanding of life and its meaning? Conversely, is it correct to assume that duty stresses a community or social approach?

Which of the examples above best expresses your own ideal interpretation of life?

Is it necessary to balance love and duty? Are they exclusive of one another? If one must dominate, which do you think it should be?

If the concerns of the individual or the society cannot be perfectly balanced, which should dominate? What does your answer say of love and duty?

[11]John Noss, *Man's Religions*, 4th ed. (New York: Macmillan, Inc.), p. 285. Copyright © 1969 by John Noss.

[12]Christopher Noss, *Tohoku, The Scotland of Japan* (Philadelphia: Board of Foreign Missions of the Reformed Church in the United States, 1918), pp. 87–88; quoted in John Noss, *Man's Religions*, p. 33.

UNIT 63   Act and Motive

The social context within which individuals live requires the development of inter-personal relationships which are expressed through particular acts and attitudes, be they positive or negative. The interaction between particular acts (such as doing some service for a neighbor) and the motivations (love, duty, and so on) for such acts is the topic of the discussion that follows.

As they develop, societies normally create codes of moral conduct for their members. These codes consist of a set of prescribed actions that the individuals, depending on their social status (the various roles occupied in society—husband, wife, father, mother, uncle, warrior, and so forth), must perform, and a set of taboos (acts forbidden to all, or some). In less complex societies, the role of the taboo is very significant in its control of individuals' actions. The following passage, for example, describes some of the taboos in Navaho society.

A

A very high portion of all the acts which arise out of convictions about beings and powers are negative in character. Thus lightning-struck trees must be avoided. Coyotes, bears, snakes, and some kinds of birds must never be killed. The eating of fish and of most water birds and animals is forbidden, and raw meat is taboo. Navahos will never cut a melon with the point of a knife. They never comb their hair at night. No matter how crowded a hogan may be with sleeping figures, no Navaho may step over the recumbent body of another. Mother-in-law and son-in-law must never look into each other's eyes. Any kind of sexual contact (even walking down the street or dancing to-gether) with members of the opposite sex of one's own or one's father's clan is pro-hibited. Most technical processes are hedged about with restrictions: the tanner dare not leave the pole on which he scrapes hide standing upright; the potter and the basket-maker work in isolation, observing a bewildering variety of taboos; the weaver shares one of these, the dread of final completion, so that a "spirit out-let" must always be left in the design.[13]

While taboos, often unconsciously appropriated, continue to be operative in more complex societies, they tend to be replaced in importance by elaborated sets of rationally formulated, often written, moral rules. In Judaism, the earliest simple set of rules, the Ten Commandments, were elaborated into 613 specific laws governing all aspects of life. Similarly, for Muslims, the Koran contains a specific set of rules for life; the Eightfold Path of the Buddha is elaborately defined in the Buddhist scriptural commentaries.

Sets of rules inherently raise the problem of motivation and intention, how-ever. If one simply follows the rules without understanding the motivation or the reason for a particular act required by the rules, they tend to degenerate into a legalism readily compromised or avoided. Therefore, with the elaboration of rules defining most actions in life, many societies also experienced a developing interest in the motivation and intention for following the rules.

In Judaism, for instance, it is not enough to fulfill the duties, moral or cultic,

---

[13]Clyde Kluckhohn and Dorothea Leighton, *The Navaho* (Cambridge, Mass.: Harvard University Press, 1946), pp. 139–40.

that the law prescribes: One must fulfill them with a right heart or a right spirit—for the right reasons and with the right intention. One should fulfill the law because of gratitude and love toward God. The following passage, an abridgment of and commentary on a halakhic discourse from the Talmud, shows how Jewish ethical reflection attempted to clarify the relation of motive (or intention) and action.[14]

B

The Mishna states: "IF SOMEONE BLOWS THE *shofar*[a] IN A CISTERN, IN A CELLAR, OR IN A BARREL, IF ONE HEARD THE SOUND OF THE *shofar*, HE HAS FULFILLED HIS OBLIGATION; BUT IF HE HEARD THE ECHO, HE HAS NOT FULFILLED HIS OBLIGATION." Then it adds: "AND ALSO, IF ONE WAS PASSING BEHIND A SYNAGOGUE, AND HE HEARD THE SOUND OF THE *shofar* OR THE READING OF THE *megillah*,[b] IF ONE SET HIS MIND TO IT, HE FULFILLED HIS OBLIGATION; IF ONE HAS NOT, HE HAS NOT FULFILLED HIS OBLIGATION—EVEN THOUGH THE ONE HEARD AND THE OTHER HEARD, THE ONE SET HIS MIND TO IT, BUT THE OTHER DID NOT SET HIS MIND TO IT."

The subject to be explored, then, is "intention" or to be exact, whether in the carrying out of a religious duty it is necessary to intend to carry out the duty or not.[15]

[a]The ram's horn sounded in the services on Rosh Hashana, the New Year. On the requirement to hear the sound of the *shofar*, see Leviticus 23:24 and Numbers 29:1.

[b]The Book of Esther, read on the festival of Purim.

Clearly, the Jews came to understand that one's motivation for particular acts was as important as the act itself.

The same concern for relating motive to act was raised by Christian theologians and philosophers like Augustine (353–430) and Abelard (1079–1142). Although both insisted that right actions are important, for both the intention or motivation behind the act was even more important. According to Augustine, the traits of character—habits or dispositions—that Greek philosophy held to be the highest virtues—temperance, fortitude, justice, and prudence—are empty of value, are "splendid vices," unless they flow out of and are motivated by proper love of God and neighbor. The emphasis on motive—inner attitude or disposition—as at least partly determining the value of act and pattern of life had been present in Christianity from the beginning, as the following words of Jesus show:

C

"Listen to me, all of you, and understand this: nothing that goes into a man from outside can defile him; no, it is the things that come out of him that defile a man." When he had left the people and gone indoors, his disciples questioned him about the parable. He said to them, "Are you as dull as the rest? Do you not see that nothing that goes from outside into a man can defile him, because it does not enter into his heart but into his stomach, and so passes out into the drain?" Thus he declared all food clean. He went on, "It is what comes out of a man that defiles him. For from inside, out of a man's heart, come evil thoughts, acts of fornica-

[14]The Talmud contains both Halakha—reflections on the requirements of the Jewish law carried on in characteristically legal style of reasoning—and Hagada (or Agada)—nonlegal material including folklore, philosophical and theological speculation, parables, prayers, historical and legendary tales, and so forth.

[15]*The Living Talmud*, trans. Judah Golden (New York: The New American Library, 1957), p. 30.

tion, of theft, murder, adultery, ruthless greed, and malice; fraud, indecency, envy, slander, arrogance, and folly; these evil things all come from inside, and they defile the man." (Mark 7:15–23, NEB)

Compare the following Zen Buddhist story, "Muddy Road," with the examples given above:

D Tanzan and Ekido were once travelling together down a muddy road. A heavy rain was still falling. Coming around a bend, they met a lovely girl in a silk kimono and sash, unable to cross the intersection. "Come on girl," said Tanzan at once. Lifting her up in his arms, he carried her over the mud. Ekido did not speak again until that night when they reached a lodging temple. Then he could no longer restrain himself. "We monks don't go near females," he told Tanzan, "especially not young and lovely ones. It is dangerous. Why did you do that?" "I left the girl there," said Tanzan. "Are you still carrying her?"[16]

Consider the words of Archbishop Thomas Becket in T. S. Eliot's *Murder in the Cathedral*:

E The last temptation is the greatest treason:
To do the right deed for the wrong reason.[17]

In everyday decision making, are persons normally more aware of acts or of the motives for actions?

Why are religious moral thinkers more concerned with motivation than with particular moral acts?

Why is it that moral instruction is often reduced to a series of prescriptions relative to particular acts?

[16]Paul Reps, ed., *Zen Flesh, Zen Bones* (Tokyo: Charles E. Tuttle Co. Inc., 1960) p. 18.
[17]T. S. Eliot, *Murder in the Cathedral*, in *The Complete Poems and Plays of T. S. Eliot* (New York: Harcourt, Brace and Company, 1952), Part I, p. 196. Used by permission of Harcourt Brace Jovanovich, Inc., publishers and Faber and Faber Ltd.

15 _____

The Corporate Expressions
of Ethical Concerns

INTRODUCTION

The previous chapter focused on individual responses to personal and social settings. The material that follows discusses relationships characteristic of groups of people, and relationships between the ethical norms of a society (and its religion) and the social issues that arise within that society.

When considering a society and its ethical relationships, attention must be given not only to broad principles of right and wrong but also to the ethical norms of particular subgroups within a society. These groups have many organizing principles including political, economic, and religious factors. Each group develops a "corporate identity" which influences the individuals within it. As such, it applies norms of ethical behavior to the social issues it confronts. In determining the norms for any such group or the society as a whole many questions arise, such as the following:

Is the ethical character of a group the simple sum of the character of its members? Does each member of the group exercise equal influence upon the decision-making process, good or bad, of the group itself? Does the group have needs and goals which transcend the individual members? Is the process of corporate identification the same regardless of whether the group be religious, political, cultural, social, or economic? How does a group maintain its integrity in the face of conflicting claims? The answers given to these questions determine how individuals and groups respond to particular issues.

In the units of this chapter, several ethical and social issues are examined in the light of social and religious norms. Most of the examples used are drawn from Western sources, but many of the issues reflect universal concerns. The difficulties of giving simple religious answers to the questions raised by these issues should be obvious. The necessity of careful and considered response in applying religious principles and norms is equally obvious. The first two units are concerned with the relationship between human need, justice, love, conflict, and peace on the collective—social and international—level. The next two units are concerned with an issue present in every society, though awareness and recognition of it have frequently been present only in modern or modernizing societies—the status of women as participants in society. The last two units deal with racial and ethnic differences as sources of conflict or creative opportunity in contemporary societies. With all of these issues, the major focus will be on their interaction with the religious perspectives of what a society, or subgroups within it, hold to be of pivotal value or ultimate concern.

UNIT 64 Love and Justice

How does one love a million needy people?

A Here is precisely the serious difficulty of love. How are its favors to be distributed among so many beneficiaries? We never have one neighbor at a time. How are we to love justice, how are we to be just about love, how are love and justice re-lated? If to love is to seek the neighbor's welfare, and justice is being fair as between neighbors, then how do we put these two things together in our *acts* in the situation.[1]

B Various systems of Christian ethics have related love and justice: love *versus* justice (opposites), love *or* justice (alternatives), love *and* justice (complements).[2]

Joseph Fletcher, contemporary ethicist, claims that "love and justice are one and the same." He emphasizes "that love is justice or that justice loves . . . To be loving is to be just, to be just is to be loving."[3] To him, love = justice; justice = love.[4] Fletcher explains what he means in the following paragraph:

C Justice is Christian love using its head, calculating its duties, obligations, opportunities, resources. Sometimes it is hard to decide, but the dilemmas, trilemmas, and multilemmas of conscience are as baffling for legalists as for situationists. Justice is love coping with situations where distribution is called for. On this basis it becomes plain that as the love ethic searches seriously for a social policy it must form a coalition with utilitarianism. It takes over from Bentham and Mill the strategic principle of "the greatest good of the greatest number."[5]

[1] Joseph Fletcher, *Situation Ethics: The New Morality* (Philadelphia: The Westminster Press, 1966), p. 88.
[2] *Ibid.*, p. 93.
[3] *Ibid.*
[4] *Ibid.*, p. 95.
[5] *Ibid.*

愛は正義のことはとす.

Fletcher points to Paul Tillich as one who comes close to expressing his understanding of the relation of love and justice. He does not feel, however, that Tillich goes far enough in equating love and justice. Tillich states that the "relation of love to justice in personal encounters can adequately be described through three functions of creative justice, namely, listening, giving, forgiving."[6]

All persons, in one way or another, yearn to be heard, to make known their claim for justice. One who loves another or others will listen and learn in order to act justly toward them.

The second step one takes in exercising creative justice is giving. Every one we meet lives with the right to call for us to meet his or her needs. The minimum of giving in certain situations may drive toward the maximum self-sacrifice. Sacrificial giving serves the love that makes whole and creates new life in another.

"The third and most paradoxical form in which justice is united with love is forgiving."[7] Here Tillich is speaking in Pauline terms of justification by grace. This means "to accept as just one who is unjust."[8] How contradictory this seems to us! The good news of Christian teaching, however, goes beyond our usual way of viewing unjust persons as subjects deserving retribution, and instead demands reconcilation, acceptance of another into the wholeness and unity provided only by forgiveness.

In the light of what Fletcher and Tillich say about the relationship between love and justice, reflect further upon Reinhold Niebuhr's interpretation as explained by Gordon Harland, contemporary church historian. Harland explains Niebuhr as follows:

D

What then is the relation between *agape* and justice? The first thing to be said is that they cannot be simply identified. *Agape* is transcendent, heedless, and sacrificial. Justice is historical, discriminating, and concerned with balancing interests and claims. Love and justice are never simply the same thing. But if they must be distinguished, they cannot be torn asunder. Justice is the relative social embodiment of love and as such it is an approximation of love. Justice is love finding a relatively complete expression in the world. The terms are not interchangeable. But justice is never something apart from, or independent of, love and pertaining to another realm.

Love Demands Justice. For justice is not alien to love, it is love making its way in the world. Love thus prompts us to seek ever wider and more inclusive structures of justice. One simply cannot say that he is concerned that love may be expressed but not concerned with politics, economics, laws, and customs. To be unconcerned for the achievement of more equal justice is to deny the claims of love. Justice is the embodiment of love in complex human relations.

Love Negates Justice. For love always transcends justice. This is true for our ideas of justice as well as for historical structures of justice. Justice is discriminating, it must always calculate and weigh conflicting interests. Love transcends the calculation of more and less and does not reward according to deserts. Thus every structure and every idea of justice stand under the higher judgment of love. Justice, to remain justice, can thus never be complacent, because the norm is not in itself but in *agape*. . . .

[6]Paul Tillich, *Love, Power and Justice* (New York: Oxford University Press, 1954), p. 84.
[7]*Ibid.*, p. 86.
[8]*Ibid.*

Love Fulfills Justice. Only love can illumine and meet the special need. "A sense of justice may prompt men to organize legal systems of unemployment insurance through which a general sense of obligation toward the needy neighbour is expressed. But no such system can leave the self satisfied when it faces particular needs among those who are the beneficiaries of such minimal schemes of justice." Love fulfills justice also because love alone can meet the other in his uniqueness and freedom. "The other has special needs and requirements which cannot be satisfied by general rules of equity." Love fulfills justice because *agape* is redemptive. . . .

Agape, which demands that we ever seek justice, which judges and finds wanting our highest achievements, also redeems and thereby fulfills what remains incomplete and distorted by sin.

Love demands, negates, and fulfills justice. Thus, although love and justice are not the same they do not exist apart from each other; when they are sought apart from each other, each is destroyed.

Justice without love ceases to be justice. "Any justice which is only justice soon degenerates into something less than justice." Thus as mutual love needs *agape* to keep it from degenerating into a calculation of interests, so "Justice," as Niebuhr once so cryptically put it, "without love is merely the balance of power."

Love without justice ceases to be love. It becomes a vague sentimentalism that fails to come to grips with the realities of experience. Or it issues in a perverse lovelessness by refusing mistakenly, in the name of love, to deal realistically and courageously with the fact of power upon which the securing and the maintaining of justice depend. Or it becomes corrupted by being defined in terms of attitudes, and love is thereby restricted to personal relations and exercises of philanthropy, and thus the universal kingship of the Lord of the Cross is reduced to a pleasant deed transacted in a corner.

Love and justice must never be sharply separated, though they must always be clearly distinguished. They exist together in a dialectical relation of tension.[9]

LIBERATION THEOLOGY AND JUSTICE

An illustration of how to distribute love justly has been sharply focused in recent decades by "liberation theologians." Struggling with the vast inequities of the modern world between wealthy and poor nations, as well as class and economic differences within particular nations, liberation theologies seek to find new ways to apply justly the insights of love in modern societies. Liberation theologies have received impetus especially among Latin Americans and ethnic minorities of the United States who have called us to begin to do theology from a nontraditional starting point: the poor.[10] While utilizing the tools of the social sciences in analyzing the reality of conflict between the oppressed poor and the oppressors in a society in which the very structure of society is unjust and evil, liberation thinkers call for the engagement of *praxis*, a method of action and reflection by the community in the light of Scripture. Just love is action demanding reflective interpretation by Christians in group discussion that then compels even more just acts of love, which in turn call for reflection again, and so on in a continuous circle.

[9]Gordon Harland, *The Thought of Reinhold Niebuhr* (Oxford University Press, Inc., 1960), pp. 23–26. Copyright © by Gordon Harland. Used with permission.
[10]Robert McAfee Brown, *Theology in A New Key: Responding to Liberation Themes* (Philadelphia: Westminster Press, 1978), p. 60.

Liberation theologies mandate that injustices be viewed through the eyes of the poor, who have often been disenfranchised and voiceless in society, for God is to be found among the poor and marginalized of society. Liberation theologies claim that God is calling and can empower the poor of the world to exercise responsibility for the future and seek to modify and eliminate social and economic structures that presently enslave them in poverty.

④ The justice that comes with liberation, according to liberation theologians, will be a transformation not only of individuals in bondage to inward and personal sin but also of the evil structures and institutions of society that dehumanize and perpetuate poverty and corporate injustice. Further, it should be emphasized that the God in Christ revealed through the struggle of the poor is the force to liberate not only the oppressed, but also the oppressors, who, perhaps unknowingly, are also enslaved to the unjust structures of power.

UNIT 65 Peace or Justice?

A relationship as intricate as that between love and justice emerges when the principle of justice is applied to the issue of peace and its price in a modern society.

A   If peace at all costs and any price be America's foreign policy, we sacrifice justice; if the protection of justice is singly pursued, by whatever means at hand, we endanger the peace.[11]

⑨ The dilemma of choice between peace and justice is a constant problem in Christian ethical theory. Several positions have emerged over the years which reveal the variety of Christian answers. The following table with some attention to the difficulties involved in each may serve as a basis for discussion.

B

ABSOLUTE PACIFISM	NUCLEAR PACIFISM	MUTUAL DETERRENCE	PREVENTIVE WAR	ALL-OUT WAR
Refusal to resort to any violence	Refusal to use weapons of mass destruction	Armistice maintained by balance of power, threat of nuclear weapons	Police action in trouble spots, under UN auspices, conventional weapons	Unilateral action, using conventional or nuclear weapons

No position is purely right: there are troubles with each one. In dealing with the absolute pacifist, for instance, it is important to ask whether (1) he intends his position only as one of witness and protest by himself as an individual, or (2)

[11]Waldo Beach, *The Christian Life* (Richmond, Virginia: The Covenant Life Curriculum (CLC Press, 1966), p. 281.

whether he would also want his nation to adopt pacifism as its foreign policy. ("Vocational" pacifism is the name sometimes given to the former position.) If the vocational pacifist acknowledges that the State Department has to act out a different ethic than the pure way to which he witnesses, this would seem to be split-level ethic, inconsistent between public policy and private conviction. On the other hand, realism prompts the doubt as to whether he has the right to ask his nation to junk all its military defenses. Would this not default on obligations to allies and the protection of the weak?

The nuclear pacifist draws his main moral line between *kinds* of weapon. He might agree that his country should employ conventional weapons, since they can be kept within the moral rules of a just war, but nuclear weapons—never. They are totally destructive, therefore entirely immoral. Ever since nuclear fission was achieved, it has been the physicists who have been the most urgent and solemn in their pleas for the nuclear pacifist's position, reminding the nation that there is no effective defense against nuclear weapons. Hence the alternative becomes nuclear disarmament or total destruction. One possible moral weakness in the nuclear pacifist position, however, as it appears to the absolute pacifist, is this: If human life be sacred, a machine-gun blast destroys life just as finally and tragically as radioactive dust. Is it not quite arbitrary to draw a line between proper and improper weapons of destruction?

The balance of power position (to move one jog further on the line) is based on the same dread of nuclear weapons as provokes the nuclear pacifist to his stand. But it argues that since we now have nuclear weapons on both sides of the East-West controversy, the best chance for preserving the peace is to maintain an equilibrium of nuclear strength, so that neither side would dare to strike for fear of retaliation. This policy provides at best a precarious armistice, but it has served . . . to keep the peace and deter aggression. The moral dangers of this position are great: the escalation of nuclear weapons, war by miscalculation, the "nth power problem." (How many major powers can be allowed to join the nuclear club before the equilibrium is tipped over?) The consequence "peace," if it can be called that, is based on a community of fear, of negative trust resting on an inversion of the Golden Rule: "Don't do unto others what you would not want them to do unto you." . . .

Any position along the spectrum on the far right becomes impossible to justify on a Christian or humanitarian ground. Unilateral military action on the part of the United States, even limited to conventional weapons at the start and intended to head off a major aggressive move by another power, would be regarded under almost any conceivable circumstances as itself aggressive and would move quickly beyond the point of no return. Neither peace nor justice would be served by such action. Therefore, the alternatives for conscience are those on the left and at the middle of the spectrum.[12]

Past discussions of the moral problem of war have focused on several issues: (1) How can one be even reasonably sure that the cause for which a war is undertaken or risked is just? (2) Can any war between independent nation states in a world where any international conflict *might* lead to nuclear war be justified? (3) Under what conditions is a revolutionary uprising (civil war) against an aggressive or tyrannical government justified? (4) Can a counterrevolutionary war, aided by outside powers, fought to preserve a stable international balance of power, be justified,

[12]Waldo Beach, *The Christian Life, Teacher's Book* (Richmond, Virginia: The CLC Press, 1966), pp. 210–12.

even if it means keeping an oppressive government in power against the wishes of a large part of the population in the country involved?

The traditional "just war" theory, worked out by Christian moral theologians during the time from Augustine (fifth century) to the seventeenth century, held that the following conditions must be met before a war can be considered just or justifiable:

1. War must be authorized and waged under the authority of a legitimately established government. It cannot be initiated by private citizens.
2. War can be undertaken only if there is a just cause, a grave and unjustifiable injury done to the people of a country by the government or citizens of another country.
3. War must be waged with right intention—the intention of seeking a better, more just peace than would exist if the unjust situation were left uncorrected. (The war should also be fought with a proper motive, aiming at doing good to all who will be affected, including the enemy.)
4. War must be waged with proper means. Especially, the lives and safety of noncombatants must be protected from direct attack or harm.
5. War must be undertaken as a last resort only after all possibilities of peaceful settlement have been exhausted.
6. War can be undertaken only when there is a reasonable expectation that the just side will prevail—otherwise great harm would be done without a correction of the original evil.
7. War can be undertaken only when the good (to all affected parties) that will result from correcting the unjust situation will be greater than the destruction that the war will produce.

Can these conditions ever be fulfilled? Can they be fulfilled in modern war on the international level? Are they realistic or unrealistic?

Recent discussions of the morality of war have focused more and more on the apparently increasing threat of total destruction in nuclear war and on the apparently increasing dangers of nuclear war because of open-ended build-up of weapons in the arms race between the Soviet Union and the United States. In an influential study, *The Fate of the Earth*, Jonathan Schell questions the moral reasoning that equates death in conventional wars with death in a possible nuclear war. Since all-out nuclear war between Russia and the United States would likely destroy the possibility of survival of human life on earth, there is, he argues, a qualitative difference between just war calculations for nuclear war and those for conventional war.[13]

Religious groups and leaders are closely examining these issues. A pastoral letter of American Catholic Bishops that many observers consider epoch-making has urged reconsideration of just war arguments that favor retention of a defense based on nuclear weapons. The continued reliance on a nuclear arsenal for deterrence purposes can be justified, the bishops suggest, only if governments and individuals make it a matter of first priority to move away from the nuclear balance of

[13]Jonathan Schell, *The Fate of the Earth* (New York: Avon Books, 1982).

terror through negotiation and disarmament.[14] Similarly, a noted Protestant theologian, Gordon Kaufman of Harvard University, has argued that the possibility of humankind's self-destruction through nuclear war of every possible future necessitates a complete reexamination of Christian theological concepts concerning God, God's providence, God's will, and God's relation to humanity. Nuclear war, according to Kaufman, would represent major defeat for God and possibly total defeat for humanity; therefore, the most important moral and religious duty of our time is to work for nuclear disarmament and the prevention of nuclear war.[15]

Some religious and secular thinkers argue that Schell, the Catholic Bishops, and Kaufman have gone too far, exaggerating both the likelihood and the dangers of nuclear war; on the other hand, many are responding positively to the new sense of urgency about the nuclear threat, expressing themselves in a moral commitment, based either on pacifism or just war thinking, to work for peace.

How can anyone decide morally about war?

Are religious groups and religiously motivated individuals right in thinking that religious beliefs and religious teachings can give insight into these questions?

Are there some situations in which peace is more important than justice?

Are there situations in which achieving justice is more important than preserving peace?

What are your reasons for responding to these questions as you do?

UNIT 66   Religion and the Social Status of Women

This unit and the next one consider a very important social issue demanding responsible treatment from society's corporate entities and its individual members.

One of the first books of poetry by a North American writer—and the first published work by a North American poet whose works are still recognized as having literary merit—was published in England in 1650. The writer was Anne Bradstreet, daughter of Thomas Dudley, the second governor of the Massachusetts Bay Colony, and wife of a man who, after her death, also served as governor of the colony. Anne Bradstreet was the mother of eight children, devoutly Puritan in her religious outlook, well-read in religious, historical, and scientific writings. She particularly admired the poetry of Sir Philip Sidney and of the French Calvinist poet Guillaume Du Bartas, well-known Puritan writers of the period.

Anne Bradstreet did not think of herself as a poet. She wrote poetry for recreation and for the edification of herself and her friends and family. The manuscript of her book *The Tenth Muse* apparently was taken to England by her brother-in-law, John Woodbridge, without her knowledge, and given to a publisher. In his "Epistle to the Reader," published as a foreword to the book, Woodbridge wrote:

[14]The National Conference of Catholic Bishops, *The Challenge of Peace: God's Promise and Our Response, A Pastoral Letter on War and Peace*, May 3, 1983 (Washington: United States Catholic Conference, 1983).

[15]Gordon D. Kaufman, *Theology for a Nuclear Age* (Manchester: Manchester University Press, 1985).

A

I might trim this book with quaint expressions . . . but I fear 'twill be a shame for a man that can speak so little, to be seen in the title-page of this woman's book, lest by comparing the one with the other, the reader should pass his sentence that it is the gift of women not only to speak most but to speak best.

Woodbridge then goes on to suggest that male readers will not be envious of the "excellency of the inferior sex" unless "men turn more peevish than women."

It would be interesting to know what Anne Bradstreet's reaction was to this half-derogatory—"women speak most"—half self-effacing mock compliment from her brother-in-law.

Another Massachusetts poet, Nathaniel Ward, had written these lines, again without Anne's knowledge, in his introductory verse published at the beginning of *The Tenth Muse*:

I muse whither at length these girls will go;
It half-revives my chill frostbitten blood,
To see a woman once do ought that's good.

In her poems, Anne often wrote as if she did in fact accept the belief, recommended for good Christian women of her time—and other times—that women are "the inferior sex." But Anne often seems to have accepted this belief with irony, and in at least one poem, her poem on Queen Elizabeth, she wrote:

Nay say, have women worth? or have they none?
Or had they some, but with our Queen is't gone? . . .
Let such as say our sex is void of reason
Know tis a slander now, but once was treason.

Apparently Anne Bradstreet was not entirely convinced that women really *were* the inferior sex, who only occasionally—or *once*—could come up to the high standards of the male sex.[16]

Anne Bradstreet's subtle questioning of a cultural assumption—female inferiority—has been replaced in modern America with vociferous denials of that time-honored tradition. Recently, many women involved in the feminist movement have criticized the attitudes and practices of Christian and Jewish religious organizations as based on a belief in male superiority and, correspondingly, in the inferiority of women. The tendency of Judaism and Christianity to represent and

---

[16]The materials in this unit dealing with Anne Bradstreet are partly based on Adrienne Rich, "Anne Bradstreet and Her Poetry" and Jeannine Hensley, "Anne Bradstreet's Wreath of Thyme," in *The Works of Anne Bradstreet*, ed. Jeannine Hensley (Cambridge, Mass.: Harvard University Press, 1967), pp. ix–xxxv.

describe God in severely masculine terms has been criticized by some. More concretely, the exclusion of women from the priesthood and the ministry, the denial of full participation in decision making, and the explicit or implicit assumption of male superiority have been attacked.

In 1970 the Roman Catholic Church named two of its female saints, Teresa of Avila and Catherine of Sienna, to a very small, select group of theologians—fewer than forty—from the whole history of Catholic theology who have been given the awesome title "Doctors of the Church." No other women had ever been given this title. In recent years several Protestant denominations have accepted the position that women may be ordained as ministers on a basis of complete equality. Some denominations had already accepted full equality for women in the ministry. Other Protestant groups are now debating this issue. Some of the more conservative denominations do not believe ordination of women to be biblically sound, very often claiming that women follow in the lineage of Eve, who committed the first sin (Genesis 3:1–13). Thus, as a tainted gender, women cannot render a pure ministry (I Timothy 2:11-15). More moderate liberal Christians reject such an interpretation, pointing out that women have rendered effective ministries through the ages. Roman Catholics and some Anglicans also refuse to ordain women because of church principles, which assert that apostolic succession is limited to men. However, ordination of women has become widely accepted in America's Episcopal Church since its introduction in the 1970s. In the mid 1980s, an opinion survey indicated that bishops, clergy members, and laity heavily supported ordination of women to the priesthood. This represents a major change in attitude during a decade.

B

Plato, in his *Republic*, is one of the few, perhaps the only figure in the ancient Western world, who argued for complete equality of women in society. The Greek philosopher Aristotle, on the other hand, wrote:

A husband and a father . . . rules over wife and children, both free, but the rule differs, the rule over his children being a royal, over his wife a constitutional rule. For although there may be exceptions to the order of nature, the male is by nature fitter for command than the female, just as the elder and full-grown is superior to the younger and more immature. . . . The inequality is permanent.[17]

Writers on the history of Christianity have often claimed that the position of women—in contrast to their position in the Roman Empire of the first century—was significantly elevated in Christian teaching and practice. One text cited is Paul's saying that in Christ there is "neither male nor female" (Galatians 3:27–28, RSV). But Paul also had an elevated conception of male responsibility in the marriage relationship: he assumed that the male would be dominant. His teachings about the

[17]Aristotle, *Politics*. Book i, Ch. 12 (1259a–1259b), trans. Benjamin Jowett, in *The Modern Library* (New York: Random House, 1943).

role that women should play in the life and worship of the church reflect a conservative spirit. (See I Corinthians 14:33–35; I Corinthians 11:2–16.)

With the rise of asceticism as a major factor in the life of the church, the conservative view of the role and status of women became more pronounced. From the standpoint of the ascetic, who had withdrawn to the desert to flee the wickedness of the world, women became sources of temptation; after all, Eve had been the one responsible for Adam's fall, for the entry of evil into the world. Women were blamed by such writers as John Chrysostom and Ambrose for being immature and ignorant, conditions which, where they existed, are easily explained by the educational neglect of, and social discrimination against, women that was characteristic of the period. Clement of Alexandria, however, argued that by nature there was (and ought to be) complete equality between the sexes. (He did believe that there should be some differences in vocation.) It would be fair to say that the social position of women in the Roman Empire remained largely unaffected by the spread of Christianity. In pre-Christian Rome, women could own property and obtain divorces. In the Eastern part of the empire (and perhaps also in the West), there was a regular ordination of deaconesses. Deaconesses were allowed, however, to minister only to women, and they were not allowed to perform ecclesiastical functions thought to be proper to the male, such as teaching or praying aloud in worship services or approaching the altar. This is in stark contrast to the practice of many of the heretical sects of the period, such as Montanism, in which women were allowed more active roles. With the onset of feudalism, women lost many of the rights they had had in the urban setting of the Roman Empire.[18]

C

(Drawing by Stevenson; © 1969, *The New Yorker Magazine, Inc.* (May 3, 1969).)

" 'Cogito, ergo sum' is all very well for you, but what about me?"

[18]Based on D. S. Bailey, *Sexual Relation in Christian Thought* (New York: Harper and Brothers, 1959).

The irony of the cartoon is that, although seventeenth-century man—in this case the French philosopher René Descartes—may have seen a man's dignity as residing in his essence as a conscious (thinking) being—"I think therefore I am"—woman's socially defined status did not allow *her* to realize this essence. Only a woman placed in a socially exceptional position, such as Descartes's philosophically inclined correspondent, the Princess Elizabeth, or his patroness, Queen Christina, could become conscious of her rational essence. As a matter of fact, Descartes was not married. This may make the irony of the cartoon even more biting.

One emphasis of the contemporary feminist movement has been "consciousness development"—the overcoming by women of negative attitudes about their identity that derive from traditional stereotypes and practices based on social discrimination against women.

> *What roles in our society are regarded by society as really "first class"—as conferring maximum prestige and dignity on the individuals who fill those roles? How many women, in comparison with men, are in these roles? Are there some roles of maximum prestige value in our society that have never been filled by women?*

> *How do you explain the bias toward male superiority and female inferiority that has characterized Western society? Has a similar attitude been characteristic of other societies? What factors—social, psychological, economic, ideological—have contributed to this bias?*

Materials in this unit have been drawn mainly from Christian history. Other religions (for example, Hinduism, Islam, and Buddhism) have by and large taken an even more conservative stance toward the status and role of women. See also Units 71 and 72 for comment upon the status of women in preliterate and ancient cultures.

UNIT 67   Sexuality and Human Liberation

SALLY FORTH   **BY GREG HOWARD**

A   ("Sally Forth" by Greg Howard. Used by permission of News America Syndicate.)

Sally's phone conversation concisely focuses on major issues relating to sex roles in modern society, reflecting, on the one hand, the long-standing subservience of women to men, and on the other hand, the feminist protest against being treated as one without identity except in relation to husband or parents. In this unit we shall consider important concerns pertaining to the equality of women.

A student in a philosophy course recently proposed the following thesis: "Human sexuality is likely to be the most enduring of all philosophical topics." His line of reasoning was as follows: "In the past, differences of race, nationality, language-community, educational attainment, and religion have been held to be the basis for fundamental differences in status and treatment of human beings. We know now that these differences are not essential and that human beings can and should be treated on a basis of equality in spite of these differences, in line with one of the major moral and political goals of our time, equal opportunity and equal treatment. But one major and apparently irreducible difference between human beings does exist that seems to pose irreducible problems for the goal of equality, and that difference is the difference between the sexes."

Many contemporary speakers and writers would challenge the last statement in the student's explication of his thesis. Many feminists, spokespersons for feminist movements, would insist that the basic differences between the sexes, insofar as they bear on the social roles of persons, are man-created rather than natural or inevitable. In the preceding unit, traditional religious attitudes toward women and the role of women in society and in religion were discussed. One approach toward the role of women advocated by some religious leaders has been an appeal to "natural law" (see Unit 88). According to this line of thinking, the fact that women are naturally, biologically different from men indicates something of their proper role in society: Their biological nature as women indicates that morally they are best fitted to be mothers, supervisors of the home, protectors, comforters, and healers of husband and children. Against this view, many have argued that the traditional roles assigned to women, and the traditional characteristics considered feminine, are not the result of biological differences but are cultural creations, cultural stereotypes.

Adrienne Rich, a poet and an active feminist, has written:

B

[By "patriarchy"] I mean to imply not simply the tracing of descent through the father, which anthropologists seem to agree is a relatively late phenomenon, but any kind of group organization in which males hold dominant power and determine what part females shall and shall not play, and in which capabilities assigned to women are relegated generally to the mystical and aesthetic and excluded from the practical and political realms. (It is characteristic of patriarchal thinking that these realms are regarded as separate and mutually exclusive.) Such group organization has existed so long that almost all written history, theology, psychology, and cultural anthropology are founded on its premises and contribute to its survival. Based as it is on genital difference, its concept of sex is genitally centered; entire zones of the body (and soul) are to be used simply as means to a genital end.

At the core of the patriarchy is the individual family unit with its divisions of roles, its values of private ownership, monogamous marriage, emotional possessiveness, the "illegitimacy" of a child born outside legal marriage, the unpaid domestic services of the wife, obedience to authority, judgment and punishment for disobedience. Within this family children learn the characters, sexual and otherwise, that they are to assume, in their turn, as adults. . . .

The patriarchy looks to its women to embody and impersonate the qualities lacking in its institutions—concern for the quality of life, for means rather than for pure goal, a connection with the natural and the extrasensory order. These attributes have been classified as "female" in part because the patriarchy relegates them to women and tends to deny them—with a certain fatalism—to men. The encouragement of such qualities as intuition, sympathy, and access to feeling by a mother in her sons is deplored because this is supposed to make them unfit for the struggle that awaits them in a masculine world. Thus the "masculinity" of the world is perpetuated.

Most early feminists did not question the patriarchal family structure as such. They wanted education, changes in the marriage laws, birth control, suffrage; the struggle to prove that women could be entrusted with such dangerous tools was energy-consuming—and physically dangerous—enough without taking on the patriarchy en bloc. But recently, as a few, mostly white middle-class, women have obtained token "equality" in the form of permission to attend professional schools, to be pediatricians or psychoanalysts or to argue cases in court, their relationship to the patriarchy has become confusing.

When the professor who directs your thesis, the second professor who interviews you for a grant, the editor who hires you for the staff of his magazine, the government official who offers you a position on his committee, the chief surgeon with whom you work as an anesthesiologist, the reviewer who praises you for "logical thinking," the analyst who approves your method of dealing with patients in training, the members of the law firm in which you are the first woman partner, all are male, it is difficult to be sure when and where your "success" begins to build itself on a series of denials, small enough

in themselves, perhaps, yet accruing through the invisible process such things follow into acquiescence in a system of values which distrusts and degrades women.

I am not talking here about the loss of some fragile "feminine" quality jeopardized by excellence in reasoning and analysis, or by the desire to have original ideas. I am talking about the consciousness of self as Other which Simone de Beauvoir has described as that being toward whom man often feels fear, guilt, and hostility, and about whom he weaves his least defensible theories. Few women have grown up without this knowledge, lodged as it may be in some collective unconscious, disguised as it may be under codes of chivalry, domestic sentiment, biological reduction, or as it is revealed in poetry, law, theology, popular songs, or dirty jokes. Such knowledge— so long as women are not pressured into denying it—makes them potentially the deepest of all questioners of the social order created by men, and the most genuinely radical of thinkers. . . .

The "liberated" woman encounters male hostility in the form of psychic rape, often masked as psychic or physical seduction. It occurs overtly in the classroom where a male teacher denigrates female intellect; more subtly in the committee where she sits as token woman and where her intelligence is treated with benign neglect; in the magnanimous assumption that she is "not like other women" and for this reason is so desirable a colleague, figurehead, or adornment to the establishment (the pitting of woman against woman, woman against herself). At the same time that she is told about her "specialness" she is expected to be flattered, like all women, by flirtation. She is also expected to be flattered by man's sexual self-hatred and sexual confusion, his avowal "I can talk to women, but not to men," his romanticizing of his sexual dishonesty: "I can't talk to my wife, but I can talk to you." . . .

One of the devastating effects of technological capitalism has been its numbing of the powers of the imagination—specifically, the power to envision new human and communal relationships. I am a feminist because I feel endangered, psychically and physically, by this society, and because I believe that the women's movement is saying that we have come to an edge of history when men—in so far as they are embodiments of the patriarchal idea—have become dangerous to children and other living things, themselves included; and that we can no longer afford to keep the female principle—the mother in all women and the woman in many men—straitened within the tight little postindustrial family, or within any male-induced notion of where the female principle is valid and where it is not.[19]

What do you think Adrienne Rich is saying about the relation of men and women in contemporary society? In what ways does her discussion relate to the student's suggestion that there are "irreducible" differences between the sexes?

It is difficult to be objective in discussing these issues. Behavioral scientists are often heavily influenced by the assumptions or presuppositions they bring to research. Behaviorism, an influential trend in American behavioral research during the past fifty years, has emphasized the role of social conditioning in shaping what is often thought of as "human nature." Thus, behaviorists have tended to see human nature as relatively open and changeable. On the other hand, Freudian psychotherapists have often assumed that there are innate psychological differences between men and women which predispose them toward different personality structures and social roles. Recently a behavioral approach called "sociobiology" has emphasized genetic, biological factors that some have held fit men and women for different roles in society.

Conservative Christians sometimes appeal to the Genesis story of creation, according to which Eve was created to be a helper for Adam, so that Adam would not be alone, to argue for a basis in God's will for male superiority. In an interesting (and difficult to interpret) New Testament passage, I. Corinthians 11:8–12, Paul seems to argue that according to the original creation, woman *was* created for the sake of man and subject to man's authority, but in the new creation that has come through Christ, there is to be complete mutuality between woman and man. They are to be not independent of each other but mutually dependent.

Do you agree that in most societies women have been oppressed and are denied the opportunity to fulfill their human potential?

Is this true in our society?

Some feminists have stressed that as long as women are oppressed in our society, no one can be fully free. They thus see the feminist movement as working for complete human liberation.

Others have expressed fears about the impact of feminism on the traditional family structure. Still others have argued that the present decay of the nuclear family in our society through divorce is a symptom of the lack of mutuality in the relations between men and women.

[19]From *The New York Review of Books*, 19, no. 9 (November 30, 1972), 35–40. Reprinted with permission of the author. Copyright © 1972 by Adrienne Rich.

How do you feel about this?

Some sources that deal with the topics presented in this unit are: *Women and Philosophy*, edited by Carol C. Gould and Marx W. Wartofsky (New York: G. P. Putnam's Sons, 1976); *Religion and Sexism: Images of Women in Jewish and Christian Traditions* edited by Rosemary Radford Ruether (New York: Simon and Schuster, Inc., 1974); and Casey Miller and Kate Swift, *Words and Women* (Garden City, New York: Anchor Press/Doubleday & Co., Inc., 1977).

UNIT 68   Apartheid in South Africa

The government of South Africa claims the nation to be a Christian one, ruled by biblical principles. Central to that nation's life, however, is *apartheid*—"an Afrikaans expression that literally means separation or segregation . . ."[20] Since 1948, *apartheid* has come to connote the government's "system of racist rule, ranging from segregated washrooms, play grounds, and hospitals to the absence of nearly all black political rights and the wide gap between black and white incomes."[21]

This system of oppression against nearly twenty-two million blacks in South Africa favors the four and one-half million whites who own 87 percent of the land and nearly all of the minerals in South Africa. The "homelands" given to the blacks are unproductive, ruined by poor farming. Whites have the power of the law in their favor, the best jobs, the military strength and police force. Since South Africa's economy depends upon mineral resources and related industries requiring cheap labor in large numbers, blacks fill 71 percent of all industrial jobs.[22]

Racism permeates the political, economic, and cultural life of the whole nation. "Central to the system called apartheid is the notion that the different cultures and races of South Africa can never be an integrated whole, sharing a common citizenship."[23] One former prime minister expressed the purpose of apartheid by saying, "Our view is that in every sphere the Europeans must retain the right to rule the country and keep it a white man's country."[24] Because of such a position, Africans suffer dire poverty, humiliation, torture, land expropriation, imprisonment, shattered families, wrecked careers, deprived education, and unrelenting fear. "Even the supporters of apartheid pay a price, living in constant fear that they have created a monster and are losing basic human sensitivity."[25]

Some accounts of the inhumanity of apartheid come from South African newspapers, revealing daily injustices:

[20]Ernest Harsch, *South Africa: White Rule, Black Revolt* (New York: Monad Press, 1980), p. 56.
[21]*Ibid.*
[22]Unpublished paper, Greater Dallas Community of Churches, March, 1985.
[23]Louise Stack and Don Morton, *Torment to Triumph in Southern Africa* (New York: Friendship Press, 1976) p. 17.
[24]*Ibid.*, p. 18.
[25]*Ibid.*

White women living in western Krugersdorp have threatened to boycott the town's bus service if black drivers are used.

Bloemfontein's 2,000 African municipal employees are to be ringed in a new system to keep track of wages. The rings, which are plastic armbands fixed on the men's wrists with a machine, are color coded and bear a number. The armbands are virtually impossible to remove. . . .

Mr. Hutchinson Maholwanta has decided to employ Constance, his daughter, as a domestic, so she can stay with him. He is classified Coloured, she as an African. [*Colored* means mixed; *African* means black]

Several Black tennis officials who watched the Border Championships at the invitation of the Border Tennis president, Mr. H. W. Harrington, were asked to leave the main stand when one of the spectators objected. . . .

A 20-year-old White railway worker was yesterday sentenced by a Supreme Court judge here to 'five strokes with a light cane' for raping a 10-year-old African child. . . .

'I have witnessed with my own eyes old people, crippled with rheumatism, lying on the common of another platteland town, with nowhere to go. They had daughters living in the location but had been refused permits to join them. They had been lifelong farm laborers but were far past work on a farm or elsewhere. . . . The police were telling them to move on. But they had nowhere to go and nowhere to lay their heads. After a life of toil and poverty, the laws of their country had reduced them to the straits in which there was not a square inch of soil of their native land on which they could lawfully set foot.'[26]

What is the future for South Africa? How long will a system of such oppression remain in power? What are the Christian churches doing in the face of such injustice?

Afrikaans Dutch Reformed white churches support apartheid, claiming that native Africans are not yet civilized enough to rule. A number of white Christians say that God has called the whites to take care of the blacks.

The liberation movement among blacks in South Africa has among its leaders The reverend Desmond Mpilo Tutu, Anglican Bishop and General Secretary of the South African Council of Churches. Because of his efforts to unify various groups in the campaign to resolve the problems of apartheid, he was awarded the Nobel Peace Prize for 1984. He is considered a moderate who mediates between "rightist" and "leftist" groups. He believes that God not only has concern about individual salvation and ecclesiastical matters but also has "interest in the redemption of the socio-political and economic matrix in which individuals live."[27] He calls for the following: an "undivided South Africa" with "common citizenship" for all; the "abolition of Pass Laws," which restrict movement without identification; the halting of all "forced population removals;" and the establishment of a "uniform education system."[28] He believes in his cause and stands with courage to liberate his suffering people, as the following words indicate:

[26]*Ibid.*, pp. 51–55.
[27]Desmond Mpilo Tutu, *Hope and Suffering* (Grand Rapids, Mich.: William B. Erdmans Publishing Co., 1984), p. 38.
[28]*Ibid.*, p. 46.

We shall be free, about that there can be no doubt. The Black cause of liberation will triumph, must triumph because it is a just and righteous cause. God is on our side because He is always on the side of the oppressed. The only questions are how and when freedom will come. We want it now and we want it to come reasonably peacefully. Whites have to decide whether they want it all to happen by negotiation or through violence and bloodshed. . . .[29]

South Africa's apartheid is a vivid example of racism, but the phenomenon certainly is not limited to South Africa. Racial differences continue to produce intense conflict throughout the world. Aspects of some changes and adjustments to racial differences are discussed in the next unit.

UNIT 69 Ethnic Pluralism in Contemporary American Churches

The history of the so-called "mainline churches" in the United States indicates an exclusivism in which Anglo-American culture has dominated other cultures. Segregation in the United States has been reflected in the churches, separating people of color—especially Asians, blacks, Hispanics, and Native Americans—into congregations apart from whites. In most cases the ethnic-minority churches have been composed of those struggling to move beyond poverty. The larger, more affluent, white churches have usually been paternalistic toward Christians of color, extending occasional charity but without being inclusive.

New efforts to be inclusive began to emerge after the civil rights movement of the 1950s and '60s. Since the 1954 Supreme Court decision striking down inequality in education, a number of denominations have adopted a policy of "integration." The concept of "integration," however, has been applied for the most part from the vantage point of the more powerful white churches. Altruistic as they may have been, white Christians have tended to reflect the idea of the "American melting pot," but with a racist proviso—that the melding of races in America would still turn out white. "Whiteness" as a value indicating supposed superiority has been maintained throughout the history of Western civilization and of course has been a tragic theme in the Christian religion. "White is used to express the pure, while black expresses the diabolical."[30]

Even though minorities received invitations to join white churches, they still felt excluded. In various subtle ways, minorities were made aware of how difficult it is to cross cultural barriers and become integrated. Too often they felt that if they were to become equal in integrated white churches, they would have to be absorbed and abandon their own cultural roots.

In recent years the idea of integration has been reevaluated. Mainline de-

[29]*Ibid.*

[30]Roger Bastide, "Color, Racism, and Christianity" in *Color and Race*, John Hope Franklin (ed.), (Boston: Beacon Press, 1968), p. 34.

nominations in America have begun to propose "pluralism" as preferable to "integration." *Pluralism* connotes "diversity-in-unity and unity-in-diversity"—that is, fostering diverse cultural contributions while seeking unity in the Church. Some strong voices have sought to clarify that ethnic minorities represent vibrant cultures through which God is seeking to renew the total life of the Church. They support and seek to nurture cultural uniqueness, although in a context that affirms equally the positive contributions of all cultures.

In an address delivered in El Paso, Texas, in 1977, Woody White proposed another image to replace the "melting pot"—that of the "stewpot." Whereas the "melting pot" metaphor signifies a melding of different races and cultures into one in which each loses its original identity, the "stewpot" portrays that just as various vegetables and meats contribute to the making of a delicious stew without losing their various identities, so can ethnic minorities unite in "oneness" with each other and with the dominant culture while at the same time retaining their highly valuable cultural differences.

A factor that has strengthened pluralism as a significant way of viewing interethnic Christianity is the rapid growth of ethnic minorities in both numbers and influence in the United States. This has prompted mainline churches to reexamine church growth strategies, with an eye toward evangelizing ethnic minorities. Asian and Pacific Americans as well as Hispanics are expanding in numbers too quickly to enable them to be counted accurately. Although blacks compose the largest ethnic minority group (which is still growing) in the United States, demographic projections indicate that Hispanic increases suggest "the bronzing of America" and that Hispanics will become the largest minority in the United States, perhaps by the end of this century. Asian and Pacific Americans are immigrating by the thousands to the United States and have formed numerous new churches. Native Americans have asserted themselves throughout recent decades in search of ways to redress historical injustices against them. This has pricked the consciences of some Christians to reassess the ways in which churches relate to native Americans.

Those advocating ethnic pluralism in the churches argue that it calls for not only inclusive worship but also interethnic cooperation in all areas of church life. This is no easy task and demands that Christians of every ethnic background learn how to listen and learn from each other without racist bias but with ears tuned to hear the authentic and beautiful sounds of every culture. In a time when several mainline congregations have tended to settle into traditional modes of institutional existence and have even diminished in membership, it may well be that the influx of more people of color into various denominations will offer new life, variety, and enriched cultural perspectives through which the meaning of Christian commitment can be empowered. In recent years increasing numbers of white congregations have experienced this cross-cultural ferment as they have intentionally made contact with ethnic minority churches for cross-cultural worship, interethnic education, and the more difficult task of discussing and debating the Church's mission to a suffering world.

It has become clear that the future profile of at least some of the Christian churches in the United States will be pluralistic. This can provide both participants and observers a most creative opportunity to examine the interaction between changing patterns of culture and the norms and values of Christian religious groups as they interact in a society in which efforts affirm and elicit unique contributions of each ethnic group.

> *In your opinion, is it possible or wise to expect churches to become truly interethnic? Would such a movement reflect or counter social patterns in the rest of the culture?*

16

Religious Traditions and Social Stability

INTRODUCTION

Religious traditions may function as integrative and stabilizing forces in society (as in individual life). They may also function as agents of change or even of conflict in society (and in individual life). In this chapter we will be concerned with the role of religion as a unifying, integrative force in society, and in the next chapter with religion as a factor in social change.

We have defined religion as "reliance on a pivotal value in which the individual finds wholeness as an individual and as a person in community." The term *religious tradition* as used in this chapter refers to any complex of patterns of behavior, attitudes, and beliefs which function to express reliance on, or adherence to, a pivotal value (or values) by a group of people maintained and transmitted with some degree of continuity during a period of time.

In some cases a religious tradition will coincide with the value system of a whole society. In some cases it will be in tension with other value systems in the society. There may be conflicts *within* the value system of a religious tradition or society. In some cases a religious tradition, even that of a minority group within a larger society, endorses the dominant cultural values. Social change may come about by the adoption in the larger society of specifically religious values or attitudes belonging to what was originally a minority group. In other cases, a religious minority's system may be modified by the adoption into it of attitudes and values prevalent in the larger society.

Religious traditions, whether belonging to the whole society or majority or minority groups within it, very often encourage cultural and social stability. Sometimes religion serves as an integrating force in the society even when it encourages social changes. Often, however, religion plays a conservative role, resisting change or at least moderating its effects.

The units in this chapter deal with (1) the nature of religious community and some of its roles; (2) the role of religion in a highly unified, traditionally oriented, simply organized Brazilian tribal society; (3) the unity of the various facets of life in classical Greek culture; and (4) one of the major integrating themes or elements of Japanese society, the theme of simplicity.

UNIT 70   Community of Faith

The experience of religion is often uniquely individual. But even in those religions that most emphasize an individualistic approach to religion and that encourage individuals to develop or define their own individual beliefs, attitudes, and practices, there is a communal, or group, side to the nurturing of the individual's attitudes and to the preservation and continuity of tradition. This is true even if the tradition being handed on is one that emphasizes and promotes change. Belief in shared objects of faith, participation in shared rituals or practices, adherence to the same pivotal value or values—all these things make for community. Again, this is true even in the case of traditions in which the religious hermit is seen as the highest ideal of human life (as in Christianity in Egypt during the early centuries of the Christian era, and as has frequently been the case in Hinduism). Whatever the religious tradition, the community of faith, dependent itself on individual commitment and participation, provides support and guidance for individual believers and gives them a sense of belonging that helps to define individual identity and supports them in times of personal crisis.

Buddhism is a religious tradition that in many of its forms has been highly individualistic. Theravada Buddhism, especially, has taught that the individual finally must achieve Nirvana (complete enlightenment, fulfillment, salvation) by individual effort alone. Nevertheless, as the Buddhist monk's vow vividly shows, membership in the monastic community is indispensable as a source of discipline, sustaining order, and guidance.

A
I take refuge in the Buddha (the Ideal)
I take refuge in the Dharma (the Law or the Truth)
I take refuge in the Sangha (the Order of Monks)

Hebrew thought and experience is replete with this sense of community. One of the most ancient creeds, repeated individually through the centuries, is a striking example of the corporate nature of religion:

B

A wandering Aramean was my father; and he went down into Egypt and sojourned there, few in number; and there he became a nation, great, mighty, and populous. And the Egyptians treated us harshly, and afflicted us, and laid upon us hard bondage. Then we cried to the Lord the God of our fathers, and the Lord heard our voice, and saw our affliction, our toil, and our oppression; and the Lord brought us out of Egypt with a mighty hand and an outstretched arm, with great terror, with signs and wonders; and he brought us into this place and gave us this land, a land flowing with milk and honey. (Deuteronomy 26:5–9, RSV)

A contemporary expression of the significance of community is given by Malcolm X. A leader of the black movement in the early sixties, Malcolm X converted to the Muslim faith and traveled to Mecca to participate in the Hajj (the sacred pilgrimage).

C

> The believers indeed are brothers; so set things right between your two brothers, and fear God; haply so you will find mercy.[1]
>
> *The Koran*, Sura XLIX

Impressed, as a black man, with the oneness of the brotherhood, Malcolm X commented extensively on how common belief breaks down all lines of distinction—especially that of color. Having been asked what most impressed him in the Hajj he replied:

D

I said, "The *brotherhood*! The people of all races, colors, from all over the world coming together as *one*! It has proved to me the power of the One God. . . ."

I have reflected since that the letter I finally sat down to compose had been subconsciously shaping itself in my mind.

The *color-blindness* of the Muslim world's religious society and the *color-blindness* of the Muslim world's human society; these two influences had each day been making a greater impact, and an increasing persuasion against my previous way of thinking.

Here is what I wrote . . . from my heart:

Never have I witnessed such sincere hospitality and the overwhelming spirit of true brotherhood as is practiced by people of all colors and races here in this Ancient Holy Land, the home of Abraham, Muhammad, and all the other prophets of the Holy Scriptures. For the past week, I have been utterly speechless and spellbound by the graciousness I see displayed all around me by the people *of all colors*. . . .

America needs to understand Islam, because this is the one religion that erases from its society the race problem. Throughout my travels in the Muslim world, I have met, talked to, and even eaten with people who in America would have been considered "white"—but the "white" attitude was removed from their minds by the religion of Islam. I have never before seen *sincere* and *true* brotherhood practiced by all colors together, irrespective of their color. . . .

During the past eleven days here in the Muslim world, I have eaten from the same plate, drunk from the same glass, and slept in the same bed (or on the same

[1]Reprinted with permission of Macmillan, Inc., from *The Koran Interpreted*, by Arthur J. Arberry, Sura XLIX verse 10. © George Allen & Unwin, Ltd. 1955.

rug)—while praying to the *same* God—with fellow Muslims, whose eyes were the bluest of blue, whose hair was the blondest of blond, and whose skin was the whitest of white. And in the *words* and in the *actions* and in the *deeds* of the "white" Muslims, I felt the same sincerity that I felt among the black African Muslims of Nigeria, Sudan, and Ghana.

We were *truly* all the same (brothers)—because their belief in one God had removed the "white" from their minds, the "white from their *behavior,* and the "white" from their *attitude.*

I could see from this, that perhaps if white Americans could accept the Oneness of God, then perhaps, too, they could accept in *reality* the Oneness of Man—and cease to measure, and hinder, and harm others in terms of their "differences" in color. . . .

All praise is due to Allah, the Lord of all Worlds.[2]

Is it possible to have religion without some community of faith?

Is there a central affirmation that holds the community together in the examples given in the preceding passages?

UNIT 71 Wholeness of Life In a Simply Structured Society

The role of religion as a unifying element within society may be illustrated through study of a preliterate and simply structured society. In a book called *Tristes Tropiques*, the French anthropologist Claude Lévi-Strauss records observations made during his stay in a Bororo village in the interior of Brazil. The village, with a population of about 150, was a self-contained society, and at the time of Lévi-Strauss's observations it had been relatively little affected by the outside influences of European or Brazilian cultures.

One of the centers of Bororo life was the "men's house," a large building in the middle of the village. The young unmarried males of the Bororo tribe lived there; married males often took their meals in the men's house and spent much of their leisure time in it. It was also the place where preparations for the religious activities of the village went on: Religious chants were sung, and the closely guarded religious implements of the community (women members of the tribe were not allowed to see them) were made and stored. Married women were not allowed to enter the men's house; an unmarried woman was supposed to enter the building only once, when she came to propose marriage to her future husband.

Lévi-Strauss contrasts the Bororo attitude toward the "religious" dimension of life as he observed it in the men's house with the attitude he believed to be more characteristic of contemporary European society.

A

For the European observer, the apparently incompatible activities carried out in the men's house seem to harmonize in an almost shocking way. Few peoples are as deeply religious as the Bororo, and few have such a complex metaphysical sys-

---

[2]Malcolm X, *The Autobiography of Malcolm X*, with the assistance of Alex Haley, pp. 338–42. Reprinted by permission of Grove Press Inc. Copyright © 1964 by Alex Haley and Malcolm X. Copyright © 1965 by Alex Haley and Betty Shabazz.

tem. But spiritual beliefs and everyday habits are closely intermingled, and the natives do not appear to be conscious of moving from one system to another. I found the same easy-going religiosity in Buddhist temples along the Burmese frontier, where the priests live and sleep in the same hall as is used for worship, arrange their jars of ointment and personal collections of medicines on the ground in front of the altar. . . .

This casual attitude to the supernatural was . . . suprising to me . . . I lived during the First World War with my grandfather, who was Rabbi of Versailles. The house was attached to the synagogue by a long inner passage, along which it was difficult to venture without a feeling of anguish, and which in itself formed an impassable frontier between the profane world and that other. . . . Except when services were in progress, the synagogue remained empty. . . . Apart from my grandfather's silent prayer at the beginning of each meal, we children had no means of knowing that we were living under the egis of a superior order. . . .

Not that religion was treated with

greater reverence among the Bororo; on the contrary, it was taken for granted. In the men's house, ritualistic gestures were performed with the same casualness as all others, as if they were utilitarian actions intended to achieve a particular result, and did not require that respectful attitude which even the non-believer feels compelled to adopt on entering a place of worship. On a particular afternoon there would be singing in the men's house in preparation for the evening's public ritual. In one corner, boys would be snoring or chatting; two or three men would be humming and shaking rattles, but if one of them wanted to light a cigarette or if it were his turn to dip into the maize gruel, he would hand the instrument to a neighbour who carried on; or sometimes he would continue with one hand, while scratching himself with the other. When a dancer paraded up and down to allow his latest creation to be admired, everybody would stop and comment upon it; the service might seem to be forgotten until, in some other corner, the incantation was resumed at the point where it had been interrupted.[3]

In another passage, Lévi-Strauss describes one part of an elaborate funeral ceremony in the Bororo village:

B   Groups of men went into the forest to fetch armfuls of green palms, which were stripped of their leaves and then divided up into sections about 30 centimeters long. These were crudely tied together by the natives with dried grass, in bundles of two or three, like the rungs of a rope ladder several metres long. Two ladders of unequal length were made in this way, and then rolled up to form two solid discs, standing edgewise and respectively about 1.50 metres and 1.30 metres high. The sides were decorated with leaves held in place by a network of fine string made of plaited hair. These discs were the male and female *mariddo*, and the mak-

ing of them devolved upon the *Ewaguddu* clan.

Towards evening two groups, each consisting of five or six men, set out, one to the west, the other to the east. I followed the first group, and saw them making their preparations about fifty metres from the village, behind a screen of trees which concealed them from the other villagers. They covered themselves with leaves, like the dancers, and fixed their crowns in position. But this time, the secrecy of their preparations could be explained by the part they were playing: like the other group, they represented the souls of the dead which had come from

[3]Adapted from *Tristes Tropiqués* by Claude Lévi-Strauss. Translated by John and Doreen Weightman. English translation © 1973 by Jonathan Cape Limited. Reprinted by permission of Atheneum Publishers, U.S.A., and Jonathan Cape Limited, pp. 230–232.

their villages in the east and the west to welcome the deceased. When all was ready, they moved towards the dancing area, whistling as they went. The eastern group had already preceded them there (one group was, symbolically, going upstream, the other downstream, and the latter therefore moved faster).

Their timid and hesitant gait admirably conveyed their ghostly nature; I was reminded of Homer—of Ulysses struggling to prevent the flight of the ghosts repelled by blood. But all at once, the ceremony burst into life: men seized one or other of the two *mariddo* (which were all the heavier through having been made with fresh vegetation), lifted it high in the air and, thus encumbered, danced until they were exhausted and had to allow a rival to take it from them. The scene no longer had any mystic character; it had turned into a fair, where the young men were showing off their physical prowess in an atmosphere characterized by sweat, thumpings and gibes. And yet this sport, which exists in secular forms among neighbouring communities,—for instance, in the log races practiced by the Ge tribes of the Brazilian plateau— retains its full religious significance with the Bororo: in this mood of gay abandon, the natives feel they are playing with the dead and wresting from them the right to remain alive.[4]

For Bororo society, "the religious" is not, then, one aspect or activity of life, distinct from other aspects. There is not a specifically religious attitude different from the attitude toward everyday or secular activities and events; the religious dimension of life thoroughly penetrates and is penetrated by the nonreligious dimensions—in fact, speaking of the religious and the nonreligious or secular as two different dimensions of life would probably be foreign to the Bororo way of thinking. Nevertheless, Lévi-Strauss points out that there *is* a social division of labor in religious matters. "The women were excluded from the [religious] rites and deceived as to their true nature—doubtless to sanction the division of rights by which [women] take priority, where housing and birth rites are in question, leaving the mysteries of religion to their men.[5]

> *How does the Bororo attitude compare with the attitude of classical Greek society toward "religion" as a dimension of life?*
>
> *It is interesting that a similar social division of responsibility existed in classical Greece: women and slaves did not participate fully in the "wholeness" of Greek life, which was economically and politically more complex than Bororo society. Has this been true of most societies?*

UNIT 72   Wholeness of Life in Classical Greece

Unit 71 describes the unifying effect of religion in a simple society. This same function of unification may also be observed in more complex societies such as that of the ancient Greeks. H. D. F. Kitto, in a book that studies the life and culture of Greece, focusing particularly on the classical period (especially the sixth and fifth

[4]*Ibid.*, pp. 227–28.
[5]*Ibid.*, pp. 229–30.

centuries B.C.), has emphasized the *wholeness* of outlook that characterized Greek civilization. Typically, the Greeks of the classical period did not see different dimensions of life (like the religious and the secular, the moral and the aesthetic, the intellectual and the physical, the private and the social) as separated from one another. Many civilizations have made rather sharp distinctions among these areas of life. The wholeness, or integration, of the various areas of life in Greek civilization can be seen, Kitto thinks, if we examine some of the terms of the Greek language. The word *kalos* is usually translated as "beautiful," but *kalos* is used to describe actions that we would consider heroic or noble, traits of character we would consider morally good, instruments that are well made or useful. In fact the word means something like "worthy of warm admiration" and may be used to refer to goodness or beauty or appropriateness—anything that we might want to classify under one of the following categories: moral, intellectual, aesthetic, or practical. Kitto thinks that most civilizations, including our own, *have* made distinctions among these categories, but the Greeks did not. In the same way, the Greek word *aischros*, usually translated as "ugly," can be used to describe *morally* bad actions, *physical* ugliness, *baseness* (in the sense of lack of worth or merit), *uselessness* (in the practical sense) and, among other things, *badness* of character. To look at two other terms, Kitto notes that:

The word "hamartia" means "error," "fault," "crime" or even "sin"; literally, it means "missing the mark," "a bad shot." We exclaim, "How intellectualist these Greeks were! Sin is just 'missing the mark'; better luck next time!" Again we seem to find confirmation when we find that some of the Greek virtues seem to be as much intellectual as moral—a fact that makes them untranslatable, since our own vocabulary must distinguish. There is "Sôphrosynê," literally "whole-mindedness" or "unimpaired-mind-edness." According to the context it will mean "wisdom," "prudence," "temperateness," "chastity," "sobriety," "modesty," or "self-control," that is, something entirely intellectual, something entirely moral, or something intermediate. Our difficulty with the word, as with *hamartia*, is that we think more in departments. *Hamartia*, "a bad shot," does not mean "better luck next time"; it means rather that a mental error is as blameworthy, and may be as deadly, as a moral one.[6]

Do you find that people in modern society tend to see religious and secular activities as separate or different from each other?

Kitto finds the classical Greek understanding of life's wholeness clearly present in the Greek attitude toward athletic contests:

The sharp distinction which the Christian and the Oriental world has normally drawn between the body and the soul, the physical and the spiritual, was foreign to

[6]H. D. F. Kitto, *The Greeks*. Copyright © H. D. F. Kitto, 1951, 1957, pp. 170–71. Used by permission of Penguin Books, Ltd.

the Greek—at least until the time of Socrates and Plato. To him there was simply the whole man. That the body is the tomb of the soul is indeed an idea which we meet in certain Greek mystery-religions, and Plato, with his doctrine of immortality, necessarily distinguished sharply between body and soul; but for all that, it is not a typical Greek idea. The Greek made physical training an impor-tant part of education, not because he said to himself, "Look here, we mustn't forget the body," but because it could never occur to him to train anything but the whole man. It was as natural for the polis to have gymnasia as to have a theatre or warships, and they were constantly used by men of all ages, not only for physical but also for mental exercise.

Is Kitto right in saying that Christianity has "normally drawn" a "sharp distinction" between body and soul, the physical and the spiritual? Can you find aspects of Christian belief or practice that go against this kind of separation? Do Oriental or Eastern religions—for instance, Hinduism or Zen Buddhism—make as sharp a distinction between the physical and the spiritual as Kitto suggests? To what extent does modern society make a sharp distinction between the physical and the spiritual, the intellectual and the spiritual, or the intellectual and the moral?

But it is the Games, local and international, which most clearly illustrate this side of the Greek mind. Among us it is sometimes made a reproach that a man "makes a religion of games." The Greek did not do this, but he did something perhaps more surprising: he made games part of his religion. To be quite explicit, the Olympian games, the greatest of the four international festivals, were held in honor of Zeus of Olympia, the Pythian Games in honour of Apollo, the Panathenaic Games in honor of Athena. Moreover, they were held in the sacred precinct. The feeling that prompted this was a perfectly natural one. The contest was a means of stimulating and displaying human *aretê*, and this was a worthy offering to the god. . . . But since *aretê* is of the mind as well as of the body, there was not the slightest incongruity or affectation in combining musical contests with athletic: a contest in flute-playing was an original fixture in the Pythian Games—for was not Apollo himself "Lord of the Lyre"?

The Greek word *aretê* is usually translated to mean "virtue," but "excellence" is probably better, since in modern English, "virtue" usually means *only* "moral goodness."

It was *aretê* that the games were designed to test—the *aretê* of the whole man, not a merely specialized skill. The usual events were a sprint, of about 200 yards, the long race (1½ miles), the race in armour, throwing the discus, and the javelin, the long jump, wrestling, boxing (of a very dangerous kind), and chariot-racing. The great event was the pen-tathlon: a race, a jump, throwing the discus, and the javelin, and wrestling. If you won this, you were a man. Needless to say, the Marathon race was never heard of until modern times: the Greeks would have regarded it as a monstrosity. As for the skill shown by modern champions in games like golf or billiards, the Greeks would certainly have admired it intensely, and thought it an admirable thing—in a slave, supposing that one had no better use for a slave than to train him in this way. Impossible, he would say, to acquire skill like this and at the same time to live the proper life of a man and a citizen. It is this feeling that underlies Aristotle's remark that a gentleman should be able to play the flute—but not too well.[7]

This stress on the unity of language and on athletic competence in many sports illustrates the integration of all of one's abilities in Greek culture. Religion tended to unify or support these and other elements of life, both social and individual.

Does the fact of vocational specialization—differentiation of roles—in complex modern societies—the fact that there are religious professionals (ministers, priests, rabbis), professional athletes, military professionals, professional critics of art and literature, and so forth, necessarily lead to a division of life, a loss of the wholeness or integration of its different parts or dimensions?

UNIT 73   Japanese Fondness for Simplicity

The Japanese cherish simplicity. The fondness for simplicity has been a characteristic unifying element in Japanese culture. It has helped the Japanese adapt foreign ideas, forms of expression, and practices to Japanese life, integrating them into Japanese culture and giving them a distinctively Japanese flavor. It has also helped integrate religious traditions so that both the native religions and those imported have a particular Japanese form and character.

Fondness for simplicity is seen in most areas of Japanese life and expression. For each of the examples cited in the following discussion by Hajime Nakamura, compare Western attitudes toward simplicity or the lack of it in the areas of life or expression that correspond to those of Japanese culture.

A

Traditionally, the Japanese have been inclined to dislike fanciful, complicated expressions and to take to simple and naive expressions. The Japanese language . . . is deficient in words expressing prolix and abstract conceptions. Consequently, even to this day, they use Chinese words, in most cases, to express abstract ideas.

In art, also, this tendency can be discerned clearly. The Japanese are very fond of the impromptu short verse, like the *haiku* and *tanka*. In the history of Japanese poetry, the long verse . . . is reduced to a short one (*tanka*), and then to a still shorter one (*haiku*). The extremely short form of artistic expression is characteristically Japanese and the like of it cannot be found elsewhere. . . . In Japanese literature, lyric poems and scenery sketches have been highly developed, but poems of grand style, with dramatic plots full of twists and turns, have made only a poor start.

Not only in poetry but also in archi-

---

[7]*Ibid.*, pp. 173–74.

B

The Ise Shrine, in Japan, is the National Shrine of Japanese Shintoism. (Courtesy Ministry of Foreign Affairs, Government of Japan.)

tecture, we can recognize the characteristic love of simplicity. The Japanese imported various formative arts from Indian Buddhism, indirectly through the hands of Chinese and Koreans. As seen in the magnificent splendor of golden Buddhist altars and mural paintings of temples, the complicated sculptures of transoms, the fantastic statue of the Goddess of Mercy . . . with a thousand arms, the square diagram of figures (Mandala) with its intricate and delicate composition—all of them had, in general, a very elaborate structure. But, such an art could hardly penetrate into the life of the common people. The Japanese could not abandon the simple and unpainted wooden architecture of ancient style, in many shrines as well as in the Great Shrine of Ise. And, even in the architecture of Buddhist temples, the various sects of the Kamakura period [1185–1333] turned to a rather simple style. Also, in the Zen-influenced taste of the tea-ceremony house, we can discern a naive simplicity. . . . In some cases, especially under the influence of the Zen cult, the Japanese endeavored to infuse unlimited complexity into this simplicity. This tendency emerged especially in such arts as architecture, drawing, and poetry. For example, the void of empty spaces or of silent pauses is often not devoid, in fact, of important meaning. Even in the etiquette and conversation of everyday life, silence can be a very

positive expression at times. This ideal fusion of the complex and the simple was realized by the Chinese people, who loved complicated thinking and whose spiritual life was greatly influenced by the Zen cult. When introduced into Japan, however, this, too, was altered by greater simplification. . . .

Thus, because complicated symbols were not used by the Japanese in their thinking, the philosophical theories of Indian and Chinese Buddhism were too profound, abstruse, and complicated to penetrate into the life of the common people in Japan. Consequently, they had to be simplified.

The Japanese, in assimilating Buddhism, did not depend upon its philosophical doctrines. Of course, the clergymen of large temples were engaged in philosophical debates and wrote a great number of books. The common people, however, demanded concrete and empirical clues rather than philosophical theories. . . .

The tendency to fondness for simple symbols appeared in the process of adoption of Buddhist ideas by Japanese Shintoists in ancient and medieval times. . . . Shintō, in the process of its development as religion, advanced from the cleanness of the body to the idea of cleanness of spirit. This "internal cleanness" was expressed by moral virtues of "sincerity" and "honesty." The virtues of gods of

Shintō were admired through these virtues. But we can find these terms in the Buddhist sūtras. Besides, the benevolence and wisdom, admired as virtues of gods, are, of course, Buddhist terms. Therefore, it is not too much to say that almost all of the terms of the central virtues of medieval Shintō were derived from Buddhist sūtras. It must be pointed out, however, that Shintoists never adopted the doctrines of Buddhism indiscriminately. Only the virtues, which had originally existed as germs in Shintō, were brought to definite consciousness and expression by the help of Buddhist philosophy. The Shintoists did not take in the speculative, schematized, and generalized classifications of virtues of the Indian Buddhism. . . . They took in directly those virtues which happened to appear congenial to Shintō. Consequently, they hardly endeavored to interpret the relations among these virtues systematically and speculatively.

"Virtues of the Indian Buddhism" refers to such teachings as those contained in the Four Noble Truths and the Eightfold Path. See Unit 21, "Gautama's Quest for Nirvana."

We have tried to demonstrate that through the process of assimilation of Buddhism many Japanese people are inclined to give direction to their practice through very simple symbols. This tendency reappeared, it seems, in the introduction of Christianity from the period of the Civil Wars [which lasted for a century] to the beginning of the Tokugawa period in the 17th century. The Japanese Christians [Roman Catholics] devoted themselves to such simple symbols of Christianity as the cross. The trampling of the holy image *(Fumi-e)* sufficed, on

c

Sacred image, a copper or wooden tablet with a crucifix or the Virgin Mary, used by the Tokugawa government to suppress Christianity. All who refused to tread on such an image (the test was conducted every New Year after 1628) were executed as Christians. (Tokyo National Museum. Reproduced by permission.)

this psychological ground, as a loyalty test at the time of the Christian Inquisition in Japan.

We may say that religion is always simplified when it is popularized. . . . If we look back to the trend of Japanese thought in recent years, we can realize that the complete reliance upon simple symbols has been one of the most deep-rooted attitudes of the Japanese people.[8]

Tanka—a thirty-one-syllable poem

Haiku—a seventeen-syllable poem

The *haiku* is extraordinarily *simple*, but it is highly symbolic and suggestive. Here is an example by the poet Matsuo Bashō (1644–1694):

> Breaking the surface
> of a still pond a frog jumps—
> The silence echoes

---

[8]Hajime Nakamura, *Ways of Thinking of Eastern Peoples: India-China-Tibet-Japan* (Honolulu, Hawaii: East-West Center Press, 1964), pp. 564–65; 572–73. By permission of the University Press of Hawaii.

17

Religious Traditions
and Social Change

INTRODUCTION

In the last chapter we dealt with religious traditions and their relation to social stability. In this chapter we will seek to examine the relationship between religious traditions and the process of social change.

As society becomes more open, urbanized, and heterogeneous, social stability becomes more difficult to maintain. At the same time, religious institutions themselves cannot remain unaffected by this change. They respond to it either positively or negatively—that is, either by coming to terms with the new problems or by resistance and withdrawal from them.

In this chapter we present aspects of the response religious institutions may make to the problems relating to social change. The first unit is centered on the challenges presented to religious traditions by population growth and the resultant mass hunger. In the second unit, the rapid increase in the growth of technology and the implications for change it suggests are considered. Next, the process of secularization is considered. The stress between forces of change and the reluctance of some in every society to identify with change is the focus of the consideration of fundamentalism. The patterns and character of modernization and the alienation it, and other forces in a society, creates are the topics of the final units.

UNIT 74 The Challenge of World Hunger

A

(Jacques Bakke)

The problem of hunger is acute and promises to become more so with each passing year. Concerned persons throughout the world ponder the complexities of the world food crisis, what has led to its more rapid development, and what avenues to solution may be found. This unit looks at some of the issues raised by the problem of hunger as it causes rapid social change. The responses of different religious traditions reflect their particular social contexts and understandings of nature and the universe.

One of the Major Causes

B

Almost two centuries ago, in 1798, an Englishman named Thomas Malthus warned that the population would race ahead of the food supply. It would do so, he argued, because we can only *add* to the food supply, while the population *multiplies*. At that time the world's population of less than one billion was growing at a rate of about one-half of 1 percent annually. Now the growth rate is about 2 percent for the world and 2.5 percent for poor countries as a whole. These percentages may seem small, but the increase makes a dramatic difference.

By 1930 the world had two billion people. If you were born in 1930, the world's population has already doubled within your lifetime; and if you live to the turn of the century, you will be able to add still another two or three billion people. *During your lifetime the earth's living population will have more than tripled its previous total achievement.*

That is an explosion.

It explains why the population graphs show a horizontal line veering suddenly upward—as though a cyclist, riding along a barely noticable slope, began pedaling straight up a cliff.

The world is presently adding 70 million persons each year to its numbers: the equivalent of the entire U.S. population every three years. Most of this growth is taking place in the poor countries, among hungry people. Today's poor countries already contain more than two-thirds of the earth's population. Soon they will contain three-fourths, and by the turn of the century, four-fifths of the human race. All the while demand for the world's food supply will climb sharply each year, and—barring unprecedented global efforts—increasing numbers will wind up in the "hungry" category. No wonder the mother from the Bronx and a great many other U.S. citizens are saying: "The only solution to the hunger problem is birth control."

Consider the evidence, however:

Lower death rates, not higher birth rates, are responsible for today's population growth. Poor countries as a whole have actually lowered their birth rates slightly over the past several decades—but death rates have dropped more sharply, and that achievement has touched off the population boom. Advances in medicine and public health, along with increases in food production, account for most gains against early death. For example, while Malthus wrote his *Essay on Population*, a fellow Englishman named Edward Jenner was discovering a vaccination for smallpox. This discovery foreshadowed a long series of steps in disease control that cut back death rates.

The population explosion began in Europe. Not the "inconsiderate poor" of Asia, Africa and Latin America, but our own ancestors touched it off. A few simple statistics show this. In 1800 about 22 percent of the human race was Caucasian; but by 1930 (only five or six generations later) that percentage had jumped to about 35. This happened because the new technologies that pushed back the death rate occurred in the West. During that time the white, European peoples had two enormous advantages:

1. *Industrial growth kept ahead of population increases.* Because gains in public health occurred gradually, population growth rates also increased gradually. The Industrial Revolution had begun earlier, so the population increase was usually needed in the cities by industries, which depended upon a growing supply of unskilled workers. Although the Industrial Revolution imposed cruel hardships on those who moved from farms to sweatshops and urban slums, the suffering would have been greater and the social situation far more explosive had the population raced ahead of industrial jobs. But the jobs usually got there first.

2. *New lands opened up for colonization.* New lands, including North America, offered an important outlet to population stresses that did develop. For example after the potato famine ravaged Ireland in the 1840s, almost a million Irish came to our shores within five years.

When periods of unemployment occurred, new lands provided a place to seek work. They also handed European peoples an impressive psychological advantage by keeping hopes alive.

Poor nations face a sharply different situation today. Two centuries of public health gains were made available to them more rapidly, so their populations began to soar almost without warning. Their people now pour into the cities long before industries can possibly supply them with jobs; and for all but a few there simply is no frontier, no new lands to colonize, no safety valve.

Population growth was cushioned in the West (1) because the death rate receded gradually, and (2) because people became economically more self-sufficient and less dependent upon their offspring for security. Today's poor countries have moved quickly into the first stage: Public health measures and modern medicine have reduced the death rate—but much faster than in the West, causing their populations to multiply more swiftly. *But the second stage is not taking hold.* A majority of people in the poor countries are *not* moving toward the point where their sense of security is clearly related to having fewer children. Instead the opposite usually applies: more children mean more security."[1]

What Is Hunger?[2]

Hunger is a weakened condition brought about by the prolonged lack of food. There are four basic types of hunger:

C

1. Chronic Undernutrition

Undernutrition results when people do not consume sufficient calories and protein over a prolonged period of time. This is the most widespread but least recognized form of hunger. It is invisible, persistent, and debilitating. The headlines capture dramatic images of acute starvation, but the vast majority of the hungry suffer in quiet obscurity through chronic undernutrition. The effects include:

Decreased mental attentiveness
Permanent mental retardation
Listlessness
Emotional stress
Decreased productivity
Increased susceptibility to disease

2. Malnutrition

Malnutrition results from specific deficiencies in essential vitamins and minerals vital to good health. Malnutrition is closely related to undernutrition, but the physical manifestations are more obvious. Common effects include:

[1]Arthur Simon, *Bread for the World* (New York: Paulist Press, 1975), pp. 28–31. Used by permission.
[2]Items C, D, E, and G of this unit are drawn from *The Hunger Primer*, a publication of *Food for the Hungry*. Used by permission.

Blindness: Up to 100,000 children become blind each year because of insufficient Vitamin A.

Anemia: Five hundred million women in developing countries are anemic due to a lack of iron in their diets.

3. Famine

Famine is the widespread, extreme scarcity of food, affecting an entire region. Often it is closely associated with disaster situations such as drought, flood and war, which disrupt the availability of food to an area. Without the institutional ability to handle the crisis, famine results. No more than 10% of hunger-related deaths are due to famine. Food may exist in an area struck by famine, but the deep poverty of the people, combined with over-inflated prices, make the food available only to the wealthy. Much of the "surplus" is then exported to countries that can pay the higher prices.

4. Seasonal Undernutrition

Seasonal undernutrition occurs annually, as harvests stored from the previous year are depleted before the new crops can be harvested. Families may go hungry for weeks, or even months at a time.

What Is the Magnitude of Hunger?

D

One out of every eight people in the world is hungry most of the time.

450 million people, one-fourth of the developing world, suffer from undernutrition.

Every year, almost 13 million people die as a result of hunger and starvation—the equivalent of all the children under five in the United States.

One billion people in the world have various degrees of brain damage because of inadequate consumption.

More people have died of hunger in the past five years than have been killed in all wars, revolutions, and murders in the past 150 years.

Who Are the Hungry?

E

Children

One-third of the children in developing countries die of malnourishment before age 5.

Of the 24 people that die from hunger each minute, 18 are children.

One out of every four children in the developing world dies by the age of five from hunger and hunger-related causes.

Rural Poor

Three-quarters of the hungry live in rural areas.

Over 600 million people live in rural households that are either completely landless or near-landless.

In Latin America, 7% of the farmers own 93% of the land, and more than 60% of the rural poor are landless altogether.

Urban Poor

One-fourth of the hungry live in burgeoning urban slums.

Slums form up to 75% or more of the cities in some developing countries, with as many as 20 people living in one room.

Millions of rural landless have moved to cities in hopes of finding work, but discover jobs are not available.

Refugees

A refugee is a person who flees his home to escape invasion, oppression or persecution.

Currently, over 10 million people are classified as refugees.

At least one million people a year are added to the list of refugees in the world.

850,000 refugees have resettled in the United States.

Some Moral Dimensions in Solving the Problem

F

Although world food output has expanded impressively over the past generation, population growth so far has absorbed all but a fraction of the increase. Hundreds of millions of the world's people still do not have enough food to fully realize their genetic potential as human beings. In a situation of global food scarcity, if some of us consume more, others must of necessity consume less. The issue that some of us are forced to confront in a world where we are dependent on common resources of energy and fertilizer to produce food is whether we can realize *our* full humanity if we continue to overconsume in full knowledge that we are thereby contributing to the premature death of fellow human beings. Former Chancellor Willy Brandt of West Germany summed up this point effectively in his first address before the U.N. General Assembly in the fall of 1973: "Morally it makes no difference whether a man is killed in war or is condemned to starve to death by the indifference of others."

Altruism is a hallmark of civilized society. But in a world transformed from a collection of relatively independent, isolated nation-states to one of complex interdependence, reliant on the sharing of often scarce resources, our concept of altruism must be adjusted. It is no longer merely a matter of alms-giving but of abstaining from excessive consumption when that consumption jeopardizes the very survival of human beings elsewhere in the world. For a man with only one crust of bread, a second crust may ensure survival, but for one with a loaf of bread, an additional crust is of marginal value. What is at issue in the global politics of food scarcity is who will get the additional crust—affluent consumers in the United States and the Soviet Union, who do not need it, or those on the brink of survival in the Indian subcontinent and in the sub-Saharan countries of Africa. . . .[3]

Both conventional wisdom and economics have long held that the more the rich countries consume, the greater the markets will be for products of the developing countries. This is still true in some situations, but only to a degree. If the supply of a given resource cannot be expanded easily, continuing growth in consumption in the affluent countries will drive the price beyond the reach of the poor countries.

Our intent here is not to suggest that all affluent Americans, Russians, Europeans, or Japanese should abandon their automobiles or abstain from eating meat; it is to urge those who are more affluent

[3]Lester R. Brown, *By Bread Alone* (New York: Praeger Publishers, 1974), pp. 250–51. Reprinted by permission of Praeger Publishers, a Division of Holt, Rinehart & Winston.

to re-examine the link between their consumption of material goods and their own well-being. We need to ask whether a 20 percent increase in income indeed brings a 20 percent increase in well-being, a 10 percent increase, or any increase at all. It has been said that there are two sources of unhappiness: not getting what we want, and getting it. Many of us may be in a situation where the only real satisfaction can come from trying to improve the lot of the world's most seriously deprived: those living in the Fourth World. Indeed, this could be the new moral and social frontier for mankind.[4]

What Are the Causes of Hunger?

G It is difficult to attribute hunger to a single cause. Today, however, most experts agree that the main cause of hunger is *poverty*, or a lack of financial, material and educational resources: The world's poor do not have enough of these resources to provide a subsistence livelihood for their families. However, hunger and poverty are not due to a simple lack of resources. Inequitable use of resources, poor stewardship, and systems that perpetrate this inequality do not allow the poor to have access to the resources that are available.

> Disparate patterns of land ownership in developing countries, aggravated by unjust trade policies, concentrate resources into the hands of the wealthy few.
> Technology appropriate to the needs of Third World agriculture and the necessary training to implement this technology are not made available to the rural poor.
> These factors culminate in the wide income disparity found in developing countries today.

However, even this assessment does not go far enough. Hunger and poverty are much broader than the mere physical and are not confined only to the Third World.

Hunger, like poverty, can be found in all aspects of human need: physical, emotional, intellectual and spiritual.

> Around the world, not only in the poor countries, I have found that the poverty of the West is so much more difficult to remove.

—Mother Theresa

What attitudes toward hunger might one expect among Buddhists, Hindus, and Christians?

What does it mean to be ethically responsible in this crisis?

UNIT 75 Religion, Humanity, and Technology

A prehominid, a manlike primate, is toying with a large bone from a long-dead animal; while manipulating, he accidentally discovers a function for it. He makes of it a tool, a weapon. Another step is taken in the process of learning to manipulate

[4]*Ibid.*, p. 251.

environment in order to satisfy personal or group needs. Others learn from him this new skill and a new stage in the sophistication of the species begins.

Humans embark upon the long journey to the planet Jupiter in a complex, computer-operated spacecraft. The newest accomplishment of human technology has reached an unprecedented level of sophistication. Without the efficient functioning of the intricate computer system, the life-support system as well as the transport to the distant planet would not be possible. Enroute, complications develop which result in the decision by the computer system to sacrifice human beings in the interest of completing the mission for which it was programmed. Human technology is then beyond control and the passengers are at its mercy.

Stanley Kubrick, in his fascinating film *2001: A Space Odyssey*, seems to have voiced a protest against humanity's allowing itself to become a slave to its technology. As human beings develop new tools in order to meet their needs in the exploration and understanding of their immediate and distant environment, must they not discern those points where technology no longer serves its creative purpose, or where it even dehumanizes the species? The following materials elaborate on the problems raised by technology and some responses given to them.

How do different religious traditions look at technology? The answer to this question can be found perhaps by asking how the different religious traditions look at humanity in relation to nature and history. How do the different religious traditions view historical change? Will human beings have a role in shaping the future? If they do, is this a way of fulfilling their destiny or is it a kind of impiety, a way of disrupting the divinely or naturally ordained patterns of life?

The Protestant theologian Harvey Cox has argued that the Judeo-Christian tradition has been inconsistent or ambivalent in answering these questions. He has found three different positions about the role of humanity in shaping the future. Sometimes persons within the Jewish or Christian tradition have held an "apocalyptic" view that foresees an imminent catastrophe brought about by direct divine intervention. This view carries a negative evaluation of the present world, of humans' ability to shape the future through their own efforts, and therefore of their own technology. A second view within the Jewish and Christian traditions is the "teleological." It sees the future as the certain unfolding of fixed purposes built into the structure of the universe. According to the teleological view, present technological efforts, as a part of the automatic movement to the future, may be valued highly. But the human responsibility to exercise critical judgment about which technological possibilities to develop and how to use them tends to be ignored. Finally, some persons within the Jewish-Christian tradition have held a position described by Cox as "prophetic." The prophetic tradition, he believes, has emphasized that the future is open and that it will become what the human race makes of it. Thus, both human technology and responsibility to use it wisely, with concern for its effects on the whole human community, are stressed.[5]

Cox's analysis gives us a typology defining how Protestant Christianity has responded to the problem. Two popes of the Roman Catholic Church in recent

[5]Harvey Cox, "Tradition and the Future," Parts I & II, *Christianity and Crisis*, 27, nos. 16–17 (1967).

years have issued encyclicals which present a particular Christian position regarding human technology in relation to God's will and purposes.

A

Peace on earth, which men of every era have most eagerly yearned for, can be firmly established only if the order laid down by God is dutifully observed.

The progress of learning and the inventions of technology clearly show that, both in living things and in the forces of nature, an astonishing order reigns, and they also bear witness to the greatness of man, who can understand that order and create suitable instruments to harness those forces of nature and use them to his benefit.

But the progress of science and the inventions of technology show above all the infinite greatness of God, who created the universe and man himself. He created all things out of nothing, pouring into them the abundance of His wisdom and goodness, so that the holy psalmist praises God in these words: *O Lord, our Lord how glorious is your name in all the earth.* Elsewhere he says: *How manifold are your works. O Lord! In wisdom you have wrought them all.*

God also created man in his own *image and likeness*, endowed him with intelligence and freedom, and made him lord of creation, as the same psalmist declares in the words: *You have made him little less than the angels, and crowned him with glory and honor. You have given him rule over the works of your hands, putting all things under his feet.*

Nevertheless, in order to imbue civilization with sound principles and enliven it with the spirit of the gospel, it is not enough to be illumined with the gift of faith and enkindled with the desire of forwarding a good cause; it is also necessary to take an active part in the various organizations and influence them from within.

And since our present age is one of outstanding scientific and technical progress, one cannot enter these organizations and work effectively from within unless he is scientifically competent, technically capable and skilled in the practice of his own profession. . . .

In other words, it is necessary that human beings, in the intimacy of their own consciences, should so live and act in their temporal lives as to create a synthesis between scientific, technical and professional elements on the one hand, and spiritual values on the other.[6]

B

All of you who have heard the appeal of suffering peoples, all of you who are working to answer their cries, you are the apostles of a development which is good and genuine, which is not wealth that is self-centered and sought for its own sake, but rather an economy which is put at the service of man, the bread which is daily distributed to all, as a source of brotherhood and a sign of Providence.

With a full heart We bless you, and We appeal to all men of good will to join you in a spirit of brotherhood. For, if the new name for peace is development, who would not wish to labour for it with all his powers? Yes, We ask you, all of you, to heed Our cry of anguish, in the name of the Lord.[7]

Each of these encyclicals calls for active involvement in the changes wrought by technology by persons committed to a religious perspective so as to influence the changes.

C. P. Snow, a twentieth-century novelist who was trained as a physicist,

[6]Pope John XXIII, *Pacem in Terris* (Peace on Earth) (New York: The American Press, 1963), pp. 3–4; 46–47.

[7]Pope Paul VI, *Populorum Progresso* (On the Development of Peoples) (Boston: St. Paul Editions, 1967), pp. 50–51.

expressed concern about what he understood to be a dangerous gulf between the scientific-technological world and the rest of human experience and expression (in academic terminology, the area of the humanities). Discussing the complicated question of how we can best utilize scientific-technological-industrial developments in a social and human world, he wrote:

C

Industrialisation is the only hope of the poor. I use the word "hope" in a crude and prosaic sense. I have not much use for the moral sensibility of anyone who is too refined to use it so. It is all very well for us, sitting pretty, to think that material standards of living don't matter all that much. It is all very well for one, as a personal choice, to reject industrialisation—do a modern Walden, if you like, and if you go without much food, see most of your children die in infancy, despise the comforts of literacy, accept twenty years off your own life, then I respect you for the strength of your aesthetic revulsion. But I don't respect you in the slightest if, even passively, you try to impose the same choice on others who are not free to choose. In fact, we know what their choice would be. For, with singular unanimity, in any country where they have had the chance, the poor have walked off the land into the factories as fast as the factories could take them. . . .

The industrial revolution looked very different according to whether one saw it from above or below. It looks very different today according to whether one sees it from Chelsea or from a village in Asia. To people like my grandfather, there was no question that the industrial revolution was less bad than what had gone before. The only question was, how to make it better.

In a more sophisticated sense, that is still the question. In the advanced countries, we have realised in a rough and ready way what the old industrial revolution brought with it. A great increase of population, because applied science went hand in hand with medical science and medical care. Enough to eat, for a similar reason. Everyone able to read and write, because an industrial society can't work without. Health, food, education; nothing but the industrial revolution could have spread them right down to the very poor. Those are primarily gains—there are losses too, of course, one of which is that organising a society for industry makes it easy to organise it for all-out war. But the gains remain. They are the base of our social hope.[8]

These examples suggest that efforts must be made to direct the use of technology in appropriate, humane ways. One can argue that scientific and technological advances are themselves based on values. They are expressions of human goals for the individual and society. As such, they improve humanity's condition. Nevertheless, they also disrupt and modify our patterns of living. Inevitably, these changes cause conflict between traditional ethical values and the new possibilities offered by technology. Some of the questions scientific and technological developments pose include the following:

Should our technology determine our future as a culture? How shall we use our technology? To what extent should it shape the direction of our lives? Who should make these decisions?

Does the use of technology *need to be regulated?*

[8]C. P. Snow, *The Two Cultures: And A Second Look* (New York: Cambridge University Press, 1959, 1963), pp. 30–32. Used by permission.

Should religious and ethical values regulate the use of findings of scientific investigation?

Should technological changes and advances be made merely because they are now possible?

Can we expect whole societies to have the knowledge and interest to resolve these questions according to democratic decision-making procedures?

UNIT 76   Secularization

The changes and modifications in the relationship of religion to society are often referred to as "secularization." Depending upon one's perspective, this word takes on varied meanings. To some, secularization may mean the fragmentation or breakup of the religious values that undergirded past experience. To others, it may mean progress in religious understanding, the movement beyond antiquated and irrelevant values.

Paul Ricoeur, a contemporary French philosopher and Christian layman, has commented on secularization as follows:

A   We mean by secularization an institutional phenomenon: the emancipation of most human activities from the influence of ecclesiastical institutions. In this first sense, secularization is synonymous with laicization: the community no longer coincides with the parish, political authority dissociates itself from religious authority. This transfer of power from the churchman to the civil servant and politician has been marked by a series of crises in which communities, hospitals, and schools have been successively affected.

In a second sense secularization is characterized by the erasing of the distinction between the spheres of the sacred and the profane. This distinction, applying to time (religious and non-religious holidays), space (holy places and public buildings), social roles (the priest and the layman), the world-view (the heavens and the earth), the emotions (piety and justice) has tended to disappear for modern man. Its disappearance characterizes modernity as such. To this loss of distinction is connected the dissolution of peculiarly religious traditions, which today have become merely cultural provincialisms resistant to the universal industrial society.[9]

Harvey Cox, another contemporary Christian thinker, in his book *The Secular City*, commented on this sense of secularization in a similar way:

B   Recently, *secularization* has been used to describe a process on the cultural level which is parallel to the political one. It denotes the disappearance of religious determination of the symbols of cultural integration. Cultural secularization is an inevitable concomitant of a political and social secularization. Sometimes the one precedes the other, depending on the historical circumstances, but a wide imbalance between social and cultural secularization will not persist very long. In

[9]David Stewart and Joseph Bien, eds., *Paul Ricoeur, Political and Social Essays* (Athens: Ohio University Press, 1974), pp. 182–83.

the United States there has been a considerable degree of political secularization for many years. The public schools are officially secular in the sense of being free from church control. At the same time, the cultural secularization of America has come about more slowly. The Supreme Court decisions in the early 1960s outlawing required prayers pointed up a disparity which had continued for some years. In Eastern Europe, on the other hand, the historical process has been just the opposite. A radically secular culture has been imposed very quickly in Czechoslovakia and Poland, but religious practices Americans would find strikingly unconstitutional still obtain. In Czechoslovakia, for example, all priests and ministers are paid by the state. In Poland, in some instances religious instruction is still permitted in public schools. These discontinuities are due in part to the disparate pace with which social and cultural secularization occur. . . .[10]

There have been debates among religious thinkers as to whether secularization is a good thing or a bad thing from the religious point of view. Some have lamented the legally required removal of religious practices and symbols (such as prayer in schools or manger scenes in city parks) from American public life as leading to a deterioration of traditional moral and religious values held to undergird our society.

In the nineteenth-century United States, there were many efforts to effect a legal, constitutional connection between religion and the state. One proposal would have made the United States officially a "Christian Commonwealth," with the right to vote restricted to "genuine Christians" (defined as Presbyterians, Congregationalists, Episcopalians, Methodists, and Baptists). In Massachusetts, Catholic children who had been told by their parish priests not to participate in reading aloud from the King James version of the Bible (regarded as a Protestant translation) were ordered by public school officials to be beaten until they agreed to take part in Bible reading. In response to a controversy concerning Bible reading in the public schools in Cincinnati, Ohio, Judge Alfonso Taft in 1870 ruled as follows:

> Legal Christianity is . . . a contradiction of terms. When Christianity asks the aid of government beyond mere impartial protection, it denies itself. Its laws are divine and not human. Its essential interests lie beyond the reach and range of human governments. United with government, religion never rises above the merest superstition; united with religion, government never rises above the merest despotism; and all history shows us that the more widely and completely they are separated, the better it is for both.[11]

Historically, some have favored secularization because they have believed that legally established religion has a harmful effect on government and violates the liberties of individuals and groups within society. Judge Taft obviously believed that both government and religion benefit from the separation that we have described in this unit as resulting from secularization. Many then, and probably many now,

[10]Reprinted with permission of Macmillan, Inc., from *The Secular City*, rev. ed. by Harvey Cox. Copyright © Harvey Cox 1965, 1966.

[11]Quoted in Perry Deane Young, *God's Bullies: Power, Politics, and Religious Tyranny* (New York: Holt, Rinehart and Winston, 1982), p. 170.

questioned this. In the present-day United States, some Catholics and Protestants, including but not limited to those sympathetic to the New Protestant Fundamentalism, the Moral Majority, and the pro-life (anti-abortion) movement, have argued that divine and human law cannot be separated in an absolute or final way. They have argued that some legally permitted rights of religious expression (such as limited times of prayer in public schools that do not require participation by those unwilling to participate) should be recognized when they are desired by a majority of citizens (see Unit 77).

On the other hand, the religious thinkers previously quoted, Paul Ricoeur and Harvey Cox, believe that the secularization process is inevitable. They, like Judge Taft, see value for both religion and government in the resulting separation.

Still others have seen both losses and benefits for religion and for modern societies in the secularization process as just described. This issue is discussed further in the following unit.

> *How do the sentiments relative to the relationship of religion and society expressed in item A of this unit compare to those found in Units 71 and 72?*
>
> *What might be the value for religion and government in the separation process that results from secularization?*

UNIT 77 Fundamentalism in America

Major religions of the world have conservative strains that for the most part have stressed a life set apart from the political and social involvements of society. In recent decades, however, some conservative traditions have become increasingly involved in the political and social arena—for example, Buddhist monks burning themselves in Vietnam, Shiite Muslims taking aggressive measures to resist modernization, conservative Catholics in Latin America and other areas joining protests against political tyranny.

Fundamentalism, the name for extremely conservative Christianity in the United States, arose during the debate between conservatives and liberals over the fundamentals of "the Faith." The controversy raged, especially during the 1920s and 1930s, with the "fundamentalists" defending Christianity against the threat of the theory of evolution and higher criticism of the Bible, both of which religious or theological liberals supported.[12]

Fundamentalists held to "premillennial eschatology"—that Christ's return would occur before the biblically predicted thousand-year rule of peace and that times would worsen before Christ returns to establish the millennium.[13] Liberals abhorred such pessimism, believing in the progress of society under the influence of Christian teaching.

---

[12]Maria J. Selvidge, ed., *Fundamentalism Today: What Makes It So Attractive?* (Elgin, Illinois: Brethren Press, 1984) p. 13.
[13]*Ibid.*, p. 14.

Fundamentalism in its early decades was mostly apolitical and "other worldly," and was highly critical of church involvement in politics and the "worldly" structures of society. This has changed in recent decades, however, under the leadership of Jerry Falwell, the Moral Majority, and others. During the 1970s, Falwell and his followers came to feel that liberalism had undermined the crucial Christian values of America, and that this was especially evident in the pro-abortion decision of the Supreme Court.[14] Endorsing Ronald Reagan as president, fundamentalist groups have fought the Equal Rights Amendment, called for legalized prayer in public schools, supported United States military build-up, fought pornography, and stood against positions that seem soft on communism.

Peggy Leu Shriver, an analyst of fundamentalism, represents her understanding in the monologue of an imaginary fundamentalist whom she claims represents an authentic interpreter of fundamentalism. Excerpts from her statement follow:

. . . I love America and am proud to be an American,. . . But we have got to get this country back on track, make it a Christian nation once again, . . . I hold the liberals and secular humanists responsible for a lot that has gone wrong in this country. . . . I've not been much of a person to get involved in politics, but it's time some of us God-fearing folk stood up and put things back to rights . . . I look to the Bible for what's right. It's all written there, plain for anyone with common sense to see . . . From it we can use the scientific method of deduction to know whatever we need to know about the world . . . Some scientists today ignore the most basic "facts" available—the Bible itself. They think they are really scientists! Especially the evolutionists . . . Now the scientists are beginning to look pretty silly—look what a mess they've gotten us into by not taking the Bible facts as seriously as nature . . . It used to be that you could count on the public school to teach Christian values but, thanks to the liberals and humanists, you can't anymore . . . Fortunately, we have some good colleges and lots of Bible colleges we can send our children to, and they can be a part of a Campus Crusade program or Youth for Christ fellowship . . . It's time we got rid of the moral pollution on the TV . . . I have a great vision for this nation, but I think lots of people have lost it . . . As a Christian na-

tion America can lead the rest of the world into democracy and Christianity . . . That means we must be militarily strong. The forces of evil constantly try to pull down God's chosen ones. My preacher says that Russia and Communism are the anti-Christ, that the tribulation is almost upon us, and it probably means a nuclear war . . . Sometimes places like New York seem more like Babylon than the new Israel . . . You can tell churches that are loose in doctrine by noticing where they stand on moral issues and whether they indulge in worldly behavior. The two go together. . . . If we don't save the family, which is the cornerstone of American society, the whole country may fall. Just think of what is happening in many American households today. Children talk back to their parents. Sons or daughters run off and live together brazenly . . . And our own government has legalized many of the things historic Christianity has declared to be immoral and evil so that our children are confused. One of the worst things that is happening is that girls no longer know what it is to grow up to be women . . . Of all the things to be confused about, one ought at least to know the God-given place of a woman as a support and helpmate to her husband . . . God's truth is given once-and-for-all through the Bible. Those who see the truth as

[14]*Ibid.*, pp. 17–19.

changing are just trying to take hard truth and make it soft so they don't have to strain to obey it. They are even trying to rewrite the Bible to suit themselves! . . . We need to return to the Bible to the fundamental facts of Jesus' virgin birth, the substitutionary atonement, Jesus'

bodily resurrection, the authenticity of the miracles, and the inerrancy of Scripture. On these five fundamentals I stand, and there is no changing them. It is all common sense, and it is all in the Bible.[15]

Compare the fundamentalist's concern for society with that of liberation theologians (see Unit 64). In what ways are they similar and different?

UNIT 78 Characteristics of Modernization

The inevitability of rapid and comprehensive change differentiates a modern society from traditional societies. This is the basis of the process of secularization, as noted in a previous unit. Though change has always been part of any culture, it has become so accelerated that it is now a central feature of modern societies. To change is to modernize. In light of this, the following list indicates some of the factors that sociologists have suggested are characteristic of modern societies.

1. *Urbanization:* Modernization implies not just that people live in cities (people have lived in cities since 3000 B.C.) but that the great majority of the population is not engaged in agricultural (primary) production but in industrial (secondary) and service (tertiary) occupations. The overcoming of the necessity for a majority of the population to be engaged in production of food and basic raw materials for clothing and shelter has been one of the keys to the transition from a traditionally oriented to a modernized society.

2. *Atomization:* Modernization has resulted in a breakdown of traditional family structures and group relationships. This is seen in the shift from extended family (or clan) groupings in traditionally oriented societies to the nuclear family (parents and children). It is also seen in the tendency of modern society for one's economic role ot be separated from family relationships—the family group does not work together as an independent economic unit. Individuals also find themselves more and more independent and capable of determining their own patterns and relationships; thus they are more like individual atoms in a larger molecular structure.

3. *Rationalization:* Activities of individuals and organizations tend to be coordinated systematically in modern societies, either by semiautomatically functioning mechanisms (the "market" in the economic sphere in capitalist societies) or by deliberately created agencies (bureaucracies). All activities tend then to be structures in interconnected, interacting patterns that demand rational/systematic responses.

4. *Differentiation:* One of the characteristics of modernizing societies, accord-

[15]*Ibid.*, pp. 73–76.

ing to a number of contemporary sociologists—including the Americans Talcott Parsons and H. W. Pfautz and the German Joachim Matthes— is that the basic institutions of the society—political, economic, educational, and religious— undergo a process of differentiation. According to Parsons, all human institutions and all aspects of human life undergo processes of development in the course of social, cultural, and personal change. There is both internal differentiation (expansion and diversification) and differentiation in relation to (change of relation to) other factors in the system of interaction. Thus, as society evolves, the religious element (the sacred) becomes separated, or differentiated, from the nonreligious elements (the secular). Religion tends to lose some of its earlier functions—for instance, as in Western society, some of its educational, charitable, and political functions. This process is exemplified, Parsons held, in the Protestant Reformation's extension—or transfer—of autonomous responsibility, traditionally lodged in the church, to individual Christians for their activities in their secular roles. According to Parsons, in modernized European and American societies, the Christian church's role is no longer "parental." The ethical principles that had been institutionalized within the church now became the responsibility of the individual. And the present church system typical of America, which Parsons called "denominational pluralism," was interpreted by him as a farther extension of the "institutionalization of Christian ethics"—each denomination differentiates and establishes its own ethical pattern.

A   The denomination . . . shares with the church type the differentiation between religious and secular spheres of interest. . . . Both may be conceived to be subject to Christian values, but to constitute independent foci of responsibility for their implementation. . . . The denomination shares with the sect type its character as a voluntary association where the individual member is bound only by a responsible personal commitment, not by *any* factor of ascription.[16]

5. *Institutionalization of innovative attitude*: One further characteristic of modernizing societies, in contrast to traditionally oriented societies, is that change not only is expected, it is encouraged. This underlies the role of science and technology in modernizing and modernized societies. Life is lived with the expectation that newer and better methods of doing things will be invented, that newer and truer knowledge will be discovered. John R. Platt has argued that modern societies are in the process of creating a "steady-state" world, a world of societies in which there will be nothing static: "What will begin to be steady is our acceptance of . . . new ways of creative leisure and interaction as being the most interesting and most satisfying ways of life."[17] Allan R. Brockway has written:

B   The cliche . . . [that the only certainty is change] points to the essential character of the age into which we are moving today. Change is no longer causing the so-

[16]Talcott Parsons, "Christianity and Modern Industrial Society," in *Sociological Theory and Modern Society* (New York: The Free Press, 1967), p. 413.
[17]John R. Platt, *The Step to Man* (New York: John Wiley & Sons, Inc., 1966), p. 200.

cial and psychological disruption it once produced. . . . Change, even very rapid change, is being assimilated by contemporary men and women with a facility that would have been extremely puzzling . . . to people only a few generations ago.[18]

The implications of this understanding of modernization and change for the world's religions are many. Traditional formulations of religious truths and traditional patterns of ritual will have to be constantly modified. New technological innovations which change life patterns and styles will require rethinking ethical applications of religious insights. Traditional patterns of religious institutions will need adjustment. These suggestions are not intended to be exhaustive, but it should be clear that any religion, to remain relevant to a changing society, will need significant adjustments in the formulation and application of its central and unchanging truths.

What changes in medical technology require rethinking religious and ethical definitions and teachings?

What effect does it have on religion to say "change is a way of life?"

Why is change so much more important to religion now than it has traditionally been?

What effect do the changes in military technology have on religious concepts of, and teachings about, war?

UNIT 79 Alienation

In a modern society where modernization, change, and secularization are prominent features, persons often become "alienated" from other persons, traditional codes of behavior, and various social institutions. The concept of alienation, although a traditional idea in religious thought, takes on new importance when it becomes a significant aspect of modern culture.

Alienation means separation, estrangement, a feeling of isolation, loneliness, strangeness, foreignness, helplessness, hopelessness. At least this is the way the term has been used by contemporary novelists, psychologists, and existentialist philosophers. Sociologists have described societies in which alienation is prevalent as being characterized by widely sensed feelings of normlessness (there is no generally accepted set of rules to follow) and powerlessness (many members of the society feel that they have no ability to influence it significantly).

The *term* has been used by philosophers at least since the nineteenth century, when Hegel and Marx gave alienation a large role in their writings. But the *concept* of alienation—even if the *term* wasn't used as widely as at present—has been important in philosophical and religious writings in the West at least since the Greek philosopher Plato (fourth century B.C.).

---

[18]Allan R. Brockway, *The Secular Saint* (Garden City, New York: Doubleday & Co., Inc., 1968), pp. 22–23.

Plato

For Plato, a thing is alienated when it does not conform to its essence. Essences are eternal and objectively real universal concepts in which specific individual things participate. Since the essence, or essential being, of humans is fulfilled in individuals only when they fully realize their rational potential by coming to know and commune with eternal truth, individuals become *alienated* when they seek their ultimate interests or goals in the changing realm of sense experience. Persons who seek fulfillment through pleasure, prestige, wealth, or power do not realize their true, innate human nature. Human nature is fulfilled when individuals rise above interest in the uncertain and impermanent realm and gain knowledge of unchanging reality (such as mathematical and scientific truth; knowledge of the essences of things, including knowledge of human nature, involving insights into ethical, political, and esthetic truth; but especially an overall and comprehensive spiritual vision of the unity of all essences and truths in the comprehensive Form of the Good). Self-alienation results in social alienation, since justice and social cooperation cannot exist unless they are based on unchanging, objective reality. Otherwise, humans will seek false satisfaction in material possessions, sensual pleasure, and personal power. If such goals are sought as ways to attain satisfaction, then individuals are divided against themselves and against other individuals, and all societies are always either potentially or actually at war with all other societies.

Augustine

For the fifth-century Christian theologian Augustine, human alienation is caused by the rebellious refusal to recognize God as the source of all life. Each individual participates in the "original" rebellion of Eve and Adam against God and personally repeats that rebellion. All humans reject their creaturely finitude and want to become "as gods." This results in alienation from God, self, and neighbor and produces human societies full of strife and injustice. There is Platonic influence in Augustine's thought, but Augustine rejected Plato's mind/body dualism as the cause of alienation. He located the cause of alienation in the rebellious will, the denial of creaturely finitude. According to Christianity, the cure for alienation is to be found in God's own restoration of human nature through the death and resurrection of Jesus Christ, and in concrete, personal participation in these events by individual humans.

Hegel

For the nineteenth-century German philosopher Hegel, alienation was a necessary stage in the self-realization of God, or Absolute Spirit. The essence of Spirit is to be free, but Spirit, unless embodied concretely, is empty and abstract. History is the progressive unfolding of Spirit. The physical world is Spirit alienated from itself—concrete but unfree. It is through the world of human cultural activity—in the political and legal system, and particularly in religion, art, and philosophy—that Spirit (freedom) becomes objectively and consciously expressed.

Humans participate in freedom and in Spirit through social roles; as citizens; through education and vocational roles; through family and other relationships; and especially through devotional, creative, and reflective awareness in religious, artistic, and philosophical activity.

Marx

In many ways Marx agreed with Hegel, but he was a materialist instead of an idealist. By nature, according to Marx, human beings are creative, and their creative abilities allow them to transform the world by creative work into a place of freedom—to give it a human image. But in a society in which the majority (or even some) are not free, all are alienated from their true human nature. Alienated humans are not free to choose social or economic roles—the work they will do—and are not free to control what they produce (it is taken from them by their capitalist employers). They are also alienated from their fellow humans since there are no authentic human relationships except between free individuals. Marx thought true freedom would come only by a revolution that would abolish economic and social inequality and alienation of individuals from themselves, their fellows, and their societies.

The Existentialists

Most nineteenth- and twentieth-century existentialists accept elements of the positions just discussed. The existentialists have seen humans as depersonalized in the modern world by the acceptance of social conformity and by the refusal to make an authentic personal commitment or choice about the meaning of their own lives. For most existentialists, the crucial thing is for each individual to make authentic commitments, to decide personally what values and purposes will be authentic for that individual. Thus, for the existentialist, in contrast to Marx, Hegel, Augustine, and Plato, alienation is overcome by subjective decision rather than by objective activity, either on the part of human beings (Marx, Hegel, Plato) or on the part of God (Augustine).

Jürgen Moltmann

A contemporary Protestant theologian, Moltmann has attempted to give a contemporary Christian interpretation of *alienation*. He argues that Platonic and modern dualistic understandings of what it means to be human—the soul/body dualism—and the manipulative orientation of technological civilization have produced alienation.

Man regards his body as his possession, but he is no longer identified with his *bodily* life. His bodily and social life is something that he *has* and that represents him, but . . . is not he himself. An environment takes shape in which all things are replaceable and all human relationships interchangeable. . . . This leads people to play it cool in everything and to enter human relationships without love and their jobs as though they were the roles of an actor in the theater. In love we identify ourselves with our bodily and social existence. But that makes us vulnerable. It is therefore a self-defense to play a role with one's life, while at the same time . . . holding back one's soul. Identification of the self with bodily and social existence has been replaced by the category of having and possessing, [causing] an increasing differentiation between man and the reality of his life.[19]

Because of this alienation in contemporary life, one can, Moltmann thinks, understand the "youth protest" movements of the recent past, in which "the children of protest" sought their social and bodily identity in the battle against the repressions of "present society." One can find both authentic and inauthentic elements expressed in contemporary protest. According to Moltmann, Christian faith, directed to concrete historical happenings—what God has done in the past and what he will do in the future—is the basis for the concrete hope of overcoming alienation, hope that demands present commitment, involvement, and action. The Christian resurrection does not deny the importance of our earthly life by making us dream "of some kind of disembodied spiritual life. It makes us ready to accept our mortal life and to identify with it. This hope does not differentiate between body and soul like the Greek concept of immortality, but makes us ready to animate the mortal body and thus also to humanize the repressive society of having."[20]

Other religions not of the Western tradition, from which these analyses of alienation were drawn, have pointed to a similar phenomenon in their cultures. Gautama Buddha's enlightenment included the realization that humanity is subject to suffering—a form of alienation. The cause of alienation for Buddha was selfish desire, to be overcome by following the Eightfold path. Hinduism incorporates similar concepts in its teaching that humanity is entrapped—alienated from true self—by the illusory material world. Other religions have corresponding concepts.

Perhaps alienation is simply a part of life, as some authors suggest; but it is clear that change, because it disrupts accepted ideas and practices, often produces *feelings* of alienation in individuals and groups more intense than those experienced in more stable times. Possibly social change also produces new *forms* of alienation. The comments in this unit suggest that philosophical and religious thinkers constantly attempt to offer not only explanations but also solutions to alienation.

Which of the positions given is the most adequate explanation of alienation?

Is it true that alienation is part of the human condition?

Will alienation be lessened because modern society accepts the fact that change is normal and natural?

[19]Reprinted by permission of Charles Scribner's Sons from *Religion, Revolution and the Future*, p. 56, by Jürgen Moltmann. Copyright © 1969 Jürgen Moltmann.
[20]*Ibid.*

18

Interpretation and Verification of Religious Knowledge

INTRODUCTION

Plato, in his dialogue Theaetetus, may have suggested that when persons claim to know something—"I know that it rained last night"—they mean to assert at least three things: (1) that what they claim to know is true—"It really did rain last night"; (2) that they believe it is true; and (3) something else, something that the participants in Plato's dialogue were not able to define to their satisfaction—something that expresses a difference between *mere* belief and belief based on adequate evidence. There are many things that most people would say that they believe but would not claim to know. When we claim to know something, we generally mean that we have good reasons for believing it, that our belief is more than mere belief: it is based on adequate evidence.

Every society has well-established methods of determining whether different kinds of statements—proposed beliefs, proposed knowledge—are true or not. Even within a single society there are widely different ways of verifying or testing the truth of different kinds of statements. Some of the different ways of verifying beliefs depend on the kind of statement involved. (We use different methods for deciding whether it is true that "It rained last night" and " 'Beauty is truth, truth beauty'— that is all/Ye know on earth, and all ye need to know.") Sometimes differences in ways of testing beliefs depend on the context of the statements being considered. (For some of our beliefs the statement "Well, I've always been told that" might count as good evidence, but it would not count as good evidence in a court of law.)

There are many sides to participation in any religious tradition. Most religions include a code of conduct. Most religions involve participation in some form of worship, though this may range from communal observances to solitary meditation. But religions also involve beliefs, and every religious tradition accepts some methods as legitimate ways of interpreting and verifying religious knowledge. The religious tradition must be able to give guidance to its adherents about how to find religious truth; otherwise, a crisis of belief, a crisis of truth, would result.

A particular religious tradition may appeal to wisdom or revelation handed down orally through the generations as containing ultimate truth. It may appeal to written documents—Judaism, Christianity, and Islam are often referred to as "religions of the Book." A religion may appeal to those who have had especially intense experiences of religious ecstasy or who have followed special religious disciplines as its interpreters of truth, or to persons who have been specially trained and selected by the official agencies of the group or to those with whom the spirit of the Divine seems to reside in a striking way. It may appeal to criteria of rational acceptability, or to scientific methods of observation. But each of these sources of arriving at truth requires a continual effort of interpretation, for traditions must be continually interpreted and reconciled to one another. (The Navaho American Indians often explain divergences in oral tradition by saying, "Well, that's *one* story, that's *his* story.") Scriptures like the Jewish Torah and the Christian New Testament must be interpreted: Jews and Christians and Muslims must ask themselves first what the scriptures actually *say*, what they *mean*; then they must ask how the teachings of the scripture are to be applied in present situations. Even the criteria of rational acceptability and scientific testability require a continuous effort at further clarification, reflection, and experimental observation.

Most religious traditions would insist that not all religious truth can be verified, adequately tested, established, or refuted by ordinary common-sense methods of observation or by scientific methods of experimentation. Some religious traditions insist that much religious truth transcends and surpasses human reasoning capacities and thus cannot be fully understood or tested by methods of reason or sense observation alone. Nevertheless, every religious tradition will make provision for methods of finding and testing proposed religious truth. It is worth noting that, in a time when many feel that contemporary societies are experiencing a profound crisis of belief, a crisis of truth, the suggestions religious traditions give about sources of truth and methods of arriving at testing it may be of the greatest value and relevance.

It is also worth noting that most religious traditions contain a variety of different kinds of beliefs—all of which are accepted by adherents of that tradition as containing genuine knowledge. For instance, some Christian beliefs are *historical* statements ("Jesus suffered under Pontius Pilate, was crucified, dead and buried"). Some are *metaphysical* statements ("God is the sole Creator of all that exists, and He created it out of nothing"). Some, though they sound like *predictions* or *forecasts*, are more likely intended to be understood as *promises, assurances* to sustain faith and commitment.

The chapters in this section are intended to present several aspects of the question of religious knowledge. In this chapter, some aspects of the problem of interpreting and verifying religious knowledge are explored. In the first unit, the distinction between what in ordinary usage we sometimes call "factual statements" and other kinds of expressions is examined. Many religious traditions hold that important aspects of religious truth are not subject to factual or observational tests in the sense described, yet are nevertheless both true and capable of being tested and proved—verified—by those who have had appropriate religious instruction or experiences.

The second unit in the chapter deals in a more general way with the concept of verification; however, a number of questions are raised specifically with respect to application of the concept and its criteria to the realm of religious knowledge.

Perhaps no topic has been more thoroughly investigated by contemporary theologians and philosophers of religion than the question of the "logic" of religious language. By this is meant the question of *how* language expressing aspects— feelings, attitudes, value judgments, beliefs—of the religious dimension of life (the dimension of ultimate or pivotal concern and commitment) behaves.

Very roughly—since the issue is extremely complex—there have been four major positions taken about the logic of religious language. (1) The logical positivists, of whom A. J. Ayer is a notable example, insisted that religious language (as well as moral, ethical, and aesthetic language) expresses *only* people's feelings and attitudes and therefore there is no need to be concerned about how religious statements might be tested for truth value. Religious language does not even make claims or assertions about reality. This view has been called emotivism.

The other three views are willing to grant that some religious language may be claiming to assert truth. To oversimplify, the views might be characterized as follows: (2) Some hold that there is no problem about the logic of testing the truth of at least some religious statements: We would use exactly the same kinds of procedures to discover whether they are true as we do to test statements in the realm of the sciences, history, or ordinary sense experience. (3) Some hold that at least some religious language makes statements that claim to be true, but the method of testing them for truth is totally unique (perhaps depending on a special kind of authority or on some inner revelation or illumination). (4) Others have argued that, though at least some expressions in the language of religions claim to give true accounts of the way things are, their logical status is neither wholly like nor wholly unlike that of statements in other areas of discourse. Although there may be some analogies between the claims made by a religious affirmation—once we have come to understand its intent and significance, say an article of the Apostle's Creed—and the expression of a scientific hypothesis, there may also be disanalogies, dissimilarities. People who hold to this fourth view may argue that, though it is useful to compare the way religious statements function and are verified with the way statements in science, history, ethics, aesthetic appreciation, and the law function and are verified, there should be no attempt to impose the logic of the statements of one field on statements belonging to other fields.

Obviously, Unit 81, on verification, can only begin to explore some of the dimensions of this important topic, a topic that not only has been of interest to contemporary students, but also has excited the intellects of the great thinkers of the Jewish-Christian-Islamic Middle Ages, as well as of great Hindu thinkers like Śankara and Ramanuja.

UNIT 80 Factual Statement

"That is a factual statement."

This statement, commonly made, means that the speaker has related something observable and verifiable, something that could be checked by talking with persons who were present when the incident occurred.

Yet seldom do we find in a statement only a description of the occurrence. Other components are almost inevitably present. The purpose of this discussion is to explore some of the components present in a "factual" statement and to see if there is only one type of "fact." The reader will then be encouraged to analyze other material, using the methods of this exploration.

As the raw material for our exploration we will use the following statement.

The Church received a letter from a couple that visited our church several Sundays back. Every pastor is eternally looking for new reasons to encourage folks to come to Church. Try this one for size:

> Dear Friends:
> There is more to the story of our stopping in Pecos and attending your church than you realize. We stopped near the church and entered our trailer to change from traveling to church clothes. We were going north on 385 to 66. We got as far as Littlefield that Sunday evening. If we had not stopped that 1½ hours for church we would undoubtedly have been in Hereford for the night . . . the night the tornado struck there. Therefore in our opinion it pays to go to church on Sunday even on vacations and trips.
> Sincerely,
> Mr. & Mrs. . . .[1]

The letter contains "fact" in that it refers to occurrences that could be verified by other persons present.

[1]Bulletin (Pecos, Texas: The United Methodist Church, 1971).

```
                                                          line
        Dear Friends,                                       a
             There is more to the story of our              b
        stopping in Pecos and attending your                c
        church than you realize. We stopped near            d
        the church and entered our trailer to change        e
        from traveling to church clothes. We were           f
        going north on 385 to 66. We got as far as          g
        Littlefield that Sunday evening. If we had          h
        not stopped that 1½ hours for church we             i
        would undoubtedly have been in Hereford for         j
        the night . . . the night the tornado struck        k
        there. Therefore in our opinion it pays to          l
        go to church on Sunday even on vacations            m
        and trips.                                          n
             Sincerely,                                     o
        Mr. & Mrs. . . .                                    p
```

Do you think this accurately isolated the data that could have been verified by other persons, assuming they were present when the occurrence took place?

Observation: In most instances, the factual nature (verifiable possibility) is clear. In places, however, the data seem to begin to move out of the category of verifiability by external witnesses.

Examples:

Line f   The words "from traveling to church" have been deleted because they probably reflect the subjective judgment of the writer of the letter. Yet, assuming that the couple wore ragged, patched, or sloppy clothes while traveling, it could be a verifiable fact. But we do not know that.

Line p   "Mr. & Mrs. . . ." indicates a married relationship that presumably can be verified by examining municipal records, assuming the marriage is not by common law. Yet this type of verification, requiring special effort and intent, is to a degree different from that required from the other facts contained in this statement.

These occurrences are referred to as facts because they are known, or could be known, to have happened. They are real, true, have existence. But what about the rest of this letter? How can we characterize this material?

The remainder of this letter refers to aspects that might not be able to be verified, even by persons present.

```
                                                          line
        Dear Friends,                                       a
             There is more to the story of our              b
        stopping in Pecos and attending your                c
        church than you realize. We stopped near            d
        the church and entered our trailer to change        e
        from traveling to church clothes. We were           f
        going north on 385 to 66. We got as far as          g
        Littlefield that Sunday evening. If we had          h
        not stopped that 1½ hours for church we             i
```

would undoubtedly have been in Hereford for   j
the night . . . ~~the night the tornado struck~~   k
~~there.~~ Therefore in our opinion it pays to   l
go to church on Sunday even on vacations   m
and trips.   n
      Sincerely,   o
      Mr. & Mrs. . . .   p

One striking thing about the material not marked out is its diversity; all that is shared is the impossibility or difficulty of externally verifying its content. A more specific analysis may be useful.

Lines a, o   The words *dear* and *sincerely* indicate attitudes allegedly held by the authors of the letter. Yet can such attitudes be demonstrated with certainty? Or are these merely customary and ceremonial ways of beginning and ending letters that need not be taken to involve attitudes or factual claims at all? Yet they do point to attitudes that the authors might, if asked, espouse. Are there objective tests for determining whether others have affection for us, even if they say they do?

Line a   The consideration just discussed applies somewhat to the term *friends*, but it also differs. This term indicates an interpersonal relationship that may be difficult to verify by observation of external behavior. Perhaps referring to the church members as "friends" is merely a conventional mode of address, just as someone else might have said, "Hi fellows." Does anything in the letter lead you to believe that the letter's authors really *feel* friendship for the people of the church in Pecos?

Lines e to f   The words "to change . . . clothes," by syntax as well as meaning, indicate a motive on the part of the authors. Now it may be that that is exactly what they did. But the actual observable occurrence does not necessarily prove the motive.

Line f   The actions referred to by the words "from traveling to church," commented on above may possibly have been observable. The words may indicate, however, a value judgment on the part of the authors.

Lines h to k   The words "If we had not stopped . . . for the night" represent an assumption of an occurrence on the part of the authors. Obviously it did not happen. It is equally true that it might not have happened—the car might have broken down, caught fire, had a flat; the trailer might have come loose from the car; one of the persons involved might have become sick; and so forth. Yet the authors assume that none of these possibilities would have occurred. Rather, they assume that a fact that could have been verified by anyone would have occurred. This may represent a projection, based on their own intentions.

Lines l to n   The words "therefore . . . trips" clearly indicate the conclusion the couple drew from that which is related. The word "therefore" labels the inference, and the words "in our opinion," the couple's acceptance of the inference. The main inference is "it pays to go to church on Sunday," an inference that they believe to hold true even in special circumstances, "even on vacations and trips." This then represents an interpretation of "fact"; that is, a convincing understanding of observable occurrences and their relationship. Do you find it convincing? Do you think it found universal acceptance? Does the pastor who quotes the letter seem to accept it? To the couple, the answers to these questions might not matter—to them it is convincing.

Line d   The words "than you realize" reveal that the authors of the letter assumed that the readers did not see the full significance of the occurrences. This means that they assumed that the readers lacked insight, which they were providing.

The unverifiable or difficult-to-verify material, therefore, deals with different dimensions:

attitudes allegedly held by the authors of the letter
assumed interpersonal relationships
alleged motives
value judgments by the authors
assumptions about possibly observable occurrences
interpretive inferences convincing to the authors
assumption of a lack of insight on the part of others

The term *fact* is not commonly applied to this type of information. Yet is not the material in section 2 real, true? Does it not have existence for the couple, and for others who accept the accuracy of their assumptions? Is it accurate to say that these aspects of the event their story describes did not "happen"?

Is experience made up of the combination and interaction of verifiable and nonverifiable components? Or do we use many methods for verifying or attempting to verify different kinds of beliefs about different aspects of experience?

In the analysis of the letter, it may have seemed that we can often make a clear distinction between "facts" that everyone can observe and interpretations of those facts by various observers. The examples that follow are meant to suggest that such a distinction may be very difficult to make.

A Each of the following statements, except the first, involves interpretation, and all (except perhaps the last) claim to be factual. (They are all to be taken as intended descriptions of the same group of events.)

1. It seems to me that his body appeared in the room and that when it appeared, it jerked convulsively.
2. When his body appeared in the room, it jerked convulsively.
3. When he walked into the room, he jumped.
4. When he walked into the room, he jumped for joy.
5. When he walked into the room, he jumped in a startled, terrified way.
6. When he walked into the room, he jumped joyfully, fulfilling the saying of the prophet, "The Lord shall come leaping like a young deer."

It should be noted that statements 4 and 5 are incompatible with each other; 5 is also incompatible with 6, and 4 is compatible with all except 5. Obviously, much more interpretation seems to be occurring in statements 5 and 6, or even 4, than in 1, 2, or 3. What is the source, or what are the sources, of the claimed significance the interpreter finds in the more "interpreted" examples?

B All of the following statements describing essentially the same event, the publication of a book, involve interpretation, and each might claim to be factual. (Statement 3 is incompatible with statements 2 and 4, but is compatible with 1.

Statements 2 and 4 are compatible with each other, 4 entails 2, though 2 does not entail 4, and both 4 and 2 entail 1, though 1 does not entail either 4 or 2.)

1. At the age of thirty-six, X, then professor of philosophy at Y college, published his first book, *The New Phenomenology*.

2. At the age of thirty-six, X, then professor of philosophy at Y college, published his first book, a significant, indeed a magisterial, contribution to American philosophical thought. This epoch-making work was titled *The New Phenomenology*.

3. At the age of thirty-six, X, then professor of philosophy at Y college, published his first book, a confused hodgepodge of logical fallacies and linguistic errors, infected by the German Hegelian and post-Romantic existentialist tradition of scorn for clarity and analytic precision. The contribution of this book, titled *The New Phenomenology*, to significant philosophical discussion was precisely zero.

4. At the age of thirty-six—the age at which Hegel published his epoch-making first work, *Phenomenology of Spirit*—X, then professor of philosophy at Y college, published his first book. Like the Swabian Master, X had written a number of incomplete early works, but until the publication of the significantly titled *New Phenomenology*, his prestige as a philosopher had been eclipsed by the fame of his more sensational younger contemporaries. Nor was the significance of either work recognized at once. Both philosophers remained relatively unknown for years—each languishing as high school principals—before receiving permanent university appointments—Hegel at the University of Berlin, X at Harvard. Each initiated a new age in the history of our comprehension of Being. Once, when asked by a graduate student if *The New Phenomenology* represented a twentieth-century fulfillment of the project that Hegel had carried up to the year 1807 in his *Phenomenology*, X said, "Have you read the book? What did you find in it? Did you find the activity of God as it has unfolded presented, analyzed, made available for human consciousness?" Those who have thoughtfully read *The New Phenomenology*, those who have thought on it long and have tested it against our perceptions of the times, know that a new Hegel, a greater Hegel, did appear in twentieth-century America.

Some of these statements attribute much more significance to the event being described than others do. Statement 3 expresses a sense or feeling of disgust for the book and the person who wrote it. Statement 4 describes the author with almost religious reverence. Are these merely subjective reactions, or are they objective or at least partly objective differences of opinion? How does one decide about the significance of events? In interpreting events, what are the *basic* sources that allow us to make judgments of significance? How would you decide whether reading Professor X's book would be worth the time it might take to understand it, or whether it would be a useless waste of time?

Can there be an absolute distinction between the merely factual description of an event and the significance—goodness or badness, importance or unimportance—an interpreter judges it to have, or do all descriptions to some extent contain interpretatioins of the event's meaning or significance? We would probably think that one characteristic of *religious statements* is that they are evaluative, interpretative of the significance of what they describe or attempt to describe. Does this mean that they are more subjective than other kinds of statements? Or does it mean, rather, that they may be more complex or profound? This question is discussed in more detail in the next unit.

UNIT 81 Verification

As indicated in the introduction to this chapter, the question of whether and how religious expressions can be judged to be *true*—whether they make truth claims and if they do, how it can be determined whether the claims they make are in fact true—is one of the most frequently discussed issues in contemporary theology and philosophy of religion. This unit discusses the verifiability of statements expressing religious belief in the context of verifiability, or verification in general.

Some students of religious uses of language have warned us that it may be a fundamental mistake to *ask* whether uses of religious language are true or verifiable. Many twentieth-century philosophers and theologians have stressed *noncognitive* uses of religious language—that is, uses in which the speaker does not and may not intend to convey information.

A   Rather, noncognitive use of language expresses feeling, makes a commitment, helps to cement the bonds of solidarity of a group, or does any other of innumerable possible things about which it would be ridiculous to suppose that questions of truth or falsity arise, as they would if the language use were assumed to have cognitive content (*i.e.*, to claim to convey information). As has often been pointed out, when a minister says the words in a marriage ceremony, "I now pronounce you united in holy matrimony," or in a baptismal service, "I baptize you in the Name of the Father, Son, and Holy Ghost," no one would think that the purpose of the minister's expressions is to give information. Rather, the minister is using language performatively, to accomplish something. Still, the position asserted by some that *all* religious language is noncognitive seems extreme and would not be accepted by most religious persons.[2]

If some religious language *is* cognitive—that is, makes claims to be true—by what methods or sources do we verify its truth claims? When is a belief *merely* a belief and when is it knowledge? When is a belief a "fact" and when is it merely opinion?

Ordinarily we say that we *know* a belief is true, or we say that a belief is a fact, when we possess good reasons—a sufficient amount of the right kind of evidence (that is, a sufficient amount of relevant *other* beliefs that we have good reason to accept as true).

Philosophers have sometimes attempted to establish that there are *some* facts that we know with absolute certainty, facts (beliefs) that we do not need to justify by appealing to other beliefs (facts) to support them. One candidate for a type of absolutely certain belief—a pure "fact"—has been the kind of factual statement based on immediate sense experience. How can I be mistaken that I am now seeing a patch of white, or feeling a sharp pain? These philosophers argued that, on the basis of such immediate sensations, we *construct* a theoretical world of objects: we infer that, because we see patches of white, there is an object present *causing* us to

---

[2]Robert C. Monk and Joseph D. Stamey, *Exploring Christianity: An Introduction* (Englewood Cliffs, N.J.: Prentice-Hall, Inc., 1984), p. 129.

have the experience of seeing white. The theoretical world we construct may be a world of common-sense objects—tables and chairs—or it may be the abstractly conceived, rigorously precise world of theoretical physics.

Other philosophers have argued that there is no clear-cut line between what we observe or experience and the theoretical interpretations we create to explain what we observe and experience. Ordinarily, we do not *see* patches of white, we see white objects. Thus Marx Wartofsky, a contemporary philosopher of science, points out that what we *observe* will be dependent on the language, the set of predicates, we choose to interpret the observed (and the observable).

B

Thus, determining what are observables may be reduced to the question of choosing the so-called basic predicates of [our] reconstructed language. For example, if one chooses as basic predicates such "phenomenal" terms as *red, heavy, hot, loud*, and such "phenomenal" relations as *longer than*, or *brighter than*, then this fixes such terms as denoting the observables for that system. The only question is whether the theoretical terms of a science may somehow be reduced to these, and thus tied to observation as stipulated. On the other hand, one may choose terms of physical measurement as the basic predicates, so that everything would in principle be reducible to such predicates as measured distances, time intervals, or measurements of mass, or of electrical charge.

It is on pragmatic or instrumental grounds, according to this view, that one chooses among alternative languages— on grounds relating to the methodology of science, involving what scientists do when they observe, measure, etc. Nor does one simply choose among prevailing languages, which may have developed haphazardly in the history of science; rather one constructs artificial languages, ideally reconstructed languages, choosing the terms and even the logical structures best suited to scientific frameworks.

What appears as an utter relativism concerning "observation" thus has certain constraints. Although someone may choose anything at all as his basic or ob-

servation predicates, in practice the choice is not haphazard. When scientists talk about observing something, the context and the operation have been delimited by the culture of science, just as when observing is spoken of in common usage there is a consensus on what this means and how it is done. The mystic may claim to have observed the face of God in his private revelation; and in delirium, someone may perfectly sincerely claim to observe figures and objects which we take to be hallucinatory. Yet we do not take these as the normal cases of observation, though we may grant that to the person involved, all the features of normal attentive perception or observation were present. The reason is that we take observables to be common and public; we begin with the expectation that what we see is what anyone would see if he were looking; and thus we take observation to be constrained by the check of reference to public objects. . . .

The public quality of observation (what we might facetiously call the communism of the observable, where no property is private and all is commonly owned; and where the maxim holds: "From each according to his ability, to each according to his need"), this open availability to all comers, is then a criterion which excludes certain experiences, such as revelation or hallucination, from being observational. Beyond this, it seems, no other contraints are definitive.[3]

[3]Marx W. Wartofsky, *Conceptual Foundations of Scientific Thought* (New York: Macmillan, Inc., 1968), pp. 112–13. Copyright © 1968 by Marx W. Wartofsky.

Wartofsky emphasized the condition of being publicly verifiable that holds for what will be considered "observable." But *similar*, though perhaps less rigorously measurable, criteria of verification are often appealed to in the realm of religious experience. Thus though the experience of *satori* (enlightenment) in Zen Buddhism is ineffable and incommunicable, the Zen Master is able to validate or verify the occurrence of this experience in his disciples, presumably by seeing whether the change in manner and attitude of the disciple is coherent with the Master's sense of the meaning of the experience.

A further example is given by Carlos Castaneda in *The Teaching of Don Juan: A Yaqui Way of Knowledge.*[4] The book is an autobiographical account of an anthropology student's attempt to learn the techniques of sorcery from a Yaqui Indian sorcerer. To interpret his experiences, the author Castaneda makes a distinction between ordinary consensus—the methods we have learned to use to arrive at true (or probable) belief based on criteria of publicly observable features of factors of a situation—and "special consensus." Special consensus is a method for verifying or establishing the truth of beliefs by means of tests and methods that would not depend on objective or public criteria of observation.

Thus, in one instance, Don Juan gives Castaneda peyote to eat and, under the influence of the drug, Castaneda frolics with a dog. Afterward, Don Juan tells Castaneda that it was not really a dog but the god Mescalito who had "played" with him. Don Juan claims to have seen or recognized the god. Castaneda asks if the other persons present saw Mescalito or only a dog, and Don Juan seems to suggest that what the others *saw* is irrelevant: It was the god because Don Juan had gone through certain esoteric experiences that allowed him to *know* this.

Don Juan gave Castaneda elaborate instructions on what he could *expect* to experience under the influence of the various hallucinogenic plants administered to him. At one point, he taught Castaneda how to turn himself into a crow and fly with other crows. Under the influence of the sacred mushroom *(psylocybe mexicana)*, Castaneda did seem to himself to turn into a crow. Afterward, he asked Don Juan whether *other* observers would have seen him as a crow, or as himself. Again, Don Juan dismissed the question as irrelevant. The special consensus—the set of beliefs held by Don Juan and communicated to Castaneda *and* the experiences induced in Castaneda through use of the hallucinogenic plants *counted* for Don Juan as sufficient verification for the belief that Castaneda had actually become a crow.

Apparently, the *meaning* of a belief to the one who holds it can be discovered by asking what that person would consider good evidence—enough evidence of the relevant kind—to establish the truth of the belief for him or her.

The American philosopher Charles S. Peirce wrote:

> Consider what effects, that might conceivably have practical bearings, we conceive the object of our conception to have. Then, our conception of these effects is the whole of our conception of the object.[5]

[4]Carlos Castaneda, *The Teachings of Don Juan: A Yaqui Way of Knowledge* (Berkeley, Calif.: The University of California Press, 1968).

[5]James Mark Baldwin, *Dictionary of Philosophy and Psychology* (New York: Macmillan Inc., 1902).

What are some of the beliefs you hold? What evidence—what kinds of evidence—do you consider to be good evidence in favor of those beliefs?

Are different kinds and different amounts of evidence involved in testing the truth of different kinds of beliefs?

19 _____

Authority and Tradition

INTRODUCTION

The previous chapter examined some of the cognitive dimensions involved in interpretation of events from a religious point of view and methods of verifying religious beliefs. This chapter continues the discussion of religious knowledge, focusing particularly on the ways in which religious interpretations may be mediated in particular structural frameworks.

Every religious community includes some concept of authority, some concept of source or sources—it may be persons, institutions, documents, or experience of some kind—of authority. *Authority*, in this sense, refers to that which is accepted as orthodox, stable, fixed. As such it becomes the touchstone of belief and action. It is used to settle questions of religious truth, questions about right conduct and right belief. The first unit of this chapter discusses the role of authority in religion.

In this book we often use the words *religious tradition(s)* to refer to the many facets of a distinct religion. Used in this manner, *tradition* incorporates reference to beliefs, leaders, distinctive events, structural patterns, and the host of other aspects that make up a particular religion such as Christianity, Hinduism, or Islam (See Unit 6 for a discussion of religious tradition used in this sense). *Tradition* has other meanings, however, one of which is its reference to the means by which a particular religion conveys to each new generation the knowledge and experience gained within a religious community. It is this understanding of tradition that will be the focus of our attention in the second unit of this chapter.

While authority and tradition are principal elements in the authentication and conveyance of religious knowledge, there is another aspect of knowledge that plays an important role in religious development—this is doubt. The problem of doubt is critical for any society—"Can we trust our leaders?" "How do we know the media tell us the truth?" Some doubt may be beneficial to society, may promote scientific discovery, reform in society, and the healthy development of inquiry. In the same way, doubt may play an important role in clarifying and investigating religious truth—matters of ultimate importance and ultimate concern. The last unit in the chapter discusses the role and significance of doubt for religious knowledge.

UNIT 82   Authority in Religion

Søren Kierkegaard, a nineteenth-century Danish thinker, was brought up by his father in a tradition of strict Lutheran orthodoxy. For a time he rebelled against the strictness of his religious upbringing, but later he embraced it fully, rejecting humanistic and liberal elements that had become popular in academic Protestant circles in his day. The humanistic liberals stressed human capacity to understand God. They emphasized human reason and conscience and human creativity as sources of religious truth. Kierkegaard rejected all this. In the following passage he argues that genuine religious truth must come from God, by revelation. Thus a prophet or an apostle, like Paul—persons who are instruments of God's revelation—is in a very different category from wise or learned or brilliant or well-educated persons whose teachings, however brilliant they may be, are simply productions of finite human capacities. The prophet and the apostle possess authority from God; the others do not.

Kierkegaard thought that a true understanding of Christianity depended on seeing that it is paradoxical, that it negates human expectations and accomplishments—human intellect, knowledge, insight, and virtue are *not* the key to religious understanding—at the same time that it fulfills the deepest hopes by speaking of a God who reaches out to humans to bring them into the presence of his love. The paradox is that truth and fulfillment come by unexpected means and in ways that shock and surprise and humble. In the following passage, Kierkegaard's critique of the liberals (referred to as clergymen) leads him to the forceful statement of his own interpretation of religious authority.

A   When the sphere of paradoxical religion is abolished or explained back into the ethical, then an apostle becomes nothing more nor less than a genius—and then good-night Christianity. *Esprit* and spirit, revelation and originality, a calling from God and ingeniousness, an apostle and a genius, all coalesce . . . one not infrequently hears clergymen . . . in all learned simplicity, prostitute Christianity. . . .

They talk in lofty tones of the cleverness and profundity of St. Paul, of his beautiful similes, etc.—sheer aesthetics. If Paul is to be regarded as a genius, it looks very bad for him. Only to clerical ignorance could it occur to praise Paul aesthetically, because clerical ignorance has no standard but thinks in this wise: If only one says something good about Paul, it's all to the good. Such good-humored and well-intentioned thought-lessness is to be referred to the fact that the person in question has not been disciplined by qualitative dialectics, which would have taught him that an apostle is not served by saying something good about him when it is crazy, so that he is recognized and admired for being what in an apostle is a matter of indif-ference and what essentially he is not, while with that what he is is forgotten. It might just as well occur to such thought-less eloquence to laud Paul as a stylist and for his artistic use of language, or still better, since it is well known that Paul practiced a manual trade, to maintain that his work as an upholsterer must have been so perfect that no upholsterer either before or since has been able to equal it—for, if only one says something good about Paul, then all is well. As a genius Paul can sustain no comparision with Plato or with Shakespeare, as an author of beautiful similes he ranks rather low, as stylist his is an obscure name, and as an upholsterer—well, I may admit that in this respect I don't know where to place him. One always does well to transform stupid seriousness into jest—and then comes the real serious thing, the serious fact that Paul was an apostle, and as an apostle has no affinity either with Plato or Shakespeare or a stylist or an upholsterer, who are all of them (Plato as well as the upholsterer Hansen) beneath any com-parison with him.

A *genius* and an *apostle* are qualita-tively distinct, they are categories which belong each of them to their own qualita-tive spheres: that of *immanence* and that of *transcendence*. . . . The genius may

well have something new to contribute, but this newness vanishes again in its gradual assimilation by the race, just as the distinction "genius" vanishes when one thinks of eternity. The apostle has paradoxically something new to contrib-ute, the newness of which, precisely be-cause it is paradoxical and not an antici-pation of what may eventually be de-veloped in the race, remains constant, just as an apostle remains an apostle to all eternity, and no immanence of eternity puts him essentially on the same plane with other men, since essentially he is paradoxically different. . . . The genius is what he is by reason of himself, i.e., by what he is in himself: an apostle is what he is by reason of his divine author-ity. . . . A genius may perhaps be a cen-tury ahead of his age and hence stands there as a paradox, but in the end the race will assimilate what was once a paradox, so that it is no longer paradoxical.

Quite otherwise with the apostle. The word itself indicates the difference. An apostle is not born, an apostle is a man called and sent by God, sent by him upon a mission. . . .

An apostle can never in such wise come to himself that he becomes con-scious of his apostolic calling as a stage in his life's development. The apostolic call is a paradoxical fact which in the first as well as the last moment of his life stands paradoxically outside his personal identity with himself as the definite person he is.

A genuis is appraised on purely aesthe-tic grounds, according to the content and specific gravity his productions are found to have; an apostle is what he is by reason of the divine authority he has. The *divine authority is the qualitatively* decisive fac-tor.[1]

Because the authority of the prophet or apostle rests for Kierkegaard in the Divine, and these persons are unique representatives of the Divine, their words become distinctive and binding. Only a few persons are so called and serve as instruments of God's revelation.

In seventeenth-century England, the Quakers held a view of religious author-

[1]Selections from Soren Kierkegaard, *On Authority and Revelation: The Book on Adler, or A Cycle of Ethico-Religious Essays*, trans. Walter Lowrie (copyright 1955 by Princeton University Press), pp. 103–107. Reprinted by permission of Princeton University Press.

ity which, like Kierkegaard's, stressed the presence of the Divine but was also quite different. The Quakers declared that all persons were blessed with divine authority—each believer experiences the indwelling Spirit of Christ, the Inner Light, as a source of all religious truth. Embracing the Light present in all, all believers had within themselves the full religious authority of Christ. An authority on the religious history of the time has written the following:

B

Many of the [seventeenth-century] Quakers took [the] doctrine of the indwelling Spirit to what by most of the [other] Puritans was felt to be a dangerous extreme. The Spirit was to be the guide by which everything, Scriptures included, was to be judged. William Penn corrected misunderstandings when he wrote: It is not our Way of Speaking to say that the Light within is the Rule of the Christian Religion; but the Light of Christ within us is the Rule of true Christians, so that it is not our Light but Christ's Light that is our rule.[2]

In the understanding of Kierkegaard and the Quakers, religious authority resides in the Divine even when exemplified in a human personality. Yet the words, works, and writings of those who possess divine authority often become sources of religious authority. Paul's writings, and those of other apostles and prophets, came to be accepted as sacred scripture because of the divine authority which they possessed. Nevertheless, as scripture, these words assumed an authority of their own. They represent the presence and the will of the Divine. Similarly, religious authority often resides in several aspects of community experience: Particular historical events take on religious authority—Gautama's enlightenment; Jesus' life, death, and resurrection. Great teachers and leaders become authorities—Confucius, Buddha, the Pope in Roman Catholicism, Martin Luther in Protestantism. Orthodox beliefs are formulated into creeds and confessions—the Three Refuges of Buddhism, the Apostles' Creed of Christianity, the confessions of the *Koran*. Authoritative moral codes define proper life—the Ten Commandments in Judaism and Christianity, the Eightfold Path in Buddhism, the Five Great Relations in Confucianism. Each of these sources of authority points beyond itself to the Divine, but for the ordinary believer each constitutes meaningful and real authority, defining belief and action. In so doing, these sources exemplify the multifaceted nature of religious authority as experienced in daily life.

How does Kierkegaard's understanding of authority relate to the discussion (in Unit 34) of general and special revelation? Would it be accurate to say that Kierkegaard rejects the validity of the idea of general revelation?

What are the most significant sources of authority in the religious groups and traditions with which you are familiar?

Who can speak with authority in matters of religious truth? Those who are specially trained or appointed (ordained)? Those who live the best lives, morally or religiously? Those with a unique or distinctive religious experience? What do the main religious groups with which you are familiar say about this?

Does ultimate religious authority reside in the written words of a document (such as the Bible or the Koran)? Does it come from a special experience, such as an illumination of the heart by revelation? Does it come from some other source?

[2]Hugh Martin, *Puritanism and Richard Baxter* (London: SCM Press, 1954), p. 79.

UNIT 83   Tradition: Its Meaning and Function

Because of the brief span of our national history, our mobility, and the fact that we are a land of immigrants, Americans have sometimes been "antitraditional"—making a virtue out of newness and often discarding the old. Only recently have we begun to understand and appropriate our traditions in the manner that most cultures have throughout history. It may be difficult for Americans to appreciate the significant role tradition has played in human history, yet its importance can hardly be overstated.

The term *tradition* is derived from the Latin word *traditio*, which literally means "a handing over." In Latin culture and in later cultures, this term was used to indicate (1) content—information, teachings, doctrine, behavior patterns, or other thoughts and/or practices received from previous generations—and at times (2) the process by which such material was handed down. The term thus embraces customs, doctrines, and concepts, as well as action.

Tradition understood in this way has been an ever-present reality in the great religious movements of the world. It has been the central means by which religions ensured the transmittal of religious experience, information, beliefs, and moral codes to each new generation of believers.

Tradition is so important in Judaism that in the musical *Fiddler on the Roof*, set in a late nineteenth-century Russian Jewish community, it was idealized as perhaps *the* means of defining life and its relationship to God.

A

A fiddler on the roof,
   Sounds crazy, no? But in our little village of Anatevka you might say everyone of us is a fiddler on a roof, trying to scratch out a pleasant simple tune without breaking his neck. It isn't easy.
   You may ask, "Why do we stay up there if it's so dangerous?" We stay because Anatevka's our home. And "How do we keep our balance?" That I can tell you in one word: tradition.
      Tradition! Tradition! Tradition!
      Tradition! Tradition! Tradition!

Because of our traditions we've kept our balance for many years. Here in Anatevka we have our traditions for everything—how to eat, how to sleep, how to work, even how to wear clothes. For instance, we always keep our heads covered; we wear these little prayer shawls. This shows our constant devotion to God. You may ask "How did this tradition get started?" I'll tell you, I don't know. But it's tradition. Because of our traditions everyone here knows who he is and what God expects him to do.[3]

Tradition plays an important part in Judaism in yet another way. Its festivals and holy days are to a large degree the means by which Jewish faith, life, and history are perpetuated. This is evident in the Passover celebration, in which, among the components of the ceremonial practices, there is a section that recites the ancient "four questions," usually asked by the youngest male present.

[3]"Tradition," from *Fiddler on the Roof*, a musical play based on Joseph Itkin, *Fiddler on the Roof*. Copyright © 1964 Joseph Stein. Used by permission.

B   Why is this night of passover different from all other nights of the year?
On all other nights, we eat either Chomaytz or Matzoh,
> but on this night we eat only Matzoh.

On all other nights, we eat all kinds of herbs,
> but on this night we eat only Moror.

On all other nights, we do not dip even once,
> but on this night we dip twice.

On all other nights, we eat either sitting or reclining,
> but on this night we eat reclining.

The eldest male, usually the father, answers:

Once we were slaves to Pharaoh in Egypt, and the Lord in His goodness and mercy brought us forth from that land, with a mighty hand and an out-stretched arm. Had he not rescued us from the hand of the despot, surely we and our children would still be enslaved, deprived of liberty and human dignity.

We, therefore gather year after year, to retell this ancient story. For, in reality, it is not ancient, but eternal in its message, and its spirit. It proclaims man's burning desire to preserve liberty and justice for all.

The first question asked concerns the use of Matzoh. We eat these unleavened cakes to remember that our ancestors, in their haste to leave Egypt, could not wait for breads to rise, and so removed them from the ovens while still flat.

We partake of the Moror on this night that we might taste of some bitterness, to remind ourselves how bitter is the lot of one caught in the grip of slavery.

We dip twice in the course of this Service, greens in salt water and Moror in Charoses, once to replace tears with gratefulness, and once to sweeten bitterness and suffering.

The fourth question asks why, on this night, we eat in a reclining position. To recline at mealtimes in ancient days was the sign of a free man. On this night of Passover, we demonstrate our sense of complete freedom by reclining during our repast.[4]

Note that in both these examples, tradition does not necessarily depend on cognitive or conscious transmission of information or patterns of behavior, but rather is incorporated in the dynamic interplay of daily life; therefore, it is often unconsciously appropriated. Tradition plays a similar role in all religions. In Chinese and Japanese religions, tradition has been as important as duty (see Unit 62) in defining life. Even to an outsider, the importance of traditions of Hinduism in Indian society are obvious.

Christianity, as other religions, depends greatly on tradition to define and interpret beliefs and life-styles. Roman Catholicism and Eastern Orthodoxy heavily depend on tradition, insisting on its continuing role in defining belief and action. The following statement by the Catholic theologian Karl Adam expresses this function:

[4]*Haggadah for the American Family*, English Service with directions by Martin Berkowitz. Copyright © 1958, 1963 and 1966 by Martin Berkowitz. Used by permission of the copyright owner.

C   The Church affirms, completely and entirely, the whole of holy Scripture, both the Old Testament and the New. . . .

And by the side of the holy Scripture stands extra-scriptural Tradition. The Gospel itself is based upon oral teaching, upon the preaching of Christ, of his disciples and of that apostolic succession of teachers which began with the first pupils of the apostles. Therefore the formation in the Christian communities of a living stream of tradition was natural and inevitable. The New Testament is certainly an important expression, but it is by no means an exhaustive expression, of this apostolic tradition which filled and permeated the whole consciousness of the Church. Oral tradition, the apostolic teaching alive and active in the Christian communities, that is prior to and more fundamental than the Bible. It attests the Bible, both in its inspiration and in its canon. It is more comprehensive than the Bible, for it attests a mass of ritual and religious usage, of customs and rules, which is only slightly indicated in the Bible. And it possesses a quality which the Bible as a written document has not and cannot have, and which constitutes its pre-eminent merit, namely, that living spirit of revelation, that vitality of revealed thought, that "instinct of faith" which stands behind every written and unwritten word, and which we call the "mind of the church."[5]

What principal traditions can you identify within the religious communities with which you are familiar?

Is it possible to sustain a religion from generation to generation without the use of tradition?

Given the definition of religion used in this book, is it possible for a person to be religious with little or no dependence on tradition?

What might be the relationships, if any, between tradition and personal religious experience?

UNIT 84 Doubt

Although some religions may look upon doubt as a dangerous enemy to recognized sources of authority and even to faith itself, doubt may be seen by others as a necessary stage on the way to religious maturity.

A student once asked her college chaplain, "Is it wrong to doubt faith and god? I've been religious all my life, but now I doubt my religion. It troubles me to doubt." This student raised questions that trouble many people. What is the role of doubt in life? How do individuals and groups deal with the doubt that may arise in the course of the study and practice of their religion? Ignore it? Condemn it? Welcome it? If doubt cannot be ignored, how can it be dealt with? Can they affirm with Tennyson that more faith resides in "honest doubt than in all the creeds?"

In the past four centuries, many so-called permanent values that gave certainty to believers have been called into question. Not only has the scientific picture of the universe changed, but some philosophers and even religious thinkers have

[5]Karl Adam, *The Spirit of Catholicism*, trans. Dom Justin McCann, O. S. B. (New York: Macmillan, Inc., 1954). Used by permission of Sheed & Ward Ltd. and the Ampleforth Abbey Trustees.

affirmed that God has died. Thus, doubts abound. If doubt cannot be eliminated by condemnation or avoidance, some have held that it can be dealt with effectively by an honest acceptance—embracing doubt bravely.

Different levels of doubt should be recognized. The theologian Paul Tillich has described four types of doubt: scientific, skeptical, existential, and redemptive.

Scientific Doubt

Scientific doubt is necessary to scholars and scientists; it is a part of their method for discovery of truth. If they failed to doubt established facts and conclusions in the academic world, there would be no advancement in knowledge and study. The process of learning involves continual question raising about views of the universe. When Copernicus doubted that the earth was the center of the universe, he paved the way for the scientific revolution of the seventeenth century, a new astronomy, a new physics, and the technology that transformed Europe. Because the Wright brothers doubted the commonly held belief in the impossibility of successful flying machines, it has now become possible for humans to fly to the moon. Scientific doubt is essential to scientific and technological development. It has been one of the major sources leading to discovery of the laws of nature.

Skeptical Doubt

Another level of doubt is skeptical doubt, defined by Tillich as "an attitude of actually rejecting any certainty."[6] Not to be refuted logically, this attitude may reveal indifference, a superficial refusal to take serious questions seriously, or it may be an expression of genuine despair about finding anything to believe in. Skeptical doubt of "everything" may be a game that people play to protect themselves from serious claims of involvement.[7]

This level of doubt can be destructive if it crystallizes into negativism about every aspect of life. The cynic tends finally to be self-negating, to find no exit from a feeling of worthlessness in a meaningless universe. Suicide or mental breakdown may become alternatives if the liberating function of skeptical doubt fails.

Implicit in skeptical doubt is the demand to doubt *doubts* and thus move to dimensions of doubt as a redemptive reality. If this positive aspect of skeptical doubt emerges, the doubter engages in what Tillich calls "existential doubt."[8]

Existential Doubt

The word *existential* refers to existence—the vitality and reality of life at any one moment; therefore, existential doubt operates at a different level than skeptical doubt or scientific doubt. Existential doubt is doubt about the meaning of an individual's life. It is felt in a very personal way, involving the individual's questioning of the validity of his or her own life and of its ultimate purpose or meaning. It

[6]Paul Tillich, *Dynamics of Faith* (New York: Harper and Brothers, Publishers. 1957), p. 19.
[7]*Ibid.*
[8]*Ibid.*, p. 20.

usually arises when the individual has begun to doubt those things that have given meaning to life. "It does not question whether a special proposition is true or false. It does not reject every concrete proof, but it is aware of the element of insecurity in every existential truth."[9] Doubt about the *meaning* of existence pertains to one's ultimate concern. Tillich calls this the doubt "which is implied in faith."[10] It is the doubt inherent in *every* human venture, in every risk of faith or commitment. It may never rise to the surface. It may be repressed or ignored; when it does emerge, it may cause panic or despair, or it may offer redemptive possibilities.

Redemptive Doubt

According to Tillich, then, doubt can become a redemptive element in faith. When existential doubt becomes the basis of a new willingness to commit oneself in faith and trust at a deeper level, it becomes redemptive. Faith can embrace doubt. Theistic believers may see their doubts as gifts from God. Here, faith means trusting, or risking one's life in commitment that does not close its eyes to uncertainty. Although trust emphasizes confidence, risk is always involved, and the awareness of risk brings conscious or unconscious doubts. Even the skeptic is involved in risk in holding the skeptical position. The skeptic who begins to doubt skepticism can open the door to the existential doubt that may lead to the courageous risk of faith. In the process of doubting, redemption from self-negating cynicism or indifference may be at hand.

In this unit, potentially positive as well as negative effects of doubt in relation to religious belief and commitment have been examined. An important question, then, for any religious authority system will be: *How does it deal with existential doubt when its adherents are faced with the crises of life?* In the preceding unit we examined the role of tradition in religion as one of the main means by which religious continuity is established. It may not be an exaggeration to say that the strength and vitality of tradition in religion provide one of the major means of dealing with the problem of doubt in the religion's adherents, sometimes even circumventing the appearance of doubts of any kind.

[9]*Ibid.*
[10]*Ibid.*

20 _____

Order and Origins

When we speak of "nature," "the natural word," and "the universe" we refer not only to the immediate physical, psychosocial, and cultural setting of human activity; in one sense we refer to the whole of reality that can be comprehended or imagined by finite rational-experimental processes. When we use the term *natural universe*, we may at times mean the realm that we apprehend through the senses. We may also mean the realm studied by the various sciences. We will also see that religions and religious traditions show an interest in the natural realm. Most religious traditions have included among their cognitive features (their beliefs) concepts about the nature, origin, goal or destiny, and significance of the natural universe.

In considering the natural world, religion and science are often viewed as two separate ways of understanding reality; however, we assume that scientific understanding and religious understanding must be considered within a common context, especially since both religious vision and scientific method have influenced the modern view of the natural order.

Several modes of understanding the universe and its relationship to religion are investigated in this chapter. In asking the question of whether the meaning of the natural order has significant implications for one's religious understanding, two important considerations emerge. The prevailing view of modern science that reality is a process may give us tools for appropriating conflicting religious views about the universe. As the Eastern and Western views of life come into closer contact, their views concerning the nature of the universe become more relevant.

How will contemporary persons deal with the differences between the Hebraic affirmation of the natural order as basically good and the Hindu view of the world as illusory or unreal? What is the origin of the universe and how have various religious traditions described its beginning?

The relationship of science and religion remains, in the minds of many, an important question. Kepler and Copernicus represent giant minds in the modern scientific revolution, yet we must quickly note that, though they were scientists, they depended heavily upon religious interpretations in spelling out their new view of the universe. In more recent times, thinkers diverse in other ways—Alfred North Whitehead, Pierre Teilhard de Chardin, Michael Polanyi—represent a similar spirit. You may want to consider the following question as you read this unit: Can science and religion work together to lead to richer and deeper understanding of the universes of our experience—the inner universe that we know in feeling and achieved self-consciousness and the external universe that we know through sense experience and the imaginative constructions of intellect? Both religion and science involve powerful impulses to creative and imaginative expression. Perhaps the connections between the two realms are becoming clearer now than ever before in human history.

UNIT 85 Religious Views on the Origin of the Universe

As noted in the chapter introduction, though we may sometimes contrast religious approaches to the understanding of the natural universe with scientific or secular (the terms may not be interchangeable) approaches, it is important to realize that there have been and are contrasting religious attitudes toward the nature and origin of the universe.

How the universe, at least in its present configuration, originated, what its present stage of development is, and toward what future states it may be evolving—these questions have fascinated thoughtful and imaginative persons in many ages. In contemporary astrophysics, the field of cosmology—the study of the structure and development of the universe—has grown excitingly in the past two decades. Scientists have been fascinated with concepts of an expanding universe. The model known as the "big-bang" theory—that the expansion of the universe began as a result of the explosion of densely packed matter some billions of years ago—currently seems to have won the day, but theorists continue to elaborate the concept.

Concepts and images relating to the origin and development of the universe have appeared in the world's religions, too. Integral to the religions has been an interest in understanding, or at least in recognizing, the power(s) or being(s) that activate(s) the process. Such interest often finds expression in images of God(s) as creator(s) and sustainer(s) of the universe. These images are numerous and yet varied in their understanding of the Divine, the process of creation, and humanity's place in it.

Egyptian Hymn to the Creator (1300 B.C.E.)

Pharaoh Amenhotep IV, in the fourteenth century B.C.E., consolidated ancient Egyptian worship into worship of one God—the sun god, Aton. The following passages praising Aton stress his creativity, which is seen as a continuing process constantly renewing itself.

A

Thy dawning is beautiful in the horizon of the sky,
O living Aton, Beginning of life!
When thou risest in the eastern horizon
Thou fillest every land with thy beauty.
Thou art beautiful, great, glittering, high above every land,
Thy rays, they encompass the lands, even all that thou has made.
Thou art Re, and thou carriest them all away captive.
Thou bindest them by thy love.
Though thou art far away, thy rays are upon earth;
Though thou art on high, thy footprints are the day. . . .

Creator of the germ in woman,
Maker of seed in man,
Giving life to the son in the body of his mother,
Soothing him that he may not weep,
Nurse even in the womb,
Giver of breath to animate every one that he maketh!
When he cometh forth from the body . . . on the day of his birth,
Thou openest his mouth in speech,
Thou suppliest his necessities. . . .

How manifold are thy works!
They are hidden from before us,
O sole God, whose powers no other possesseth.
Thou didst create the earth according to thy heart
While thou wast alone:
Men, all cattle large and small,
All that are upon the earth,
That go about upon their feet;
All that are on high,
That fly with their wings,
The foreign countries, Syria and Kush,
The land of Egypt;
Thou settest every man into his place,
Thou suppliest his necessities,
Every one has his possessions,
And his days are reckoned.
The tongues are divers in speech,
Their forms likewise and their skins are distinguished.
For thou makest different the strangers.[1]

[1]"The Hymn to Aton," trans. J. H. Breasted, in *Development of Religion and Thought in Ancient Egypt* (New York: Charles Scribner's Sons, 1912).

Compare this "hymn" with the Hebrew Psalm 104.

Arising from a common geographical and cultural matrix around the same time as the Egyptian passage above were two well-known stories of the creation process. The Babylonian *Enuma elish'* epic may be fruitfully compared with the Hebrew story as found in Genesis 1. The similarities as well as the differences are striking and attest to the distinctive religious perspectives from which each account is written.

Babylonian Story of Creation (about 2000 B.C.E.)

The story begins with a picture of the earliest imaginable period of primordial time, when only the divine pair, Apsu, the fresh water, and Tiamat, the salt water, existed. Out of their commingling, the younger gods arose. When they began to cause disturbances, Apsu determined to destroy them, but they were able to kill him. Tiamat, the primordial salt water, set out to avenge him. Marduk, one of the younger gods, was chosen to fight her. After extensive preparation, he engaged the primordial mother-god in battle. Marduk, referred to as "Sun of the heavens," succeeded in destroying her. What follows is the description of what he did with her body.

B

Then the lord [Marduk] paused to view her dead body,
That he might divide the monster and do artful works.
He split her like a shellfish into two parts:
Half of her he set up and ceiled it as sky,
Pulled down the bar and posted guards.
He bade them to allow not her waters to escape.
He crossed the heavens and surveyed the regions.
He squared Apsu's quarter, the abode of Nudimmud,
As the lord measured the dimensions of Apsu.
The Great Abode, its likeness, he fixed as Esharra,

The Great Abode, Esharra, which he made as the firmament.
Anu, Enlil, and Ea [gods] he made occupy their places.
He constructed stations for the great gods,
Fixing their astral likeness as constellations.
He determined the year by designating the zones:
He set up three constellations for each of the twelve months. . . .

In her belly he established the zenith.
The Moon he caused to shine, the night (to him) entrusting.
He appointed him a creature of the night to signify the days: . . .
When Marduk hears the words of the gods,
His heart prompts (him) to fashion artful works.
Opening his mouth, he addresses Ea
To impart the plan he had conceived in his heart:
Blood I will mass and cause bones to be.
I will establish a savage, "man" shall be his name.
Verily, savage-man I will create.
He shall be charged with the service of the gods
That they might be at ease! . . .

The most guilty of the gods is then selected to be killed as material for the creation of man.

> It was Kingu who contrived the uprising,
> And made Tiamat rebel, and joined battle.
> They bound him, holding him before Ea.
> They imposed on him his guilt and severed his blood (vessels).
> Out of his blood they fashioned mankind.
> He imposed the service and let free the gods,
> After Ea, the wise, had created mankind,
> Had imposed upon it the service of the gods.

Finally, after building a lofty shrine in Babylon, the gods feast.

> The great gods took their seats,
> They set up festive drink, sat down to a banquet.[2]

Hebrew Story of Creation (After 1300 B.C.E.)

In the beginning God created the heavens and the earth. The earth was without form and void, and darkness was upon the face of the deep; and the Spirit of God was moving over the face of the waters.

And God said, "Let there be light" and there was light. And God saw that the light was good; and God separated the light from the darkness. God called the light Day, and the darkness he called Night. And there was evening and there was morning, one day.

And God said, "Let there be a firmament in the midst of the waters, and let it separate the waters from the waters." . . . And it was so. And God called the firmament Heaven . . . a second day. And God said, "Let the waters under the heavens be gathered together into one place, and let the dry land appear." And it was so. God called the dry land Earth, and the waters that were gathered together be called Seas. . . . And God said, "Let the earth put forth vegetation, . . ." And it was so. . . . And God saw that it was good . . . a third day.

And God said, "Let there be lights in the firmament of the heavens to separate the day from the night; and let them be for signs and for seasons and for days and years, and let them be lights . . . upon the earth." And it was so. . . . And God saw that it was good . . . a fourth day. And God said, "Let the waters bring forth swarms of living creatures, and let birds fly. . . ." And God saw that it was good . . . a fifth day. And God said, "Let the earth bring forth living creatures. . . ." And it was so. . . . And God saw that it was good.

Then God said, "Let us make man in our image, after our likeness; and let them have dominion over the fish of the sea, and over the birds of the air, and over the cattle, and over all the earth, and over every creeping thing that creeps upon the earth." . . . Male and female he created them. And God blessed them. . . . And it was so. And God saw everything that he had made, and behold, it was very good. And there was evening and there was morning, a sixth day.

Thus the heavens and the earth were finished, and all the host of them.

And on the seventh day God finished his work which he had done, and he rested on the seventh day. . . . So God blessed the seventh day and hallowed it. . . . (Genesis 1:1–2:3, RSV)

[2] "The Creation Epic," from "Akkadian Myths and Epics," trans. E. A. Speiser in *Ancient Near Eastern Texts Relating to the Old Testament*, by James B. Pritchard (ed.) 3rd ed., with Supplement. (Copyright © 1969 by Princeton University Press), pp. 66–69. Reprinted by permission of Princeton University Press.

What is the reason for creation in each of these stories?

The nature or character of the God(s) is reflected in these stories: How is it similar or different in each?

What is the character of the human being described as having been created in each account? What is the purpose for which the human was created?

What materials are described as having been used in creation? What is their origin said to have been?

These stories comment on the beginning of the universe; creation is an event in the past. Many interpreters regard these stories, whether Egyptian, Babylonian, or Hebrew, as attempts to express in symbolic language a basic religious understanding of the relation of the Divine to the natural universe and human life and activity. There are other ways to understand creation, as the following passage shows. Martin Luther (1483–1546 C.E.) believed that the creative process continues; it is not something that happened only in the past.

D Even as God in the beginning of creation made the world out of nothing, whence He is called the Creator and the Almighty, so His manner of working continues still the same. Even now and unto the end of the world, all His works are such that out of that which is nothing, worthless, despised, wretched and dead, He makes that which is something, precious, honorable, blessed and living. Again, whatever is something, precious, honorable, blessed and living, He makes to be nothing, worthless, despised, wretched and dying. After this manner no creature can work; none can produce anything out of nothing.[3]

Luther also stressed the sustaining nature of God's activity.

E "I believe in God the Father Almighty, Maker of heaven and earth." What does this mean? Answer: I believe that God has made me and all creatures; that He has given me my body and soul, eyes, ears, and all my members, my reason and all my senses, and still preserves them; also clothing and shoes, meat and drink, house and home, wife and children, fields, cattle, and all my goods; that He richly and daily provides me with all that I need to support this body and life; that He defends me against all danger and guards and protects me from all evil; and all this purely out of fatherly, divine goodness and mercy, without any merit or worthiness in me; for all of which it is my duty to thank and praise, to serve and obey Him. This is most certainly true.[4]

When we turn our attention from Western concepts of creation to those of the East, other distinctive aspects arise. Because Hindus stress the union of an individual's soul (Atman) with the world-soul (Brahman), they are less concerned with concepts of time and history (see Unit 11). Nevertheless, the importance of the creative processes does not escape attention, as the following passage from the *Mundaka-Upanishad* shows. Notice the reincarnation and reunion motifs that underlie the statement.

[3]Martin Luther, "The Magnificat," *The Works of Martin Luther*, Vol. III (Philadelphia: Muhlenberg Press, 1930), 127.

[4]Martin Luther, *Smaller Catechism* (St. Louis: Concordia Publishing House, © 1943), p. 6.

F

_This is the truth. As from a blazing fire sparks, being like unto fire, fly forth a thousandfold, thus are various beings brought forth from the Imperishable, my friend, and return thither also.

That heavenly Person is without body, he is both without and within, not produced, without breath and without mind, pure, higher than the high Imperishable.

From him (when entering on creation) is born breath, mind, and all organs of sense, ether, air, light, water, and the earth, the support of all.

Fire (the sky) is his head, his eyes the sun and the moon, the quarters his ears, his speech the Vedas disclosed, the wind his breath, his heart the universe; from his feet came the earth; he is indeed the inner Self of all things.

From him comes Agni (fire), the sun being the fuel; from the moon (Soma) comes rain (Parganya); from the earth herbs; and man gives seed unto the woman. Thus many things are begotten from the Person (purusha).

From him come the *Rig*, the Sâman, the Yagush, the Dîkshâ (initiatory rites), all sacrifices and offerings of animals, and the fees bestowed on priests, the year too,_ _the sacrificer, and the worlds, in which the moon shines brightly and the sun.

From him the many Devas too are begotten, the Sâdhyas (genii), men, cattle, birds, the up and down breathings, rice and corn (for sacrifice), penance, faith, truth, abstinence, and law.

The seven senses (prâna) also spring from him, the seven lights (acts of sensation), the seven kinds of fuel (objects by which the senses are lighted), the seven sacrifices (results of sensation), these seven worlds (the places of the senses, the worlds determined by the senses) in which the senses move, which rest in the cave (of the heart), and are placed there seven and seven.

Hence come the seas and all the mountains, from him flow the rivers of every kind; hence come all herbs and juice through which the inner Self subsists with the elements.

The Person is all this, sacrifice, penance, Brahman, the highest immortal; he who knows this hidden in the cave (of the heart), he, O friend, scatters the knot of ignorance here on earth._[5]

Mundaka-Unpanishad

Although Hinduism's picture of creation magnifies the mystery of the Brahman-Atman nature, Japan's ancient Shinto religion embodies a creation myth or story comparable to those found in many Western traditions. Concerned only with the islands of Japan and not the universe, it accounts for creation from a distinctively nationalistic viewpoint. The following summarization of this complicated Japanese tradition is that of John Noss.

G

The Japanese islands are a special creation of the gods. After the primal chaos had in the course of events separated into heaven and ocean, various gods appeared in the heavenly drift-mist, only to disappear without event, until finally there came upon the scene the two deities who produced the Japanese islands and their inhabitants. These were the primal male and female, Izanagi, the Male-Who-Invites, and Izanami, the Female-Who-Invites. Their heavenly associates commanded them to "make, consolidate, and give birth to" the Japanese islands. These two beings descended the Floating Bridge of Heaven (a rainbow?), and when they reached its lower end, Izanagi pushed down his jeweled spear into the muddy brine and stirred it until the fluid below them became "thick and glutinous." Then he drew the spear up, whereupon "the brine that dripped down from the end of the spear was piled up and became an island." Stepping down on the island,

[5]*The Unpanishads*, trans. E. Max Müller, Vol. II (New York: Dover Publications, Inc., n. d.), 34–35.

they came together, and Izanami bore from her womb the eight great islands of Japan. . . . [After the creation of a number of lesser deities Izanami dies and goes to the underworld. Izanagi unsuccessfully attempts to rescue her and a period of conflict and disorder ensues. During this period Izanagi produces the goddess of the sun, the moon-god, and the storm-god.]

Years later, we find the sun-goddess, Amaterasu, looking down from her seat in heaven and becoming concerned about the disorder in the islands below. The storm-god's son was ruling there, but she was not satisfied. She finally commissioned her grandson Ni-ni-gi to descend to the islands and rule them for her. . . . [In later times Ni-ni-gi's great grandson Jimmu Tenno became the first human emperor of the islands and established his capital on the central island, Honshu, in 660 B.C]

Meanwhile, the leading families of Japan and the whole Japanese people descended from the minor deities, or lesser kami, residing on the islands.

Thus, we are to understand that the emperor of Japan is a descendant in an unbroken line from the sun-goddess, Amaterasu, and that the islands of Japan have a divine origin, and so also the Japanese people.[6]

Why have the world's religions been occupied with the attempt to explain the origin of the universe? How many different accounts of the "nature and destiny of humanity and natural order" do you find in the accounts in this unit? What is the relation of humans to God and to the natural universe in each account?

Recent scientific developments have added great interest to questions about the origin and nature of the universe. There is now perhaps a greater awareness of "cosmology" than has existed since the time of Copernicus, Kepler, Galileo, and Newton. In the next unit we will examine the role of religious components in the creation of a "new cosmology" in the scientific work of one of the great scientific investigators of an earlier period and in the relation of scientific thought to religious vision in our time.

UNIT 86   Religious Vision and Scientific Method

In the previous unit we noted some similarities and contrasts between scientific and religious interpretations of nature, but focused on similarities and differences between contrasting religious interpretations. This unit attempts to illustrate the role that religious concepts and images have had as a basis for scientific work and to suggest that such concepts and images may well be continuing to function in creative imagination leading to scientific discovery.

Johann Kepler was one of the founders of exact modern science, an astronomer who not only championed but corrected and refined the Copernican

[6]John B. Noss, *Man's Religions*, 4th ed. (New York: Macmillan, Inc., 1969), pp. 320–21. © John B. Noss, 1969. Used by permission.

model that placed the sun, rather than the earth, at the center of our planetary system. E. A. Burtt has described how a number of essentially religious conceptions about the nature of the universe (or cosmos) influenced Kepler to adopt the revolutionary new theory. Burtt, discussing Kepler's theories, writes:

A

In his subsequently expressed reasons for accepting Copernicanism this central position of the sun is always included, usually first. This ascription of deity to the sun was covered over by Kepler with such mystical allegorization as was necessary to give it a hearing in the prevailing theological environment, with especial reference to the doctrine of the Trinity. The sun, according to Kepler, is God the Father, the sphere of the fixed stars is God the Son, the intervening ethereal medium, through which the power of the sun is communicated to impel the planets around their orbits, is the Holy Ghost. To pronounce this allegorical trapping is not to suggest, of course, that Kepler's Christian theology is at all insincere; it is rather that he had discovered an illuminating natural proof and interpretation of it, and the whole attitude, with its animism and allegoriconaturalistic approach, is quite typical of much thinking of the day. Kepler's contemporary Jacob Boehme, is the most characteristic representative of this type of philosophy. . . . But the connexion between Kepler, the sun-worshipper, and Kepler, the seeker of exact mathematical knowledge of astronomical nature, is very close. It was primarily by such considerations as the deification of the sun and its proper placing at the centre of the universe that Kepler in the years of his adolescent fervour and warm imagination was induced to accept the new system: But, his mind immediately proceeded, and here his mathematics and his Neo-Pythagoreanism come into play, if the system is true, there must be many other mathematical harmonies in the celestial order that can be discovered and proclaimed as confirmation of Copernicanism, by an intensive study of the available data. This was a task in exact mathematics, and it was very fortunate for Kepler that he was just plunging into

such profound labours at the time when Tycho Brahe, the greatest giant of observational astronomy since Hipparchus, was completing his life-long work of compiling a vastly more extensive and incomparably precise set of data than had been in the possession of any of his predecessors. Kepler had joined Tycho Brahe the year before the latter's death and had full access to his magnificent accumulations. It became the passion of his life to penetrate and disclose, for the "fuller knowledge of God through nature and the glorification of his profession," these deeper harmonies, and the fact that he was not satisfied merely with mystical manipulation of numbers, or aesthetic contemplation of geometrical fancies, we owe to his long training in mathematics and astronomy, and in no small degree to the influence of the great Tycho, who was the first competent mind in modern astronomy to feel ardently the passion for exact empirical facts. . . . Both Copernicus and Kepler were firmly convinced for religious reasons of the uniformity of motion, *i.e.*, each planet in its revolution is impelled by a constant and never failing cause, hence Kepler's joy at being able to "save" this principle as regards the areas even though it had to be surrendered as regards the planet's path. But the discovery which yielded Kepler the most inordinate delight and to which he referred for many years as his most important achievement, was the discovery published in his first work, the *Mysterium Cosmographicum* (1597), that the distances between the orbits of the six planets then known bore a certain rough resemblance to the distances which would be obtained if the hypothetical spheres of the planets were inscribed in and circumscribed about the five regular solids properly distributed between them. Thus if a cube be inscribed in the sphere of Saturn, the sphere of Jupiter will approximately fit within it, then between Jupiter and Mars the tetrahedron, between Mars and the earth the dodecahedron, etc. Of course, this performance has remained entirely unfruitful—the correspondence is rough, and the discovery of new planets has quite upset its underlying assumptions—but Kepler never forgot the pristine enthusiasm which this achievement awoke in him.[7]

Kepler wrote:

B The intense pleasure I have received from this discovery can never be told in words. I regretted no more the time wasted; I tired of no labour; I shunned no toil of reckoning, days and nights spent in calculation, until I could see whether my hypothesis would agree with the orbits of Copernicus or whether my joy was to vanish into air.[8]

Following is Kepler's own discussion of what seemed to him the significance of his discovery.

C In the first place, lest perchance a blind man might deny it to you, of all the bodies in the universe the most excellent is the sun, whose whole essence is nothing else than the purest light, than which there is no greater star; which singly and alone is the producer, conserver, and warmer of all things; it is a fountain of light, rich in fruitful heat, most fair, limpid, and pure to the sight, the source of vision, portrayer of all colours, though himself empty of colour, called king of the planets for his motion, heart of the world for his power, its eye for his beauty, and which alone we should judge worthy of the Most High God, should he be pleased with a material domicile and choose a place in which to dwell with the blessed angels. . . . For if the Germans elect him as Caesar who has most power in the whole empire, who would hesitate to confer the votes of the celestial motions on him who already has been administering all other movements and changes by the benefit of the light which is entirely his possession? . . . Since, therefore, it does not befit the first mover to be diffused throughout an orbit, but rather to proceed from one certain principle, and as it were, point, no part of the world, and no star, accounts itself worthy of such a great honour; hence by the highest right we return to the sun, who alone appears, by virtue of his dignity and power, suited for this motive duty and worthy to become the home of God himself, not to say the first mover.[9]

Kepler's close identification of religion and science has often been lost in the modern world. Many persons see a conflict between the knowledge gained through scientific investigation and that found in religious insights.

Particularly in the eighteenth and nineteenth centuries, many educated persons felt that there was conflict and antagonism between the Newtonian concept of the natural order—often interpreted as leading to a view of the universe as a completely mechanical, "clockwork" deterministic machine—and religious views of the universe as alive and the scene of encounter between the human spirit and

---

[7]E. A. Burtt, *Metaphysical Foundations of Modern Physical Science*, 2nd rev. ed. (London: Routledge and Kegan Paul Limited, 1932), p. 48. Used by permission of Humanities Press, Inc., New York.

[8]*Ibid.*, pp. 47–52.

[9]*Ibid.*, pp. 51–52.

the Divine. The revival of attacks on Darwinian concepts of evolution by "scientific creationists" reflects the belief of some Christians that there are conflicts between biblical accounts of creation and God's role in it and widely accepted results of modern scientific inquiry.

Yet this understanding of a conflict—alleged or real—is not shared by all. Interpreters of Hinduism and Buddhism have pointed to what they consider to be profound analogies between modern scientific cosmology and microphysics and concepts of Hinduism and Buddhism involving space, time, the evolving universe, and the self. After an initial impulse within late nineteenth- and early twentieth-century theology to separate science from religion by saying that science deals with facts whereas religion deals with values, or value-laden interpretations of the significance of facts, an increasing number of Jewish and Christian thinkers have been interested in exploring the relationship between religious belief and the new science.

The Catholic priest and paleontologist Pierre Teilhard de Chardin (d. 1955) interpreted the evolutionary process, as disclosed in geological, biological, and cosmological sciences, as under the guidance of the divine Spirit and believed that contemporary scientific insight can sensitize us to the Divine's presence and purposes.[10]

The writings of another contemporary thinker, Michael Polanyi, also contain interesting speculations concerning the relation in contemporary scientific work of an intuitive vision of reality to exact scientific procedures. In *The Tacit Dimension*, Polanyi explores a dimension, or process, of mind that he calls "tacit knowing." According to Polanyi, tacit—intuitive, nonreflective—knowing plays an essential role in scientific discovery, especially in guiding scientists to the problems that lead to new discoveries. Flashes of insight, hunches, lucky guesses, and intuitions are examples of tacit knowledge emerging into consciousness—in much the same way that new forms of life emerge from simpler forms.[11]

Alfred North Whitehead was another twentieth-century thinker who shared Polanyi's belief that exact scientific theorizing begins at an intuitive, feeling-level relationship to nature that may be called *religious*, since it involves a sense of a relationship that can never be given complete and exact conceptual expression to the *whole* and potential *wholeness* of things. Mathematician, logician, philosopher of science and metaphysician, Whitehead wrote:

D   Nature is a process. As in the case of everything directly exhibited in sense-awareness, there can be no explanation of this characteristic of nature. All that can be done is to use language which may speculatively demonstrate it, and also express the relation of this factor in nature to other factors.

It is an exhibition of the process of nature that each duration happens and passes. The process of nature can also be termed the passage of nature. I definitely refrain at this stage from using the word "time," since the measurable time of sci-

[10]See especially Pierre Teilhard de Chardin, *The Future of Man* (New York: Harper & Row, Publishers, Inc., 1964).

[11]See Michael Polanyi, *The Tacit Dimension* (New York: Doubleday & Co., Inc., 1966) and *Personal Knowledge* (Chicago: University of Chicago Press, 1958).

ence and of civilised life generally merely exhibits some aspects of the more fundamental fact of the passage of nature. I believe that in this doctrine I am in full accord with Bergson, though he uses "time" for the fundamental fact which I call the "passage of nature." Also the passage of nature is exhibited equally in spatial transition as well as in temporal transition. It is in virtue of its passage that nature is always moving on. It is involved in the meaning of this property of "moving on" that not only is any act of sense-awareness just that act and no other, but the terminus of each act is also unique and is the terminus of no other act. Sense-awareness seizes its only ·chance and presents for knowledge something which is for it alone.[12]

Many have found that not only the new cosmology, with its vision of a dynamic universe that embraces evolutionary processes on a physical-universal as well as biological-terrestrial scale, but also the newer theories of the microcosm, begun with Max Planck's and Albert Einstein's quantum physics (1900–1905) and continuing to the latest experimental and speculative theories concerning the physics of elementary particles, partly derive from and possibly support a dynamic religious vision of reality.[13]

Some time ago, one of the authors of this book asked a friend, an outstanding physicist, what an atom looks like. With great patience he replied, "I don't know; I've never seen one. I can't tell you where one is. I can only tell from a cloud chamber where something has been." From subatomic particles to clusters of galaxies, all are examined, not in terms of what they are as static entities, but as interacting participants in a cosmic drama. For many, contemporary physics discloses a sense of grandeur and mystery in its emerging vision of reality. Such grandeur and mystery constantly challenge traditional interpretations of the relationship of science and religion, and perhaps leave room for a much closer identification of religion with science than has often been assumed.

> *Is Polanyi's theory about "tacit knowing" at least in part a theory about the role of religious vision in scientific knowledge?*
>
> *Do Polanyi's and Whitehead's theories about tacit, or intuitive, knowing rest on a religious vision—or at least an intuitive vision about reality, the nature of human life, and its relationship to the rest of nature?*
>
> *Examine how the discussion of Kepler's scientific theorizing illustrates the interaction of religious and aesthetic values with the observational and mathematical exactness so often considered the special characteristics of scientific method.*

[12]From Alfred North Whitehead, *The Concept of Nature* (Cambridge: Cambridge University Press, 1920), pp. 53–54. Used by permission of publisher.

[13]See especially, from the scientific side, such recent works as Nigel Calder, *The Key to the Universe* (New York: The Viking Press, 1977), Robert Jastrow, *God and the Astronomers* (New York: Warner Books, Inc., 1978), Gary Zukav, *The Dancing Wu Li Masters: An Overview of the New Physics* (New York: Bantam Books, Inc., 1980), John Gribbin, *In Search of Schrödinger's Cat* (New York: Bantam Books, Inc., 1984), Ilya Prigogine, *Order Out of Chaos: Man's New Dialogue with Nature* (New York: Bantam Books, Inc., 1984) and John Boslough, *Stephen Hawking's Universe* (New York: William Morrow and Co., Inc., 1985). See also, from the side of religion, Roland Muskat Frye, (ed.), *Is God A Creationist?* (New York: Charles Scribner's Sons, 1983).

21

Human Response
to the Natural Process

The two units in this chapter focus on the religious dimensions of attitudes toward the place of human beings in the natural order. The chapter stresses contrasting attitudes—feelings, images, concepts—that different societies have taken toward nature and its impingement on and relationship to human life.

In some cultures the natural process has been viewed with warmth and acceptance, in others as something impersonal to be used, and in others as something to be downgraded and dispensed with in the human search for truth.

We can easily recognize how attitudes toward nature in the West have fostered problems of pollution and other forms of environmental violence. We have refrained from including descriptive material on these problems because of lack of space and the abundance of materials elsewhere. Instead we have sought to penetrate the attitudes prevalent in the West that have produced the disruptive actions concerning nature. We have also sought to relate these attitudes and concepts to the religious traditions that have transmitted them. A wealth of resources, contemporary and traditional, exists that will allow the reader to go beyond the fairly limited discussion of this chapter.

UNIT 87   Humanity and the World

A

(*Rick O'Shay* by Stan Lynde. Copyright © 1970 by *The Chicago Tribune.* Used by permission.)

What is the relationship between humanity and the natural process? Different cultures and different individuals have responded to this question in diverse ways. Some responses have been analytical; some descriptive; and still others imitative. Some have emphasized the cognitive dimension; others the affective. Some responses have been given consciously; others unconsciously. This probe will seek to isolate and tentatively explore three types of responses, each type a basic perspective concerning the natural process:

(1) symbiosis
(2) apobiosis
(3) diabiosis

Symbiosis

This term, derived from the field of biology—the study of living things—is widely used to stress the interrelatedness that exists between all living things. The prefix *sym-* is a Greek preposition used as part of a compound word, and signifies "together, interdependent, mutual, reciprocal." The morpheme *-bios-* in Greek signifies "life in all of its appearances and expressions." Hence the term *symbios-* literally means "life together, interdependent life, life lived mutually or reciprocally." When used to characterize a type of attitude toward the natural process, *symbiosis* denotes the accommodation of humanity to the natural process in a relationship of harmony, unity, organic wholeness. Symbiotic persons regard themselves as one with the natural world, from which they draw their sustenance and meaning with a minimum of disruption and interference.

This type of relationship is exemplified by the relationship of most animals to their natural environment. Few animals kill for the sake of killing. Animals will kill out of hunger, sometimes out of fear, in self-defense, or perhaps as a part of a life ritual, such as mating. But few ravage for the sake of ravaging.

Some cultures strongly reflect this type of primary understanding. The cultures of the American Indians are and were symbiotic in relation to the natural process. Likewise, the Chinese and Japanese cultural ethos, the bygone culture of ancient Egypt, and many isolated Western cultures today reflect this mentality. More developed expressions of symbiotic awareness may be found in aspects of popular Hindu religion—veneration of animals, especially the cow; reverence toward rivers and lakes, especially the Ganges; the recognition of the process of life/death, creation/destruction, within the natural process, as mediated through the worship of Shiva; ahimsa, nonviolation of living things; and the extremely profound recognition of the continuity and interdependence of human existence, samsara, rebirth/redeath. This symbiotic attitude is not absent, however, in Western culture. Embodiment is readily at hand: Rod McKuen's *The Earth* and other poems, much of Robert Frost and Thoreau, the strain of nature-mysticism within Christianity. Even the preoccupation of many Westerners with sex—including its mutation in advertising—may be but a disguised expression of the ancient, symbiotic nature/human fertility cult. But on the whole, Western culture, unlike the cultures of the East, has not been dominated by the symbiotic consciousness.

This mentality, therefore, is seldom found in pure form. Even in the cultures and for those individuals most shaped by the symbiotic awareness, a distinction is noted—in varying degrees—between humanity and the rest of nature. The totem of an Eskimo tribe may be one of the community, even as in prehistoric Nile culture a village appears to have identified with a particular animal; but the existence of the totem itself reflects at least an unconscious awareness that the totem animal or plant is distinguishable from the group. Black Eagle (note the name) in the Rick O'Shay cartoon expresses this. Even where the affirmation of the natural process is depicted in religious or divine imagery, the distinction between humanity and the world is preserved. Yet the symbiotic perspective persists as the dominant tone of humanity's sense of relationship to the natural process. And this perspective values stability and order, and tends to encourage the status quo. Change—when it means interference or manipulation or reordering of natural process—is resisted. One is encouraged to observe and to adjust to the natural process rather than to manipulate it.

From a religious perspective, this mentality is based on the perception of divine power or force, which is considered immanent in the natural process, including humanity. This divine power or force may be depicted in many ways: the Japanese veneration of kami, the pre-Communist Chinese reverence for Heaven and the ancestors, shaktism in India, the love of natural order and beauty in the West, the experience of the psychic powers of sexuality. These are but a few examples. In any case, nature itself—including humanity—is considered an expression or materialization of the divine presence.

B

Nature is an indispensable part of me, especially mountains. I am really looking forward to this summer when I can again be in the mountains. It is in the mountains where I find real peace. I can feel life and really be aware of it, and not just take it for granted. I feel closer to God when I am alone in the mountains than any other time. Then I know there is a God who is still active whereas at other times I'm not really sure.[1]

Apobiosis

This term, coined for our purposes, signifies the antithesis of symbiosis. The prefix *apo-* is the Greek preposition meaning "apart, separate from, alienated." Hence the compound *apobiosis* denotes that attitude which emphasizes humanity's apartness, its separation, its lack of oneness with the natural order. Or more positively, persons see themselves as detached from the natural process, and not only free from it, but impelled to oversee, manipulate, and exploit the natural process for their own ends.

This mentality is one of the wellsprings of the technological thrust of European and North American culture, and has at least two sources in the history of

---

[1]Unpublished student journal of Beth Utton. Used by permission.

Western culture: on one hand, the affirmation in Greek culture of man's capacity to understand and to order phenomena through reason; on the other hand, the conviction drawn from the Jewish tradition and mediated through Christianity that God and man stand somewhat apart from the natural process. Examples of this attitude are seen in the "naming" of the animals in the creation story of Genesis 2 and the injunction to man to "fill . . . subdue . . . have dominion" in Genesis 1. Both of these components issued eventually in the rebirth called the Renaissance; in exploration, settlement, and development of new political and social patterns; in the industrial revolution; and in the awesome development of modern science and technology. The apobiotic mentality is a requisite for the conquest of space, disease, and all other frontiers.

Yet it is striking that only in Western Europe and North America do we find the birth of science and technology; only recently, along with the spread of Western culture, do we find its appearance in India, China, and Japan. Nor has it been present in the Near Eastern countries. The reason for this may be found in the observation that, although Islam has a deity who is transcendent, a human being is not understood as an independent agent, manipulating and ordering the natural process. At this point we need to distinguish between the apobiotic mentality and modern scientific mentality. The Muslim cultures have not given birth to modern science in the full sense of the term. Yet in these cultures persons often see themselves as opposed to the natural process; they are reconciled to it only through submission to the sovereignty of Allah, who has created, controls, and provides for those who abide by his covenant. As Harvey Cox has noted (see quotation), both the Jewish and the Christian heritages contain a strong emphasis on a transcendent deity. Cox sees in this conviction the basis for the disenchantment of the natural process. This is correct, at least in part. A transcendent deity to whom humanity is related does issue in a semitranscendent understanding of humanity in these religious traditions. And it is with respect to the understanding of humanity that Judaism and Christianity differ from Islam. But not until the Renaissance—and the rediscovery of the Greek emphasis on rationality—did the Jewish and Christian understanding of humanity generate the apobiotic mentality that is reaching its fruition in Western science and technology. Technology means "building-knowledge," and apobiotic persons are the builders.

Again, one may not find a pure expression of apobiosis. The contrast with symbiosis lies not in the means but in the objective. Both rely on observation (note how Black Eagle calls Rick O'Shay only by the name "Yellow Hair"). But symbiotic persons observe in order that they may participate. Apobiotic persons observe in order that they may manipulate. Yet in their apobiotic efforts, they are often caught up in the order and beauty they are seeking to understand and then harness. Affective involvement fostering harmony and identification with the natural process has no place in a scientific experiment or a technological application. The astronauts of the Apollo series, looking out at the lunar terrain, may have been awestruck by the sight, but this was extracurricular as far as their mission was concerned: they were after rocks, not scenery. Their response to the moonscape was symbiotic, but their mission was apobiotic. As men they combined the two. The apobiotic mentality aims at conquest, change, harnessing the powers (no longer divine) of nature. Exploitation, frustration, disorder, or failure may occur, but only as the price of humanity's creativity, a creativity which itself transcends the natural order.

Thus the natural process itself does not contain a divine power of presence. Humanity, by becoming master of nature, shares in the transcendent power of God.

C

Presecular man lives in an enchanted forest. Its glens and groves swarm with spirits. Its rocks and streams are alive with friendly or fiendish demons. Reality is charged with a magical power that erupts here and there to threaten or benefit man. Properly managed and utilized, this invisible energy can be supplicated, warded off, or channeled. If real skill and esoteric knowledge are called into play, the energies of the unseen world can be used against a family foe or an enemy of the tribe. . . .

Many historians of religion believe that this magical world-view, although developed and organized in a very sophisticated way, was never really broken through until the advent of biblical faith. The Sumerian, Egyptian, and Babylonian religious systems, despite their fantastically complicated theologies and their enormously refined symbol systems, remained a form of high magic, relying for their cohesion on the integral relation between man and the cosmos. . . . Both god and man were part of nature.

This is why the Hebrew view of Creation signals such a marked departure. It separates nature from God and distinguishes man from nature. This is the beginning of the disenchantment process. . . . Whereas in the Babylonian accounts, the sun, moon, and stars are semidivine beings, partaking the divinity of the gods themselves, their religious status is totally rejected by the Hebrews. . . . None of the heavenly bodies can claim any right to religious awe or worship.

Nor is man tied to nature by kinship ties. The lines of kinship in the Bible are temporal, not spatial. Instead of reaching out to encompass kangaroos and totem shrubs, they reach back to the sagas of the fathers and forward to the fortunes of the children's children. . . . Just after his creation man is given the crucial responsibility of naming the animals. He is their master and commander. It is his task to subdue the earth. Nature is neither his brother nor his god. As such it offers him no salvation. . . . For the Bible, neither man nor God is defined by his relationship to nature. This not only frees both of them for history, it also makes nature itself available for man's use.[2]

The contrast between symbiosis and apobiosis may be illustrated by the response to the following life situation:

A certain city was located on a large river which received water from a large watershed. At intervals the watershed far above the city would receive large amounts of rainfall, causing the river, without perceptible reason, to overflow, causing severe damage to the urban area.

The symbiotic inhabitants tried to combat the problem by clearing the channel of underbrush and building their houses on stilts. Yet to a large measure, they remained vulnerable to the threat of the river.

The apobiotic inhabitants were not opposed to the above measures, but, in

[2]Harvey Cox, *The Secular City* (New York: Macmillan, Inc., 1965, pp. 21–23. Copyright © Harvey Cox, 1965, 1966.

addition, sought to build dams upstream to control the flow of water. In so doing, they created an even greater hazard in the event that one of the dams should break.

Both had at least one thing in common: Both symbiosis and apobiosis regard the natural process as having reality. The third mentality differs on this point.

Diabiosis

This term, also coined for our purposes, is compounded from the noun *bios* and the prepositional prefix *dia-*. This preposition is used in Greek sources to signify movement through a place, duration throughout a time, or the agent or instrument by which something is accomplished. *Diabiosis*, therefore, signifies an attitude toward the natural process which regards nature as that through which one must move if one is to reach reality. In this view, the natural process is regarded as changing, impermanent, imperfect, and of secondary importance at best. The diabiotic person believes that one must penetrate or survive the natural order in order to arrive at that which is real and eternal.

The culture of India most consistently exhibits diabiosis as the dominant mentality. As Heinrich Zimmer states, the natural process, including human existence itself, is considered "as fugitive and evanescent as cloud and mist." Humanity may be deluded by the seductiveness of *maya* but, in the end, that which is ultimate and real can be known only when the illusion dissolves. This Indian perspective continues in the movement of Mahavira, Jainism. In this tradition, the natural process is identified with "matter," which attaches itself to the soul through sin and can be purged only through asceticism and the practice of nonviolence toward all living things. Only then can the soul become free. Another child of Indian culture, Buddhism, also exhibits this mentality toward the natural process, including humanity's ego and culture: Gautama, the initiator, regarded not matter but destructive craving as that which perpetuated one's egoistic existence and bound him to the world of illusion. Later Buddhists held to this position. Yet, unlike Gautama, they returned to the conviction that beyond this illusory existence is cosmic reality, be it compassion or energy, and only by penetrating through maya can this reality be reached. In the philosophical form of Taoism in China we also encounter the conviction of a reality beyond. Yet unlike Indian culture, this reality—or Tao—is also within the natural process. Thus the knowledge of Tao informs and transforms one's relationship to the natural process. Nature, then, is not unreal; rather, it is dependent for its existence and meaning upon the Tao inherent in it.

But this diabiotic mentality is not absent from Western culture. It appeared especially within the Christian tradition. From the very earliest times some Christians have reviewed the natural process as irretrievably corrupted by human sin. The natural process, therefore, is regarded as temporary, as that which must soon pass away. Persons, in this view, are at best pilgrims in a strange land, and at worst victims of the natural order. The Revelation to John of Patmos is the strongest New Testament example; contemporary examples may be found on the radio and in the newspapers. Other non-Christian Western expressions of this diabiotic view may be noted in Greco-Roman times in Platonism and neo-Platonism, Stoicism, Gnosticism, and Manicheanism. Modern non-Christian Western expressions may be found in the alcohol and drug cultures, in which one attempts to escape the world as one experiences it.

Diabiotic persons seek release from a natural process which is regarded as corrupt, illusory, or secondary. One seeks reality beyond. Such a mentality may neglect and abandon societal problems and values. The quest is an individual one, for no one can accompany them. One is primarily concerned with saving oneself, and the rest, if necessary, must look out for themselves.

D

The *māyā* of the gods is their power to assume diverse shapes by displaying at will various aspects of their subtle essence. But the gods are themselves the productions of a greater *māyā*: the spontaneous self-transformation of an originally undifferentiated, all-generating divine Substance. And this greater *māyā* produces, not the gods alone, but the universe in which they operate. All the universes co-existing in space and succeeding each other in time, the planes of being and the creatures of those planes where natural or supernatural, are manifestations from an inexhaustible, original and eternal well being, and are made manifest by a play of *māyā*.

. . . Māyā is Existence: both the world of which we are aware, and ourselves who are contained in the growing and dissolving environment, growing and dissolving in our turn. At the same time, Māyā is the supreme power that generates and animates the display: the dynamic aspect of the universal Substance. Thus it is at once, effect (the cosmic flux), and cause (the creative power). In the latter regard it is known as Shakti, "Cosmic Energy." . . .

. . . Enthralled by ourselves and the effects of our environment, regarding the bafflements of Māyā as utterly real, we endure an endless ordeal of blandishments, desire and death; whereas, from a standpoint just beyond our ken (represented in the perennial esoteric tradition and known to the illimited, supraindividual consciousness of ascetic, yogic experience) Māyā—the world, the life, the ego, to which we cling—is as fugitive and evanescent as cloud and mist.[3]

It should be noted again that most societies manifest contrasting attitudes toward nature. Perhaps nowhere would *one* of the three types discussed in this unit be found in an entirely pure form. However, cultures may, over a long period of time, be characterized in a fairly definite way by one of the forms. India, for instance, and the Europe of the Patristic and early Middle Ages, were essentially diabiotic in attitude and ideology, if not always in life-style. A society like that of contemporary Japan is interesting. With its mixture of Eastern religious traditions—Shinto (symbiotic) and Buddhism (with Zen, especially, characterized by both diabiotic and symbiotic streams)—with the emulation of Western technical-manipulative attitudes (apobiotic), one finds a stimulating, sometimes confusing, and possibly fruitful intermingling of attitudes. Do you find one dominant attitude, a conflict of attitudes, or a mixture of attitudes about the relation of human beings to the natural order in contemporary American society?

[3]*Myths and Symbols in Indian Art and Civilization* by Heinrich Zimmer, ed. by Joseph Campbell, Bollingen Series VI (copyright © 1946 by Bollingen Foundation), reprinted with permission of Princeton University Press, pp. 24–26.

UNIT 88   Nature and the Natural

As we have seen in previous units, there is a profound religious dimension to our concepts of, and attitudes toward, the natural realm. Even our feelings about nature express this. When we respond to nature—whether we mean the world that the astronomer and physicist present in their highly abstract theories or the concrete experience of a sunset—the way that we *feel* embodies our commitment to, and understanding of, what seems to us to be of supreme value. In this unit, we attempt to explore some of the ambiguities—the many not always harmonious meanings— of the term *nature* as reflected in contrasting religious attitudes.

What do the terms *nature* and *natural* mean? Is nature the word of living things that the biologist studies, or is it the abstract, mathematically stated laws that the physicist gives us as descriptive of "reality"? Is nature what Romantic poets like Wordsworth wrote about? Is nature the realm of the sounds, scents, and colors that we experience? Or is it only the motion and interaction of events, waves, and particles—sound waves rather than sounds? Is it the sunsets and mountain peaks that the tourist sees? Is it what the hippie or the hermit who has abandoned the world of suburbia or the industrial centers returns to, a realm of cosmic and personal harmony? Is it the world of the jungle that the explorer seeks to conquer, where animal species struggle for survival?

Does nature include humanity's social institutions: Are civilizations, humane societies, "natural"? Or is nature whatever exists independently of, or apart from, human activity? We speak of natural rather than artificial (man-made) products. But are persons a part of nature? Or do they stand over against it, different from it, opposed to it? Are persons at war with nature? Or is nature, in persons, at war with itself? Some religious traditions speak of humanity as evil by nature. Others speak of humanity as naturally good. One thing is certain: Not only must we ask whether different cultures and different traditions (or the same cultures in different moods or at different periods of time) have a *positive* or a *negative* attitude toward nature; we must also ask what they think of as *natural*, and what they think *nature* includes.

Alfred North Whitehead has described the view of nature and the meaning of the term that arose with modern Western scientific thought. Whitehead wrote:

A   Nature is that which we observe in perception through the senses. In . . . sense-perception we are aware of something which is not thought and which is self-contained for thought. This property of being self-contained for thought lies at the base of natural science. It means that nature can be thought of as a closed system whose . . . relations do not require the expression of the fact that they are thought about.[4]

This rather abstract definition is perhaps a typical understanding of what nature, as described by the laws of physics, has meant since the seventeenth century for many Western thinkers.

[4]Alfred North Whitehead, *The Concept of Nature* (Cambridge: Cambridge University Press, 1920), p. 3. Used by permission of publisher.

Describing the view of nature held by such seventeenth-century philosophers and scientists as Galileo, Descartes, Locke, and Newton, Whitehead wrote:

B

We then ask in what sense are blueness and noisiness qualities of the body. By analogous reasoning, we also ask in what sense is its scent a quality of the rose.

Galileo considered this question, and at once pointed out that, apart from eyes, ears, or noses, there would be no colours, sounds, or smells. . . . The occurrences of nature are in some way apprehended by minds, which are associated with living bodies. Primarily, the mental apprehension is aroused by the occurrences in certain parts of the correlated body, the occurrences in the brain, for instance. But the mind in apprehending also experiences sensations which, properly speaking, are qualities of the mind alone. These sensations are projected by the mind so as to clothe appropriate bodies in external nature. Thus the bodies are perceived as with qualities which in reality do not belong to them, qualities which in fact are purely the offspring of the mind. Thus nature gets credit which should in truth be reserved for ourselves: the rose for its scent: the nightingale for his song: and the sun for his radiance. The poets are entirely mistaken. They should address their lyrics to themselves, and should turn them into odes of self-congratulation on the excellence of the human mind. Nature is a dull affair, soundless, scentless, colourless; merely the hurrying of material endlessly, meaninglessly.

However you disguise it, this is the practical outcome of the characteristic philosophy which closed the seventeenth century.[5]

The Romantic poets Wordsworth and Coleridge, at the end of the eighteenth century, reacted against this way of conceiving nature, as did Whitehead himself in his philosophical writings. The Romantics and Whitehead conceived of nature as dynamic and alive, as a realm of feeling and meaning and value in which we are involved not first as abstract observers but as sentient participants.

In contrast to both these Western approaches, in the Hindu civilization of India, nature has been viewed negatively, as illusory or unreal—and this included the whole of existing reality belonging to the natural *and* the social spheres. In Chinese civilization, nature has been viewed positively. According to the Confucian emphasis, nature is thought of as inclusive of the social order and its institutions and relationships: One is living "naturally" (harmoniously, as one ought to live) when one lives according to the rational and traditional precepts that make one a properly and actively functioning member of the social order. On the other hand, the Taoist emphasis in Chinese culture has regarded the world of social institutions and moral precepts as artificial: Humanity lives naturally when it returns to the passive and harmonious simplicity of communion with mountain, flower, animal and stream.

Even before the post-seventeenth-century tendency to look at nature abstractly (described in the two previous Whitehead quotes), there had been an ambivalence toward nature in Western thought. Both Judaism and Christianity emphasize that the created order—including the social order—is (or should be) good.

[5]Whitehead, *Science and the Modern World* (New York: Macmillan, Inc., 1948), pp. 78–80.

C And God saw all that He had made, and it was very good. (Genesis 1:31, NEB)

This is certainly true of the "natural" world of cosmos and minerals, plants and animals (see Genesis 1). But Christianity especially has been inclined to suggest that nature—in the sense of cosmos and mineral, plant and animal realms—has been involved in the calamity of humanity's historical (individual and social) fall from its true nature. Thus not only has humanity, through its sin, become alienated from nature (its own and that of the rest of the universe) but the rest of nature has suffered.

D And to the man God said:
   "Because you have . . . eaten from the tree which I forbade you, accursed shall be the ground on your ac- count. . . . It will grow thorns and this- tles for you, none but wild plants. . . ."
(Genesis 3:17–18 NEB)

Paul in Romans 8:19–23 writes that the whole creation, which has been subject to bondage and decay, is longing to be set free. Other Christian thinkers—for instance, John Milton in Adam's speech in the Tenth Book of *Paradise Lost*—develop the idea that nature and its order have been upset as a result of Adam's sin. Both Paul and Milton also suggest that nature is in fact being restored through God's redemptive activity in Christ.

Not only Romantic poets and writers like the American transcendentalist Thoreau but also contemporary poets have suggested that participation in a complex urban and industrialized society represents a fall from a harmonious relationship with nature and have called for a return to "natural simplicity." The American poet James Dickey has said:

E I'm much more interested in a man's re- lationship to the God-made world, or the universe-made world, than to the man- made world. The natural world seems in- finitely more important to me than the man-made world. I remember a state- ment of D. H. Lawrence's; he said that as a result of our science and industrializa- tion, we have lost the cosmos. The parts of the universe we can investigate by means of machinery and scientific empir- ical techniques we may understand better than our predecessors did, but we no longer know the universe emotionally. It's a great deal easier to relate to it as a collocation of chemical properties. There's no moon goddess now. But when men believed there was, then the moon was more important, maybe not scientifi- cally, but more important emotionally. It was something a man had a personal rela- tionship to, instead of its being simply a dead stone, a great ruined stone in the sky. The moon has always been very im- portant to me. The astronauts have intro- duced me to a new kind of mythology about the moon. This may in the end be greater than the old Greek one.[6]

In contrast, according to Enid Starkie, the nineteenth-century French poet Charles Baudelaire believed

[6]From *Self Interviews* by James Dickey, pp. 67–68. Copyright © 1970 by James Dickey. Pub- lished by Doubleday & Company, Inc.

F   that art existed only by reason of what man added of his own substance, of his own soul, to the raw material of nature. He could not endure the Romantic idealisation of nature, nor the Rousseau myth of the nobility of natural man, uncorrupted by civilisation. He believed, on the contrary, that the only value in man consisted in his spiritual essence, which only self-discipline and self-culture could develop, and that this was of greater price than anything which could be discovered in nature. . . . Baudelaire . . . tried to put nature in her proper place, for he thought that man lost his pride and dignity by being too humble with her. The violence of his opinions is due to his reaction against sentimentality.[7]

As noted in the quotations and in the illustrations, how one understands nature profoundly affects how one lives and thinks. Religion and every other aspect of life are influenced by one's understanding of nature.

[7]Enid Starkie, *Baudelaire* (New York: New Directions, 1958), p. 293.

22 _____

Time and Eternity

INTRODUCTION

Crucial to human views of nature and natural processes is the concept of time. In human settings an interest in time is related to human purposes: We measure time as we do because we are interested in temporal sequences related to our hopes, fears, needs, goals, and desires. Time in nature also often seems measurable in terms of purposive sequences. As the Jewish Scriptures say, "There is a season and a time for everything under heaven . . . a time to plant, and a time to harvest what has been planted" (Ecclesiastes 3:1–2).

Thus nature itself, in the seasonal cycles and the seemingly endless generational cycles of birth, growth to maturity, and procreation, seems to show that the passage of time measures an orderly sequence. But in the natural order that transcends our own earth, the cosmos itself, time must certainly be understood differently; it is not limited by the rotation of our earth, the basis of our earthly time structures. Similarly, many human societies have questioned whether in the larger, universal order of nature the passage of time is purposive, meaningful, goal oriented. This question reveals a religious dimension to the human experience of time.

In considering the question of whether time in its passage has religious significance, one must consider several possibilities. Is it leading toward an ultimate fulfillment, as has been commonly understood in Western religions? If so, what aspects of human reality that involve time can be eternal? What realities of human

317

life are not involved in, or affected by, time? What realities are beyond time? Is time only a convenient human construct that has no relevance to ultimate realities or meanings?

The purpose of this chapter is to probe the religious dimensions of the human experience of time and of the concepts of time and the eternal as they have been expressed in a variety of religious-cultural traditions. Here again we are using the term *religious* in the broad sense that denotes belief in a pivotal or supreme value—the fundamental purpose(s) to which individuals or groups may be committed.

The first unit examines concepts of time, giving attention to the distinction between typical Eastern and Western views and attitudes. The second unit considers a possible contrast between traditions that emphasize time, history, and a personalized concept of the Divine and those that stress a timeless eternal, the natural order, and the concept of an impersonal deity.

UNIT 89 The Mystery of Time

What is time? Do we exist in time? Is time a reality? Numerous questions may be asked regarding the mystery of time. Such questions are both asked and answered differently in the Eastern and Western worlds.

Hermann Hesse, in his novel *Siddhartha*, provides us with the flavor of an Eastern response to the question of time.

A

"When the Illustrious Buddha taught about the world, he had to divide it into Samsara and Nirvana, into illusion and truth, into suffering and salvation. One cannot do otherwise, there is no other method for those who teach. But the world itself, being in and around us, is never one-sided. Never is a man or deed wholly Nirvana; never is a man wholly a saint or a sinner. This only seems so because we suffer the illusion that time is something real. Time is not real, Govinda. I have realized this repeatedly. And if time is not real, the dividing line that seems to lie between this world and eternity, between suffering and bliss, between good and evil, is also an illusion."

"How is that?" asked Govinda, puzzled.

"Listen, my friend! I am a sinner and you are a sinner, but someday the sinner will be Brahma again, will someday attain Nirvana, will someday become a Buddha. Now this 'someday' is illusion; it is only a comparison. The sinner is not on the way to a Buddha-like state; he is not evolving, although our thinking cannot conceive things otherwise. No, the potential Buddha already exists in the sinner; his future is already there. The potential hidden Buddha must be recognized in him, in you, in everybody. The world, Govinda, is not imperfect or slowly evolving along a path to perfection. No, it is perfect at every moment; every sin already carries grace within it, all small children are potential old men, all sucklings have death within them, all dying people—eternal life. It is not possible for one person to see how far another is on the way; the Buddha exists in the robber and dice player; the robber exists in the Brahmin. During deep meditation it is possible to dispel time, to see simultaneously all the past, present and future, and then everything is good, everything is perfect, everything is Brahman."[1]

[1]Herman Hesse, *Siddhartha*, trans. Hilda Rosner. Copyright 1951 by New Directions Publishing Corporation. Reprinted by permission of New Directions Publishing Corporation. Pages 114–45.

B

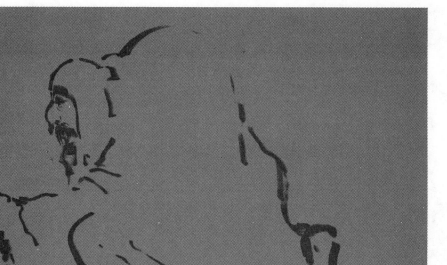

(*Jacques Bakke*)

Conversely, Westerners emphasize time as real and of great importance. Let us consider some of the issues significant to the Western frame of reference.

We are constantly reminded by clocks, calendars, and schedules that we exist *in* time and that time is in us. Whereas non-Western religions tend to deemphasize time, Western religions experience the Divine as revealed in time, in and through events of history.

> Time, a problem pervading our existence
> Demands our allegiance,
> But remains a mystery eluding our understanding.

The ancient Greeks pictured time in two figures: *Chronos*, an old gray-headed man, bent with a burden of time grown old, and *Kairos*, a young man running swiftly, the back of his head shaven smooth with only the forelock remaining. Chronos, old Father Time, represents our preoccupation with clock-time, the time that passes and sucks us into the past. Through the eyes of Chronos we see the world growing

C

(Jacques Bakke)

old, and we become weary with the burden of time. If we run with Kairos we know time as opportunity, to be seized in the moment that it comes to meet us. Through the eyes of Kairos we see the significance of the present and the future. Kairos will run by us if we do not grasp his forelock quickly at the right moment.

Paul Tillich comments on the *mystery* of time.

D

Augustine points to the depth of this mystery, when he says, "If nobody asks me about it, I *know*. If I want to explain it to somebody who asks me about it, I do not know." There is something unspeakable about time, but this has not prevented the most profound religious minds from thinking and speaking about it. . . .

Mankind has always realized that there is something fearful about the flux of time, a riddle which we cannot solve, and the solution of which we could not stand. We come from a past which is no more; we go into a future which is not yet; *ours* is the present. The past is ours only in so far as we have it still present; and the future is ours only in so far as we have it already present. We possess the past by memory, and the future by anticipation. But what is the nature of the present itself? If we look at it closely, we must say: it is a point without extension, the point in which the future becomes the past; when we say to ourselves, "This is the present," the moment has already been swallowed by the past. The present disappears the very instant we try to grasp it. The present cannot be caught; it is always gone. So it seems that we have nothing real—neither the past nor the future, nor even the present. Therefore, there is a dreaming character about our existence, which the psalmist indicates, and which religious visionaries have described in so many ways.

Time, however, could not even give us a place on which to stand, if it were not characterized by that second mystery, its power to receive eternity. There is no present in the mere stream of time; but the present is real, as our experience witnesses. And it is real because eternity breaks into time and gives it a real present. We could not even say "now," if eternity did not elevate *that* moment above the ever-passing time. Eternity is always present; and its presence is the cause of our having the present at all. . . . In every moment that we say "now," something temporal and something eternal are united. Whenever a human being says, "Now I am living; now I am really present," resisting the stream which drives the future into the past, eternity *is*. In each such "now," eternity is made manifest; in every real "now," eternity is present. Let us think

for a moment of the way in which we are living our lives in our period of history. Have we not lost a real present by always being driven forward, by our constant running, in our indefatigable activism, toward the future? We suppose the future to be better than any present; but there is always another future beyond the next future, again and again without a present, that is to say, without eternity. According to the Fourth Gospel eternal life is a *present* gift: he, who listens to Christ, has eternity already. He is no longer subject to the driving of time. In him the "now" becomes a "now eternal." We have lost the real "now," the "now eternal"; we have, I am afraid, lost eternal life in so far as it creates the real present.

There is another element in time, its third mystery, which makes us look at the future; for time does not return, nor repeat itself: it runs forward; it is always unique; it ever creates the new. There is within it a drive toward an end, unknown, never to be reached in time itself, always intended and ever fleeing. Time runs toward the "future eternal." This is the greatest of all the mysteries of time. . . . The eternal is the solution of the riddle of time. Time does not drive toward an endless self-repetition, nor to an empty return to its beginning. Time is not meaningless. . . . It brings about a hidden reality—the new creation. The infinite significance of every moment of time is this: in it we decide, and are decided about, with respect to our eternal future.[2]

Although Tillich supports the goal-oriented view of time emphasized in the West, he seeks to correct false hopes for future fulfillments by stressing the "now" in which eternity is present. Meaningless waiting or frantic striving for unfulfilled futures can be transformed into "meaning-filled" moments uniting the temporal and eternal when one affirms "now" as real. In his understanding of "now," eternity is present; the temporal and the eternal unite when a person affirms "now" as real. Here Tillich criticizes the way Westerners push toward the future and thus fail to realize the gifts of the present. Tillich does not neglect the future, however. He sees time as

[2]Reprinted by permission of Charles Scribner's Sons from *The Shaking of the Foundations*, pp. 34–37 by Paul Tillich. Copyright 1948 Charles Scribner's Sons.

dynamic, moving toward the "future eternal" wherein the mystery of time is solved. Since that "future" has not arrived, time remains a mystery.

> *In what ways do we constantly run into a future? Can the present moment be all-significant, as Tillich suggests? How do you understand a meaningful present? In what ways do we run from time? In what ways do we confront time?*

UNIT 90   The Temporal and the Eternal

With respect to the understanding of time and eternity in relation to the Divine, religions may be divided into at least two distinct types: those that understand the Divine as wholly or primarily eternal and those that emphasize that the Divine has significant temporal as well as eternal aspects.

The Divine as Personal

Judaism, Zoroastrianism, Christianity, and Islam illustrate the first type. These religions speak of the Divine in terms derived from personal experience, interpersonal relations, and the interaction of nations. Generally understood as a *personal deity*, the Divine may be characterized with words descriptive of human personality and can enter into personal relationships with individuals and groups. Being thus related to human concerns, he acts within the setting of earthly existence; therefore, he acts within time. This fact infuses time itself with divine significance.

There are numerous examples of this interplay and personal contact between the Hebrew leaders and Yahweh, the God of the Israelites. In Genesis 18, Yahweh is described as having decided to destroy the cities of Sodom and Gomorrah because their inhabitants have participated in gross moral sin. He shares his intent to destroy the cities with Abraham. The following conversation ensues:

> Then Abraham drew near, and said "Wilt thou indeed destroy the righteous with the wicked? Suppose there are fifty righteous within the city; wilt thou then destroy the place and not spare it for the fifty righteous who are in it? Far be it from thee to do such thing, to slay the righteous with the wicked! Far be that from thee! Shall not the Judge of all the earth do right?" And the Lord said, "If I find at Sodom fifty righteous in the city, I will spare the whole place for their sake." . . . Then he [Abraham] said, "Oh let not the Lord be angry, and I will speak again but this once. Suppose ten are found there?" He [Yahweh] answered, "For the sake of ten I will not destroy it." And the Lord went his way, when he had finished speaking to Abraham; and Abraham returned to his place. (Genesis 18:23–33, RSV)

This example of an interpersonal relationship, wherein Abraham is not only in God's presence and talking to him but even challenges him to be fully righteous, suggests how clearly the Israelites understood their relationship to God to be one of direct, personal contact, much like that with other humans. Note that the example suggests that Yahweh—the transcendent, all-powerful God of all creation—acts directly in history, creating, destroying, ruling, chastening. Yet it is clear that Yahweh is not understood by Abraham as an equal: Abraham is anxious not to anger God. God is transcendent, not bound by human affairs or human history. Abraham may speak his mind and be heard by God, but it is God who acts in and controls history.

In contrast, the Israelite realization of the transcendent nature of Yahweh, wherein the Divine is beyond comprehension or description, is expressed in the following passage from the prophet Isaiah:

> Have you not known? Have you not heard?
> Has it not been told you from the beginning?
> Have you not understood from the foundations of the earth?
> It is he who sits above the circle of the earth,
> and its inhabitants are like grasshoppers;
> who stretches out the heavens like a curtain,
> and spreads them like a tent to dwell in;
> who brings princes to nought,
> and makes the rulers of the earth as nothing.
> Scarcely are they planted, scarcely sown,
> scarcely has their stem taken root in the earth,
> when he blows upon them, and they wither,
> and the tempest carries them off like stubble.
> To whom then will you compare me,
> that I should be like him?
> says the Holy One,
> Lift up your eyes on high and see: who created these?
> . . . .
> The Lord is the everlasting God,
> the Creator of the ends of the earth.
>
> (Isaiah 40:21–26, RSV)

As Isaiah indicates, the transcendent aspect of God is as important to Hebrew understanding of God as is the concept of his relating to persons and the nation on a personal basis.

As these two examples suggest, God is understood by the Israelites as transcending creation—including time—*and* at the same time as being involved in time and history. Such a concept is not without its tensions, for it requires a timeless transcendent Deity, unbound by creation and its time sequence, to be involved in the very history of that creation. In this tension, timeless transcendence threatens to overwhelm the concept of a personal historical involvement by God and the significance of human beings, creatures confined with the limits of time. Yet the Hebrews, along with Christians, Muslims, and Zoroastrians, maintain that the Divine manifests both elements so that adherents to the religion experience a personal God who is nevertheless transcendent; therefore, human beings can enjoy the fruits of a personal relationship to the Divine.

The Divine as Impersonal

Hinduism, Buddhism, philosophical Taoism, and Shinto illustrate the second type of understanding of time and eternity. These religions speak of the Divine in terms derived from natural process. Generally understood as an *impersonal* power, the essence of the Divine is characterized with words not associated with human personality. Being impersonal, it does not enter into personal relationships with individuals and groups. Thus the essence of the Divine transcends this existence, and is therefore timeless, without beginning and without end. Time itself becomes but a passing episode in an unending, eternal process.

Heinrich Zimmer calls attention to an intriguing story in one of the *Puranas*, a story which speaks forcefully to our concern. It is entitled "The Parade of Ants." The story opens with the figure of Indra, King of the Gods, after he has slain the Dragon who pent up the life-giving waters. Indra, to express and celebrate his kingly glory and splendor, has ordered Vishvakarman, the god of arts and crafts, to build splendid gardens, palaces, lakes, and towers. As he works, Indra's vision of what he desires gets bigger and bigger, so that finally Vishvakarman, in desperation, appeals to the "demiurgic creator, Brahmā, the pristine embodiment of the Universal Spirit, who abides far above the Olympian sphere of ambition, strife, and glory," for help. Brahmā himself appeals to Vishnu, the Supreme Being, who by a mere nod of his head indicates that the wish of Vishvakarman will be fulfilled. The next day a brahmin boy, "slender, some ten years old, radiant with the luster of wisdom," appears at Indra's gate. After inviting the boy into his palace, Indra asks, "O Venerable Boy, tell me the purpose of your coming."

A

This beautiful child replied with a voice that was as deep and soft as the slow thundering of auspicious rain clouds. "O King of Gods, I have heard of the mighty palace you are building, and have come to refer to you the questions in my mind. How many years will it require to complete this rich and extensive residence? What further feats of engineering will Vishvakarman be expected to accomplish? O Highest of the Gods,"—the boy's luminous features moved with a gentle, scarcely perceptible smile—"no Indra before you has ever succeeded in completing such a palace as yours is to be."

Full of the wine of triumph, the king of the gods was entertained by this mere boy's pretension to a knowledge of Indras earlier than himself. With a fatherly smile he put the question: "Tell me, Child! Are they then so very many, the Indras and Vishvakarmans whom you have seen—or at least, whom you have heard of?"

The wonderful guest calmly nodded. "Yes, indeed, many have I seen." The voice was as warm and sweet as milk fresh from the cow, but the words sent a slow chill through Indra's veins. "My dear child," the boy continued, "I knew your father, Kashyapa, the Old Tortoise Man, lord and progenitor of all the creatures of the earth. And I knew your grandfather, Marichi, Beam of Celestial Light, who was the son of Brahmā. Marichi was begotten of the god Brahmā's pure spirit; his only wealth and glory were his sanctity and devotion. Also, I know Brahmā, brought forth by Vishnu from the lotus calix growing from Vishnu's navel. And Vishnu himself—the Supreme Being, supporting Brahmā in his creative endeavor—him too I know.

"O King of Gods, I have known the dreadful dissolution of the universe. I have seen all perish, again and again, at the end of every cycle. At that terrible time, every single atom dissolves into the primal, pure waters of eternity, whence originally all arose. Everything then goes back into the fathomless, wild infinity of the ocean, which is covered with utter darkness and is empty of every sign of animate being. Ah, who will count the universes that have passed away, or the creations that have risen afresh, again and again, from the formless abyss of the vast waters? Who will number the passing ages of the world, as they follow each other endlessly? And who will search through the wide infinites of space to count the universes side by side, each containing its Brahmā, its Vishnu, and its Shiva? Who will count the Indras in them all—those Indras side by side, who reign at once in all the innumerable worlds; those others who passed away before them; or even the Indras who succeed each other in any given line, ascending to godly kinship, one by one, and one by one, passing away? King of Gods, there are among your servants certain who maintain that it may be possible to number the grains of sand on earth and the drops of rain that fall from the sky, but no one will ever number all those Indras. This is what the Knowers know.

"The life and kingship of an Indra endure seventy-one eons, and when twenty-eight Indras have expired, one Day and Night of Brahmā has elapsed. But the existence of one Brahmā, measured in such Brahmā Days and Nights, is only one hundred and eight years. Brahmā follows Brahmā; one sinks, the next arises; the endless series cannot be told. There is no end to the number of those Brahmās—to say nothing of Indras.

"But the universes side by side at any given moment, each harboring a Brahmā and an Indra: who will estimate the number of these? Beyond the farthest vision, crowding outer space, the universes come and go, an innumerable host. Like delicate boats they float on the fathomless, pure waters that form the body of Vishnu. Out of every hair-pore of that body a universe bubbles and breaks. Will you presume to count them? Will you number the gods in all those worlds—the worlds present and the worlds past?"

A procession of ants made its appearance in the hall during the discourse of the boy. In military array, in a column four yards wide, the tribe paraded across the floor. The boy noted them, paused, and stared, then suddenly laughed with an astonishing peal, but immediately subsided into a profoundly indrawn and thoughtful silence.

"Why do you laugh?" stammered Indra. "Who are you, mysterious being, under this deceiving guise of a boy?" The proud king's throat and lips had gone dry, and his voice continually broke. "Who are you, Ocean of Virtues, enshrouded in deluding mist?"

The magnificent boy resumed: "I laughed because of the ants. The reason is not to be told. Do not ask me to disclose it. The seed of woe and the fruit of wisdom are enclosed within this secret. It is the secret that smites with an ax the tree of worldly vanity, hews away its roots, and scatters its crown. This secret is a lamp to those groping in ignorance. This secret lies buried in the wisdom of the ages, and is rarely revealed even to saints. This secret is the living air of those ascetics who renounce and transcend mortal existence; but worldlings, deluded by desire and pride, it destroys."

The boy smiled and sank into silence. Indra regarded him, unable to move. "O Son of a Brahmin," the king pleaded presently, with a new and visible humility, "I do not know who you are. You would seem to be Wisdom Incarnate. Reveal to me this secret of the ages, this light that dispels the dark."

Thus requested to teach, the boy opened to the god the hidden wisdom. "I saw the ants, O Indra, filing in long parade. Each was once an Indra. Like you, each by virtue of pious deeds once ascended to the rank of a king of gods. But now, through many rebirths, each has become again an ant. This army is an army of former Indras.

"Piety and high deeds elevate the inhabitants of the world to the glorious realm of the celestial mansions, or to the higher domains of Brahmā and Shiva and to the highest sphere of Vishnu; but wicked acts sink them into the worlds beneath, into pits of pain and sorrow, involving reincarnation among birds and vermin, or out of the wombs of pigs and animals of the wild, or among trees, or among insects. It is by deeds that one merits happiness or anguish, and becomes a master or a serf. It is by deeds that one attains to the rank of a king or brahmin, or of some god, or of an Indra or a Brahmā. And through deeds again, one contracts disease, acquires beauty and deformity, or is reborn in the condition of a monster.

"This is the whole substance of the secret. This wisdom is the ferry to beatitude across the ocean of hell.

"Life in the cycle of the countless rebirths is like a vision in a dream. The gods on high, the mute trees and the stones, are alike apparitions in this phantasy. But Death administers the Law of time. Ordained by time, Death is the master of all. Perishable as bubbles are the good and the evil of the beings of the dream. In unending cycles the good and evil alternate. Hence, the wise are attached to neither, neither the evil nor the good. The wise are not attached to anything at all."

The boy concluded the appalling lesson and quietly regarded his host. The king of gods, for all his celestial splendor, had been reduced in his own regard to insignificance.[3]

In this story the Divine Reality is timeless, impersonal, solitary, removed from the passing into existence and passing out of existence of the multitudinous universes. The Divine is oblivious to and detached from the concerns of "ambition, strife, and glory," exemplified by the god Indra.

Yet it is significant that the concern of the story is the meaning of individual—Indra's—identity, as expressed in his desire for palaces, gardens, lakes, and towers celebrating his glorious achievements. Thus within the world view that espouses timeless, eternal reality, one of the pressing problems is the significance of time and human achievement.

B

Meanwhile, another amazing apparition had entered the hall.

The newcomer had the appearance of a kind of hermit. His head was piled with matted hair; he wore a black deerskin around his loins; on his forehead was painted a white mark; his head was shaded by a paltry parasol of grass; and a quaint, circular cluster of hair grew on his chest: it was intact at the circumference, but from the center many of the hairs, it seemed, had disappeared. This saintly figure strode directly to Indra and the boy, squatted between them on the floor, and there remained, motionless as a rock. The kingly Indra, somewhat recovering his hostly role, bowed and paid obeisance, offering sour milk with honey and other refreshments; then he inquired falteringly but reverently, after the welfare of the stern guest, and bade him welcome. Whereupon the boy addressed the holy man, asking the very questions Indra himself would have proposed.

"Whence do you come, O Holy Man? What is your name and what brings you to this place? Where is your present home and what is the meaning of this grass parasol? What is the portent of that circular hair-tuft on your chest: why is it dense at the circumference but at the center almost bare? Be kind enough, O Holy Man, to answer, in brief, these questions. I am anxious to understand."

Patiently the old saint smiled, and slowly began his reply. "I am a brahmin. Hairy is my name. And I have come here to behold Indra. Since I know that I am short-lived, I have decided to possess no home; to build no house, and neither to marry nor to seek a livelihood. I exist by

[3]*Myths and Symbols in Indian Art and Civilization* by Heinrich Zimmer, ed. by Joseph Campbell, Bollingen Series VI (copyright © 1946 by Bollingen Foundation), reprinted with permission of Princeton University Press, pp. 4–8.

begging alms. To shield myself from sun and rain I carry over my head this parasol of grass.

"As to the circle of hair on my chest, it is a source of grief to the children of the world. Nevertheless, it teaches wisdom. With the fall of an Indra, one hair drops. That is why, in the center all the hairs have gone. When the other half of the period allotted to the present Brahmā will have expired, I myself shall die. O Brahmin Boy, it follows that I am somewhat short of days; what therefore, is the use of a wife and a son, or of a house?

"Each flicker of the eyelids of the great Vishnu registers the passing of a Brahmā. Everything below that sphere of Brahmā is as insubstantial as a cloud taking shape and again dissolving. That is why I devote myself exclusively to meditating on the incomparable lotus-feet of highest Vishnu. Faith in Vishnu is more than the bliss of redemption; for every joy, even the heavenly, is as fragile as a dream, and only interferes with the one-pointedness of our faith in Him Supreme.

"Shiva, the peace-bestowing, the highest spiritual guide, taught me this wonderful wisdom. I do not crave to experience the various blissful forms of redemption: to share the highest god's supernatural mansions and enjoy his eternal presence, or to be like him in body and apparel, or to become a part of his august substance, or even to be absorbed wholly in his ineffable essence."

Abruptly, the holy man ceased and immediately vanished. It had been the god Shiva himself; he had now returned to his supramundane abode. Simultaneously, the brahmin boy, who had been Vishnu, disappeared as well. The king was alone, baffled and amazed.[4]

This portion of the story not only reinforces the previous emphasis but declares that not only humanlike Indra but the Creator-God Himself—Brahmā—is ruled by the timeless, inexorable wheeling of eons.

Yet the story does not end here. And the ending itself underscores the demand within timelessness for temporal significance.

C The king, Indra, pondered; and the events seemed to him to have been a dream. But he no longer felt any desire to magnify his heavenly splendor or to go on with the construction of his palace. He summoned Vishvakarman. Graciously greeting the craftsman with honeyed words, he heaped on him jewels and precious gifts, then with a sumptuous celebration sent him home.

The king, Indra, now desired redemption. He had acquired wisdom, and wished only to be free. He entrusted the pomp and burden of his office to his son, and prepared to retire to the hermit life of the wilderness. Whereupon his beautiful and passionate queen, Shachi, was overcome with grief.

Weeping, in sorrow and utter despair, Shachi resorted to Indra's ingenious house-priest and spiritual advisor, the Lord of Magic Wisdom, Brihaspati. Bowing at his feet, she implored him to divert her husband's mind from its stern resolve. The resourceful counselor of the gods, who by his spells and devices had helped the heavenly powers wrest the government of the universe from the hands of their titan rivals, listened thoughtfully to the complaint of the voluptuous, disconsolate goddess, and knowingly nodded assent. With a wizard's smile, he took her hand and conducted her to the presence of her spouse. In the role, then, of spiritual teacher, he discoursed sagely on the virtues of the spiritual life, but on the virtues also, of the secular. He gave to each its due. Very skillfully he developed his theme. The royal pupil was persuaded to relent in his extreme resolve. The queen was restored to radiant joy.

This Lord of Magic Wisdom, Brihas-

[4]*Ibid.*, pp. 8–10.

pati, once had composed a treatise on government, in order to teach Indra how to rule the world. He now issued a second work, a treatise on the policy and stratagems of married love. Demonstrating the sweet art of wooing ever anew, and of enchanting the beloved with enduring bonds, this priceless book established on sound foundations the married life of the reunited pair.

Thus concludes the marvelous story of how the king of gods was humiliated in his boundless pride, cured of an excessive ambition, and through wisdom, both spiritual and secular, brought to a knowledge of his proper role in the wheeling play of unending life.[5]

About this story, Zimmer says,

D

The two great gods, Vishnu and Shiva, instruct the human hearers of the myth by teaching Indra, king of the Olympians. The Wonderful Boy, solving riddles and pouring out wisdom from his childish lips, is an archetypal figure, common to fairy tales of all ages and many traditions. He is an aspect of the Boy Hero, who solves the riddle of the Sphinx and rids the world of monsters. Likewise an archetypal figure is the Old Wise Man, beyond ambitions and the illusions of ego, treasuring and imparting the wisdom that sets free, shattering the bondage of possessions, the bondage of suffering and desire.

But the wisdom taught in this myth would have been incomplete had the last word been that of the infinity of space and time. The vision of the countless universes bubbling into existence side by side, and the lesson of the unending series of Indras and Brahmās, would have annihilated every value of individual existence. Between this boundless, breathtaking vision and the opposite problem of the limited role of the short-lived individual, this myth effected the reestablishment of a balance. Brihaspati, the high priest and spiritual guide of the gods, who is Hindu wisdom incarnate, teaches Indra (i.e., ourself, the individual confused) how to grant to each sphere its due. We are taught to recognize the divine, the impersonal sphere of eternity, revolving ever and agelessly through time. But we are also taught to esteem the transient sphere of the duties and pleasures of individual existence, which is as real and as vital to the living man, as a dream to the sleeping soul.[6]

The contrast between the world view based on time and that based on timelessness is sharply drawn in the following passage from Zimmer.

E

This vast time-consciousness, transcending the brief span of the individual, even the racial biography, is the time-consciousness of Nature herself. Nature knows, not centuries, but ages— geological, astronomical ages—and stands, furthermore, beyond them. Swarming egos are her children, but the species is her concern; and world ages are her shortest span for the various species that she puts forth and permits, finally, to die (like the dinosaurs, the mammoths, and the giant birds). India—as Life brooding on itself—thinks of the problem of time in periods comparable to those of our astronomy, geology, and paleontology. India thinks of time and of herself, that is to say, in biological terms, terms of the species, not of the ephemeral ego. The latter *becomes* old: the former *is* old, and therewith eternally young.

We of the West on the other hand, regard world history as a biography of mankind, and in particular of Occidental

---

[5]*Ibid.*, pp. 10–11.
[6]*Ibid.*, p. 22.

Man, whom we estimate to be the most consequential member of the family. Biography is that form of seeing and representing which concentrates on the unique, the induplicable, in any portion of existence, and then brings out the sense-and-direction-giving traits. We think of egos, individuals, not of Life. Our will is not to culminate in our human institutions the universal play of nature, but to evaluate, to set ourselves against the play, with an egocentric tenacity.[7]

In this unit we have discussed, on the one hand, the way the Divine is conceived as personal, temporal, and in interaction with persons and nations, noting especially how Christianity, Judaism, Islam, and Zoroastrianism reflect this perspective. On the other hand, we have shown the Divine to be timeless and impersonal as understood by Hinduism, Buddhism, and Taoism. Thus we have set the contrast between the temporal and the eternal in the world's major religions; we would emphasize, though, that all religions apparently maintain a dialectic between the temporal and the eternal to one degree or another.

[7]*Ibid.*, pp. 20–21.

Index of Names

Index of Religious Traditions

Index of Subjects